Relocations

SEXUAL CULTURES
General Editors: José Esteban Muñoz and Ann Pellegrini

For a full list of titles in the series, www.nyupress.com

Relocations

Queer Suburban Imaginaries

Karen Tongson

NEW YORK UNIVERSITY PRESS

New York and London

NEW YORK UNIVERSITY PRESS
New York and London
www.nyupress.org

References to Internet websites (URLs) were accurate at the time of writing. Neither the author nor New York University Press is responsible for URLs that may have expired or changed since the manuscript was prepared.

Library of Congress Cataloging-in-Publication Data

Tongson, Karen.
Relocations : queer suburban imaginaries / Karen Tongson.
p. cm. — (Sexual cultures)
Includes bibliographical references and index.
ISBN 978–0–8147–8309–2 (cl : alk. paper) — ISBN 978–0–8147–8310–8
(pb : alk. paper) — ISBN 978–0–8147–8408–2 (e-book : alk. paper)
1. Gays—United States—Social conditions. 2. Suburbs—United States—
Social conditions. 3. Homosexuality—Social conditions—United States.
I. Title.
HQ76.3.U5T66   2011
306.76′620973091733—dc22   2011005582

New York University Press books are printed on acid-free paper,
and their binding materials are chosen for strength and durability.
We strive to use environmentally responsible suppliers and materials
to the greatest extent possible in publishing our books.

Manufactured in the United States of America
c   10 9 8 7 6 5 4 3 2 1
p   10 9 8 7 6 5 4 3 2 1

For my parents, James and Elizabeth Dykes,
and my grandmother, Linda Katindig

Contents

Illustrations

Preface and Acknowledgments

THIS BOOK ABOUT relocations through space and time—in some situations by choice, and in others through circumstances beyond one's control—has been guided from the outset by my own circuitous journeys to, through, and between many places, as well as among the many people who made these locations truly significant to me, not only intellectually but also affectively. The way I *think* the locations in this book, in other words, belongs to those who made me *feel* these spaces more acutely, even long after "being there" was transposed into memory.

While my enthusiastic and effusive citational practices in *Relocations* offer certain signposts to the figures who have compelled, enriched, and enlivened this project, I would like in this preface to dispense with some of the more formal methods of mapping academic worlds; instead, I would like to acknowledge not only *who* has inspired me but also *how* they have done so. At times their presence is felt through the language I use in this book, in my experiments with an aspirational lyricism that grasps toward "the condition of music" (to invoke Walter Pater), which I hope succeeds as often as it can, considering that such reaching is bound to fail. Their presence is also conjured in the convivial, conversational tone that erupts in the clumsy afterglow of such strivings. I imagine them—imagine you—talking *with* me as much as *through* me about the scenes, histories, events, gestures, haunting melodies, and tangled theoretical coincidences that constitute the placeness of a place.

Though located in many institutions, the excursions and sometimes even dead-ends that we've shared together have always exceeded the institution-as-framework. For this disruption of boundaries and dispensing of formalities, I have many great teachers to thank. First and foremost, I have to acknowledge those who got me in this mess to begin with: the public school teachers of the RUSD (Riverside Unified School District), namely, Kathy Rossi and Keith Lloyd at Sierra Middle School, and Richard McNeil, Richard Zeiner, Rick Woodbury, Katie Mackey, and Robin Speer at Ramona High School. They taught me to love literature, music, performance, and writing. Little did they know what they might ultimately unleash on the world when they indulged this immigrant kid, newly arrived to the suburbs, in my earliest experiments with cultural studies (like the time I brought in a newspaper clipping of Wham!'s arrival in China as a "significant international event" for a history assignment). I share my chapter on the Inland Empire with them, along with the friends who played on those school yards with me, smog alerts permitting: Keri Williams, Heather Lott, Joseph Spagna, Paul Jacques, Carey Thacker, Natalie Patterson, Jessica Learned, Craig Swart, Sarah Parry, and last but certainly not least, Jennifer Stoever-Ackerman, who continues to share the school yard with me now as my colleague in this wider world of the academy.

I am also indebted to the scholars and friends who guided me through my undergraduate years at UCLA and who shared my first encounters with the sprawling city that continues to both captivate and confound my imagination: "Kvang," Cali Linfor, Andrew Peck, Erin Coburn, John Tain, Elina Shatkin, Carolyn Clark, Janel Munguia, Kharon Hathaway, Holly Heaven, Robert N. Watson, Thomas Wortham, Joseph Bristow, Karen Wallace, and the late Paula Gunn Allen, whose fierce irreverence modeled for me what it meant not only to be a better scholar but also a better person.

During my graduate studies at the University of California, Berkeley, I was trained as a Victorianist and learned the methods of New Historicism. Though I never actually grew up to *be* a Victorianist by trade, I hope my mentors and teachers—Catherine Gallagher, Sharon Marcus, Celeste Langan, and Pheng Cheah—will nevertheless read within these pages a commitment not only to what they taught me, but also *how* they taught me to do it. I also thank Robert Kaufman and Rei Terada for encouraging me to believe in my work not despite but *because* of its tendency to move askew into unwieldy directions.

When I left Los Angeles and arrived in the Bay Area for grad school (in a tiny apartment on Page and Buchanan in "The City"), I have to admit I cried the whole first night. Soon enough—or maybe it took all seven years—I grew accustomed to Northern California's more petite geographies and superior air quality. I came to appreciate L.A.'s northern adversary thanks in no small part to my coterie of friends, intellectual interlocutors, and athletic heroines at Berkeley and beyond, particularly Gia Kim, Mai-lin Cheng, Gillian Harkins, William Bishop, Thierry Nazzi, Joon Lee, Gil Hochberg, Keri Kanetsky, Mel Chen, Homay King, Catherine Zimmer, Emma Bianchi, Trane Devore, Susan Zieger, Gayatri Gopinath, Elizabeth Freeman, Amy Kautzman, Kimberly Nalder, Michael Silver, and the Cal women's softball team (2002–2005).

Of course, my time at Berkeley—including numerous international destinations with SFO as their point of origin—was made all the richer, more complex, more adventurous, and more loving by the companionship of Katrin Pahl. I thank her for sharing her worlds and her family with me, and for continuing to be a close and treasured friend.

As I explain throughout *Relocations*, one's arrival in or return to the suburbs is more often than not thought to herald the end of creativity. This was far from my experience, especially when I returned to Southern California as a President's

Postdoctoral Fellow in Literature at the University of California, San Diego, and as a Residential Fellow at the Humanities Research Institute at the University of California, Irvine. Though this project began in the waning years of my graduate studies at Berkeley, *Relocations* truly blossomed during this interstitial time, in these supposedly interstitial suburban environments. My sincerest gratitude goes to Judith Halberstam and John D. Blanco for serving as my postdoctoral mentors at UCSD, and to Judith and David Theo Goldberg for inviting me to join the "Queer Locations" working group at the University of California Humanities Research Institute from January to June 2004, in the fine company of Alicia Arrizón, Tom Boellstorff, Roderick A. Ferguson, Glen Mimura, Chandan Reddy, and Jennifer Terry. As a result of living and working in Irvine, I also had the opportunity to meet scholars at UCI (or based in "the 'Vine") whose work continues to inspire me, and whose friendship—intellectual and otherwise—has only affirmed my belief that strange and beautiful things can flourish in the suburbs, namely, Vicky Johnson, Lucas Hilderbrand, Lauren Steimer, Kelly Wolf, Adria Imada, Bliss Cua Lim, and Laura Kang.

In many respects, the University of Southern California is an ideal place for me and for this project to have landed. Not only has the university been kind enough to fund my research and writing with an Achievement in the Humanities and Social Sciences Grant, as well as a Provost's Visions and Voices Grant (which brought the work of Butchlalis de Panochtitlan and Hector Silva to campus), but the intellectual community at USC has fueled my research and thinking in ways that are unquantifiable. Special thanks are owed first and foremost to David Román and Judith Halberstam for their guidance during my earliest years at USC. The Department of English, the Program in Gender Studies, and the Department of American Studies and Ethnicity have provided warm and inviting homes for my scholarship, and I would like to thank the respective chairs of these departments, Margaret Russett, Lisa Bitel, and John Carlos Rowe. I am also grateful to Sarah Banet-Weiser for asking me to join the "BrandSpace" working group, which she leads at the Norman Lear Center at the Annenberg School for Communication, and to Josh Kun for inviting me to share the music behind my scholarship at the Popular Music Project, also at the Lear Center. I am honored and thrilled to call both of them dear friends as well as colleagues. Tania Modleski, David Lloyd, and Tara McPherson have shepherded me through the final stages of this project, and I am deeply grateful to them for knowing how to ease my spirits, even as they pushed me to cross the t's and dot the i's when I neared the finish line.

The sheer number of excellent friends and colleagues I have at USC precludes me from naming them all here, but given this project's propensity for sprawling out, I will at the very least make an effort to name those who have read, commented on, or inspired this project in one way or another: Kara Keeling, Janelle

Wong, Dana Johnson, Rebecca Lemon, Akira Mizuta Lippit, Ellen Seiter, Aniko Imre, Bruce Smith, Richard Meyer, William Handley, Alice Gambrell, Emily Anderson, Dorinne Kondo, Henry Jenkins, Michelle Gordon, Shana Redmond, Macarena Gomez-Barris, Maria Elena Martinez, and Sarah Gualtieri. My many exceptional graduate students at USC have also coaxed this work into new directions, and I would like to acknowledge them here, especially those who enlivened my seminars on "Queer Provincialisms and Suburban Sociabilities," "Queer of Color Critique," "Feeling Theory," and "Relocating Empire." My research assistant, Alex Wescott, not only performed the perfunctory task of gathering the materials I asked for, but also brought me supplementary ephemera "just in case." These materials especially enhanced my chapter "Behind the Orange Curtain," and for that I am eternally grateful. Thanks also to Krista Miranda in Performance Studies at NYU for her research assistance during the final stages of formatting and securing permissions for this manuscript.

The irony that this book was finally submitted far away from Southern California during my only time in residence in New York City—and to NYU Press to boot—is not lost on me. Though New York takes a well-deserved hit in several of my chapters, particularly "Relocating Queer Critique," I have to admit that the place and its people do have their charms. To my fearless editor at NYU Press, Eric Zinner, for his generous and careful reading of my manuscript: thank you for getting *me* as well as my work. Thanks also to Ciara McLaughlin at NYU Press for shepherding the manuscript through its final stages of production in what felt like a New York minute.

My deepest gratitude is also owed to José Esteban Muñoz and Ann Pellegrini, not only for pursuing *Relocations* for the Sexual Cultures series, but also for being instrumental in bringing me to NYU's Department of Performance Studies at the Tisch School of the Arts for a visiting professorship in spring 2010. Because of this opportunity, I had the pleasure of spending time with some amazing minds and spirits in the city, namely, John Andrews, Jasbir Puar, Deb Schwartz, Karen Shimakawa, Nao Bustamante, Ricardo Montez, Alina Troyano, Ela Troyano, Dr. Virginia Chang, Lisa Duggan, Tavia Nyong'o, Barbara Browning, Camille Robcis, Yael Kropsky, Ellis Avery, Sharon Marcus, Karen Jaime, Taylor Black, Peggy Lee, Sonjia Hyon, Logan Jardine, Jeanne Vaccaro, Vincenzo Amato, Alexandra Vazquez, and Lynne Chan. I thank you all for the hospitality, conviviality, jazz hands, warmth, and song that made this Angeleno love New York despite my skepticism. Because of you, I no longer simply transpose "Empire State of Mind" into the key of I.E.

As much as these acknowledgments and the chapters that follow might seem to insist on the fact that collegialities, friendships, and intimacies are inextricably bound up with particular coordinates, I am also irrefutably attached to the affective potential of dispersal. And the sprawl of my broader intellectual and affective communities reaches out to many elsewheres and affinities that radiate across space and time. It is in the spirit of the remote intimacies I write about in *Relocations* that I send my affections and appreciation to Sarita See, Scott Herring, Shane Vogel, Kandice Chuh, Daphne Brooks, David Eng, Patricia White, Heather Sias, George Haggerty, Alex Espinoza, Kyle Behen, Ricky T. Rodriguez, Martin Manalansan, Michelle Erai, Marcia Ochoa, Christina Hanhardt, Ricardo Ortiz, Rembert Hueser, Verena Mund, Genevieve Love, Eric Weisbard, Ann Powers, and R. Zamora Linmark.

To my sisters of elsewhere who have shared the music of everywhere, past, present, and future with me, Christine Bacareza Balance and Alexandra Vazquez: I always read, write, think, and sing along with you, with your irrepressible spirits at my side.

As you will come to read, *Relocations* begins and ends with home—with the places from which we emerge, as well as those to which we unwittingly find ourselves moved, and moved by. Home began as Manila, which continues to be the place that haunts my daily movements to, through, and between the many elsewheres that have mapped my life's journeys. To my family here and there—to the Moraleses, Katindigs, and Tongsons—and to the dear friends always here or there, especially Joy Escobar and Bliss Cua Lim: thank you for everything, but most of all for reacquainting me with the home from which my first relocation estranged me. To my grandmother, Linda Katindig, for coming here, even when you had everything there: thank you for first revealing the mysteries of writing to me when you sat for hours at a time in front of the typewriter at 7 General Capinpin Street, spinning radio melodramas as I twirled deliriously on the lazy Susan in front of you. To my parents, James Dykes and Elizabeth "Maria" Katindig-Dykes, for taking me on the road with you as you made music, instilling in me a contradictory desire for going and for settling: yours is the music that will forever score my movements, and I am grateful for everything you have ever given me, especially your unconditional love.

For much of my adult life, home has been Southern California, and my daily commutes on its concrete arteries have only affirmed to me that "home" exists in plural, among the many spiritual companions I have found across the region's seemingly nebulous landscapes. Home is with Jennifer Terry, Surina Khan, Rosie, and their tambourine of death in Long Beach. With Jennifer Doyle at the cliff's edge, and with the ladies of Lucile Avenue, Genevieve Yue and Emily Perez. With the Balance-Gabisans, Anjali Arondekar, and Lucy Mae San Pablo Burns in the LF. With the Mod-Loves in WeHo, Gabriela Martinez in HP, and Hector Silva and Napoleon Lustre in Pomona. With JK, LK, CBB, and KK at "da club." With Deanna Erdmann in Little Armenia, and Deanna Maclellan and Emma Gaze in the SFV. With the Ahns and the Cutlers in the Valley and on the Westside. With Heather Lukes and Molly McGarry on the twilight-dappled terraces of Easterly and Sanborn. With Mari Garcia, Claudia Rodriguez, and Raquel Gutierrez, wherever you may take me, up, down, around, and straight to the heart of a "lesser Los Angeles." With Holstein—affectionately known as "The Stein"—my compassionate, companion species born on the streets of L.A., who has inhabited every one of my homes, shared every love, and warmed every desk from my undergrad honors thesis to this book.

Home, everywhere, elsewhere, and nowhere will always be with Patty Ahn. No one I know shares a deeper and more abiding love of this landscape than you—from the Red Lobster to the Smog Cutter. And it is with you in my heart and at my side that this journey has been all the more worthwhile.

1 Relocations
Queer Suburban Imaginaries

THIS BOOK FLOWS from beginning to end through the freeway tributaries that tenuously bind the sprawling counties of Southern California's suburban landscape. We enter these counties that glow at night like neat sherbet grids from the twisted surfaces of concrete cloverleaves, the elaborate off-ramps that spiral toward "home" past earnestly edged lawns, big-box shops, and tawdry strip malls looking wan beneath layers of worn stucco, yet teeming with more than mere commerce. Contained in these boxes, little and large, are the unacknowledged urgencies, desires, and encounters meant to be kept out of these meticulously planned geographies: queers, immigrants, "gangstas," minimum-wagers, Others who find the notion of a "nuclear family" as toxic as it sounds.[1]

Before we take this ride together, allow me to offer you a map of this introduction. By design, the Southern California suburbs leaves a lot of ground to cover, and the presumed conformity of its landscapes leave little in the way of route markers to prevent getting lost. Add to that the layers of customization this project demands—from the suburbs' forms real and imagined, to the queer theories that animate this intervention, to the imperial histories paved over by suburban architectures of convenience—and the sprawl grows with no distinct landmarks in view. I ask that you activate your architectural imagination as you take this journey of relocation to places that will seem all too familiar yet will become utterly unrecognizable.

Think of the first half of this introduction as the foundation and frame for the structures of suburban sociability and aesthetic practice I hope to make legible throughout *Relocations*. Contemporary scholarly and media discourses about the suburbs converge with queer theoretical debates about urbanity, rurality, regionalism, and transnationalism to establish the stakes of remapping queer of color topographies in Southern California, a region redolent with the residue of American imperial ambitions. The second half of this introduction completes the facade and finishes the interior by turning to the modes, technologies, and practices of suburban representation in books, on television, and in popular music. We will not so much read, look at, or listen to books, TV shows, and songs *about* the suburbs, but rather read, look, and listen *into* and *through* the suburbs as they shape, and are shaped by, the queer imaginaries that reside there.

One of the frustrations of driving through suburban space is arriving at cul-de-sacs (dead ends by a fancier name), meant to impede drivers in search of shortcuts while maintaining the tranquility of subdivisions impervious to outsiders. The end of this introduction may, perhaps, irritate you with an outro that refuses the convenience of chapter summaries, the tidy paragraphs that provide a shortcut through the sprawl of *Relocations'* disparate landscapes, from Orange County, to the Inland Empire, to East and Southeast Los Angeles. The profound figures in my own queer of color suburban imaginary—the focal subjects and objects of this book—appear instead in cameos throughout this introduction. They announce themselves at key instances, when a topic or theory calls them out to join individually or collectively. This approach is less for the sake of tranquility as it is a sincere appeal to your interest as a reader, one with the generosity to follow *Relocations* through its contours and flows. Though I know it may be a fantasy to expect everyone to read from cover to cover about the sprawling spaces that ritually disabuse us of the concept of "boundaries," I'm determined to luxuriate in this delusion as a form of tribute to these landscapes without end that are said to herald the end of everything.

Stylistically, the first half of this introduction may not seem all that glamorous in its workmanly efforts to offer a sturdy structure for the embellishments and improvisations that a beautiful facade and warm interior demand. But if you pardon the construction and await the stillness of the machinery coming to a halt, you may hear the music coming from another place you mistook as home.

Framing the Suburbs

Through a range of scholarly discourses—from literary history and media studies, to critical geography, social history, and cultural studies—we have learned that the American suburbs, post–World War II, were meant to achieve the architectural embodiment of peaceful similitude.[2] The postwar suburbs would serve as sanctuaries of the good life where racial and economic homogeneity guaranteed "safety," while satisfying the white middle classes' desires for a lived environment that struck a delicate balance between privacy and community. As the media studies scholar Lynn Spigel notes in her watershed study *Welcome to the Dream House:* "At the center of suburban space was the young, upwardly mobile middle-class family; the suburban community was, in its spatial articulations, designed to correspond with and reproduce patterns of nuclear family life. . . . Older people, gay and lesbian people, homeless people, unmarried people, and people of color were simply written out of these community spaces, and were relegated back to the cities."[3] As I argue throughout *Relocations*, the predictable routes of transit meant to keep the white middle classes at a reassuring remove from nonnormative subjects have been dramatically rerouted. I invoke the spatial containments mapped by Spigel's work, known colloquially as the logic of "white flight," as a starting point for this book's efforts to forge a reparative, queer relationship to the suburbs:[4] one that might help rewrite the many others "relegated back to the cities" (especially queers of color) back *in* to an ever-sprawling suburban cultural history that may or may not want them.

At the heart of *Relocations* are two critical interventions that merge and weave in tandem. First, the book tackles and radically revises prevailing national discourses about the suburbs that perpetuate the mythos of its racialized, classed, and sexualized homogeneity. Though the mass suburban migration previously known as white flight has recalibrated its coordinates since the places Jane Jacobs famously identified as "great American cities" have undergone massive "rehabilitation" efforts in the last several decades, perceptions about the suburbs' lack of economic, racial, and sexual diversity have endured.[5] Second, *Relocations* intervenes in a queer theoretical discourse that relies on these same normative, suburban, white flight narratives to route an opposite trajectory for queer subjects who are—for cultural, political, and stylistic reasons—compelled to leave ostensibly homogenous suburban spaces to find more active (and implicitly activ*ist*) lifestyles in the urban "gay meccas" of the national imaginary, including San Francisco and New York.

On a national scale, the changing demographics of the suburbs have been the focus of volumes of work in numerous disciplines, from critical geography, to ethnic studies, to suburban studies itself. The most comprehensive collection of suburban studies to date, Becky M. Nicolaides and Andrew Wiese's *The Suburb Reader*, culls from this vast interdisciplinary and representational archive to animate the historical, legal, political, and aesthetic debates that have reconfigured the American suburbs since their inception in the nineteenth century and their mass proliferation after World War II. Four sections of the reader with over thirty individual excerpts reconstruct several pivotal moments in the American suburbs' transformation, from "Ethnic Diversity in Early Suburbia" (chap. 7), to "Postwar Suburbs and the Construction of Race" (chap. 11), to "Recent Suburban Transformations, 1970–2000" (chap. 14), to "Inclusion and Exclusion in Recent Suburbia" (chap. 15). The genealogy Nicolaides and Wiese construct in *The Suburb Reader* offers an instructive snapshot of how American ideology, civic legislation, immigration laws, and intensified forms of late-capitalist privatization have flowed in and through U.S. suburbs. Early conflicts about the political ramifications of white, working-class immigrants buying into capitalist ideologies of home ownership, for example, are juxtaposed with Supreme Court debates about restrictive covenants discriminating against African Americans and other communities of color in the late 1940s.[6] The diversification of the American suburbs after the momentous changes in U.S. immigration law in 1965 is also contextualized alongside the thinly veiled variations on restricted covenants in contemporary gated communities.[7] Yet other excerpts focus on the lived experience of new immigrants and people of color moving into suburbs that exclusively cater to such "niche" communities.[8]

The contemporary media has also focused anew on the suburbs in the last decade as, simultaneously, a design-worthy destination for thirtysomething hipsters in pursuit of mid-century nostalgia and a simmering cauldron of racial and economic tension portending the meltdown of the "American dream." Glossy magazines like *Details* ("Why the Suburbs Are Cooler Than Downtown," November 2007) and *Dwell* ("The New Suburbanism," December 2007/January 2008) provide stylish primers for the penny-wise "bourgeois bohemian" (or "Bobo") on how to settle suburbs as the next "hot spots" after certain flip-worthy urban neighborhoods have reached their apex.[9] In April 2000, the *New York Times Magazine* produced a special issue titled "Suburbs Rule: How the New Suburban Majority Is Changing America." Chock-full of essays by an eclectic assemblage of nonfiction writers and media superstars like Michael Pollan, Martha Stewart, and David Brooks, as well as fiction writers like T. C. Boyle, Amy Bloom, Chang-rae Lee, A. M. Homes, George Saunders, and Manil Suri, this supplement did its best to represent the changing demographics of the suburbs in think pieces like "Migration of the Melting Pot" (by Lawrence Osborne) while revisiting some of its more durable character motifs of bored teenagers and licentious housewives.[10] Exposés on gang wars "invading" the suburbs appear nightly on news programs (notably in *Nightline*'s September 2005 piece on the Salvadoran Mara Salvatrucha gang, in greater Washington DC), while their root causes of social inequality are considered in more sustained forms, like the investigative journalist Sarah Garland's book *Gangs in Garden City: How Immigration, Segregation, and Youth Violence Are Changing America's Suburbs*.

Given such expansive, neatly collated, and meticulously documented evidence to the contrary, how then does the gestalt of the suburbs remain largely unchanged in the American imaginary? There are, of course, numerous answers to this question, most of which can be attributed to enduring representations of the suburbs as a ticky-tacky void in literature, television, popular music, media, and the arts. As Andrew Blauvelt, one of the curators of the groundbreaking *Worlds Away: New Suburban Landscapes* exhibit, remarks in the extensive catalog for the show (held at the Walker Art Center in Minneapolis and then the Carnegie Museum of Art in Pittsburgh), "Most of what we think we know about suburbia has been shaped by its portrayal in various media—film, music, literature, and television in particular—where it has been depicted alternately as an idyllic setting for family life in TV sitcoms, for instance, and a dysfunctional landscape of discontent in Hollywood movies."[11] As *Relocations* will show throughout its many pages mimicking, at certain instances, suburbia's tidy yet nebulous sprawl, even *this* representational field has been marred by strange and wild things growing where they shouldn't. But before tackling this larger and more intricate problem of representation through reading, watching, and listening, I want to turn our attention to another theoretical conjecture, one very specific to this project, for why even the postmillennial suburbs remain the presumed natural habitat for normativity: that of queer studies.

Throughout its institutional history, queer studies has produced its share of spatial Others for the sake of maintaining its urbane reputation and cosmopolitan orientation. From George Chauncey's groundbreaking study of *Gay New York*, to contemporary projects attentive to lesbian cosmopolitanisms, like Diane Chisholm's *Queer Constellations: Subcultural Space in the Wake of the City* and Julie Abraham's *Metropolitan Lovers: The Homosexuality of Cities*, queer studies has self-consciously undertaken the task of documenting its rich urban histories and metropolitan forms of cultural production.[12] In her important book *In a Queer Time and Place: Transgender Bodies, Subcultural Lives*, Judith Halberstam assigns a neologism to describe this urbanist legacy in queer studies: "metronormativity." As Halberstam argues, her term "reveals the conflation of 'urban' and 'visible' in many normalizing narratives of gay/lesbian subjectivities," creating a compulsory narrative of migration for queer subjects that marks the development of "previously closeted subjects who 'come out' into an urban setting."[13] The more that metronormativity takes shape conceptually in Halberstam's book, the more it comes to describe the dialectic—experienced both psychically and spatially—between the rural and the urban in queer studies. As I discuss further in my chapters on Lynne Chan's JJ Chinois projects and on Southern California's Inland Empire, Halberstam's critique of metronormativity opens the possibility of opting out of a compulsory queer movement toward "the city," a move predicated on acquiring a greater sense of "pride," "liberation," and safety for queer subjects thought to be in emotional, aesthetic, and physical peril in nonurban environments.

Yet unlike other scholars of queer rurality or of the queer peripheries more broadly defined, Halberstam inevitably refuses to relinquish "the city" as the emblematic habitat for queers. She writes, "*In a Queer Time and Place* both *confirms* that queer subcultures thrive in urban areas *and* contests the essential characterizations of queer life as urban."[14] Eschewing the either/or of the urban/rural binary for an either/and, Halberstam instead calls on other queer scholars to explore the different "truth[s] to this division between urban and small-town life [and] between hetero-familial cultures and queer creative and sexual cultures," without "occlud[ing] the lives of nonurban queers."[15] *In a Queer Time and Place* focuses primarily on a rural "horror of the heartlands" mythology at the core of representational debates about the transgender icon who was a martyr of rural violence, Brandon Teena (subject of the well-known documentary and subsequent feature film). Beyond her chapter on Teena, however, Halberstam leaves the task of documenting the complex interrelations of queer life beyond metropolitan subcultures to other scholars.

Of course, numerous scholars documented queer life outside metropolitan centers long before Halberstam's study of homo- and heteronormative approaches to time and space.[16] Lauren Berlant's *The Queen of America Goes to Washington City* reminds us, for example, that even the most radical of urban queer activist groups, such as Queer Nation and San Francisco's SHOP (the Suburban Homosexual Outreach Program), staged some of their more spectacular and performative "invasions" in suburban shopping malls.[17] Nevertheless, the spatiotemporal concept of metronormativity and Halberstam's emphasis on subcultures and queer lifestyles has had a legible and significant impact on how contemporary queer scholarship envisions its interventions into queer urbanism, despite Halberstam's residual attachments to urban settings for subcultural expression.

In subsequent chapters of *Relocations*, I grapple with some of these residual fantasies about urban queer subcultures and their purported "radicality" in the sphere of queer aesthetics and politics. Even after metronormativity was named, in other words, queer studies has remained reliant on the forms and formalisms of urbanist subcultural idioms in ways that often preclude a serious consideration of the more problematic forms of racialized and classed desires for the "backward," aesthetically and politically "conventional," or "mainstream." In the introduction to his remarkable work *Another Country: Queer Anti-Urbanism*, Scott Herring fashions a discursive jukebox out of some of queer studies' greatest hits: the urbanist one-liners used to dismiss the hicks and small-town queers (as well as the Podunks they came from) from a special class reserved for metropolitan minds and mind-sets. With line after line, hit after hit from scholars like Michael Warner and George Chauncey, Herring sketches the "entwined urbanism that bridges the givens of everyday lesbian and gay metropolitan life in the United States and the shared assumptions of U.S.-based queer studies that have been produced since the 1980s."[18] Herring focuses on a "queer rural stylistics" that countervails and thwarts the queer urbanist logic that assumes liberation comes with leaving behind one's nowhere place of origin—in his project, "the country"—to arrive in "the city." *Another Country* offers a substantial contribution to the "as-yet unwritten cultural history of U.S. metronormativity," finding at once the fissures and breaks in what has appeared to be a seamless national narrative about queer life that locates its inventiveness and political interventions in urban environments like New York.[19] Proposing an alternative *queer* anti-urbanism that, in his own words, threads "a delicate needle" between undoing the encompassing symbologies of "the city" for queer subjects—while still acknowledging that the force of urbanism persists in its negative articulations through rural stylistics—Herring crafts a contingent politics open to various registers of failure, from the aesthetic to the ideological. This "paper cut politics," as Herring describes it, "rarely does significant damage since it never punctures the body's deep tissue. It does, however, cause a considerable amount of discomfort, often more annoying than dire."[20] He conceives of paper cut politics as the means toward a disruptive "nuisance" to "the idealizations of any urbanized lesbian and gay imaginary," employing his own rhetoric of sassy rurality as a weapon against the "aesthetic intolerance" of grandly declarative, metronormative queer discourses.

Relocations' efforts to confront queer metronormativity with irritating (and irritable) incisions in its master-narratives of aesthetic and stylistic superiority are in keeping with Herring's recent efforts in *Another Country*. And yet, while I sometimes wish that I, too, could shake my inner Sugarbaker with the vigor of Herring's Southern sass, I know full well that the suburbs by design merit less passion than the age-old spiritual and stylistic showdown between the country and the city.[21] Thus my approach is far less incisive than paper cut politics and noticeably more sprawling (true to suburban design, or the lack thereof) in its attempt to encompass the disparate, if strikingly familiar and repetitive, articulations of how the suburban imaginary functions in queer and normative national discourses. While the first relocation tracked in this book revisits the metronormative trajectory of the queer subject from "nowhere" to "somewhere"—more precisely, from the California suburbs to New York City in Lynne Chan's JJ Chinois projects—*Relocations* also stays put (as suburban objects and subjects are wont to do) in some of Southern California's emblematic landscapes, such as amusement parks ("Behind the Orange Curtain"), strip malls ("Empire of My Familiar"), and freeways ("There Is a Light That Never Goes Out"). Rather than get caught up in the fierce battle that's been raging for ages between the country and the city in queer studies and beyond, *Relocations* takes pleasure and pause in the storied commute and vexed communion between the suburban and the urban.

Theoretically and conceptually, this book's intervention into queer urbanism is inspired by the perilous cloverleaf freeway interchanges that opened this introduction. Once created to keep the flow of traffic moving on and off the major arteries of transit to and from cities and suburbs, cloverleaves now (as many other architectures created with convenience in mind) have become the source of what they sought to prevent: congestion, confusion, and aggravation.[22]

Cloverleaf freeway interchange, ca. 1950s, Los Angeles. Courtesy of the Los Angeles Public Library Photograph Collection.

Cloverleaf interchanges require an elaborate choreography between vehicles and drivers. Rather than merging directly onto the flow of traffic with the aid of lights and signals, the cloverleaf offers an interstitial lane on which vehicles traveling at different speeds and at cross-purposes—some exiting, others entering—negotiate their transactions of motion within a death-defying instant. During my earliest experiences on Southern California's freeways as a newly licensed sixteen-year-old driver, cloverleaves terrified me the most. Careening onto a single lane to exit the freeway at high speeds, or trying desperately to merge while keeping control of a car hurtling with the centrifugal force of a twisting on-ramp, challenged my ability to see beyond the blind spots these structures aggravated. But once I learned how to use them—to see the other cars, time the traffic, and adjust my speed according to another's flow—I took a pleasure and thrill in the dangerous transaction, the elaborate dance between drivers destined for different directions, yet forced by design to notice one another as if their lives depended on it, because they do for that instant. The suburban and the urban, queer narratives and normative ones, history and theory, may be at cross-purposes and propelled by different velocities toward different destinations, but I force them to interact in *Relocations* as if they were on one of these cloverleaves: they meet transiently, aware they're inhabiting one another's blind spots, and yet they are willing to yield their right of way to take the risk of crossing in time and space together, lest there be a fatal and catastrophic collision.

By definition, the suburbs are an intermediary space between the rural and the urban, a nether zone that (as of this writing) doesn't even have its own U.S. census category.[23] Whereas the rural and the urban are each other's stalwart opposites, the suburban cannot even exist etymologically without the "urban." The American suburbs may have functioned historically as spaces of escape from the decline of its industrial cities, but the two have nevertheless shared, over time, a codependent relationship.[24] Never too far apart, and yet seemingly worlds away, suburbs and cities are—as the joke goes about many longtime companions—beginning to resemble each other. As Andrew Blauvelt observes:

> City dwellers and suburbanites need each other to reinforce their own sense
> of place and identity despite ample evidence that what we once thought were
> different places and lifestyles are increasingly intertwined and much less
> distinct. The revenge of the suburb on the city wasn't simply the depletion of its
> urban population or the exodus of its retailers and office works, but rather the
> importation of suburbia into the heart of the city: chain stores and restaurants,
> downtown malls and even detached housing. . . . Suburbia has returned to the city
> just as more suburbs are experiencing many of the things about city life it sought
> to escape, both positive and negative: congestion, crime, poverty, racial and ethnic
> diversity, cultural amenities, and retail diversity. At the same time, cities have taken
> on qualities of the suburbs that are perceived as both good and bad, such as the
> introduction of big box retailing, urban shopping malls, and reverse suburban
> migrations by empty nesters who return to the city to enjoy the kind of life they
> lived before they had kids to raise.[25]

The rerouted paths of migration, commerce, and sociability of the United States' normative subjects—of the heterosexual couples who cultivated nuclear families in suburban spaces they imagined were at a safe distance from the racialized dangers and perversions of big cities—have changed the stakes of contemporary debates about whether cities still nurture the Others who were economically quarantined from the suburban good life during the age of white flight. Cities have, since the boom of technologically driven "creative" industries in the mid-1990s, become the preferred destination for a new species of normative Americans alternately called the "creative class" or the "bourgeois bohemians." In the introduction to his best-selling book *Bobos in Paradise: The New Upper Class and How They Got There*, David Brooks anoints this hybrid species of elites the new American standard: "These are highly educated folk who have one foot in the bohemian world of creativity and another foot in the bourgeois realm of ambition and worldly success. The members of the new information age elite are bourgeois bohemians. . . . These Bobos define our age. They are the new establishment. Their hybrid culture is the atmosphere we all breathe. Their status codes now govern social life. Their moral codes give structure to our personal lives."[26] In so far as queer studies positions itself against normativity, as well as normative temporalities and geographies, part of the intervention I offer in *Relocations* is simply to recognize that normativity itself is no longer a stable category found in fixed spatial environments. Normativity has a new face and has proved itself adaptable to different landscapes, including the cities it once abandoned for the good life in the suburbs. In the twilight of suburbia we have awoken to realize that this new face bears a remarkable resemblance to our own queer visages. Berlant and Freeman warned at the height of queer studies' institutional emergence that "queer culture's consent to national normativity must itself be made more provisional."[27] As their prophecy came to fruition during the United States' transition from the economic prosperity of the Clinton era into George W. Bush's troubled two-term regime, Lisa Duggan urged us to reevaluate the saliency of "queer" in the wake of what she named "homonormativity," or a "demobilized gay constituency and a privatized, depoliticized gay culture anchored in domesticity and consumption."[28]

Relocations underscores the connection between metronormativity and homonormativity. But rather than resting with the assumption that homonormativity remains within the purview of gays and lesbians who strive to mimic some of the United States' more traditional institutions of citizenship (e.g., marriage, domesticity, and family life) in their most predictable settings (e.g., the suburbs), I want to emphasize how much the new "creative" and "Bobo" forms of normativity crib their iterations of subcultural capital, consumption-based multiculturalism, and rehabilitative urbanism from gays, lesbians, and even those who identify as queer. Among the questions *Relocations* considers throughout its pages are the following: How do we measure normativity in the wake of these changes? How do we delineate subcultural production when its stylistic and spatial boundaries have been broached? How do we enumerate normative time after the rise of what Richard Florida, in concert with David Brooks, calls the "creative class"—a class to which we as queer scholars may inevitably belong?

In a series of books, Richard Florida has characterized an emergent, postindustrial, creative class of workers involved in "knowledge industries" not bound to the forty-hour workweek.[29] The creative classes—including economically prosperous gays and lesbians—helped intensify corporate and civic efforts at urban gentrification with their preference for city living, due in large part to the amenities it offers, including "diversity" itself.[30] A more pointed discussion of Florida's promulgation of the lifestyle politics of gentrification unfolds in the coda to *Relocations*, which focuses on the queer performance ensemble Butchlalis de Panochtitlan's theatrical confrontation with creative classers in the remodeled queer, racialized, and working-class social spaces of "lesser Los Angeles."[31] I gesture toward Florida's body of work here because the critique of queer urbanity I offer in *Relocations* focuses on just how deeply, if unintentionally complicit, certain subcultural logics of queer urbanity are with these newly normative, "creative" processes of gentrification.[32] Queer urbanites as well as their normative counterparts have contributed to the latter-day suburban migrations of communities of color from more traditional, ethnic urban enclaves deeper into suburbia.

The spatial designation "suburbia" has its origins in ancient Rome where, as Robert Bruegmann explains, "*suburbium* mean[t] what was literally below or outside the city walls."[33] Whereas American suburbanites after World War II fled cities in search of the "good life," their ancient Roman counterparts left because "they could not afford to live in the city and so had to forgo urban services and the protection of the walls."[34] What Bruegmann describes as ancient custom in the history of sprawl resurfaces as a historical echo of the suburban relocations transpiring more recently in the fluctuating real estate environments of Southern California, which are the primary coordinates for *Relocations*. Suburban migrations in Southern California have come as a consequence of several key socio-economic and cultural factors, including: post-1965 U.S. immigration, the local migrations instigated by globalization and several real estate booms and busts from the 1980s onward, as well as the displacements wrought by the ethos of urban renewal and gentrification enacted through official channels by civic legislation and corporate redevelopment, all the while spearheaded *un*officially by creative-class lifestyle cultures.[35]

Southern California's variegated and racially marked suburban counties pose a historical challenge to perpetually whitewashed imaginaries of the suburbs.[36] But as I mentioned above, portraits of suburban similitude persist in queer, homonormative, and heteronormative cultural and theoretical discourses. The queer cosmopolitanism that disavows the suburbs for its homogeneity still relies on the traditional urban rubrics of density, diversity, and verticality offered by New York and San Francisco. Instead of orienting another inquiry toward the historical queer destinations of New York or San Francisco, *Relocations* looks anew at the postmillennial models of sprawl typically associated with Los Angeles and its horizontal conglomeration of seemingly "centerless" landscapes. As critical geographers and urban theorists like Edward Soja and Mike Davis have observed, the ever-expanding form of Los Angeles' amorphous urbanism is often conflated with the spatial, economic, and spiritual *sub*urbanization of the nation and the world.[37] Suburban-style development in Los Angeles has arguably inspired the proliferation of the "post–third world" megalopolis in sites throughout Asia, South Asia, and Latin America, thus contributing globally to what was initially conceptualized as the Western, primarily U.S. problem of suburban sprawl.[38] With its eye on global development in Southern California, the regionalism of my study aims to accomplish more than offering a local addendum to national narratives about queer lifestyles and representations. Instead, *Relocations* explores how the Southern California suburbs from Orange County to the Inland Empire have functioned as a conceptual and topographical nexus for an American empire bound up with histories of sexuality, race, and desire.

In *When America Became Suburban*, Robert A. Beauregard argues that American global ascendancy and the growth of the suburbs after World War II "was not about subjugation or territory. Neither colonialism nor expansion was the goal. Rather the United States hoped to establish itself at the center of an international economy based on free trade."[39] Beauregard is only half correct in his assertion, in so far as free trade took its place as the engine of American international policy after the war. But as Inderpal Grewal, Amy Kaplan, and Victor Bascara, among many others, have rightly insisted, free trade and global capitalism cannot be imagined as projects distinct from the growth of the American empire. Indeed, American imperialism distinguished itself from earlier imperial models in part by its refutation of European forms of bureaucratic and administrative colonialism, favoring instead the liberal (and now neoliberal) spread of capitalism and free trade.[40] As Bascara writes, "Gone is the fleeting legitimacy of the 'benevolent assimilation' of 'little brown brothers,' or the uplift and Christianization of the heathen, or even the opening of 'the China Market.' That arrogance has since been displaced by a different type of arrogant conception of modernity that champions development and globalization, as well as multiculturalism and its forms of diversity management."[41]

Despite Beauregard's disavowal of the term "imperialism" to mark the United States' global economic expansion after World War II, he quite accurately depicts how the suburbs reflected American imperial exemplarity on the global stage in the mid-twentieth century: "The daily life of the 'average' American became a model for people around the globe. Suburban life anchored a standard of living commensurate with the nation's status as the leader of the 'free world' and established the country's economy and form as the best hope for affluence, democracy, and world peace. Life in the suburbs was a mark of American exceptionalism and a model to which all nations could aspire."[42] In other words, the picture of normativity captured in the suburbs—of a white, nuclear family surrounded by their possessions, especially their comfortable home—became not only an American standard, but also was exported globally as a touchstone for "freedom" and "prosperity" in the so-called developing world. The suburbs of the twentieth century symbolized the United States' imperial transition from a production economy to one of consumption. The American dream of a good life, replete with consumer conveniences in the suburbs, became a significant aspect of the nation's *cultural* imperialist rhetoric of freedom during the Cold War, an era formative to the Orange County amusement cultures I describe in this book.

As I discuss in more depth in "Behind the Orange Curtain," the region's economic growth from the 1960s onward was spurred simultaneously by the rise of its military and defense industries, and its amusement cultures at Disneyland and Knott's Berry Farm. The dual imperatives of security and amusement combined in Orange County to foment a consumer ethos that was disseminated globally through emblematic pop icons like Disney's Mickey Mouse—the cuddly, if rodentious, emissary of American cultural imperialism.[43] Despite decades of wealth and unprecedented prosperity, Orange County's spectacular financial collapse during the early 1990s (the municipality declared bankruptcy in December of 1994),[44] symbolically augured the fate of today's suburban empires: a fall experienced many times over by its aptly named neighbor to the east, the Inland Empire. Hubristically oversized suburban dream houses are lost everyday to bankruptcy and foreclosure as Southern California's suburban empires are slowly but surely turning to rubble.

In 2009, *Time* magazine announced that the "American suburb as we know it is dying. . . . Thanks to changing demographics, including a steady decline in the percentage of households with kids and a growing preference for urban amenities among Americans young and old, the suburban dream of the big house with the big lawn is vanishing."[45] As queers invested in the architectures of normativity coming to ruin, we may too hastily rejoice in *Time*'s declaration of the suburbs' end, accompanied by eerie portraits of empty retail behemoths and abandoned big-box shops. The service economies engendered by these massive chains throughout the suburbs have also, in the wake of post-industrialization and the booms and busts of the technologically driven "creative" economy, come to provide a primary source of income for many of Southern California's immigrants, migrants, and working-class communities.[46] As Marcelo M. Suarez-Orozco explains, immigrants "escaping economies that more or less 'broke' during the global restructuring . . . are drawn by the service sector of the U.S. economy where there seems to be an insatiable appetite for foreign workers."[47] The United States' mid-twentieth-century transition from a production to consumption culture in the suburbs then, paradoxically, created the conditions for the suburbs' and the American empire's undoing half a century later. The American suburbs have been globally restructured, reconstituted as service economies, and repopulated as residential apartment communities for low-wage immigrant workers reliant on service sectors for sustenance. When we as queer theorists, cosmopolites, and denizens of creative urbanity cheer the vanquishing of the contemporary suburbs, the vestiges of U.S. cultural and economic imperial ambition, *whose* demise are we celebrating?

As I argue in my chapter on the Inland Empire, Southern California's suburbs have become—and in many respects already *were*—a repository for the subjects scattered by the United States' latent imperial ambitions in the twentieth century, and as a consequence of the nation's collusion with other imperial projects during earlier ages of empire. From the Spanish missionary culture coinciding and conflicting with the United States' westward expansionism before ultimately colliding head-on with the nation's nascent imperialism at the turn of the twentieth century, to the British capital paired with "American ingenuity" in the agricultural expansion of the inland region's "Orange Empire" at the close of the nineteenth century, Southern California's suburbs have served as test-sites for imperial projects that have both "succeeded" and gone terribly awry. The imperial legacies of the late nineteenth century that encompassed "territories" like Mexico, Cuba, Puerto Rico, and the Philippines, followed up by the United States' Cold War ethos of containment-through-incursion in places like Korea and Vietnam in the mid-twentieth century, dramatically transformed the demographies, architectures, and cultural life of the Southern California region. Thus the arcane term "empire," rather than its newer variations and forms such as "globalization" or "transnationalism," emerges as a key word throughout the pages of *Relocations* to describe the flows of bodies, cultures, and systems of power that delineate the migrations to, through, and within Southern California's suburbs.

By acknowledging the residual effects, affects, and echoes of empire in the suburban landscapes of Southern California, *Relocations* shares in Inderpal Grewal's project of reexamining the "new centers" and nodes of American imperialism in the age of transnationalism. Whereas Michael Hardt and Antonio Negri insist that no single nation can be imagined as an imperial leader in the "decentered" and "deteritorizalized" regime of management, which "scrambles" the spatialized order of so-called first through third worlds installed by nation-states and sovereign-ruling imperial*ists* of the nineteenth and early twentieth centuries, Grewal reminds us of the United States' imperial adaptability as it has been harnessed through transformations of capital.[48] As Grewal explains, "The United States remained a hegemon, and its source of power was its ability to generate forms of regulation across particular connectivities that emerged as independent as well as to recuperate the historicized inequalities generated by earlier phases of imperialism."[49] This oscillation between discourses of freedom and American exceptionalism, and the United States' complicity with an imperialism that it has stridently disavowed, can be traced throughout the chapters of *Relocations*, from the migrant destinies paid tribute to (as well as parodied) in Lynne Chan's JJ Chinois projects, to the nascent narratives of "homonationalism" set in the Inland Empire, like Alex Espinoza's novel *Still Water Saints*.

Poised somewhere between Grewal's painstaking attention to networked forms of power in *Transnational America* and Hardt and Negri's ecstatic utopianism for a "new cartography . . . waiting to be written—or really . . . being written today through the resistances, struggles, and desires of the multitude,"⁵⁰ *Relocations'* own goals are more modestly scaled to the micro-intimacies that forge everyday irruptions in the contemporary imperial landscapes of Southern California's suburbs. From the laughter coaxed by Lynne Chan's ludic remapping of queer discovery through chain stores and convenience marts, to the awkward group dancing staged by teens of color on amusement park dance floors, to the car-ride sing-alongs hosted by the Butchlalis de Panochtitlan en route to the nowheres that have since been made over into somewheres by the urban hips-terati, *Relocations* revels in the transient and unruly glimmers of possibility amid empire's incursions into local spaces.

Irreverence, and the unruliness that comes with a humorous response to serious matters, is a governing affect and key metacritical feature of *Relocations*. Inspired by the laugh-out-loud infectiousness of these works in their creative responses to suburbia, my own prose, and indeed my own theorization, strives to capture how crucial humor is to the *techne* of survival for queer of color suburban subjects. Whereas irony and referentiality have been the governing tropes of post-modern analysis, especially in relation to popular objects, figures like JJ Chinois and the Butchlalis de Panochtitlan in *Relocations* mobilize humor as an ameliora-tive mode in their work. In other words, instead of using humor or irony to make themselves distinct, or to stand out and apart from the popular mainstream, they cull from the popular to forge unlikely sociabilities, relationships, and alliances between themselves and the spheres of living and referentiality they are meant to be excluded from—particularly the suburbs as both a cultural and spatial entity. This humor is also always freighted by something "heavier," something deeper and potentially more catastrophic. In many respects, their use of humor—and my own throughout this book—can be imagined as activating the "joke work" Freud famously conceived in *Jokes and Their Relation to the Unconscious*. Only instead of figuring this labor as an elaborate set of negotiations *within* the uncon-scious between the superego, ego, and id, the joke work of *Relocations* traces a set of material relations between and among built environments, subjects circulating in those environments, and the objects that form sociohistorical connectivities in these historically determined settings.⁵¹

In keeping with its dual emphasis on the superficial and the profound as it manifests in contemporary queer migrations, then, the title for this book, *Reloca-tions*, taps into the range of meanings the term both promises and threatens, from its purely descriptive attributes and silly euphemistic function in the real estate industry, to its more violent overtones of forced martial and imperial displace-ments. In the parlance of the suburban real estate economy, "relocation" offers an innocuous, if gussied up, way to describe people—mostly families—moving from one place to another, often because of a new job. Companies and real estate firms offer "relocation experts" linked across the Internet, ready to help business-people and their families find the right neighborhood, in the right school district, with the right grocery stores and other conveniences, within the right proximity to their new jobs. Full-service relocation experts boast of how much time and money can be saved by consulting their collated databases. Local realtors in turn spare advertising dollars, because by signing up with a relocation service they no longer have to commit ad money to disparate markets. One business journalist and a proponent of full-service relocation, Harry Feinberg, offers an illustrative scenario:

> Imagine this. You're a real estate broker in Tuscaloosa (God forbid). You need your listings to reach every rare and precious professional who is asked to relocate to your tiny berg. You have two choices. Choice one, you can buy expensive ads in the NY and LA Times and pray that someone from Hollywood or Gotham sees your ad the day they get the joyous news that corporate HQ is moving to your little slice of heaven. Choice two, (the better choice) is that you can sign a deal with a national relocation company that moves thousands of employees annually (some of whom actually may be forced to move to your undiscovered gem of a town).[52]

Setting aside Feinberg's colorful description of the specific sites in question—he manages to insult both rural "folks" and shallow urbanites with his quippy asides about Tuscaloosa, Gotham, and Hollywood—we acquire a glimpse at how the business practice of relocation works. Relocation experts serve as local informants and transitional consultants for the legions of workers whose movements are predicated by regional and global corporate economies. These movements are sometimes consensual and at other times coerced. Further, corporate relocation agencies, real estate relocation consultants, and do-it-yourself books like Beverly Roman and John Howells's *Insiders' Guide to Relocation* also offer families advice on how to cope psychologically and emotionally with uprooting from one place to start anew in another.[53]

The psychological pitfalls connoted in contemporary, commercial uses of "relocation" are haunted by, if blissfully ignorant of, the brutal legacy of the term as it has been deployed in a long American (imperial) history of coerced displacements and topographical quarantines. From the 1830 Indian Removal Act forcibly moving First Nations populations from the East to the West during one of many legislated landgrabs in American expansion; to the internment of Japanese Americans during World War II in an effort to sequester potential "enemies within"; to the violent dispersals wrought by slavery and its aftermaths, from the slave trade and the "great migration," to "white flight" and Hurricane Katrina; to the quarantining of "enemy combatants" at Guantanamo Bay (who were then "rendered" in elsewheres we have yet to discover) after September 11, 2001, in the name of "national security"—"relocation" has functioned as a polite euphemism for imperialist aggression masquerading as commonsense policies for the prosperity, safety, and welfare of the "American people."[54]

Relocations does not attempt to forge facile analogies with these violent events in American history; rather, it traces how the imperial policies and principles behind them are reanimated in contemporary American landscapes, from the gentrification of urban neighborhoods as a result of new "landgrabbing" economies in which queers are also complicit, to the "crabgrass apartheid" that apportions Southern California's suburbs through zoning laws and other civic policies while erecting gates to protect "fortress communities" from the encroachment of less prosperous immigrants and communities of color that build them and keep them clean.[55] As Meiling Cheng reminds us in her work *In Other Los Angeles: Multicentric Performance Art*, "With the surges of multiethnic and multinational populations throughout the region's history came various *purges* of differences."[56] This book's focus on immigration and migration to and through Southern California's suburban landscape also cannot be abstracted from the *queer* theoretical labor that compels its efforts to create alternate cartographies of sexuality and race in the region. Thus *Relocations* engages with, and hopes to contribute to, an ever-expanding conversation about "purges of differences" overlapping with queer diasporas and regionalisms.[57]

Relocations, as the title strongly suggests, shifts our cartographies of the queer/ immigrant imaginary by reorienting our spatial perspective to account for *local* migrations that intersect with queer of color regionalisms in the United States. My critical motivation for situating *Relocations* in Southern California is to explore the rich intersections among queer immigrant communities from Latin and Central America and the Pacific Rim while seeing how variegated modes of transit, arrival, and departure inform these colliding imaginaries. Further, gender remains a crucial framework for reevaluating the aesthetic and political economies of queer lifestyles in a Southern California landscape where hemispheric regionalisms collide. My first chapter, on "Relocating Queer Critique: Lynne Chan's JJ Chinois," for example, provides a genealogy for how the urban cultural history of queer communities in the United States and abroad perpetuates a gendered divide between gay men and lesbians along the axes of style. As Gayatri Gopinath has argued in her work on "Queer Regions," many accounts of queer diaspora are still burdened by urbanist and cosmopolitan frameworks that look to cities as sites of "first contact" for immigrant populations.[58] Such gestures toward more encompassing, metropolitan global accounts of queer life end up replicating the separation of gendered spheres in queer lifestyles. Promoting queer regionalism as an adjustment to queer diaspora, Gopinath offers the possibility that

shifting our critical lens from male public cultures of the global city such as
Mumbai, Delhi, London, or New York, to nonmetropolitan locations that are
just as saturated by global processes although they may appear to be "purely local,"
allows us to foreground those spaces and bodies that are elided within dominant
narratives of global gayness. These "other" sexual cultures may not be readily
intelligible as either "public" or "gay": they may well be enacted by female subjects
and take place not in the bar or the club but rather the confines of the home, the
beauty parlor, the women's hostel.[59]

With all due respect to the serious work Gopinath accomplishes by animating
queer diaspora in its variegated forms, I offer instead my own cheeky (and as
some have said, cheesy) neologism, "dykeaspora," as a disposable counterpoint to
the notion of queer diaspora, in order to describe the translocal movements of
queer female bodies within the United States. The term's vicissitudes, failings,
and modest successes are explained at length in my chapter on "Relocating Queer
Critique," but I want to register here the priority given to "dykes" in my project.
"Dykeaspora" underscores my project's critique of the gendered discourses of
queer space that locate gay men at the center of the action in desirable and desire-
drenched cities while relegating female queers to potentially mundane and reproductive homonormative existences in unspecified elsewheres.

Turning to local sites like Orange County's amusement parks and the Inland
Empire's strip malls, *Relocations* revisits spaces that may on the surface seem
to be reserved for families and consumers, but which inevitably become transformed as spaces of queer of color encounter and social transaction. Concluding with the dyke performance ensemble Butchlalis de Panochtitlan's disparate performances and media interventions, *Relocations* explores the affective
potential of butch lesbian intimacies amid the incursions of both hetero- and
homonormative social and spatial "rehabilitators" in East and Southeast Los
Angeles. By approaching queer regionalisms through some of these ephemeral,
queer, and specifically dyke of color performances and social practices, *Relocations* constructs itself as cultural study in the broadest sense. *Relocations* thus
includes historical and sociological dimensions, but it ultimately absconds
from a strictly demographic approach to queer space—something that previous projects about the "gay suburbs," such as Wayne Brekhus's *Peacocks, Chameleons, Centaurs: Gay Suburbia and the Grammar of Social Identity*, and the Urban
Institute's *Gay and Lesbian Atlas*, have already accomplished. Such critical findings will instead be brought to bear on the spatial *imaginaries* perpetuated, disseminated, and culturally produced in a range of representational media, such
as performance, popular music, literature, television, and new media, as well as
in the genre of criticism itself.[60]

Throughout the twentieth century, and reaching as far back as the eighteenth century in England and the United States, the suburbs have been considered an aesthetic vacuum, a place where art and creativity are domesticated and inevitably disappear altogether. Catherine Jurca underscores this in the opening to her book *White Diaspora: The Suburb and the Twentieth-Century American Novel*, when she takes on Edith Wharton's remark that "The Great American Novel" would never be at home, so to speak, in the mundane confines of suburban spaces.[61] What Jurca's project exposes is the cultural argument that "art" and "innovation" could never be cultivated in the spiritual and spatial void typified by suburban contexts.[62] The cultural conservatism modeled by Wharton—one that paradoxically employs "avant-gardist" criteria to dismiss suburban space—strikingly resembles a queer cosmopolitanism that also politicizes certain avant-gardist and subcultural aesthetic practices while diminishing "pop," "mass," and "folk" approaches to the queer imaginary, thus continuing to gender and hierarchize cultural spheres of production for a purportedly radical queer politics.

This project's account not only about *where* we locate queer activism, radical politics, and ethics, but also of *how* we go about doing so, is bound up with recent debates about queer temporality and its propensity toward the *avant*. Elizabeth Freeman's important work on "temporal drag," for example, inspires my project's take on the sometimes evocative, citational, and repetitive nature of queer of color suburban practices.[63] Temporal drag manifests in Freeman's essay as a "stubborn identification with a set of social coordinates" that exceed one's own contemporariness.[64] She uses as an example the "gravitational pull that 'lesbian' sometimes seems to exert upon 'queer' not only stylistically, but historically (e.g., through stubborn attachments to supposedly 'outmoded' and essentializing forms of feminism), and also performatively (through the simultaneous expression of incongruous historical and political effects and affects)."[65] While Freeman's freighted temporality sets the time signature for this book, my chapter on the Inland Empire creates an interface between Freeman's gendered account of queer belatedness, and postcolonial critiques of temporal progress confused as progressive*ness*.

Suburban environments are presumed to fluctuate wildly between stasis and rapid development. In the suburbs, everything remains, or at the very least *appears*, the same. And yet the suburbs also function as modernity's laboratory—as an environment where homes, shops, objects (like televisions, radios, or kitchen appliances), and even people are constantly being replaced, paved over for something newer, bigger, and more convenient. As we turn the corner for a closer look at the representational and aesthetic practices of the queer of color suburban imaginary, I would prefer not to *say* anything more about temporal drag so that we might collectively inhabit its certain stillness as it waits to break its pose: that "pull of the past upon the present," and the stubborn if sometimes incongruous reiterations of what we think we know about the suburbs, and what we may never come to understand about its aesthetic practices. Do forgive the repetition you may find here of what we have seen and heard before: it may contain within it what we never thought we would see or hear.

Reading, Watching, Listening

We have read about the suburbs before in novels, memoirs, magazines, and newspapers—that is, before print was declared dead (again), and before newspapers ceased to clutter doorways and driveways as dailies both distinguished and disposable began to fold, one after the other. In the most sustained literary analysis of the suburbs to date, Jurca's *White Diaspora*, we learn about how the suburbs came to be the exemplary setting for the crisis of American normativity. Paradoxically, the privilege that cohered in the suburbs throughout the twentieth century—the bourgeois seclusion afforded to whiteness, masculinity, femininity, and childhood within the tidy confines of suburban domesticity—also became the prosperous white American's most profound burden. Jurca "marks the systematic erosion of the suburban house as a privileged site of emotional connection and stability," revealing through her supple readings of various novels, from Sinclair Lewis's *Babbit* to John Updike's "Rabbit" series, how the house ceases to be a spiritual "home" for the twentieth-century novel's anguished, primarily white, male protagonists.[66] She writes that "even as an 'indigenous ideal of suburban residence and home ownership' has become crucial to and equated with the achievement of the 'American dream' in this century, an ongoing strain of the American novel has insisted that the suburb and suburban house cheat characters out of the very thing that is supposed to be their white, middle-class, property-owning due."[67]

As much as we may derive a certain satisfaction from the spectacle of American normativity's spiritual unraveling in the master-planned communities meant to protect its prosperity, we can never forget that the structure of feeling made legible by Jurca's reading of the suburban novel—an ennui born of comfort and convenience—is also a privilege exclusive to normative subjects. The people, characters, and personae that populate *Relocations*—the Bakersfield-born, Coalinga-raised, transgender superstar JJ Chinois; the Buena Park teens who danced all night at Studio K in Knott's Berry Farm; the lost souls of the Inland Empire seeking healing in a strip-mall botanica (in Alex Espinoza's novel *Still Water Saints*); the trio of brown butches cruising for amusement through lesser Los Angeles (the performance ensemble Butchlalis de Panochtitlan)—refuse to luxuriate in this ennui. They simply cannot afford to. Instead they laugh, sway, watch, and sing along, focusing less on what is their due, understanding all the while that their task and their pleasure is to *make do* with a suburban world designed to keep them at bay or to expel them from its boundaries. They are the relocated: the queers, immigrants, and people of color who know that inhabiting the suburbs promises privilege but experience it otherwise.

The relocated (sometimes by choice, at other times by circumstance) are not as often found in literature as they are read in and through queer theory: in the incidental moments of queer imagining we happen upon through the yearnings and formative moments of discovery that may theoretically lead to elsewheres, but which bring us inevitably back to those shared, secret nowheres. For me it begins, appropriately enough, with a young provincial girl named Eve seeking a destiny elsewhere in other bodies and through others' desires. In the retrospective 1992 preface to her 1985 volume *Between Men: English Literature and Male Homosocial Desire*, Eve Kosofsky Sedgwick confesses, "There was something . . . irrepressibly *provincial* about the young author of this book." She writes about the special "incredulity" born of the realization that there was something avowedly *not* normal about her own provincial desires:

> As each individual story begins in the isolation of queer childhood, we
> compulsorily and excruciatingly misrecognize ourselves in the available mirror of
> the atomized, procreative, so-called heterosexual pre- or ex-urban nuclear family
> of origin, whose bruisingly inappropriate interpellations may wound us—those
> resilient or lucky enough to survive them—into life, life of a different kind. The
> site of that second and belated life, those newly constituted and denaturalized
> "families," those tardy, wondering chances at transformed and transforming self-
> and other-recognition, is the metropolis. But a metropolis continually recruited
> and reconstituted by having folded into it the incredulous energies of the
> provincial. Or—I might better say—the provincial energies of incredulity itself.

Even as she reinscribes the coordinates *Relocations* strives to unravel—that "chord that stretches from provincial origins to metropolitan destinies"[68]—she finds herself rerouted, pulled back to the incredulity, the naïveté and perhaps even euphoria that animates provincialism as it struggles to survive the toxic habitats of normativity. I like to imagine that this provincial incredulity is what inspires her later turn to the "reparative," the "additive and accretive" impulse of theoretical labor that eschews virtuosic displays of mastery, ambition, and knowing, in the spirit of intellectual and affective compromise.[69] As if writing across time to other provincial subjects seeking another way to read themselves in, with, and through space, time, and the problematic baggage of their formative moments from elsewhere, she concludes that "what we can best learn from such practices are, perhaps, the many ways in which selves and communities succeed in extracting sustenance from the objects of a culture—even of a culture whose avowed desire has often been not to sustain them."[70]

Other queer theorists have read, written, and forged reparative archives from the detritus of provincial, suburban pasts. Jennifer Doyle finds a source for the "sex objects" that would come to compose her scholarly archive in the daily offerings of porn catalogs left by a horny teenage neighbor in her family's mailbox in suburban New Jersey. In *Sex Objects: Art and the Dialectics of Desire*, the title *Moby Dick* (shared by a porn video as well as Melville's venerable novel) becomes a sign that activates the dialectics of her scholarly labors and fantasies, which mediates between high and low, the provincial and cosmopolitan, pornography and art, naïveté and knowing.[71] In *Disidentifications: Queers of Color and the Performance of Politics*, José Esteban Muñoz recalls his own formative moments of "suburban spectatorship," when "talk-show deviants . . . would appear long after I was supposed to be asleep in my South Florida home." These "deviants," televised and teleported to his suburban bedroom, awakened his ability to read into and otherwise. Through these late-night assignations with the small screen, Muñoz was able to "get it"—"it" referring to the "exhilarating" and "terrifying" languages of queer innuendo beamed in from the metropole.[72] There are surely other moments, other anecdotes that slip between the lines in the tomes of queer theory devoted to other places, objects, and subjects. I've tracked these incidents here not merely for the sake of revealing an otherwise-unwritten genealogy of provincial, suburban moments through Sedgwick and her pupils, thereby implying a through line of reparative, queer suburban thought that each may prefer to disavow. I follow these moments, these flash points that have captivated *my* attention across time in queer theory, because they also offer within them a genealogy for reception within the emergent queer suburban aesthetics I offer throughout this book. We move with and through each of them as they grasp toward other archives and places by reading books, looking at pictures, and watching TV.

We have seen the suburbs on TV—before and after network television was declared dead (many times over) and quality cable programming offered seductive new cul-de-sacs of fantasy and vérité. Lynn Spigel's remarkable *Welcome to the Dream House* traces the twin emergence of television and the postwar American suburbs. In many respects, TV is the emblematic suburban medium: a technology designed for the lived environment it helped to engender and subsequently reshape from the mid-twentieth century onward. From the ideal nuclear families who glowed as exemplars on shows like *Ozzie and Harriet* (1952–1966) and *Leave It to Beaver* (1957–1963), to their bizarre Goth doubles on *The Munsters* (1964–1966) and *The Addams Family* (1964–1966), TV has grappled with the social transformations of a suburbia that it played a tremendous role in creating.[73] Nothing is impossible in the suburbs on American television. TV assimilated encroaching monsters and hillbillies into the suburban neighborhood, paving the way for postmillennial soccer-mom drug dealers (on *Weeds*, 2005–) and dysfunctional mob bosses (on *The Sopranos*, 1999–2007), whom we actually pay extra to watch on premium cable. Although *Relocations* pauses for prime-time programming throughout its pages, with the occasional nod to the Norman Lear oeuvre and an extended side trip to the sun-dappled splendor of *The O.C.* (2003–2007), it is less invested in enumerating small-screen representations of the suburbs than it is tuned into the archives of affect inspired by the intimate viewing practices of the book's central figures. From Lynne Chan's appropriation of names, places, and products in her creation of JJ Chinois, to the incidental, televised debut of Studio K at Knott's Berry Farm, to the imperial reimaginings of British bands on MTV's earliest music videos in the Inland Empire and among the Butchlalis de Panochtitlan, TV belongs to the queer suburban imaginary as a node for what Jennifer Terry has called "remote intimacy."

In the earliest versions of Terry's current manuscript in progress, "Killer Entertainments: Militarism, Governmentality, and Consuming Desires in Transnational America," she defined the concept of remote intimacy as the "transmission of sentiments through designed uses and creative appropriations of telemediating devices."[74] While Terry focused primarily on the Internet and the multiuser, multiplayer platforms harnessed to work out the feelings that arose in the aftermath of George W. Bush's declaration of the "War on Terror"—from the "pro-military, imperialist attitudes" it inspired, to the "violent spiritualist reactions *against* it"—I want to hold on to some of the literalism she offers in the term, without relinquishing some of its harsher implications. Terry has given me license "to run with the concept," to remake it into a theory as well as praxis for queer of color suburban subjects. My own customized version of "remote intimacy" offers a friendly supplement and a reparative improvisation to Terry's concept. Television, and what is seen and heard on it, becomes one of the key telemediating devices on which I focus, because it remains a significant medium of "creative appropriation" for the queer of color suburban artists and figures in *Relocations*. Beyond fomenting what Benedict Anderson has famously called an "imagined community" through the simultaneous moments of consumption made possible across long distances with communication technologies (his concentrated on print), "remote intimacy" registers more acutely the temporal and spatial paradoxes of communion such shared consumption may offer.[75]

Remote intimacy, for example, is not contingent on a simultaneity either actual or imagined. Subjects consuming certain television archives may or may not watch and look at the same time, or even at or within the same era, especially since televisual recording technologies—from Betamax and VHS, to digital video recorders (DVRs), to web platforms like Hulu, have made it possible to relinquish what TV scholars have called "appointment viewing."[76] But one needn't look as far into the contemporary moment as TiVo, Netflix, YouTube, or whatever the next big thing is to make this point about TV. Syndication and repeats already afforded asynchronous temporalities of viewing and enabled what could be called archival practices of consumption for generations historically removed from the original run of certain formative programs, like network sitcoms (one of JJ Chinois's touchstone shows is *Good Times*) or prime-time soaps (like *Falcon Crest*—a BdP favorite).[77] And yet these artifacts of viewing continue to resonate in the queer of color suburban imaginary, creating collective intimacies out of what may have been solitary viewing practices in the past. This configuration and sentiment of "remoteness"—of watching or listening alone as an isolated subject of suburban sprawl—also haunts the various chapters throughout this book, creating generative intimacies among disparate suburban subjects that are often belated. We may not have read that book, seen that show, or heard that song together, but we do so now, not in the spirit of nostalgia but as if it truly is the first time. Together, it *is* the first time.

We have heard about the suburbs before in songs on the radio, on records and tapes (before they became CDs), and on CDs (before they became MP3s), disseminated through a music industry they say is on its deathbed.[78] We have heard about them in protest songs like Malvina Reynolds's jaunty, if biting, "Little Boxes"; in poseur protest pop like the Monkees' infectious "Pleasant Valley Sunday"; in 1980s British dance pop like "Suburbia," the Pet Shop Boys' melodic homage to both Madonna and the smooth jazz flügelhorn star Chuck Mangione. We have *heard* the suburbs in the music made there in garages, basements, and living room piano lessons.[79] We hear it in Downey, California, home of both the Carpenters and Metallica's front man, James Hetfield. We hear it in a sun-drenched Orange County that grew both Gwen Stefani of No Doubt and Zack de la Rocha of Rage Against the Machine. We hear it in the Inland Empire, where Joan Baez went to high school and Etta James lives, and where the horn sections for ska bands like the Skeletones and the Voodoo Glow Skulls honed their chops in the marching bands of the Riverside Unified School District. We hear it through the records and Cassingles we bought at big-box shops like Kmart and chain stores like the Wherehouse, Music Plus, and Tower Records.[80] I hear the suburbs everyday I write this book, its synthy refrains indistinguishable from the theory I read, the histories I find, the blunt numbers of the census data I scour.

I used to think popular music posed a distraction to this project, to the labor that went into carefully calibrating the studious part of suburban cultural studies. Now I've come to realize that it is the heartbeat pulsing through all the queer relocations and remote intimacies I tried *not* to sing, but which I end up singing anyway throughout this book in a twisted form of critical karaoke. Joshua Clover introduced the concept of "critical karaoke" to participants at the Experience Music Project's 2004 Pop Conference in Seattle. We were invited to select a song and write a brief essay to be read aloud as an accompaniment that could only last for the duration of the song's recorded length. Other stylistic choices were left to us as writers and interpreters. We could time our remarks to coincide with crescendos and dance breaks if we so chose, or we could read completely through the essay without pause if we felt anxious about the clock running out. As with much of the critical apparatus of this project, the tenets of critical karaoke are not reproduced strictly or prescriptively in *Relocations*, but rather are repurposed for a queer suburban aesthetics that revels in strange echoes. Like a good karaoke singer or *American Idol* contestant—and no, "good" paired with either of those terms does not equal an oxymoron—I've tried to make it my own, not by singing closely to the melody in an effort to get every note right, but with an interpretive turn of phrase, an improvisation, or unexpected pause that rearranges the stakes and spirit of each theory, each artifact of history, each transient performance.[81]

Relocations is not about popular music per se, but the popular music I and others hear in the suburbs informs every theoretical gesture, every awkward dance move performed solo or in groups, every historical high note piercing through these pages. Theoretically and cartographically, *Relocations* participates in the "audiotopian" practices of listening and mapping elegantly charted by Josh Kun. As Kun explains, an "audiotopia" is the equivalent of a musical map, "a musical 'you are here'" that positions you within larger social worlds. Riffing on remarks made by the African American poet Jean Toomer, Kun proposes that music transports us into different worlds; even when we eventually slide back into our "own worlds," we "slide back forever changed."[82] In the spirit of singing along, as all the figures I write about in this book do at some point or another, from Lynne Chan's JJ Chinois, to the kids at Studio K, to the novelist Alex Espinoza, to the Butchlalis de Panochtitlan, I would like to add what might be an excessive melismatic flourish to Kun's notion of audiotopia by insisting that sometimes popular music is most utopian when it transports us deeper *into* the heart of our own worlds rather than to different ones. It drags us back. Not backward looking through time, but back into the spaces and times that collide in our situated presences. It reminds us of where we are, where we come from, and where we never truly leave.

The listening practices I cultivated as an immigrant kid who relocated to the Inland Empire in the early 1980s determined the coordinates—at once spatial, conceptual, material, and theoretical—mapped throughout this book. The music I heard there was not unfamiliar. It is music not especially obscure but rather straight off the rack, befitting a culture of convenience. I heard it before in Manila—where I was born to a family of musicians, and where I spent most of the first decade of my life surrounded by music both homemade and broadcast from elsewhere on American-style Top 40 radio or on actual American TV shows. I heard it again when I landed in Southern California's Inland Empire, funneled through retail, taped off the radio, still broadcast from elsewhere. I hear it now when I listen again to the music they played at Knott's Berry Farm's Studio K, the dance club reanimated in "Behind the Orange Curtain," and in the car rides staged by the Butchlalis de Panochtitlan, who score their butch intimacies to "Diamond Girl" and "There Is a Light That Never Goes Out." It is a music inspired by commutes and too much time spent in a car moving slowly toward work or pleasure. As I explain more explicitly in my chapter on Butchlalis de Panochtitlan, so much of queer suburban sociability transpires in cars, driving around, looking for something (or someone) to do. While queer cosmopolitans are likely to find such searching and confined listening abject, I would argue that there is something tremendously generative in the acts of imaginative transformation that can turn a freeway or parking lot into a social- and soundscape, without needing the crutch of cool. It is the music that turns convenience into pleasure, the music of micromigrations between blocks or between suburbs. It is the music of immigration and the American pop songs we heard elsewhere foreshadowing the love, heartbreak, rebellion, wealth, and sex we would find once we arrived, only to remind us after we got here that we're still waiting for all those things.

It is the music that inspires us to ask questions. What about queer of color desires spawned somewhere else? What about those born in the provinces and in the suburbs? In and around malls? In schoolyards after hours, or, in the words of Alexandra Vazquez, on the "slippery naugahyde seats of a . . . public school bus"?[83] Made in garages (to gesture to Christine Bacareza Balance's work on Filipino American DJ culture) or crafted in basements, attics, and on public softball fields radiant in twilight smog? It is, was, and will be in these "transnational suburban hubs" that we bump to the beat of freestyle.[84] *There* we conduct our immigrant practices of "everyday performance," like the karaoke in our parents' carport or on their back porch.[85] This music—the pop music found everywhere but heard repeatedly in the suburbs—isn't just the cry of a forgotten and (as some would argue) justifiably forgettable suburban past of arbitrary queer, brown, immigrant musical discovery. Not from a precious little record store with snobby salesclerks, but rather from the bins at big-box shops or the dazzling, direct-mail innovation that was the Columbia House Catalog—ten records for a penny! These enticing, credit-wrecking temptations came in the mail, inspiring our mothers to wait for Ed McMahon to appear at the door with a fat, novelty-sized check: the American dream, COD (collect on delivery).

This is the music that moves *Relocations*. It sometimes manifests as lyrics from a chorus, such as from Journey's anthemic "Don't Stop Believin'" in my chapter on JJ Chinois, for example, or from the Smiths' "There Is a Light That Never Goes Out" in my chapter on the Butchlalis de Panochtitlan. Sometimes popular music itself becomes the conceptual framework for reading echoes through history and across time, as it does in my chapter on the Inland Empire. At other moments popular music is the direct object of inquiry, as in my chapter on Orange County's amusement park soundscapes, "Behind the Orange Curtain." In a more general sense, music functions in *Relocations* as another technology of remote intimacy. In much the same way that remote intimacy as a viewing or reading practice offers belated opportunities for communion among disparate subjects through asynchronous encounters with popular objects, listening as remote intimacy brings people, things, and concepts together, even if suburban space and time dictates their dispersal and isolation.

The queer of color suburban archive I ask you to read, see, and hear in *Relocations*—one that commutes to and from an array of locations that are not necessarily "destinations"—is at once an archive of familiarity and incongruity, of things and situations that are utterly mundane, mainstream, predictable, or "behind the times," yet have somehow managed to remain unthinkable in both normative and queer cultural contexts. It comprises the popular forms we encountered *in* our little boxes through other little boxes, like TV sets, radios, and sedans. Queerly, all this brings us back to our bedrooms, but not in the way you might think. It brings us back alone, with a flashlight under the covers so that we can read after-hours, with a glowing TV screen as our companion, or with our headphones on in the dark. In this little box we sit, think, and dream alone until we find those precious others who've done the same, who've maybe even swayed the same in nowhere elses or in desperate elsewheres, teaching themselves every painstaking move and note until someday we can raise our lighters in unison, as unmistakable voices sing with a tender, distant sorrow.

2 Relocating Queer Critique
Lynne Chan's JJ Chinois

I hate New York. . . . It's not simply the city's awesome capacity to imagine itself as the be-all and the end-all of modern queer life (no small feat, mind you). What I really hate is the casualness with which this move is dispatched, the taken-for-granted assumption that you want to be on that tiny island (but not some of those outer boroughs) and be there soon. That you want to get there someday, somehow, and get out of this god forsaken town.

—Scott Herring, *Another Country: Queer Anti-Urbanism*

A lot has been said about JJ Chinois, and there's a lot more to be said about him. His popularity has grown enormously in the years since his first admirers started shouting, "Nice Ass." It began with the teens of course. But at JJ's debut in New York City, it soon became obvious that it's easier to skin an amoeba than to catalog the "typical JJ Chinois fan." . . . His good looks and raw-throated vulnerability bring an immediate response from fans and critics. But his story actually began a few years ago, in Coalinga, California.

—Lynne Chan, "JJ Chinois" website

Just a small town girl
Livin' in a lonely world
She took the midnight train goin' anywhere.

—Journey, "Don't Stop Believin'"

Journeys with JJ

A lot has been said about JJ Chinois since I first presented a paper about his website at the 2002 Modern Language Association Annual Convention in New York City.[1] JJ Chinois is an alter ego, superstar avatar, and long-term artistic endeavor of Lynne Chan, a queer Asian American multimedia artist based in New York but originally from Cupertino, California. The irony that this entire project on queer suburban imaginaries began, in effect, about an artist currently living and working in New York, and on a panel about "Gay New York" hosted in the proverbial belly of the beast, is not lost on me. At its best, the embryonic fifteen-minute form of this project called for a renewed focus on queer regionalisms. At its worst, the paper devolved into the same boosterist rhetoric about California that inspired so many migrations to the Golden State. Little did I comprehend then that my abundant enthusiasm masked genuine aggression. Like Scott Herring, my intellectual comrade in critical anti-urbanism (whose sassy, full-throated complaint I open with above), I get downright hateful about the developmental logics of queer relocation starting in amorphous elsewheres and triumphantly ending somewhere—in the designated "place for us" that is New York, New York.

And yet there was also something desperately wannabe about my earliest renditions of shrill West Coast cheerleading about the JJ Chinois website (http://www.jjchinois.com/) that became less about what was *wrong* with buying into the New York state of mind, and more about being "good enough" to play the big city game. As if lost in the karaoke echo chamber of a song that resonates loudly in the realms of both immigrant masculinity and jazz-hands fagulosity—"New York, New York"—my argument took up the song's climactic, gut-busting lyrics as the initial template for tracking the relocations in Chan's JJ Chinois projects: "If I can make it there, I'll make it anywhere." Overdetermined as those lyrics felt for me at that moment, in an unflatteringly lit MLA ballroom in midtown Manhattan, the object of inquiry itself—Chan's humor-driven work about a transgender pop idol discovered in Coalinga, a cattle-ranching outpost in central California—also demanded renewed efforts to transpose these lyrics into the key of the reparative rather than the paranoid.[2] Chan's mock-fansite for JJ Chinois responds to the challenge of "New York, New York" by insisting that making it *there* requires making anywhere—your characterless nowhere—into a *somewhere*. With her witty mythologizing of rural, suburban, and exurban locales in California such as Coalinga, Bakersfield, Riverside, and Cupertino, Chan's website traces JJ's multipronged migration from sites in Asia to California, and from California's suburbs to New York City.

I first posited California as New York's Other not only because Chan's art demanded it, but also because the flyover rivalry between East Coast and West is so deeply ingrained in American popular narratives about immigration, migration, and pathways to the "good life."[3] For better or worse, New York City and California serve as national endpoints, not only at the coastal edges of the mainland American expanse, but also within fantasmatic trajectories of a still-extant, if now economically ravaged, "American dream" for immigrants as well as queers.[4] From Ellis Island to Angel Island, from Fire Island to Fashion Island, New York City and California's (coastal) suburbs serve as last stops in trajectories of struggle—then triumph—for the queer aspirant as much as they are beacons for strangers from a different shore.[5] But even though Chan's JJ Chinois appears to take off with this familiar flight plan from California to the New York islands, the ameliorative effect of her work does not merely rest with recuperating certain California sites so that they may ultimately be included in a more expansive master-plan for queer metronormativity.[6]

As I have come to realize during my extended journeys with JJ Chinois, the journey itself is what ends up being important. By saying this, I'm not just recycling some feel-good California checkout-stand Zen, hoping it'll make you mellow enough to be down with whatever I say. The journey *is* crucial, not only to this chapter on Chan's work but also to this entire project. How one actually moves through space has been a key point of distinction between the urban and suburban in planning, architecture, and even aesthetics. As I illustrate throughout my subsequent chapters, the commute—our everyday micro-journeys for work, errands, escape, and pleasure—becomes the emblematic form of suburban movement and contact (or lack thereof).[7] The more protracted journeys outlined in Chan's JJ Chinois projects, from Far East to West to Out East, sets the pace for the other, ostensibly more local movements in Southern California featured throughout this book. As an aesthetic project fundamentally outlining the developmental arc in which queers and immigrants are transported from nowhere places to the United States' emblematic urban destinations, Chan's JJ Chinois website provides the broad brushstrokes for the more intricate relocations traced around corners, beneath freeway overpasses, and sometimes stuck in the middle of suburban blocks in *Relocations*.

As I introduced above, the journey is important. Through the character of JJ Chinois, Chan racializes as well as genders her approach to drag. She exaggerates Asian and white masculine iconographies that circulated with suburban cachet during her formative years in the late 1970s and early 1980s. JJ's look is famously crafted in the image of Bruce Lee, himself an avatar for interracial imaginaries about eros and masculinity. As Mimi Thi Nguyen has noted, "JJ models himself after Lee as a lover rather than a fighter, transfiguring the iconic image of Lee's masculine physicality for its sensuality and eroticism."[8] Beyond stylizing JJ after the most iconic Asian male to have "made it" as an enduring cinematic superstar and sex symbol in the latter half of the twentieth century, Chan also models JJ after figures who are, to put it kindly, somewhat *less* iconic in the Asian American popular imaginary. Another of Chan's inspirations for JJ Chinois is Steve Perry, the former lead singer of the San Francisco–based pop-rock supergroup Journey, circa early 1980s.[9] What differentiates Chan's citation of Perry's period-specific style from her homage to Lee's legendary aesthetic is that Perry's appearance is freighted by time, whereas Lee's look (by virtue of his untimely death and the mythological circumstances surrounding it) achieves timelessness. To put it another way, even though Bruce Lee died long ago, his style lives on, whereas Steve Perry lives on but his early-1980s style expired long ago.

Of course, one could protest that Perry's look occasionally resurfaces in ironized forms in hipster boroughs throughout the world, but it is precisely Chan's point to underscore the belatedness that adheres to this look's latter-day

Lynne Chan, "JJ and a Young Fan Posing Backstage at the El Rey Theater,"
2002. Courtesy of the artist. All rights reserved.

citations. Steve Perry functions, in other words, as Chan's vehicle for what Elizabeth Freeman calls temporal drag, "with all of the associations that the word 'drag'
has with retrogression, delay, and the pull of the past upon the present."[10] As I've
already emphasized in my introductory chapter, temporal drag is a key concept
that reappears in different iterations within a queer of color suburban aesthetics—in style, embodiment, and sound. Without belaboring the point here, I do
want to stress that Chan's freighted visual invocation of Steve Perry also, in effect,
activates a sonic echo that provides the perfect accompaniment to JJ's journey
across the United States: "Just a small town girl / livin' in a lonely world / she
took the midnight train goin' anywhere."

Since it first debuted in 1981 on the album appropriately titled *Escape*, Journey's anthemic hit "Don't Stop Believin'" has scored everything from movie
montages, to sports comebacks, to political campaigns, to small-screen fina-
les.[11] While legions of pop culture scribes have already written, and are sure
to write more, about the significance of Journey's enduring anthem for the
United States' small-town dreamers, Chan encapsulates the ethos of "Don't

Stop Believin'" through JJ Chinois without ever explicitly using the song on her website. What she holds on to with JJ's narrative is that melismatic "feeeliiiin'" the song implores its listeners to keep striving for. It is not necessarily "belief" that becomes the key element of JJ's journey, but rather the notion of not stopping—of perpetually yearning toward "streetlight[s], people" in a quest of "living just to find emotion."[12]

The propensity toward movement and sensation we find narrated on JJ Chinois's website, as well as in the song "Don't Stop Believin'," would seem to reinscribe a certain national romance with mobility (at once spatial and economic) endemic to an American dream intensified during the nation's suburbanization after World War II.[13] Even as the suburbs were founded on class mobility and constant movement in the form of commutes, countercultures positioning themselves against suburbanization revisited romantic and bohemian ideals about wanderlust to reclaim mobility for the spiritually depleted subject's sensational nourishment.[14] Refracted through the lens of queer migrations, meanwhile, we might also construe this sensation-seeking mobility (predisposed to bustling boulevards instead of small towns and single-family dwellings) as a form of spatial and cultural privilege that has since become de rigueur for queer subjects. Scott Herring has called this spatial momentum "compulsory urbanity," an effect of metronormativity's discursive emergence during the second half of the twentieth century.[15] While we will explore genealogies of gay urbanity later in this chapter, I want to focus here on the other genealogies of queer of color relocation made possible by Chan's *attention* to movement.

The "midnight train" Steve Perry famously falsettoed into being on Journey's *Escape* album is actually going "*anywhere*," not somewhere in particular. A striking feature of Chan's JJ Chinois website is that it, too, will go anywhere, refusing to pass over the points of transit to and from emblematic sites of migration and immigration like California and New York. While Chan's JJ Chinois does arrive at a designated destination, the route rather than the outcome becomes the focal point of the project. Further, the affective resonance of these compulsory relocations amplify the tensions between and among queer national migrations and international immigration to the United States.[16] Through JJ Chinois's journey, Chan analogizes her own migration from the suburbs to New York City with her parents' immigration to the United States from Hong Kong. By situating JJ's tour stops in chain stores and recreational centers within the so-called flyover zones of the United States, Chan also offers an imaginative remapping of local queer migrations to complement and complicate various renditions of diaspora, which have inevitably focused on clustered, nation-based relocations to urban ghettos (e.g., "Chinatowns"), rather than to rural or suburban environments.[17]

This dialectic between diaspora and what I will define later as its ludic double—dykeaspora—not only propels my analytic of queer suburban imaginaries, but also refocuses our attention onto American imperialism as it traffics across international borders (as well as within and through local landscapes and architectures). While queer scholarship has addressed the consequences of American imperialism in national and international contexts, queer studies has yet to explore in depth how U.S. imperialism coincides with *suburban* expansion after World War II and through the "conflicts" in Korea and Vietnam.[18] By placing Chan's work in conversation with scholarship on queer migration as well as suburban studies, I show how sexuality, race, and regionalism collide in American imperial narratives. As Kandice Chuh explains, "The already complex matter of understanding the position of U.S. racialized minorities is further complicated by recognizing the United States as an imperial metropole."[19] That American imperialism manifests most vividly both architecturally and ideologically in the nation's suburbs as well as its metropolitan centers develops as an important keynote of this entire book. Lynne Chan's wacky, idiosyncratic approach to imperial signifiers in various landscapes—in the rural, suburban, and urban—sets the tone for my attempt to confront imperialism by "imagining otherwise" (to invoke Chuh). Perhaps using humor and kitsch to relocate empire and diaspora in sites beyond the metropole has the potential to deflate forms of imperial power that are only enhanced by the serious languages of denial and burden.[20]

Before turning our attention completely to JJ's journey, allow me to address one of the most common complaints I received about my earlier approaches to Chan's work: that JJ Chinois's settings are not always technically suburban. Moving from sites like Coalinga (an agricultural, exurban community just outside Fresno, California) to Skowhegan, Maine (a Kennebec River Valley town with a population of about nine thousand), Chan's JJ Chinois projects show a proclivity toward what we might call spatial promiscuity. And yet I would argue that Chan's promiscuity—her conflating and combining of spatial styles and citations to conform to her site, or her virtual "lot"—is part of what establishes the very *suburbanness* of her aesthetic. Structurally and conceptually, the suburban *is* the mediation between the rural and the urban.

As of the 2000 U.S. Census, "rural" and "urban" remain the primary spatial classifications used to analyze population data. (There are data-set distinctions between "urbanized areas" and "urban clusters" that we can only assume are meant to absorb suburban environments, but no official classification for the suburbs exists at the Bureau of the Census to date.)[21] Beyond filling the amorphous population gap between "the rural" and "the urban," the suburban has always stylistically combined the romance of rusticity with urban modernity.

From recreations of the ranch house and imitations of English and Mediter-ranean country villas, to the sleek, glass-box transparency of Neutra's mid-cen-tury modern gems and contemporary loft developments on restored subur-ban main streets, the suburbs have accommodated a range of lifestyle visions inspired by both "the country" and "the city."[22] Contrary to a popular imagi-nary replete with cookie-cutter images of suburban tracts, suburban ideology has historically promoted individualization through architectural style. John Archer has traced this ideology to the republicanism spawned by the American Revolutionary War, which "presented bourgeois American men . . . both the obligation and the opportunity to engage in more intensive opportunities for self-identification through various forms of architectural house plans, stylistic rhetoric, and furnishings."[23]

This license for experimentation and customization has, depending on the aesthetic trends of any given moment, also come under attack for its random excesses, as the literary critic Barry Langford explains:

> However paradoxically, [literary] modernists were just as likely to pillory the
> conformist suburbs for a certain *excess* of (albeit illegitimate) personality: the
> vision of mile after mile of suburban semi-detached estates laid out in cookie-
> cutter uniformity, competes in the bestiary of modernist design orthodoxy with
> their contradictory flipsides, the stubborn resistance to system manifested by the
> functionally superfluous additions and flourishes, such as mock-Tudor fake half-
> timbering and excessively ebullient gables. . . . Design historians have likewise
> noted the manifold possibilities for idiosyncratic symbolic self-expression in
> such quintessential suburban domestic items such as birdbaths, garden gates,
> crazy paving, twee housenames like Bideawee or Dunroamin, and so on. The
> peculiar offence of the suburbs, then, was to be sites of *ambiguity*: specifically, the
> ambiguity that arises from the problem of personal style.[24]

Langord's emphasis on excess and ambiguity, I would add, makes it possible for us to see how this particular crisis of suburban representation is linked to the incursion of raced, gendered, and sexualized subjects into the suburban setting, where home ownership and self-expression were previously reserved for the white, male, bourgeois "master of the house." Whereas the white, male, bourgeois home owner renovates and "improves," enhancing property values through his self-expression, it is women, immigrants, and people of color (essentially all Others) who ornament and over-adorn their homes in gaudy displays of "pride," which are paradoxically guaranteed to diminish property values.[25]

Even mainstream popular culture has parodied such unwelcome develop-ments in the suburbs. *Next Friday* (2000)—the second film in the hit *Friday* franchise created by and starring the gangsta rapper turned Hollywood player Ice Cube—relocates to the suburbs only to discover (in the words of its tagline) that "the suburbs make the 'hood look good." The film unfolds amid the backdrop of the smoggy exurban enclaves east of Los Angeles dubbed the "Inland Empire": a stucco landscape of Spanish-style subdivisions where the "good life" is transformed into an extension of the "'hood life" (and the subject of a subsequent chapter in this book). *Next Friday* depicts a suburban culture clash through a series of slapstick encounters among blacks, Latinos, and Asians vying for their respective interpretations of the suburban landscape. This clash is also, fundamentally, a conflict among styles of living that rupture the architectural interchangeability and similarity that defines (often by failing to define) suburban space. During various chase scenes in the film, the characters have difficulty knowing where they're going because everything looks the same. But *Next Friday* also derives much of its humor from portraying what are expected to be generic and unmarked tract homes and strip malls as "blinged-out" ethnicized lairs for the film's characters. Chinatown tchotchkes, low-riding mini-trucks, and ghetto baroque furniture vacuum-sealed in vinyl point to the endless varieties of class and "ethnically" inflected customization that have gradually transformed the suburban environment while putting a distinctly different spin on the competitive aspiration to keep up with the Joneses.[26]

By confounding white bourgeois tastes with classed and racialized flourishes of prosperity, *Next Friday* offers a critique of suburban aesthetics while reconfiguring the suburban imaginary with its parodic take on the stylistic markers of upward mobility. Whereas *Next Friday* explores how suburban spaces and communities have been altered by the mostly lateral migrations made by urban families of color seeking more affordable housing, Chan inverts the classic "good life" trajectory from the city to the suburbs. She engages in and critiques a queer developmental narrative in which the queer subject does not come out, but rather comes *into* a queer scene by moving from a gaudy yet placeless place like the suburbs to "the city." Taking its cues from pop-cult films of the 1970s all the way up to *Next Friday* in 2000, the starting premise of Chan's revisionist narrative is to "re-Orient" her audiences to an otherwise dis-orienting suburban landscape: to show us that placeless places have their own vexed, if unarticulated, relationship to race, sexual orientation, and Orientalism.[27] As the subsequent section shows, Chan's customization of space and self—her amplification of the suburbs' excesses and ambiguity through JJ's "ethnic," transgender star persona—makes apparent the reach of an individuating suburban bourgeois ideology otherwise obscured by the veneer of conformity.

From Suburban Idyll to Suburban Idol: Inventing JJ Chinois

> It turns out we overestimated the power of architectural determinism. The
> suburbs have proved flexible enough to accommodate working mothers . . . as
> well as a great many different kinds of families and lifestyles. Since I left the
> Gates, its white nuclear families have been joined by singles and gays, Asians and
> African-Americans, people operating home businesses and empty nesters. . . . The
> world that built the postwar suburbs has passed away, and yet those suburbs still
> stand, remodeled by the press of history. What they haven't been is reimagined or
> renamed, at least not yet.
>
> —Michael Pollan, "The Triumph of Burbopolis"

> Forget Chinatown: most Asian Americans live in middle-class suburbs. The big-
> gest markets for Asian suburbanites are in western states, but more than half of
> the top-25 Asian metros are elsewhere. Asian suburbs are diverse markets, ranging
> from Filipino Daly City to Chinese Monterey Park. And while suburban Asians
> are usually assimilated Americans, they also tend to preserve ancestral customs.
> —William P. O'Hare, William H. Frey, and Dan Fost, "Asians in the Suburbs"

Despite the evolving architectural functions and demographics of the postmillennial suburbs, its twentieth-century mythos of homogeneity manages to endure.
In *White Diaspora*, a study of suburban novels from the 1930s to the late twentieth century, Catherine Jurca describes how a "suburban aesthetics" was not only
produced by the political and economic imperatives of a postwar United States
that inspired a "white flight" from cities to suburbs, but in turn produced a powerful cultural myth about suburban life that achieved saliency as a master-narra-
tive for the white middle classes. As Jurca explains, the suburban literary canon
established in the twentieth century by authors like John Updike, Richard Yates,
Sloan Wilson, and Rick Moody (among others) represented the suburbs as "the
exemplary location, not only of middle-class advantages, but of middle-class
abasement; moreover, its abasement is a function of its advantages."[28]

Encapsulating a sanitary ideal of white, middle-class homogeneity and "safety," as
well as its dark underbelly of psychic dysfunction and suffocating privilege, the suburban aesthetic has only recently begun to account for a new wave of immigrants,
queers, people of color, and working-class families (many of whom were displaced
from urban centers by encroaching gentrification and skyrocketing property values), who now form "minority majorities" in places like the California suburbs.[29] A
slew of novels and films this past decade have transposed the white, upper-middle-
class intrigue and ennui of the suburban aesthetic into dramas about immigrant
assimilation (like Jhumpa Lahiri's celebrated 2003 novel *The Namesake*) or kinetic

parables of overachievement gone bad (like Justin Lin's cinematic take on Asian American hooligan nerds in Orange County, *Better Luck Tomorrow*, 2002). As the epigraph from O'Hare, Frey, and Fost declares, the "Asian suburbs" have proliferated throughout the American West, most remarkably in Northern and Southern California, thus relocating the representational landscape for various articulations of immigrant drama.[30] While Chan begins with a reconfigured, racialized suburban landscape as a point of departure for her JJ Chinois projects, she opts out of the cycles of self-pity—or to paraphrase Jurca, the abasement of advantage—so often revisited in suburban representations.[31] Instead, humor and hyperbole are the cornerstones of Chan's project. To focus on humor is not to say that privilege (particularly the privileges enjoyed by professional-class immigrants) are simply laughed away, failing to appear in Chan's work more broadly speaking. Rather, Chan uses humor to underscore how class privilege employs certain idioms of despair and sentimentality in suburban cultural representations.

Part of Chan's reparative intervention with the suburban aesthetic, then, is to summon forth what Jurca calls the abasement of advantage without dignifying it, exposing it instead for its laughable shallowness through indirection and fantasy. In the various live and web-based incarnations of her JJ Chinois projects, Chan works to transform her suburban imaginary from sprawl to specificity by trading on an idiosyncratic repertoire of place-names and strip-mall sites. In doing so, she constructs a suburban archive of excess, as well as alternate forms of worldly knowledge. The "worldliness" of this suburban archive is contingent on the classed, racialized, and nationalized tropes of popular culture, particularly television and web culture, which function as the surrogate sites and circuits of sociability in an architecturally decentralized suburban context.[32]

Where in the World Is JJ Chinois?

Of course, Chan is not the first visual artist, nor the first *queer* visual artist, to find inspiration in the suburbs.[33] The legendary lesbian photographer Catherine Opie's body of work, for example, belies her long-term fascination with the suburban landscapes of Southern California and beyond, beginning with her MFA photographic thesis, "Master Plan" (1986–1988), which chronicles the development of a tract-home project in Valencia, California, near the Magic Mountain amusement park and the CalArts campus.[34] Opie has also documented emblematic suburban architectures like "Freeways" (1995), as well as lesbian families across the United States (2000's "Domestic" series), and ultimately her own family's scenes of domestic bliss and civic protest ("In and Around Home," 2005).[35] Like Opie, Chan also turns mini-malls into muses (Opie's "Mini-Malls" series from 1998 features black-and-white photographs of what one *New York Times* reviewer called "hideous developments . . . distinguished by their banal, low-lying construction and barrages of signs in languages from English to Korean").[36] Opie's beautifully stark portraits of freeways and mini-malls offer some level of abstraction, playing as they do with the vantage point of aesthetic spectatorship. The documentary perspective of the "Freeways" and "Mini-Malls" series in particular imparts a voyeuristic, if intimately calibrated, distance with these suburban architectures. But Chan actually inserts her persona, JJ Chinois, into the mini-mall milieu, beginning with JJ's discovery at a strip-mall dim-sum restaurant and continuing through his tour stops in various chain stores like Payless ShoeSource. Significantly, Chan accomplishes this through words rather than images, foregoing photographic depictions of the mini-mall or strip mall, opting instead to use the banal language featured on the strip mall's "hideous" signage as her medium. As we shall see below, part of Chan's purpose in taking her art to the mini-mall is to move away from abstraction in order to inhabit strip malls and mini-malls as so many immigrants do: as entrepreneurial sites and spaces of sociability.

JJ Chinois's domain is a domain name. He can be found striking his signature soft-butch, *contrapposto* pose at JJChinois.com. The borderless space of the World Wide Web plays on the fantasy of JJ's global appeal (even Chairman Mao is one of JJ's international fans) while spatially allegorizing the drama of JJ's nar-

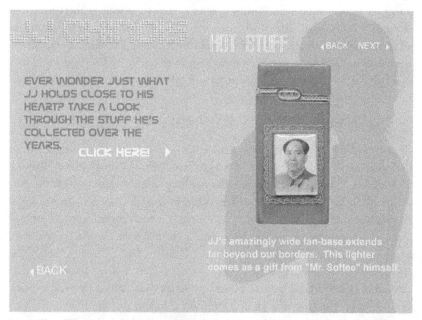

Lynne Chan, "Chairman Mao Lighter," JJChinois.com, 2002. Courtesy of the artist. All rights reserved.

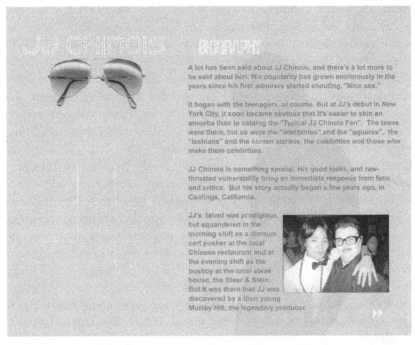

A lot has been said about JJ Chinois, and there's a lot more to be said about him. His popularity has grown enormously in the years since his first admirers started shouting, "Nice ass."

It began with the teenagers, of course. But at JJ's debut in New York City, it soon became obvious that it's easier to skin an amoeba than to catalog the "Typical JJ Chinois Fan". The teens were there, but so were the "dilettantes" and the "squares", the "lesbians" and the screen starlets, the celebrities and those who make them celebrities.

JJ Chinois is something special. His good looks, and raw-throated vulnerability bring an immediate response from fans and critics. But his story actually began a few years ago, in Coalinga, California.

JJ's talent was prodigious, but squandered in the morning shift as a dim sum cart pusher at the local Chinese restaurant and at the evening shift as the busboy at the local steak house, the Steer & Stein. But it was there that JJ was discovered by a then young Murray Hill, the legendary producer.

Lynne Chan, "Biography," JJChinois.com, 2002. Courtesy of the artist. All rights reserved.

rative of origin in another borderless zone: the California expanse somewhere between and around Los Angeles and San Francisco.

Because the type of interclass, interracial, and intersexual contact enabled by street-life and close-quarter interactions in big cities is not available to the geographically isolated queer subject,[37] the web becomes the non-space JJ Chinois uses to foment an intimacy among widely dispersed "teens," "dilettantes," "squares," "lesbians," "starlets," "celebrities," and "those who make them celebrities."[38] All supposedly compose JJ's fan base. After the Flash intro, the first page at which JJ's visitors arrive tells his biography. We learn about JJ's smashing debut in New York City engineered by the impresario and original drag king of comedy, Murray Hill, who is himself named after a little nowhere spot in Manhattan.[39] It becomes apparent that JJ has already made it there, and that we, luckily enough, are about to retrace his road to stardom.

The second page of JJ's bio informs us that "his story began a few years ago in Coalinga, California." Anyone who has ever taken a drive on the I-5 between San Francisco and Los Angeles, or who has read the *New York Times* article "The Dazed and the Bored on I-5," will recognize this place-name about midway through the route, near a corporate cattle ranch.[40] Coalinga is described on its official city website (http://www.coalinga.com/) as a place "nestled in Pleasant Valley . . . ten miles west of Interstate 5." The Coalinga website situates the town within the "urban fringe" of the city of Fresno, about sixty miles away, which the site boasts is "California's sixth largest city."[41] What comes as a surprise in JJ's bio is not just that JJ uses Coalinga as his geographical springboard, but rather the specific settings in Coalinga where JJ's "raw-throated vulnerability" is purportedly discovered. According to his bio, JJ squanders his "prodigious talents" as a "dim-sum cart pusher at the local Chinese restaurant." Meanwhile, JJ toils away during night shifts at a discount family steakhouse called "Steer 'n Stein." Chan cribbed the name from an establishment now rechristened the "Spunky Steer" in Riverside, California, a good two hundred miles south of Coalinga.[42]

By conflating, confusing, and substituting one suburban site for the next, Chan uses a familiar humorous trope that plays on the suburbs' infinite interchangeability. Places, people, and things are supposedly so similar from one suburb to the next that it matters very little whether places like the Steer 'n Stein are actually in Riverside or Coalinga: some manifestation of the kitschy cowboy steakhouse will undoubtedly be found in either place. The creative license Chan takes with locations, however, rewrites the punch line and substitutes one suburban site for another for two differently situated audiences. As Chan explains, JJ Chinois's urbane audiences are expected to find a kind of sight-gag humor in the place-name "Coalinga" without even knowing exactly what it signifies, while also assuming that the notion of Coalinga harboring a dim-sum restaurant is outlandish.[43] The site of locational knowledge for a queer New Yorker in JJ's bio would be Murray Hill, recognizable as both an homage to a place-name in Manhattan (albeit one not known as a queer locale) and the *nom de stage* of a queer entertainer who has long been based in New York City. Chan offers these place markers to a cosmopolitan audience but eventually relocates the site of "knowing" as she continues to play with place-names on the JJ Chinois website.

Unlike the cosmopolitan reader of JJ's bio, the suburban reader might not find the name Coalinga in and of itself visually humorous. But the suburbanite might revel in another level of signification and recognition. To understand the joke fully requires living or having lived the demographic specificity of what might outwardly appear to be indistinguishable suburban locales somewhere in the vast California expanse. A savvy suburbanite in California would know that the dim-sum cart pusher would most likely be found in Monterey Park, the self-dubbed "Beverly Hills for Chinese," or maybe some other densely populated Asian suburb like Rowland Heights, Walnut, Fountain Valley, or Torrance, if not necessarily in Coalinga.[44] Or rather, the Asian suburban audience who lives in Monterey Park, or who drives there for dim sum from any one of a number of other South-

Personal photo of Lynne and Leigh Chan posing in their cul-de-sac in front of the Apple headquarters, Cupertino, CA, ca. 1979. Courtesy of the artist.

ern California outposts, would realize that *this* suburb is where you might find someone like JJ Chinois.

The inside joke is also for queers oriented beyond the cosmopole. JJ Chinois's laughable open secret is not that he is a queer, transgendered, Asian performer passing as a boy in a place that fails to recognize him, but rather that Lynne Chan, now a New York City artist who has created this persona and recreated these places, shares in an intimate knowledge of suburban specificities. The cosmopolitan queer ethos, as Wayne Brekhus and Dereka Rushbrook have each suggested, relies on the repudiation of the suburbs and the glorification of urban hot spots for its veneer of stylistic and identitarian superiority.[45] Chan engages in a game of recognition with suburban queers while inviting a return of the repressed, encouraging another kind of "outing" altogether: that of a spatial familiarity with generic, nowhere spaces. JJ Chinois's narrative suggests that queers might actually come out of "nowhere," from a myriad of specifically situated and potentially embarrassing nowheres thought to be at odds with the formation of the queer, racialized subject. The topographical knowingness that distinguishes the queer cosmopolitan—where the best dim sum in the city is, or where the haute cuisine beef cheeks are perfectly done—is thus subverted by Chan's narration of JJ Chinois's discovery in such a remote setting.

Though much of Chan's website suggests that JJ Chinois rises triumphantly out of central California as a fabulous transgendered star adorned with Playboy pinkie rings and a "sexxy [sic] attitude," his actual emergence as a character in Chan's performance oeuvre is at once more quotidian yet surprisingly transnational than his web bio attests. Where it actually all began (to echo the rhetoric of JJ's web biography) is in Cupertino, California, a prosperous Silicon Valley suburb of San Jose, which is also the global headquarters for Apple Inc. Chan and her older brother, Leigh, were raised in a cul-de-sac in Cupertino in the shadow of the Apple building.

Chan's father worked as a librarian and information science specialist at a local community college. Her mother worked as a programmer in the telecommunications industry. Both were among a first wave of highly skilled and technologically savvy immigrant workers to relocate to the area in the 1970s during the region's storied boom funded by venture capitalists concentrated in nearby Menlo Park.[46] Like so many Asian immigrants, Chan's parents came to the United States separately from Hong Kong, after the passage of the 1965 Immigration and Nationality Act.[47] As many Asian American studies scholars have noted, this legislation often favored professional- and managerial-class immigrants from Asia, because East Asian nations in particular were experiencing their own economic resurgence during the post–World War II era, thereby enabling more lateral class migrations.[48] In a personal interview with Chan, she explained how her parents, like many other professional-class immigrants, were invested in the suburban ethos of upward mobility, locational safety, and assimilationist success.[49] She even jokes that the apex of her family's achievement manifested in a customized, ornamental addition to their Cupertino tract home around the time they approached retirement in the late 1990s: a neoclassical balustrade her dad was particularly proud of.

Despite her family's achievement of middle-class mobility, Chan's own daily movements were restricted by her parents' more traditional views about sociability, safety, and propriety. (Perhaps such restrictions fall within the category of what O'Hare, Frey, and Fost refer to as the tendency of suburban Asian Americans to "preserve ancestral customs.")[50] Chan describes her parents, especially her mother, as "typically overprotective," to the extent that simple excursions on her bicycle to the nearby Dunkin' Donuts with friends would have to assume the character of an elaborate subterfuge.[51] Her parents were especially concerned about "hanging out," or idling with other teens in the public sphere for no apparent purpose. For these reasons, Chan herself began to romanticize the otherwise-banal commercial sites frequented by her mostly white American peers, who "seemed so free, able to come and go whenever they wanted," for after-school socializing at strip-mall venues like fast-food restaurants, the 7-Eleven convenience store, and arcades.[52] Such parental restrictions not only applied to how often Lynne and her brother could leave the house or where they could go, but also extended to how they might present themselves in public.

While her parents "went through a phase," in Chan's words, of trying to keep her and her brother connected to Chinese culture by enrolling them in Chinese American weekend schools, her parents very rigorously adopted the policy of insisting that their children "do as much as possible to be like everyone else."[53] Paradoxically, Chan's parents wanted her and her brother to "fit in" by eradicating any possible hint of a Chinese accent, at the same time that they policed her and her brother's efforts to fit in too much by indulging in trendy styles that could be construed as immodest or improperly gendered. As Chan explains, "I was a budding tomboy (of course), and hated wearing dresses or skirts. I thought cute athletic shorts—you remember dolphin shorts?—would be OK because they were a 'unisex' trend at the time. But my mom forced me to wear culottes instead. I think people call them 'skorts' now [a contraction of 'skirt' and 'shorts']."[54]

Instead of transposing these vestiges of adolescent angst and the everyday drama of overprotective immigrant parents into something more troubling, traumatic, or studiously profound in her subsequent artwork, Chan has chosen to engage with these memories in all their fantastic ordinariness and unbridled silliness. Tone—especially a good-natured rather than withering approach to humor—becomes central to Chan's mode of customizing suburban social and commercial venues as a counterpoint to the emphasis on the home and privacy, not only in larger suburban discourses but also as it had been scripted in her family's efforts to achieve an American version of middle-class domesticity. Chan traces a pattern of queer migration from the suburbs to the city in part to eschew her immigrant parents' investment in the opposite trajectory: an "American dream" of upward mobility and a better life for their children in the suburban context.[55] She first conjured JJ Chinois as a performative alter ego after she decided to leave California altogether to pursue her career as an artist in New York in 1999. What she imagined would be her disentanglement from the sprawling suburbs, and from the overprotectiveness of her parents, actually resulted in an intensified and regenerative intimacy with both. One can see how Chan remaps her own daily micro-escapes from parental restrictions to chain stores, local franchises, and community centers like the Red Lobster, Target, the Doubletree Inn Recreation Center, the Payless ShoeSource, and the Lions Club through JJ Chinois's fantastic journey across the United States.[56]

In fact, most of the JJ Chinois website is not devoted to the glamour of the city that acts as glamour's geographical measure, New York. Nor does it narrate JJ's eventual arrival in New York City as liberation or as an attempt to flee from his nowhere places of origin. As JJ's tour dates show us, he weaves his way from the West Coast to the East by stopping at curious nowheres in between. Some of his stops include: the Veterans Building in Protection, Kansas; Dreams and Swords in Livonia, Michigan; Chien's Buffet in Sioux

Falls, South Dakota; OK Eggroll in Bowlegs, Oklahoma; the Sandollar RV Park in Sopchoppy, Florida; and the Doubletree Inn Recreation Center in Shanghai, West Virginia.

All are venues that seem like they shouldn't exist, yet all of them actually do. While not all of his tour stops are curiously Orientalist in place-name or setting, there is a running motif in which the Asian is infused into unlikely locales. Here, not only does Chan riff on the infinite substitution of the links in corporate chains, but she alludes to a racial imaginary informed by mid-century design's appropriation of "exotic" motifs for prefabricated environments in the suburbs. Among the publicity stunts employed by the developers of suburban residential outposts was to create theme environments to enliven otherwise generic and mass-produced bedroom communities.[57] The proliferation of 1950s tiki-themed bars and Oriental kitsch lounges in suburban outposts throughout the United States is but one example of how a Disney-inspired consumer imperialism manufactured a Pacific Rim exoticism that second-generation artists like Chan now exploit and celebrate as a significant component of their own racial imaginary.[58] Chan's engagement with Orientalizing replications of "Asian style" in the suburbs, meanwhile, has also been informed by, and in turn informs, her approach to JJ's sexualization in a racial continuum.

In a 2002 personal interview with Chan, she explained how her JJ persona evolved after a series of photographic experiments depicting other versions of racialized masculinity during her undergraduate work at UC Davis and UCLA.[59] Chan was initially dissatisfied with what she felt would be a requisite representation of Asian male effeminacy, so she chose to make herself up as a handlebar-mustached, butch Latino "cholo" for a series of photographic essays.[60] Pleased by how convincingly her photographs depicted masculinity (or so she imagined), Chan nevertheless began to feel ill at ease about her criteria for passing, since it reified a racialized continuum of masculinity already problematized by other artists and scholars like Isaac Julien, Richard Fung, and Kobena Mercer.[61] In this continuum that intertwines the processes of racialization and sexualization, as Glen Mimura has concisely and elegantly explained, both "Asia" and "Asianness" have been "figured as an ambivalent, mediating term between black and white, particularly as racial meaning articulates with and through the West's discourse on sexuality."[62] Chan's intersubjective experiment with "brown" instead of "yellow" masculinities parried with this Western discourse on sexuality, and it troubled Chan to the extent that she eventually chose to revisit why she disavowed performing Asian masculinities to begin with. Chan reconsidered the range of stylistic signifiers that differentiate sexual power and prowess, particularly those concerning hair:

Lynne Chan, "Tour Dates 2," JJChinois.com, 2002. Courtesy of the artist. All rights reserved.

I realized that part of what put me off of trying Asian male drag to begin with was that Asian men are imagined as hairless "soft" guys who can't grow a mustache. Given how standard-issue mustaches were in the drag scene back in the early 90s, it basically felt easier for me to put the drag on—(again, I'm such an underachiever)—by painting on an abundant mustache than it would've been for me to work with my own body to see how "man" I could be without any kind of props or embellishment. I realized it was a lot easier than I thought given how I look, and also, because when I was growing up through the late 70s and 80s, Asianness always seemed to be read androgynously if not effeminately. I wanted to play with those misconceptions.[63]

What began as an epiphany about Asian masculinity also prompted Chan to reconsider more broadly certain popular discourses about racial authenticity: "I felt pretty disconnected from any sense of 'Asianness' after having lived in Cupertino. I mean, I wasn't so keen on the whole 'Joy Luck' concept of having to experience the 'motherland,' or having to go back to China to figure out who you are. Maybe that was self-hating of me, but when I think about it, it has something to do with how many mixed signals I received not only from pop culture or 'the media,' but also from my parents who wanted us to stay Chinese, while wanting us to 'be like everyone else.'"[64]

The subjective dissonance Chan narrates in her own biography—the double imperative to remain authentically racialized while becoming "like everybody else" (implicitly the white, bourgeois subject upheld as the standard for citizenship)—is by no means out of the ordinary. Volumes of Asian American criticism, memoirs, novels, drama, and art have grappled with the very same concerns. This problematic, of course, is not exclusive to Asian American racialization in the United States, but as Kandice Chuh and Victor Bascara have most recently explained, the "model-minority" dynamic that adheres to Asian American subjects posits them as, at once, exemplary immigrants yet "foreign" in perpetuity.[65] As Chuh has argued, "The irresolution of the United States' preoccupation with the 'foreign within' manifests itself in such figures as the 'model minority.' That stereotypical image precisely bespeaks simultaneous inclusion and exclusion, thus bearing the particular function of being at once a signifier of assimilative potential and of the limitations proscribing that possibility."[66] Reading Chan's comments about her own family makes clear how this theoretical dynamic about assimilation becomes articulated and enacted in everyday modes of living, especially in spatial contexts like the suburbs that emerged as the emblematically normative habitat for upwardly mobile Americans after the United States' economic expansion post–World War II.[67]

Chan's aesthetic response to what was simultaneously a parental imperative and a culturally determined narrative for Asian American "model-minority" subjects was to fabricate a figure like JJ Chinois who, to continue riffing in concert with Kandice Chuh, emerges as a potentially "subjectless" repository for expressions of "strategic *anti*-essentialism."[68] In other words, rather than viewing Chan's experiment with subjectivity—the fantasmatic JJ Chinois—as just another queer iteration of postmodernity, excess, and reinvention, we might begin to "imagine otherwise" how these accounts of queerness resonate with an Asian American *post*-identity that Chuh has argued is always already ambiguous, imaginary, and subjectless. As Chuh proposes, "If we accept a priori that Asian American studies is subjectless, then rather than looking to complete the category of 'Asian American' . . . we are positioned to critique the effects of the various configurations of power and knowledge through which the term comes to have meaning."[69]

Chan's JJ Chinois website may, on its sparkly surface, appear to be superfluous because it relies on wordplay, referential humor, and silly jokes. But I would propose that Chan's play with surfaces, which is in keeping with suburban proclivities for facades, simulacra, and reproductions, allows us to reimagine the queer Asian American subject by humorously exposing and critiquing the "configurations of power and knowledge" called forth by the apparent fabrications and excesses of the terms "queer," "Asian," and "American." Further, the situational context of the suburbs is significant as a staging ground for the critique of power in Chan's JJ Chinois projects, because it sets into relief how "politics" itself is restricted to certain locations—more often than not urban ones—for queers, immigrants, and people of color. As we shall see in the subsequent section, Chan's ludic take on "diaspora" as a concept that weaves conceptually among race, nation, and sexuality brings to the fore the matrices of power, as well as the reparative possibilities, in and of a queer of color suburbanity conjured from out of nowhere.

Movements: From Cities to Elsewheres, from Diaspora to Dykeaspora

In the American imaginary, cities have been upheld as the emblematic spaces of arrival for both immigrants and queers. Volumes of American history offer accounts of how immigrants from all over the world first landed on the United States' shores in cities like New York, San Francisco, and even Los Angeles. But how did the city—in particular, vertical cities like New York and San Francisco—come to be viewed as the natural habitat for queers? What discursive events and institutionalized histories spawned the movements to, within, and beyond the city's parameters in the queer imaginary? Before turning to Chan's "dykeaspora"—an aesthetic approach to movement that combines narratives of compulsory relocation for both queer and immigrant subjects from suburbs and small towns to urban metropoles—we must take on how the city itself becomes a focal point in queer discourses about diversity. Not only are cities construed as sites of arrival for queers as well as immigrants, but they are upheld as exemplary locations for mingling multiple experiences and embodiments of difference. In this section, we will explore how genealogies of queer urbanity from the incipience of queer studies in the early 1990s, to more recent accounts of queer diaspora after the millennium, inform a suburban aesthetic at once critical and ludic in Chan's JJ Chinois projects.

While we certainly cannot ignore the role European sexology played in constructing "the homosexual" as a cosmopolitan, urban type—sexologists in Britain and on the Continent, such as Havelock Ellis, Richard von Krafft-Ebing, Karl Ulrichs, Charles Féré, Max Nordau, and Georg Simmel, situated their research almost exclusively in urban capitals like London, Paris, and Vienna[70]—U.S. histories of space and sexuality in the twentieth century provide collective and community models for gay identity that also establish a special character to queer urban life. The locus classicus of gay urban studies, which also comments on immigration's effects on urbanity, is George Chauncey's expansive and formidable tome *Gay New York: Gender, Urban Culture, and the Making of the Gay Male World, 1890–1940*. Published in 1994, Chauncey's social and cultural topography of New York City surfaced alongside two watershed community studies of lesbian and gay cultures also situated in the state of New York: Elizabeth Lapovsky Kennedy and Madeline D. Davis's history of lesbian life in Buffalo, *Boots of Leather, Slippers of Gold: The History of a Lesbian Community*, and Esther Newton's *Cherry Grove, Fire Island: Sixty Years in America's First Gay and Lesbian Town*.[71]

Marc Stein, who is himself a noted historian of local gay cultures in Philadelphia, makes a compelling case for how the nearly simultaneous emergence of these local histories, timed serendipitously with the twenty-fifth anniversary of the 1969 Stonewall riots, indexes regional responses to an Ur-narrative of gay identity and activism in the nation-state offered a decade earlier in John D'Emilio's 1983 book *Sexual Politics, Sexual Communities: The Making of a Homosexual Minority in the United States, 1940–1970*. As Stein explains, "D'Emilio's book, more than any other, established the framework in which most U.S. LGBT historians have operated for more than two decades. . . . Since 1983 U.S. LGBT historical scholarship . . . has developed in multiple directions, but much of it has taken the form of local studies that respond to D'Emilio's national narrative."[72]

Stein claims that such focused attention to regionalism and local phenomena from the 1990s onward becomes a method for "resisting the hegemony of the nation-state" in the production of gay "minority" histories.[73] The critique of the nation-state enacted through regional emendations of the national narrative of gay and lesbian movements (both spatial and political) remains a pivotal dimension of work produced during the nascent days of LGBT studies' institutionalization in the mid-1990s. Yet there is also a reproducibility to D'Emilio's community-building, national paradigm, which I would argue helped establish "the city" as the exemplary site for queer *politics* as well as culture in the United States, and gay men as the exemplary subjects of the nation's spatio-sexual culture.

The topography of organized activism in D'Emilio's *Sexual Politics, Sexual Communities* is routed between the United States' emblematic gay cities, San Francisco and New York. In D'Emilio's history, both the gay "movement and the subculture" congealed in San Francisco in the mid-1960s in concert with other leftist countercultural protest movements agitating for civil rights and civil liberties.[74] San Francisco's example as a site where political movements cohered and became inextricable from the subcultural life of the city ultimately "set the stage" (in Stein's words) for the Stonewall riots in New York City at the close of the decade while also anticipating "transformative mass movements of the 1970s throughout the nation."[75] In the nation-state narrative of gay identity formation and political organization, then, San Francisco and New York come to function as centers where politics and styles of living converge and achieve saliency as mutually constitutive aspects of twentieth-century gay movements, both political and cultural.

As the time line of U.S. gay and lesbian history expanded to include pre–World War II manifestations of community, more site-specific histories of gay "world making" and culture building arose as supplements to D'Emilio's history of an emergent gay identity politics. Perhaps more than any other work, Chauncey's *Gay New York* firmly established New York City as the gay *cultural* capital of the United States.[76] The rhetoric of Chauncey's book conflates a "gay *world*" writ large and the gay communities and scenes cultivated in New York City from the turn of the century to the beginning of World War II. Throughout his introduction, the phrase "gay world" is substituted for New York, implicitly establishing the patterns of association and "cultural style" historically situated in New York City as a template for a national gay ethos and culture. One among many examples of this conceptual slippage between the "gay world" and gay New York occurs when Chauncey describes the parameters of his study: "This book maps two distinct but interrelated aspects of what I call the sexual topography of the gay world in the half-century before the Second World War [and] the spatial and social organization of that world in a culture that often sought to suppress it. . . . The first project of the book, then, is to reconstruct the topography of gay meeting places, from streets to saloons to bathhouses to elegant restaurants, and to explore the significance of that topography for the social organization of the gay world and homosexual relations generally."[77] The "sexual topography" Chauncey meticulously reconstructs in his history, from the Bowery, to Central Park, to Greenwich Village, to Harlem, is what constitutes—to add emphasis to his words—"*the* gay *world*." As groundbreaking and brilliantly detailed his account of the bustling and thriving communities of New York is, his rhetoric of "world making" influenced subsequent scholars, writers, and readers to transpose the forms and styles of living he documents in *Gay New York* into a template for enriching, active, and activ*ist* modes of queer life. The specific venues and spatial contexts in which the sexual and social transactions of gay men transpire in Chauncey's narrative—the streets, saloons, bathhouses, and "elegant restaurants" of Manhattan—take on an exemplary status and register a disproportionate impact on queer spatial imaginaries, or "the social organization of the gay world and homosexual relations *generally*."[78]

To be fair, Chauncey insists that New York and its sexual culture cannot be viewed as a "typical" model: "I do not claim that New York was *typical*, because the city's immense size and complexity set it apart from all other urban areas." Yet Chauncey's study clings to the city's exceptionalism, its "complexity," and its "disproportionate influence on national culture."[79] Thus, while no other place could possibly *be* New York City, New York City nevertheless becomes the spatial coordinate and cultural standard to which all queer subjects—and perhaps even *all* Americans, given its "disproportionate influence on national culture"—implicitly orient themselves. Even though Chauncey specifies that his history is about the making of a gay *male* world, while cautiously equivocating about New York's representativeness, he ultimately concludes his introductory chapter by speculating that the city functions as an urban "prototype" for the rest of the nation's gay communities: "Nonetheless, New York may well have been *prototypical*, for the urban conditions and cultural changes that allowed a gay world to take shape there, as well as the strategies used to construct that world, were almost surely duplicated elsewhere."[80]

Of course, other histories about other cities and regions in the United States both preceded and followed Chauncey's landmark study of New York. The genealogy I'm presenting here, and the special attention paid to Chauncey's work, is by no means intended to diminish the intellectual impact of these other works, some of which deal more explicitly with lesbian community formations and cultural life that differ considerably from the forms of gay world making described in Chauncey's book.[81] Yet the crossover appeal and wide influence of Chauncey's *Gay New York* warrants this focus. It is not simply the place itself—New York City—that serves as the consummate coordinate in queer spatial discourse, but also the ways in which the place is experienced, inhabited, and lived that become touchstones for a certain quality of queer life. The "cultural style" Chauncey refers to as the primary mode for transacting and tracing gay relations in the city— codes of dress, languages of innuendo, a sophisticated system of looks and stares, a stylistic circumspection mixed with the spectacular—provides, like the city itself, a prototype for the exemplary queer: the urbane gay subject who helps enrich a metropolitan milieu.[82]

Even in subsequent revisions and addendums to the social history of queer style and queer encounter in New York, the city remains a privileged site of sexual diversity, immigrant authenticity, and aesthetic innovation. Among the most eloquent and moving works to contextualize queer encounters amid other urban diversities is Samuel Delany's *Times Square Red, Times Square Blue*, an autobiographical piece of criticism that offers inventive and discursive solutions for the diminishing interclass and interracial contact in civic life. As important as Delany's contributions are, however, his ambitious and somewhat utopian model for discursive and civic reform is possible only on the "richly variegated urban shores" of New York City—more specifically, in Manhattan.[83] For Delany, both racial and sexual diversity exists only within the context of the urban environment, and the visiting suburbanites and small-towners embody the encroachment of the white, corporate, heteronormative ideals that threaten to extinguish the democratic sociability that defines urban life. Presupposing the whiteness and heterosexuality of out-of-town visitors, Delany goes on to equate the "plague" that obliterated the populations of seventeenth-century London and Marseille with "cankle"-baring tourists in millennial Manhattan: "Here the plague may just *be* that pleasant suburban couple, lawyer and doctor, herding their 2.3 children ahead of them, out the door of the airport van and into the Milford Plaza."[84] In the coda to *Relocations*, I engage more intimately with Delany's approach to queer race and class relations, which shockingly complies, albeit unwittingly, with the aesthetics of urban gentrification (Delany's solution is to rehabilitate mixed-use urban spaces from within while retaining the "class character" of such spaces). But it is important to register here how Delany ignores the consequences wrought by the stratification of gay property ownership in the metropolis itself when he offers his vision for taking back the great (gay, interracial) American city.

Chan's JJ Chinois website undoubtedly engages with the fantasy of the city that *Gay New York* helped create and *Times Square Red, Times Square Blue* resurrected for a new millennium. Stylistically, however, we have already seen how Chan subverts certain expectations about the spaces of gay "world making" by repurposing the names of mainstream chain stores and strip-mall sites (as well as some restaurants that might be deemed less than "elegant") in her alternate mapping of queer "cultural style" and "contact" prior to and beyond JJ's arrival in New York City. JJ's fictitious fan base of teens, lesbians, dilettantes, squares, and starlets accumulates with each strip-mall stop and community-center gig across the United States. As we recall, his biographical narrative also resituates his "discovery" by the drag king impresario Murray Hill—the kind of mutually beneficial contact that Delany traces in the urban density of New York[85]—to Coalinga, California, at a local dim-sum restaurant. These events archived on the JJ Chinois website may not be real, but their effect is to relocate the queer topographical imaginary away from cities like New York that have become too expensive for queer subjects who lack the mobility of bourgeois gay men.

What has long been common lore about the different spatial circumstances of gays and lesbians—that gays live in hip neighborhoods in world cities, while lesbians generally have to traverse some bridge, tunnel, or undesirable stretch of freeway to participate in urban life—has recently been affirmed by the data in *The Gay and Lesbian Atlas* (as problematically framed as some of this data is).[86] In summarizing their findings, the atlas's editors, Gary J. Gates and James Ost, observe that "same-sex male and female couples share only five states (California, Washington, Arizona, Massachusetts, and Vermont) among their respective top 10 states . . . and the difference in location patterns is even more apparent at the county level, where only San Francisco County appears in the top 10 counties for both male and female couples."[87] *The Gay and Lesbian Atlas* further finds that "lesbian couples are less urban than their gay male counterparts, as the top 10 counties for lesbian couples are much less urbanized than the top 10 counties for gay men. While 57 percent of gay male couples live in central counties of metropolitan areas with a population of more than one million, only 50 percent of lesbian couples live in these counties. Conversely, 28 percent of lesbian couples live in areas with populations between 250,000 and one million, while only 25 percent of gay-male couples reside in these areas."[88] *The Gay and Lesbian Atlas'* map of New York City is in and of itself quite telling: lesbian couples are more scattered throughout the outer boroughs of New York, whereas gay men boast a formidable territorial presence on the West Side of Manhattan from Midtown on down. The editors speculate that there are several reasons for this, namely, that lesbian couples have lower salaries than gay male couples and are more likely to have children.[89] Part of my aim in turning to some of the statistical data on lived environments here is not to reify the "truth" of statistics as evidence, but rather to urge us to rethink the jokey queer truism that there may be a lesbian or dyke of color lifestyle and aesthetics distinct from urbanity and gay "world making." I have superimposed this data onto a discussion about Chauncey's notion of "cultural style" and Delany's "contact" because it remains an important node through which to reconsider the humorous interventions made by Chan's JJ Chinois projects. With JJ Chinois, Chan brings into perspective both the racialized and gendered dimensions of concepts like gay cultural style and queer contact by relocating their enactments to peripheral spaces. Further, while race and gender may not always neatly coincide in mappings of style and power relations, Chan's JJ Chinois website offers something of a fun house mirror in which to view the contortions of metronormative logics as they enfold the disparate concerns of race, gender, class, and sexual politics into a queer urban ethics. The metronormative dream of consolidating diversity in the urban milieu not only works in concert with both state-sponsored and privatized forms of gentrification (a topic discussed in more depth in the final chapter of this book), but it also reanimates an imperial faith in the "metropolis" to absorb conquered people, cultures, and worlds.[90]

Chan's flippant approach to listing Orientalist place-names like "OK Eggroll" within JJ Chinois's tour dates may not immediately call forth a critique of imperialism; nevertheless, she offers these funny, distorted reflections to prompt her audience to reconsider what such superficial allusions may mean. Her work on JJ Chinois actually emerged in correspondence with several significant books on race, diaspora, and queer spatio-cultural politics in the first half of this decade, including Gayatri Gopinath's *Impossible Desires: Queer Diasporas and South Asian Public Cultures*, and Martin F. Manalansan IV's *Global Divas: Filipino Gay Men in the Diaspora*. While we will return later to Gopinath's early warnings about the limitations of "diaspora" as a critical concept, especially in accounting for ephemeral queer public cultures, I would like to turn first to Manalansan's work on Filipino gay men in the diaspora as a counterpoint to Chauncey's historiography of style, urbanity, and queer politics. Manalansan's depiction of stylistic and spatial hierarchies, legislated as they are by class, race, and gender, will allow us to flesh out more fully Chan's critique of queer "cultural style" as it moves through space. Manalansan renders vividly the stylistic hierarchies that topographically divide New York City into a Manhattan-centric inside and a bridge-and-tunnel "outside" occupied by Pacific Asian gay men. Scrutinizing the mainstream gay tourist literature about New York City while conducting his own extensive ethnographic research of queer social spaces in Manhattan and the "less sophisticated peripheries" of the outer boroughs, Manalansan observes that "the mapping of gay New York City is not only about the physical layout of the landscape but is also about hierarchical and uneven spatialized imaginings where particular queers are socially and symbolically located."[91] Whereas authors like Samuel Delany have romanticized the interclass contact within the queer sexual communities of Manhattan, Manalansan reveals the harsh socioeconomic realities and embodied stylistic distinctions that keep the queer scene stratified.[92] One especially telling anecdote in Manalansan's book is of a Greenwich Village gay bar where the patrons regularly referred to a sequestered area of the establishment as the "Third World," because men of color gathered together in that spot.[93] Yet another of Manalansan's interlocutors commented on the popularity of the "grunge" look favored by stylish Chelsea boys for a brief moment in the early 1990s, observing that when gay white men wear tattered vintage clothing it looks trendy, but "when we [Filipino gay men] wear it, we just look dirty and poor."[94] By deflating the myth of inclusiveness in the gay cosmopolitan mecca of Manhattan, Manalansan brings to the fore the uneven power relations in the social, economic, and aesthetic negotiations of queer space in the city.

In many respects, Manalansan's work offers a historical addendum and a topographical corrective to Chauncey's earlier history of gay male world making in New York. But what of the racialized negotiations of space that percolate in the peripheries among queer female and transgender bodies? Where, in other words, would a transgender figure like JJ Chinois, created by an Asian American dyke artist from the California suburbs, fit into the stylistic paradigms currently available for imagining sexuality vis-à-vis space? And how does a concept like diaspora begin to account for local migrations as well as global displacements from postcolonial metropoles to "great American cities"?

The spatial and sexual orientations of dykes of color who cultivate their sexuality in the "middle of nowhere" are often misplaced and subsumed in perpetual reimaginings of global immigration, rather than properly situated in their own histories of local migration. As Gayatri Gopinath predicted early on in discussions about queer diaspora, "diaspora" itself might be a limiting term and concept in so far as it relies on "conventional ideologies of gender and sexuality" while taking for granted the spatial and aesthetic hierarchies between first and third world spaces.[95] Gopinath has since written about the "impossible desires" felt and lived by subjects both excepted and excluded from the "developmental narratives of colonialism, bourgeois nationalism, mainstream liberal feminism, and mainstream gay and lesbian politics and theory." Instead of construing "impossibility" as a liability, Gopinath gestures toward how it actually makes anti-nationalist and anti-normative critiques *possible* by forcing us to grapple with "the failure of the nation to live up to its promise of democratic egalitarianism."[96] What Gopinath describes here resonates with what was discussed in the previous section through Kandice Chuh's work, which focuses on a strategic antiessentialism and the negative potential of a paradoxically "subjectless" Asian Americanist critique. Cumulatively, both Gopinath and Chuh have inspired me to reframe these debates with their attention to the emptiness, rather than the fecundity, of certain identitarian categories and spatial orientations. This sense of shallowness is what I would like to underscore with the ridiculous neologism I've concocted to describe how Chan's JJ Chinois projects intervene in imperially driven metronormative discourses: "dykeaspora."

Dykeaspora describes the translocal and interregional queerness made legible by the movements within the United States that Chan depicts in her JJ Chinois projects. The term admittedly lacks the theoretical dignity of the word on which it plays, "diaspora," which denotes a longing for a sense of home after the dispersion from "original" sites rich with "authentic" histories and cultures. A diasporic subject is burdened with an impossible desire for ancestral authenticity that looks elsewhere, to a place of origin, for a sense of stylistic and existential originality. The nostalgia that sometimes accompanies diasporic yearnings for a placeness imbued with originality, both real and imagined, is notably muted in my vision of the suburban dykeaspora, in so far as the suburban sites that serve as points of origin for the "dykeasporic" subject demand shallow expressions of longing for silly sites that have no "real meaning" except as venues for commerce (like the Dairy Queen, Shakey's Pizza, or Denny's). Further, the dykeaspora features a vigorous distancing from the point of first contact, where the cultures imported by one's parents become assimilated into a suburban narrative of success.

It may seem superfluous to play with a word that already has a much richer theoretical valence than I have offered in my definition above. As one of my anonymous readers commented on an earlier draft of this chapter, "Neologisms are always a bit of an embarrassment"; rest assured, I've taken this point to heart. I am well aware that "diaspora" is already a term that has absorbed critical variations on its simplest meanings, from Gopinath's elegantly crafted codependency of the terms "queer" and "diaspora," to Glen Mimura's recuperation of "diaspora" as a concept capable of registering regionalisms as well as a "critical understanding of the relationship between migration and racialization across transnational spaces."[97] And yet I stubbornly cling to my embarrassing neologism, not only in the interest of reducing, reusing, and recycling, but also precisely because its absurdity—its naked dorkiness—is in keeping with the spirit of Chan's efforts to address the tandem forces of imperialism and metronormativity with suburban artifice, humor, and a winning naïveté.

Forcing "dyke" to function as a key term in Chan's rendering of JJ's migration is not only to insist on the significance of gender in the mapping of queer style, contact, and space, but also to pluck lesbianism and other non–gay male embodiments of queerness from a presumed sedentariness. Even as Chan's *transgender* persona, JJ is not exempt from these discourses about the failure to move. As Judith Halberstam has forcefully argued, the refusal of some transgender subjects to relocate given the presumed danger of life outside big cities is too often scripted as failure. Halberstam argues that Brandon Teena's self-stylization as a chivalrous middle-class American male accounts not only for his trouble—his danger and risk—but also for his pleasure. Yet Brandon Teena's reluctance to flee the Nebraska plains before his violent death can only be read by his metronormative biographers as a failure rather than as a choice: as a stubborn refusal to flee dangerous circumstances, rather than as a strategy for survival and a style of living that Halberstam speculates might be "shared by many Midwestern queers [as] a way of staying rather than leaving."[98] JJ Chinois leaves rather than stays, but like Brandon Teena his propensity toward movement is not motivated by fear or a queer, neoliberal rhetoric about choice. Instead, JJ's movements are predicated by pleasure and fantasy, as well as by a sanguine refusal to disavow "home" and the possibility of returning.

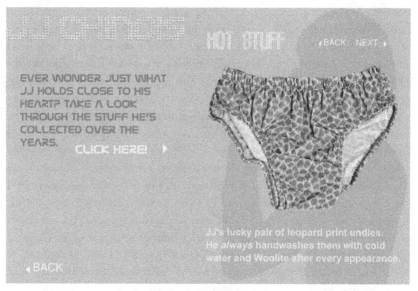

Lynne Chan, "Leopard Undies," JJChinois.com, 2002. Courtesy of the artist. All rights reserved.

The etymological failing of dykeaspora—its excision of the "dia" that signifies movement and dispersion—is, I would argue, precisely what opens the term to a critical practice that could challenge normative notions of space in queer as well as mainstream contexts. Etymologically, dykeaspora would translate into "dyke seed," a phrase that is unfortunately evocative of the lesbian baby boom, which belies a homonormative investment in bourgeois familial structures and lived environments. Yet I would like to suggest that the dyke seed contained within the term dykeaspora need not be subsumed by a reproductive imaginary. Instead, it makes legible the queer developmental narratives that underlie the queer subject's movements from suburbs and small towns to cities. Dykeaspora is an appropriately artificial term that can refer with precision to the processes of self-stylization and self-generation that initiate movements like the one Chan spectacularizes through the fantastic figure of JJ Chinois. Insisting on the term dykeaspora also paves the way for a queer regionalism and localism, because it chips away at monolithic constructions of queer cosmopolitanism that focus inevitably on gay male consumer patterns and aesthetics.[99] Resisting the national, metropolitan symbology of queerness and moving it away from representative sites like New York reveals the fragility of the imperial white, gay, male model that functions representatively when it is imported to other world cities.[100]

At the dykeasporic subject's disposal is an arsenal of styles, a set of pop culture signifiers that allude to the pervading ethos of capitalistic consumption in suburban spaces, while at the same time refusing the homogenizing imperatives of mass consumption. Indeed, we may find something more in common between a suburbanite's transformation of pop culture images, both straight and gay, and the diasporic subject's transnational relationship to these same images.[101] Chan experiments with representations of race from the suburban simulacral void. She does not turn to her parents' ancestral Hong Kong "homeland" to locate a model of Asian authenticity. Abandoning what she previously characterized as an overly sentimental "Joy Luck" ethos that romanticizes a return to the diasporic place of origin to recapture one's familial and racial "essence," Chan instead looks with longing toward California, the state of sprawl and *her* original homeland.[102] She also plays with artifacts and names of products that could very well be plucked from a suburban pantry or laundry room or picked up at any number of chain stores.

In JJ Chinois's list of answers to FAQs (frequently asked questions), for example, JJ reveals that his favorite ice cream is "mint chocolate chip," the signature flavor of the Southern California–based Thrifty drugstore chain, since taken over by Rite Aid.[103] In keeping with his penchant for chain stores, JJ Chinois also "collects Hard Rock Café menus." JJ's visual spinning wheel of collectibles and other "hot stuff" features a Playboy bunny pendant not just as a sign of his virility but also as an homage to his Chinese heritage. The text reads, "JJ also identifies by

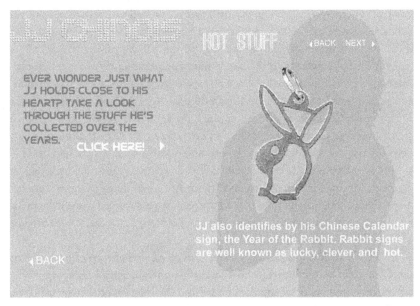

Lynne Chan, "Playboy Bunny Pendant," JJChinois.com, 2002. Courtesy of the artist. All rights reserved.

his Chinese Calendar sign, the Year of the Rabbit. Rabbit signs are well know as lucky, clever and hot."

Through JJ, Chan constantly plays with, hyperbolizes, and elevates the significance of kitschy objects as well as everyday products and sites. Yet sentimental attachments to authentic expressions of "Chineseness" are scrutinized through JJ's humorous conflation of a Chinese astrological sign (the year of the rabbit) with the iconic Playboy bunny of American raunch culture. As a result, both symbologies are altered by JJ's distorted, queer (in multiple senses of the word) reflections on the object. Without agonizing over the object or working too hard to problematize it, JJ's prized pendant offers a special alchemy of the Chinese and the American in a playfully reductive sense of both. The pendant—and by extension, its wearer, JJ—is at once "lucky" and "hot," superstitious and sordid, an homage and a parody. JJ, in other words, is deeply shallow.[104]

In Chan's work we are offered a glimpse at the suburbs as a Foucauldian heterotopia, an affective topography "referencing both the real and unreal spaces that shape social relations." Kandice Chuh has argued that "Asian America" is itself a "heterotopic formation, one that enfigures the multiple and dissimilar spaces and places of discourse and history that collectively produce what seems at first glance . . . to refer to the bounded site 'America.'"[105] JJ manages to unbind "Asia," "America," and "the suburbs" by paradoxically absorbing all their disparate meanings into a single symbolic object of consumption and decadence: the Playboy bunny pendant. In other words, JJ's quick and shallow associations through images and words are strategically *antiessentialist*, precisely because they are so overblown in their essentializing of all cultural meanings within a single talismanic object.[106]

Lynne Chan's dykeasporic punning and resignification through her JJ website happens visually as well as linguistically, relying on the sliding associations among images and words plucked from different contexts and different worlds. In this sense, Chan's work also belongs to a fin de siècle and now postmillennial Asian American aesthetic, exemplified in literature by R. Zamora Linmark's 1995 novel *Rolling the R's*. Like Linmark's groundbreaking novel, Chan employs pop culture stereotypes of queer, ethnic sexuality to explode sentimental narratives of diasporic longing for generations once, twice, or several times removed from the initial familial migration to the United States.[107] A sense of racial "authenticity" is reproduced through the citation not of sacred objects, but rather of the profane objects of everyday consumption.

Rolling the R's features a cabal of hypersexualized, prepubescent, (mostly) Filipino American kids in Hawaii who incessantly pun in pidgin while incorporating names and products from popular culture into their own special language. Take, for example, the novel's opening passage, written in the voice of one of its several protagonists, Edgar Ramirez:

So what? Like me teach you how for French kiss make hickeys, and M&M too. Dumb ass, not candies. Mutual mastication, hand-to-hand resuscitation. Learned 'em from *Afterschool Special* with Mr. Campos and latenite TV. Not Johnny Carson or Wolfman Jack. More like Pinocchio, grown-up version. . . . Yeah, my parents know I watch skin-flix. Take NoDoz, Folgers, Coca-Cola. What they goin' do? . . . Last night I had sex with Scott Baio, Leif Garrett, Matt Dillon, too. . . . Matt was in his briefs, lyin' on his side, same pose he had in the hayloft scene in *Little Darlings*. And Matt, you think that butch babe gonna go Hanes-naked and watch us play lollipops and roses? Shit, he rather oof Kristy McNichol.[108]

What is a rather common, sexually explicit scene of adolescent masturbatory fantasy may require translation for some readers, not only because of Edgar's pidgin but also because of his queer, Pinoy patois combining products, stars, and scenes from cinema and television into a kind of shorthand. The post-exchange candy treat beloved by Pinoys who lived near the U.S. naval bases, M&M's, becomes "mutual mastication," another playful variant on the M&M of mutual masturbation. ABC's *Afterschool Special*, a liberal melodrama for young adults that tackles a range of socially conscious themes from latchkey children to abusive parents, offers a sly foreshadowing of Edgar's after-school sexual shenanigans with the janitor, Mr. Campos.[109] His consumption of over-the-counter uppers—NoDoz and the caffeine in Folgers and Coca-Cola—childishly mimics the high-flying gay drug subcultures of all-night discos. And *Little Darlings*, another queer "in-joke" because it happens to be a formative film for many lesbians (who admired Kristy McNichol's budding butch scampishness), is transposed into a scene of gay male fantasy and seduction, with the male lead, Matt Dillon, lounging ever so steamily in an "all-American" setting: a hayloft at summer camp, Haynes underwear and all.

It is not merely because Linmark and Chan (through Edgar and JJ, respectively) cite popular culture that they engage in a queer, Asian American discursive practice, for citation alone is not what makes popular culture queer or "of color"—as the novels of Douglas Coupland, Nick Hornby, and other postmodern, straight-boy pop fiends make abundantly clear. Rather, it is *how* figures like JJ and Edgar cite popular culture that distinguishes their iterations as queer *and* of color. In the example I offered above, Edgar translates popular culture's terms into a language for formative sexual awakening that demands the terms stretch further, well beyond even a second layer of signification, to mean something else entirely (the M&M example is perhaps the most concise among the many that appear in the novel). While Edgar's monologue is sexually explicit, what it truly offers is a tutorial in queer innuendo that leaves the lofty gay, white, male innuendo of Wildean wit behind, cobbling together instead a poor, trashy, immigrant version of queer speech from somewhere "out there" (which in *Rolling the R's* is the rough-and-tumble service-class neighborhood of Kalihi, Oahu).

The idiomatic improvisations of the characters in *Rolling the R's* resemble what Martin Manalansan describes as *swardspeak*, a term that comes from the regional Cebuano word "sward," referring to "sissies" or homosexuals. Swardspeak, as Manalansan explains, is "the vernacular code used by Filipino gay men in the Philippines and in the diaspora," combining the layered vocabularies of Spanish colonialism, American popular culture, Tagalog words, and Pinoy provincial languages and dialects like Cebuano.[110] While the characters in *Rolling the R's* bear the linguistic traces of Pinoy postcolonialism in their conversations (with Spanish words, Tagalog, Taglish contractions, and Hawaiian pidgin), the swardspeak of which Manalansan writes is practiced in very particular ways within the gay, New York–based Filipino diasporic community that is the subject of his study.[111] In the interest of tracking some of the subtle variations of these improvisational dialects across age, space, and time, I would like to propose a crossing over between the tadpole version of swardspeak in *Rolling the R's*—practiced not only by the gay and proto-gay boys in the book, but also by its queer and proto-queer female characters—and what I have identified as the dykeasporic practices of naming, citation, and popular transposition in Chan's JJ Chinois projects.

Provincialism is a crucial element of the term and practice of swardspeak, generated as it is from the Cebuano source word and the vernacular practices of both the queer Pinoys and queer diasporic Pinoys who Manalansan includes in his genealogy. Correlatively, Chan's use of punning and other forms of wordplay participates in its own coding of provincialism: what has lately been acknowledged as the proliferation of suburban-generated neologisms in the American vernacular. "A Lexicon of Suburban Neologisms," for example, is featured in the expansive catalog for the 2008 *World's Away: New Suburban Landscapes* exhibit, co-curated by Andrew Blauvelt at the Walker Art Center in Minneapolis and Tracy Meyers at the Heinz Architectural Center of the Carnegie Museum of Art in Pittsburgh. Compiled by Rachel Hooper and Jayme Yen, who were curatorial fellows at the Walker while the catalog and exhibit were coming together, the lexicon shows how (not unlike swardspeak) suburban neologisms employ compound words and puns while riffing on objects of mass consumption, from fast food to other forms of popular culture. Some of the most illustrative examples from the lexicon include the terms "McMansion" ("A large, hastily built, cookie-cutter house with a footprint of greater proportion to its lot size"), "food cart druid" ("A satirical term coined by author Robert Lanham to describe a teenage goth or mall rat obsessed with fantasy role-playing games"), "ball pork" ("A stadium hosting privately owned sports teams and built primarily with public funds"), and "Garage Mahal" ("A large or opulent garage or parking structure").[112]

We need look no further than to Chan's own chosen name for her persona, "JJ Chinois," to see an improvisational dialect at work that is, at once, suburban,

"Asian," and "American." As a name, JJ Chinois symbolizes the intersecting racialized and classed pop culture signifiers that invoke Orientalism and imperialism as it trafficked remotely through television and other broadcast networks in the U.S. suburbs. The name "JJ" is an homage to the mainstreaming of 1970s black popular culture, an echo of Jimmie Walker's signature character JJ, the ghetto-fabulous lothario dandy with a heart of gold from the sitcom *Good Times*.[113] The surname "Chinois," meanwhile, is an effete flourish accentuating the link between cosmopolitan and imperial projects of naming. Chan cribbed it from her first wide-eyed encounter with the Asian restaurants of Paris, as well as the fusion Vietnamese restaurants of Southern California, which attempt to convey a touch of class by evoking French colonial Vietnam and a Continental joie de vivre that makes "the ethnic" palatable to discerning consumers.[114]

As Chan demonstrates, the dykeasporic subject chooses pop culture signifiers that allude to the pervading ethos of capitalistic consumption in suburban spaces while at the same time refusing the homogenizing imperatives of mass consumption. Generic strip-mall sites and corporate chain stores are transformed in the queer suburbanite of color's attempt to work with the signifying tools at her disposal. Through her JJ Chinois website, Chan complicates the facile correlations made between the "suburbs" and stylelessness by exploring the relationship between the designated site of queer culture (named in Chan's project as New York City) and its most insidious Other: the California suburbs, a vast sprawl of interlocking freeways and eight-lane Main Streets where no one walks and everyone drinks Slurpees. By contrasting the "cultural styles" and vernaculars left as imperial residue in the suburbs with those found in great American cities, Chan dramatizes the tension between urban topographical spaces—massive, vertical, centralized cities—and their sprawling counterparts on the California coastline.[115] Further, Chan endows JJ Chinois with a sanguine naïveté about rural risk and suburban ennui in an affront to metronormative discourses about queer of color safety in the city.[116] Without eschewing the metropolitan histories and desires of immigrants and queers, Chan's JJ Chinois projects reimagine peripheral spaces as potentially joyful and seductive locations of the dykeaspora, as spaces where racialized and gendered self-stylization are not fated to be marred by psychic despair at best and gruesome violence at worst.

What began as an experiment in self-stylization and topography using the fantasmatic space of the web ultimately became Chan's point of departure for a live demonstration of JJ Chinois's ability to make a scene in spaces beyond queer metropoles. In 2003, Chan introduced JJ Chinois to the townspeople of Skowhegan, Maine, where he entered the demolition derby at the Skowhegan State Fair. One of the oldest in the nation, the Skowhegan State Fair was established in 1818 to "improve the breeding of livestock, with particular emphasis

Lynne Chan, "Young Republican at the Skowhegan State Fair," 2003. Courtesy of the artist. All rights reserved.

being placed upon the betterment of breeds of horses and cattle."[117] Rather than focusing on the presumed "fear" or violence she might encounter as a queer subject entering the familial, heteronormative arena, Chan instead viewed the demolition derby as an opportunity to examine the entertainment value placed on risk and violence:

> I liked the idea of this sort of niche arena of masculine competition that combines ridiculous comedy but real violence or real risk. I wanted to tap into that collective fascination with violence and entertainment. I think the Derby proved itself to be an important counterpoint to JJ's fansite. A fansite is ultimately a bit of a safe space: it's for the already seduced, and once it's set up that fiction is set in place. I think it's one thing to talk about the web as some utopian ideal of accessing a limitless audience. But closer to the truth, a fan community is also a fiction. Actually being in public space and introducing a persona taught me about people's assumptions, and my own assumptions.[118]

As we shall see, JJ's debut in the down-home environment of the Skowhegan State Fair—an annual event that boasts on its website live appearances by such figures as "Joey Chiltwoods [of] the auto thrill show, and the nation's popular country group, Asleep at the Wheel"[119]—provides a fascinating model for reimagining the geopolitical paradigms of space that have inhibited queer movements.

The Maine Event: JJ's "Demo" in Skowhegan

The taut and tan "Young Republican" wearing the besmirched muscle shirt hunched over his customized ride in this photograph is none other than JJ Chinois. While it echoes the alluring, animated silhouette of JJ featured on the first page of his fansite, this image from the Skowhegan State Fair indulges in a more earnest and effortless rendition of JJ's working-class masculinity as he moves from the representational space of the web to a live arena. Many of the background images on JJ's fansite feature him in various shadowy profile poses, including one in which he strikes a classic muscle-mag bicep curl. In this photograph of JJ poring over his entry into the Skowhegan demolition derby, the Sha Na Na bicep curl has been replaced with just enough cocky, virile lean to reveal naturally the toned contour of his upper arm. The photograph is a study in unstudied masculinity, or at the very least, in a masculinity striving to achieve an unstudied presentation. As Chan explains, she chose JJ's demeanor and attire for the demolition derby partly as a response to the audiences she anticipated at the fair: "The Young Republican t-shirt was an in-joke on my part. It kind of summed up the look I was going for . . . white trash, patriotic, macho. All the things I went in assuming my audience would be."[120]

Indeed, various other participants in the demolition derby at the Skowhegan State Fair entered the contest for patriotic causes, like "raising money for the troops" in Iraq, so Chan's assumptions were not entirely off the mark.[121] Yet her experiences in Skowhegan in preparation for the derby and after the derby itself confounded Chan's own expectations about JJ's transition from the web to a tour stop in live space:

> JJ's tour stops on the web were an imaginary journey across mid-America or all the supposed non-places across the country. I'd never experienced a state fair with a demolition derby. . . . My interactions with the friends I made in town, and the people in the crowd, made me realize that I had my own assumptions about who my audience was. One of the most rewarding parts of entering the competition was developing friendships with people in town. I developed a genuine rapport with the elderly couple who sold me the car (Al and Betty). Ross, a mechanic in town, was the main person who helped me modify and tune-up my car. He also gave me important advice on derby strategy. Ross happened to be one of the finalists in the previous year and convinced me that the most important part of competing was "winning the crowd."[122]

Having talked the talk on the Internet, Chan wanted to walk the walk at the state fair; ultimately, she discovered that expectations on both sides of the purported culture war raging between "red states" and "blue states" during George W. Bush's two terms in office were open to reinterpretation. The red state/blue state paradigm, renamed the "retro versus metro" schism in 2004 by the eccentric liberal billionaire John Sperling in his book *The Great Divide*, is a geopolitical model both the Left and the Right used for much of this millennium's first decade to situate electoral politics within a broad cultural framework of conflicting "values."[123] Pundits to the Left and the Right have both agreed that the red or "retro" states are characterized by racially homogenous (primarily white) rural and suburban populations who preach economic and social conservatism, and who also fervently promote religion through local and statewide legislation.

As Sperling describes "retro" Americans: "These are 'God, Family, and Flag' folks politically dominated by rural, conservative, white, Fundamentalist Christian populations. Retro America is not the land of co-habiting, unmarried, hetero, or same-sex couples, or of the young seeking cultural excitement in the large Metro cities."[124] Meanwhile blue state, or "metro" populations, are depicted as racially and economically diverse, culturally "urban" and "tolerant" (even though not all "metros" necessarily live in metropolitan areas), and intellectually progressive. Sperling attempts to cast blue or "metro American states" in a thoroughly "modern" light, as places "loosely held together by common interests in promoting economic modernity and by shared cultural values marked by religious moderation; vibrant popular cultures; a tolerance of differences of class, ethnicity, tastes, and sexual orientation; and a tendency to vote Democratic."[125]

Chan acknowledges having entered the derby competition with a metro, cosmopolitan bias: a predisposition to assume her audiences might not have the critical capacity to "get the joke," even though the original web incarnation of the JJ Chinois project deliberately entertained a utopian fantasy about commonality and transformative encounters through fandom. Letting her art guide her, rather than vice versa, Chan came eventually to realize that her cyberspace account of JJ seducing the masses in heartland settings was not entirely off the mark. She speaks warmly of "Al and Betty" and "Ross the mechanic," the local figures who offered JJ support and encouragement in his quest to become the Skowhegan demolition derby champion. The quaint townsfolk who nurtured JJ's derby dreams are a far cry from the fan base described on the JJ Chinois fansite—the "teens, dilettantes, starlets, celebrities and those who make them celebrities." While JJ certainly seduced them, their earnest assistance with JJ's derby aspirations in turn seduced Chan and encouraged her to reenvision the range of JJ's fan communities. Yet even as some of these remarkable individual responses subverted Chan's assumptions about her audience, part of the thrill manufactured by JJ Chinois's participation in the Skowhegan demolition derby was not simply that certain expectations about locally marked subjects were frustrated. In fact, many of them were thrillingly *affirmed* as JJ's encounters with some locals and "retro" crowds yielded unanticipated outcomes.

As Chan reports, many of the state fair attendees were indeed "white people" gathered together from decidedly "red counties," some within the blue state of Maine, some from red states much further south along the Atlantic coast. Many of the fair participants came from suburbs, exurbs, and rural towns espousing the very ideals JJ ironically embodied in his Young Republican tee—a macho, chip-on-the-shoulder, working-class patriotism more invested in the symbols of national belonging than in critiquing the national policies installed to keep class and regional stratification in tact. In many respects, they fulfilled Chan's own queer fantasy of "the Other," an archetype of contemporary Americana with all the NASCAR trappings. JJ, on the other hand, fulfilled his audience's fantasies about a stylish and outlandish "celebrity" glamour that had to have been imported from somewhere else, and that had to represent different values: "People running the derby told me that they had 'figured I must be some kind of porn star' and Googled my website, which on some level seemed to confirm some belief about who they thought JJ Chinois was."[126]

Like the JJ Chinois site, which played with the signifiers of gender, race, and class in ways that moved beyond the drama of "passing," JJ's appearance at the Skowhegan State Fair left behind the paradigm of passing as a measure of success. Instead, Chan became more interested in staging a scene of seduction on a mass level by inviting, and potentially provoking, conflict as she inspired doubt, confusion, and even a kind of mimetic recognition with her appearance:

> I wasn't too concerned with 'passing' in this setting. I kind of naturally pass to some extent a lot of the time, and I think that I did to varying degrees to different people through the event. Yet I think JJ really won over lots of new fans by confounding expectations. I think many people probably realized on some level there was some kind of stunt going on with my appearance. Others seemed to simply accept my novelty whether it was because I was brown and dressed and acted like them, or ambiguously gendered. And then to small children I represented someone other-worldly who they could project some kind of star-status onto . . . probably the most ideal reaction I would want.[127]

JJ Chinois's live demolition derby debut presents a novel notion of "demonstration," both stylistically and politically. While it has at its core a principle of confrontation—of exposing children and adults to some kind of Other in a normative, if spectacular, setting—its larger political aim is not merely confrontation itself, or an aggressively motivated staging of incongruous differences. Neither does it work exclusively on the principles of infiltration, assimilation, or passing. In other words, working with or wooing those who hold dear normative "retro" values does not require muting the markers of queerness and race to attain an acceptance that is itself a fantasmatic ideal.[128] Yet neither does an encounter with "retro" folks demand lapsing into a suffocating "log cabin" ethos in order to prove we can be just as normal, successful, and tax-averse as everyone else. This bourgeois approach probably wouldn't fly in a setting like a state fair demolition derby.

Even though JJ dons an eagle-decal Young Republican muscle shirt and earnestly mimics the masculine gestures and poses of white, working-class masculinity, he retains an element of novelty and idiosyncrasy marked by his race and his ambiguously gendered flourishes of style: "What I quickly learned is that most people are genuinely delighted to see JJ's pink car with gold wheels with a giant waving hand. I wasn't that concerned about 'fooling' the audience about who I was. On a mass level like that, people just start to assume that you're that 'Chinese boy,' or know that you are female and don't really care."[129] More than anything, JJ Chinois's appearance at the Skowhegan State Fair reminds us that the stylishly garish spectacle of queerness has a distinctly seductive potential, even as it stakes its own claim on spaces and settings that aren't necessarily intended for us, and even when it is not employed in the service of conferring the secret of style to heterosexuals who might envy it.

Yet JJ also reminds us that queers indulge too willingly in our own preconceived notions about space, that we rest too comfortably in our urban inhibitions to reimagine the geopolitical terrain and have significant encounters with the rural and suburban "Others" we fear most in the places we fear to tread. While JJ Chinois is not likely to single-handedly lure conservatives and elusive swing voters to rally around queer causes, Chan's JJ Chinois projects at the very least enable us to redraw the urban boundaries of a queer spatial imaginary in ways that invite a mutual respect, or at the very least a potentially productive mutual curiosity. Chan's JJ Chinois projects offer a model of queer encounter that is distinctly optimistic about the queer's ability to move to, from, and through suburban and rural spaces without succumbing to the inevitable and self-fulfilling narratives of desperation and violence that haunt the spatial "peripheries." The crowds at the Skowhegan State Fair did not rip JJ to shreds or assail him with homophobic epithets and racial slurs as his pink, gold-wheeled car with a giant waving hand attached to the roof careened through the demo pit. They instead rallied around him as the underdog when his car began to take a beating in the derby. Despite having lost the derby competition, JJ accomplished the kind of victory Ross the mechanic established as the ultimate goal for his demo derby apprentice: "It's about winning the crowd."[130]

As JJ Chinois demonstrates, it might be possible for us to "win the crowd" even if we refuse to compromise the legibility of what is unapologetically, outlandishly queer. We are not obliged to transform ourselves into our tasteful, cuddlier, made-for-TV versions in order to traffic through the American heartland unscathed. How we subsequently work to transform the political landscape after staging these close encounters, however, remains to be determined. At the very least, JJ poses the possibility that we can, at once, empathize with the Other as well as invite the Other's empathy, not only in our suffering but also in our pleasures. Reflecting on JJ's "demo" in Skowhegan, Chan writes, "I wasn't so much making an ironic gesture, but finding a way of experiencing a genuine pleasure in shattering expectations about identity, race and gender in places we think of as scary, nowhere places. It was about having an audience react in confusion, but also delight."[131] This delightful confusion might only be ephemeral, might only last for the span of an evening in which irony and ridicule are suspended as the crowd sounds a roaring surge of respect for the underdog, whoever he may be, wherever she may be from. But maybe we can find a morsel of possibility in the modest vision of victory that made buddies of Ross the mechanic and JJ Chinois. Maybe it is "about winning the crowd, even if it's just for an evening."[132]

Epilogue: The Morning After, or the Exit to Somewhere

A lot has happened since I wrote my first article about JJ Chinois for a 2005 special issue of Social Text on "What's Queer about Queer Studies Now?" I opened the piece with a quote from a rising political figure, an Illinois state senator on the verge of being elected to the U.S. Senate. His soaring keynote address to the 2004 Democratic National Convention took up the challenge of remapping an American electoral landscape ravaged by Bush-era divisiveness: "The pundits, the pundits like to slice and dice our country into red states and blue states: red states for Republicans, blue States for Democrats. But I've got news for them. . . . We coach little league in the blue states and, yes, we've got some gay friends in the red states."[133] The person who famously electrified the convention floor with these words a little more than half a decade ago is now the president of the United States, Barack Obama.

Obama parlayed this rhetoric of goodwill and geopolitical utopianism into a significant electoral victory in the 2008 presidential election, becoming the first multiracial, African American president in U.S. history.[134] On his road to this "firstness" that became an important outcome for so many, Obama endured a barrage of criticism for seeming to come out of nowhere. One of John McCain's most desperate attack ads in the general election attributed Obama's rapid political rise to his global celebrity, which surged when he took an overseas tour during the presidential campaign.[135] Detractors and admirers alike have since marveled at various shirtless photos of Obama brandishing what the notorious tabloid site TMZ dubbed "Barack hard abs."[136] While a lot has been said, and there is a lot more to say, about Obama's campaign rhetoric and how it inevitably brings us back to gays, red states, and gays in the red states, I want to conclude this chapter with a theoretical shell game in which JJ Chinois's "Nice Ass" is shuffled alongside President Obama's "Nice Abs."

To invoke the words of my fellow JJ-ologist Mimi Thi Nguyen, "In my fantasy, I imagine a world in which JJ Chinois has achieved the superstardom he so rightly deserves and all his fans can participate together in adoration."[137] What Nguyen identifies as the utopian impulse of collective achievement engendered by JJ's experiments with popular culture and the affective force of stardom seems—at least in the time since Lynne Chan created her JJ persona in 2001— to have saturated broader realms of the American imaginary, including Obama's election to the presidency. Of course, to make such an expansive and ahistorical claim about JJ's powerful reach is to succumb to the hyperbole of superstardom JJ himself uses on his website.

As much as JJ culls from an expansive repertoire of popular signifiers from the 1970s and 1980s, a sense of historicity, of precedence, remains repressed in the ludic fantasy fabricated by JJChinois.com, one that constructs JJ's singularity despite his rather obvious, and indeed deliberate, embodiment of certain ephemeral archives of race, sexuality, celebrity, and consumer culture. Nguyen interprets JJ's tactics, deeply ironizing and "historically constrained," in light of "questions of labor and capital" as they coalesce around theories of queer commodity culture.[138] While I wholeheartedly agree with Nguyen's reading and feel our scholarly labors are in concert, I want to close this chapter by thinking aloud about how JJ's theoretical bromance with the president, as well as his relationship to precedents— in popular culture, in queer and immigrant history, in space and time—offers a structural context for the queer suburban imaginaries that will continue to unfold throughout this book.

The spatial imaginary offered on Chan's JJ Chinois website is at once contingent on historical precedents yet blissfully delusional about the individual's ability to transcend such precedents to emerge as the exception. JJ's arc of migration from oblivion in Coalinga, California, to superstardom in New York, New York, transforms the exemplary endeavors of the unique individual into something of greater significance, of utmost importance, for the many, including fans and anyone else who might emulate him. In other words, JJ's story is (like Barack Obama's) what we might call an American story: a narrative that relies on the rhetoric of exceptionalism and uplift to manifest itself in different iterations, from the construction of the citizen-subject, to model-minority narratives of immigrant success; from histories of queer emergence, to myths about great American cities that inspire and embrace such diversity; from the aura of celebrity, to the charisma of political leadership. Chan explores these axes of American exceptionalism through the JJ Chinois website, as well as in her more recent projects like LES FUN (on the politics of "astroturfing," or the marketing world's bastardization of "grassroots" efforts) and "New Sound Karaoke" (on the world-making potential of karaoke).[139]

It's not that hard to see how the figures of JJ Chinois and Barack Obama meet along the axes of celebrity aura, especially through their racialized embodiments and transformations of American masculinity. What might be less apparent, however, is how both manifest *political* charisma by engaging specific spatial trajectories in their (in)famous narratives of triumph and uplift. Obama's path to the White House required not only turning red states to blue ones but also, perhaps most crucially, turning out the swinging purple counties—largely suburban—that George W. Bush successfully captured in his 2004 reelection over John Kerry.[140] JJ Chinois, meanwhile, also carried on a national campaign of sorts, adopting a "fifty-state strategy" of seduction with his tour dates across the U.S. commercial landscape. Both, in effect, took back the suburbs with style. Obama wrenched the suburbs from the Republicans with his calm and confident demeanor, ending W's reign of terror. Chan, through JJ, imagined another world into being—a queer of color world unbounded by the territorial limitations of both metronormative and heteronormative claims about space, safety, and racial authenticity.

In my own overactive imaginary inspired by JJ Chinois, I like to entertain the notion that Obama borrowed from JJ's playbook by channeling the perspective of a person once-removed from parental migrations and crafting an approach that could be received as simultaneously foreign and familiar, specific and vague, audacious and simple.[141] In other words, both share an aesthetic that appeals to the suburban imaginary, calibrated as it is to the task of synthesizing the remarkable and the common. At the very least, both Chan and Obama tapped into a postmillennial zeitgeist that understood what a changing American West might mean for the geopolitics of a national imaginary still captivated by the imperial remainder, by the exception and the fantasy. By making this claim, I am not endorsing exceptionalism as a pathway to queer of color politics, or suggesting that "change" means conjuring ourselves into celebrity fetish objects for the masses, both liberal and conservative. To acknowledge that such structures of desire persist, even in moments when we want to claim our victories without any hesitation, is to keep believing in our own abilities to remain critical, not in spite of, but *because* of the fact that we are having fun. And we also have to be willing to accept that if we pursue fun with enough vigor, it will sometimes come with a price, like the bad hangover that comes when you mix it up too much in the company of everyone and anyone.

During his 2008 presidential campaign, Barack Obama visited the reddest of red counties, Orange County, California, to speak at a presidential forum hosted at the Saddleback mega-church, presided over by the antigay, antichoice, anti-Semitic pastor Rick Warren. Asked by Warren to define marriage, Obama affirmed his belief "as a Christian" that marriage is "a union between a man and a woman."[142] His remarks scored a rapturous reception from the predominantly white and conservative audience at the Saddleback Church, undoubtedly alienating some of the many "gay friends in the red states" (and quite a few in the blue) he made back in 2004. To be fair, Obama concludes the exchange by advocating for civil unions, drawing on the emotional appeal of "setting aside" his personal, religious beliefs in a gesture of empathy with same-sex couples who can't visit an ailing partner in the hospital.

Call me quaint, but I still get peeved every time—and trust me, it's often—that a Democratic presidential candidate utters these words. I know. Good political queers aren't supposed to care about same-sex marriage. Personally, I'm not invested in the issue, knowing full well our time and resources are better spent agitating on behalf of other priorities like immigration rights, health care, and labor rights. But it's the thought that counts. And taking to heart Obama's own belief in the power of words to effect change, it behooves us to remember that what one says also matters. A lot. What made *our* candidate, our *friend*, repeat that hackneyed political phrase (beyond simply excusing the political reality that he *had* to, while assuming he didn't mean it)? Obama must've known he wouldn't win Orange County, a region that hasn't voted for a Democratic presidential candidate since FDR in 1936. But Obama was in it to win it, so he made a play and came close, finishing within thirty-six thousand votes (approximately 3.8 percentage points) of his Republican competitor, John McCain.[143] In my more reparative moments, I imagine that there was simply something in the air that day at the Saddleback mega-church. That there was something about the legacy of the infamous "Orange Curtain" that made Obama play it safe that way.

In the next chapter we exit the freeways, information superhighways, and fantasmatic back roads JJ Chinois took on his queer campaign across the United States, in order to spend some quality time behind that Orange Curtain. As we shall see, Orange County's amusement industries—especially its automobile-friendly amusement parks—practically invented the notion of playing it safe.

3 Behind the Orange Curtain

On July 17, 1955, Walt Disney opened his visionary new amusement park in Anaheim, California. . . . In keeping with its founder's vision of Disneyland as an alternative to the chaotic Coney Islands of the East, with their "tawdry rides and hostile employees," clean-cut employees strove to maintain order and a friendly attitude. . . . This suburban heartland was not only home to Walt Disney's visionary new park, to thousands of new California families and new towns and cities; it was also the birthing ground of a powerful grassroots political movement. A revitalized and militant right . . . burst onto the scene nationally in the early 1960s, and nowhere more forcefully than Orange County.
—Lisa McGirr, *Suburban Warriors: The Origins of the New American Right*

My problem with "The O.C." wasn't its ignorance of the "real" Orange County, the postmodern suburban stew of multiculturalism and Mexican bashing I call *casa*. No fictional depiction of a region can possibly synthesize it entirely, John Steinbeck notwithstanding. Nor am I too bothered with out-of-towners now calling us "The O.C.," a nickname as inane as "Hollyweird." Creator Josh Schwartz's greatest sin was to transform my homeland into a synonym for avarice and vapidity—which is what Orange County's leaders want. In the eyes of America, we're now "Dallas" with better tans and a coast, and the movers and shakers of *la naranja* love it.
—Gustavo Arellano, "Headed for Reruns"

The goal was to make a record that had that feeling I got when I'd go dancing at Studio K at Knott's Berry Farm. You don't feel that anymore. . . . I wanted to make a record where every song sounds like a single . . . and every single would be someone's guilty pleasure, even if they hate me.
—Gwen Stefani, describing her debut solo album, *Love. Angel. Music. Baby.*

ON MEMORIAL DAY weekend 1984, only five months before Ronald Reagan won Orange County by four hundred thousand votes in his landslide reelection over Walter Mondale (the largest margin of victory of any county in the nation),[1] a state-of-the-art teen club designed to showcase break-dancing crews opened at Knott's Berry Farm in Buena Park, California.[2] Though these historical incidents are generationally incongruous, one might even say worlds apart, they exemplify the contradictions and odd convergences that have come to define Orange County in the American national imaginary. Orange County is at once a conservative hotbed, an immigration hot zone, and a suburban fantasyland of modern amusement.[3] In 1964, almost exactly twenty years prior to Studio K's opening, the founding patriarch of the berry farm turned theme park, Walter Knott, held his own extravaganza to help launch the presidential campaign of Barry Goldwater, the conservative senator from Arizona.[4] Co-emceed by Ronald Reagan and John Wayne and featuring such "youth-friendly" novelty acts as the folk quartet the Goldwaters and the busty, cowgirl-attired Goldwater Girls, Knott's "An Evening with Barry" drew nearly thirty thousand conservative supporters to the park.[5]

Like the other Walt, Knott's kingpin counterpart and social acquaintance Walt Disney, Walter hoped his theme park would provide a family-friendly alternative to the lascivious, immigrant pleasure zones that dotted the Eastern seaboard as well as the beaches of Southern California at the turn of the twentieth century, including the Pike at Long Beach and the Ocean Park Pier at Santa Monica Bay.[6] More significantly, both Disney and Knott were invested in the individualist frontier mythologies that helped germinate the suburban grassroots conservatism of Orange County. We see this in the region's love affair with Western heroes—or at least men who played the part, like Ronald Reagan, John Wayne (for whom the county's international airport is named, despite recent efforts to rechristen it the "O.C. Airport"),[7] and even the famously bespectacled Arizona senator Barry Goldwater.[8] As Knott became more immersed in conservative politics throughout the 1960s, joining then California gubernatorial candidate Reagan's finance committee in 1966, he left the business of Knott's Berry Farm to other family members, though not before establishing a "Freedom Center" at the park itself in the early 1960s.[9]

In a piece titled "'A Rage for Order': Disneyland and the Suburban Ideal," the historian Eric Avila suggests that Disney and other amusement entrepreneurs repurposed the amusement park for the emerging new space of the suburbs.[10] Whereas Coney Island, the Pike at Long Beach, and other turn-of-the century amusement parks appealed to immigrant communities as places of escape, licentiousness, fantasy, and the carnivalesque, Disney and Knott created recreational spaces that could contain the dangers of the noir city. Disneyland itself would be built not with public transportation in mind, like its East Coast predecessors, but with the automobile as its inspiration—the vehicle of choice for the financially mobile middle classes. Anaheim, California, was selected as the site for Disneyland because of its location on the future route of the I-5 freeway.[11] Walter Knott also expanded Knott's Berry Farm from a restaurant into an amusement park as automobile traffic increased on Route 39. And yet, as this chapter shows, the Orange County suburbs did not and could not remain unchanged, despite its boosters' and developers' best efforts to keep the region as unsullied as its pristine amusement parks. Indeed, the relentless drive for privacy, security, and profit—and the many industries it spawned, from defense plants, to real estate, and even the service sector—is actually the cause of its own spectacular undoing.

Within twenty years of Knott's Goldwater rally and Freedom Center, and on the eve of President Reagan's triumphant "morning in America," Knott's Berry Farm not only admitted but actively enlisted the "urban element" of break-dancers and other would-be participants of street and underground club cultures—read: brown, classed, "edgy," queer—to help lure more customers through its gates. How did this same "element," whom Knott and Disney once feared would disrupt the nostalgic, family-friendly atmosphere of their respective worlds, help make Studio K—and to a lesser extent, its knockoff, Videopolis at Disneyland—the club destination for teens queer and proto-queer, Caucasian and of color, in Southern California from the mid-1980s through the early 1990s?

Moving from the previous chapter's exploration of geopolitical paradigms in the artist Lynne Chan's work, this chapter looks at the constellation of political and cultural fantasies that have produced Orange County as a suburban coordinate in a queer of color imaginary. Dianne Chisholm's work on the queer city employs the concept of "queer constellations," inspired by Walter Benjamin's montage-driven city writing.[12] I use the term "constellation" here as a suburban reconceptualization of Chisholm's thesis that the "making, and unmaking, of queer society and culture share the same space as that of the modern metropolis."[13] Of use in the concept of constellation are the prismatic and seemingly coincidental convergences that Chisholm via Walter Benjamin uses to recraft accounts of urban queer life and art. But as I already argued in the introduction to this book, the primacy of "the city" in queer studies fails to take into account new destinations as well as the new migrations and immigration patterns that have radically restructured queer life, art, and sociability in late capitalism—a socioeconomic context that has thwarted neat divisions between urban, suburban, and rural lifestyles as well as architectures. Thus the constellations I map here may rely on certain *forms* of constellation, such as coincidental convergences, but they depart in spirit and spatial trajectory from the project of reinscribing city life as the touchstone for queer experience.

To chart such constellations in Orange County requires following its traces of scattered radiance, sometimes manufactured, at other times accidental, to find a shape that may not make itself apparent upon first glance or first *listen*, adding what will be an important aural as well as scopic dimension to this relocation of the queer imaginary. One of the cultural modes in which we find echoes and resonances of Orange County's tangled histories of development, migration, and immigration is in the region's many unofficial nicknames. These ephemeral, and yet stubbornly lasting, monikers reverberate with all the hopes, dreams, and cynicism about what Orange County has meant or can mean for residents and observers alike. Further, many of these unofficial place-names resonate with the amusement cultures that define the region.

The queer of color imaginary that emerges in this chapter creates playgrounds from what were, at least from the mid-twentieth century through the early part of the twenty-first century, the county's greatest tourist attractions: its theme parks. As we shall see, the visual and sonic architecture of these parks, and their short-lived dance clubs that came to life during the Reagan era, inspire us to reimagine how queer sociability might transpire in the suburbs. Knott's Berry Farm and Disneyland are both situated in the immigrant-majority and service-economy-driven "north county," which includes Buena Park and Anaheim, the towns that respectively house these parks. Scholars, journalists, and local historians often point to northern Orange County as the site of a "real Orange County" that defines the region's political and cultural significance in the contemporary national landscape, defying Disney and Knott's conservative visions. But before we return "back to life, back to reality," in the words of the British R & B band Soul II Soul (a song that provides a sonic backdrop to the amusement park clubs that soared in the mid-1980s), "Welcome to the O.C., bitch."

Naming "the O.C.": Toponyms, the Small Screen, and the Sonic Border

As the *OC Weekly* columnist and resident pop historian Gustavo Arellano remarks in one of the epigraphs that opened this chapter, the region we have come to know as "The O.C"—thanks to the eponymous teen drama produced by Josh Schwartz and Stephanie Savage for Fox in the early 2000s—has become one of the United States' most grotesque suburban spectacles, and also one of its guiltiest pleasures. In his memoir about the region, *Orange County: A Personal History*, Arellano offers a handy CliffsNotes-style survey of the recent television programming that reintroduced Orange County as a "capital of cool" in the twenty-first-century United States.[14] From August 2003 (when *The O.C.* debuted) to the present, the televisual landscape has been littered with the bodacious and botoxed bods of Orange County's rich and sensational—from the relatively short-lived teen smash *The O.C.*, to the reality programming it spawned, like MTV's *Laguna Beach: The Real Orange County* and Bravo's *The Real Housewives of Orange County* (the latter of which takes a peek behind the gates of the exclusive "south county" enclave, Coto de Caza).[15] As the journalist Kimi Yoshino describes, "Business boosters ... are rubbing their hands with glee at the prospect of increased tourism. In a strange melding of fantasy and reality, 'The O.C.' has created a national image—much as 'Dallas' and 'Miami Vice' did for their respective locales—that could outlast the show."[16]

Only The Real Housewives continues to air new episodes today, but the shows' cumulative effect was to reintroduce Orange County to the United States' living rooms, and to rebrand its tourist appeal nearly half a century after Walt Disney first used the medium to introduce Disneyland and its Orange County environs as the nation's epicenter of well-ordered amusement.[17] Even Knott's Berry Farm's teen dance club, Studio K, debuted its specially designed, tiered and mirrored dance platforms on television, when it served as the setting for the California Breakdance Competition before the club's actual opening.[18] In more recent small-screen representations of the O.C., the region has been showcased as a fantasy venue encouraging a conspicuously decadent capitalism that threatens to rupture its master-planned splendor. As Arellano explains, "Like those beautifully fraudulent orange-crate labels whose perfection masked the county's reality, but also revealed our projected self-image, during the first half of the twentieth century, the Orange County–based boob-tube programs of this millennium serve as an advertisement for an ideal but also—often unwittingly—as biting commentary on the county."[19] This representational turn on television also echoes different iterations of Ronald Reagan's vision of the United States throughout the arc of his political career: from his rise in the mid-twentieth century, thanks to the nostalgic and homespun grassroots conservative movement incubated in Orange County, to his presidential legacy as a brash world leader whose trickle-down economics inspired national avarice and rampant social inequality, from the 1980s to its most recent, spectacular collapse during the waning months of the presidential election in 2008.[20] It is no wonder that the prime-time serial The O.C. features teens born during Reagan's presidential reign reenacting many of the classed, regional conflicts that were aggravated during the county's massive expansion in the 1980s. The show approaches these conflicts through interwoven intergenerational narratives that situate the teens' seemingly frivolous and self-contained antics within the broader spatio-cultural politics of the region. In a stroke of vérité, real estate and financial speculation is how the adults of The O.C. acquire their wealth. Despite its short-lived success—The O.C. aired for only four seasons before flaming out—it effectively, if fantastically, reintroduced the region to a new national and international audience,[21] recontextualizing Orange County's political and economic legacies to the youth of the twenty-first century. In lieu of offering a more detailed industry history of how The O.C. fared on network television, the reading of the show that follows explores some of the show's recurring tropes and characterizations that helped establish "the O.C." as a toponym for the region while producing a new sonic, spatio-cultural fantasy in the American national imaginary.[22]

The ethical anchors of the adult world of *The O.C.* are Sandy and Kirsten Cohen, a kindhearted couple who fell in love as college students at the University of California, Berkeley, and continually struggle to find ways of enacting their halcyon visions of social justice. According to the show's lore, Sandy (Peter Gallagher) and Kirsten (Kelly Rowan) actually met at Berkeley while Sandy was a campus volunteer for Walter Mondale, Reagan's Democratic opponent during the 1984 presidential campaign.[23] Born in Orange County, Kirsten admits that, true to form, she is a Republican—albeit of a compassionate and moderate stripe. Unlike the other fathers of *The O.C.*, either absent or controlling, Sandy begins the series working as a public defense attorney. He reinforces his Otherness, signaled by his occupation, his Jewishness, and his liberalism (all mutually constitutive in the world of the show), by constantly referring to the spatial origins that distinguish him and his "shiksa" wife (by virtue of their college courtship at Berkeley) from the show's scheming "Newpsies" (his derisive nickname for the housewives that make up their wealthy milieu). Sandy is a working-class boy born of Jewish immigrants who lived in the Bronx. As he narrates in the pilot: "I grew up—no money, bad part of the Bronx. My father was gone. My mother worked all the time. I was pissed off." Sandy is a blue-collar Democrat turned latte liberal out of place in the Reagan and "Dubya" universe of postmillennial Orange County. He finds himself in the ethically murky atmosphere of Newport Beach, California, because Kirsten relocates their family to her hometown after her mother's untimely death. The longer they stay, the deeper Kirsten becomes embroiled in her father's rapacious land development corporation, the Newport Group, which is evocative, according to some O.C. observers, of the real-life Irvine Company.[24]

Sandy's working-class roots and his status as a stranger among the Newpsies is doubled in the lead male teen character, Ryan Atwood (Benjamin McKenzie). Upon their first meeting, Sandy tells Ryan, "We're cut from the same deck." Ryan's relocation to Newport from the "seedy" Inland Empire town of Chino—site of a real-life, notorious state penitentiary[25]—is the plot point that launches the soapy skirmishes of *The O.C.* Although Chino is only about forty miles northeast of Newport Beach, Ryan clearly comes from a different world. One character, Summer Roberts, simply replies, "Ew," after learning that Ryan hails from Chino.[26] The Inland Empire, in many respects, functions as Orange County's foil throughout the series. We witness this in the way Chino is rendered visually in the series pilot through overexposed shots of the sullied alabaster stucco of its dilapidated houses and seedy strip malls. Orange County, meanwhile, is bathed in the golden-orange hues of the Golden State. Given the show's minimal depiction of brown, racialized immigrants, Chino stands in as an unsavory point of origin, an amorphously "Other" Southern California from which Orange County gets scripted as a haven and an escape.[27] The show's class narrative, as it unfolds between these two coordinates in the Southern California landscape, substitutes and displaces the racialization of the region.

In the pilot, the smart but troubled, working-class Ryan is assigned Cohen as his public defender after being arrested for a botched attempt to steal a Camaro at his older brother's behest. Ryan first rebuffs Sandy's attempts to reform him by turning Sandy's own idealistic rhetoric about his hardscrabble origins against the lawyer: "Where I'm from having a dream doesn't make you smart. Knowing it won't come true? That does." But left with no place to go after his brother is jailed, and after his "white trash," alcoholic mother kicks him out for his run-in with the law, Ryan succumbs to Sandy's offer for help. Spirited away from Chino in Sandy's BMW, Ryan finds refuge in the well-appointed pool house of the Cohens' Newport Beach McMansion in a gated community (funded by Kirsten's earnings from the Newport Group, of course).[28] As he broodingly comes to grips with his new environs, Ryan befriends the Cohens' lonely, nerdy, yet "adorkable" son of approximately the same age, Seth (Adam Brody), and instantly sparks some romantic tension with the wan and waifish rich girl next door, Marissa Cooper (Mischa Barton). Unbeknownst to Ryan, Marissa is already attached to Luke (Chris Carmack), a towheaded water polo hunk who is the king of Harbor High, Newport's fictitious prep school. When Ryan and Seth crash a beach party hosted by Newport's cool kids, the geeky Seth gets the proverbial sand kicked in his face and the tough-guy outsider Ryan comes to his rescue. In the ensuing melee, Luke and his band of jock brothers get the better of both outcasts. While administering his final low blow to Ryan—a hard kick in the gut—Luke spits out this iconic insult to the new kid from the wrong side of SoCal: "Welcome to the O.C., bitch."

Even though Luke lasted as a main character for only the first season, his catchphrase outlived the run of the show, first becoming its tagline before entering the regional vernacular.[29] The beach brawl is also the first time viewers are clued in on why the apparently superfluous article "the" is part of the show's title: "the O.C." is what the locals call it. Never mind whether the malaprop-prone water polo studs of Newport Beach actually called Orange County "the O.C." before the show's writers wove this nickname into the county's and nation's topographical mythos. And never mind (at least for the moment) the fact that the show presents a very limited take on what it means to be an Orange County local, with its intrigue-driven portrait of white privilege.[30] Perhaps, as Arellano phrases it, "Newport Beach *is* that moneyed and aggressively ignorant about the rest of Orange County."[31] Indeed, according to the most recent census estimate of Newport Beach's population (measured in 2006), the town only accounts for about 3.5 percent of Orange County's total population. Nearly 93 percent of Newport Beach's local inhabitants are white, and the median value of owner-occupied housing units (as of the 2000 census) is $708,200.[32] The show, using its blond villain/heartthrob Luke as a mouthpiece, performatively utters the place we imagine as "the O.C." into being: a place, as the Fox network's advertising campaign for the premiere promised, that is "nothing like where you live. And nothing like what you imagine."

As far as the American and global television-viewing public are concerned, Newport Beach functions synechdocally for the entirety of the region.[33] The show's writers continued to make cheeky references to the vernacular infectiousness of appending the article "the" to numerous place-names throughout the run of the show, most notably in a second season episode featuring a spring break trip to Las Vegas—or in *The O.C.*–speak, "the Vegas."[34] Even the Inland Empire, the actual region of Southern California from which the fictitious bad boy Ryan Atwood hails, reappropriated the article-plus-initials format for its own nickname, the I.E., in a kind of jujitsu response to its constant derision on the show.

One of the Inland Empire's most lauded fiction writers, Susan Straight from Riverside, wrote a humorous piece in response to this I.E. bashing for Salon.com, titled "Dissed by 'The O.C.'"[35] The Inland Empire's rivalry with Orange County will be explored further in the next chapter. But it is important to note here how *The O.C.* renders its regional exceptionalism and recontours its borders through spatial contrasts achieved not just visually, as I already mentioned above, but also sonically. As the television scholar Patty Ahn suggests, "*The O.C.*, in its serial repetitions on network TV, helped produce a national imaginary about the actual county as a topographical character to be both seen and *heard*."[36] A running joke on the show involves Ryan's Inland Empire–inflected (read: behind-the-times) taste in popular music, as evidenced by his earnest affection for the 1980s rock band Journey.

As the show's critical reception belies, *The O.C.* is as lauded for its sound tracks and the relatively unknown bands whose careers it helped launch, as much as for its other televisual attributes. Ahn argues that the quality programming discourses in trade publications, which have distinguished the show from other teen dramas—even Arellano admits that "*The O.C.* wasn't that bad of a show as far as teenage tripe went"[37]—tend to focus on the creator Josh Schwartz's ear for music from "off the beaten track."[38] The executive producer of the show, "McG," a former music video auteur and UC Irvine graduate, went as far as to claim that the "subversive" nature of the show emerges as a result of using "music as a character."[39] Though McG's claims about the show's subversiveness are questionable, the significance of its music is undeniable. More than just serving as another character or adding sonic heft to the show's drama, the eclectic assortment of music that saturates every episode of *The O.C.* also hints at a sonic map of the greater Southern California region, and the sounds that sort one seemingly indistinguishable suburb from another. As I already noted above, a taste for Journey's anthemic "white trash" rock (see its uses in the 2003 film *Monster*, for example)[40] maps Ryan as an Inland Empire subject. Ahn traces the racialization of the show's sonic discourse through its citations of global pop, particularly K-pop from Korea, providing at least a brief glimpse of another Orange County where Asians are the majority. But to take a more mundane and local example of spatial citation and mapping, we need only to listen to the show's hit theme song "California," by the L.A.-based indie-pop band Phantom Planet.[41]

"California" accompanies the show's title sequence, which surveys the luxe suburban bluffs of Newport Beach. Though the song will forever be associated with that vantage point, it also serves as a metatext for the local migrations rendered in *The O.C.*, which have the potential to resonate more broadly with what I have described throughout this book as a queer of color suburban imaginary.

Unlike all of its subsequent episodes, *The O.C.* pilot does not open with its signature camera shot swooping upward from the Pacific Ocean to Newport's cliffs crested with housing developments. Instead, the song's introductory piano refrain enters *in media res*, as Ryan hastily gathers his belongings amid the clutter of his Chino home after a fight with his mom's abusive boyfriend. The refrain continues over an exterior shot of his squalid house, with its scraggly date palm surrounded by a barren lawn and the detritus of working-class suburbia: an abandoned armchair on the porch, a raised, early 1980s pickup parked on the lawn and filled with salvage scraps. Ryan rides off on a BMX-style bicycle to the nearest pay phone at a grubby, graffitied strip mall as the vocal melody enters for the first time: "We've been on the run / driving in the sun / looking out for number one / California here we come / right back where we started from." On the very basic level of sound track as thematic reinforcement, the lyrics emphasize how seemingly stuck Ryan is in a desperate landscape where, to paraphrase his retort to Sandy Cohen, knowing dreams don't come true is considered a mark of intelligence.

The theme song unspools while Ryan makes a series of frantic phone calls looking for refuge, and we catch a glimpse in the background of one of the Chino strip-mall vendors' signs. It's written in prop Spanish: "Restaur-nte," with a missing letter *a*. Just as he arrives at his last resort and fishes Sandy Cohen's business card out of his back pocket, the song swells with the rhythm of crashing drums to its simple, brief, but infectiously shouty chorus of sustained whole notes— "California, California! Here we come!"—as if to announce that where Ryan is now, with its graffiti and signage *en Español*, cannot possibly be California, *the*

California of so many dreams, sonic and otherwise. One verse later, Sandy Cohen arrives in his luxury sedan to take Ryan away to *that* California, and for the first and final time on the series we are offered a brief peek at the variegated suburban landscape and unsightly freeways that suture Orange County to other parts of the Southern California region.

The series' regular title sequence condenses this transition from the Inland Empire to Orange County in the reflected flicker of Ryan's passenger-seat window.[42] As Ahn notes, this moment "lyricizes the show's central narrative conflict, which is indisputably about Ryan's class and spatial migration from one suburb to another."[43] Throughout the series run, we also get to see other journeys to and from various locations, and even back to Chino. But in subsequent episodes, the route to places like Chino, Corona (an Inland Empire town on the cusp of Orange County), or even Brea (a town in northern Orange County, only twenty-five minutes away from Newport, past a few malls and mini-golf parks on Route 91) requires desolate road trips through deserts dotted with Joshua trees.[44] These rerouted journeys that transpire later in the show's run emphasize *The O.C.*'s isolation from all of the other, sordid Southern California sprawl, and literally confines the realism of classed, local migrations to a flicker, to one note. What the extended "California" of the pilot accomplishes, however, is to reveal both sonically and visually the concrete contours of another California border in the national imaginary: a fantasy border that rejects the centrifugal force of sprawl, of indistinguishable suburban landscapes bleeding together, in favor of neatly apportioned parcels that separate poverty and Spanish-language signs from a prosperous, English-only world.

At least lyrically, Phantom Planet's "California" is a contemporary echo of another song that inspired earlier migrations, one that announced previous arrivals and returns to the Golden State: "California, Here I Come," popularized by Al Jolson in his 1924 and 1946 recordings, and later revived by *I Love Lucy* in the mid-1950s.[45] It is the song Richard Nixon purportedly wanted played "softly and slowly" at his funeral, and the song the Reagans heard in 1989 when they landed at LAX after two terms in the White House.[46] Despite numerous attempts, "California, Here I Come" never became the official state song.[47] In fact, a parody of the song was released by the California League (a Republican-sponsored organization) in a vicious campaign to thwart the muckraking, socialist author Upton Sinclair's gubernatorial ambitions in 1934: "California, here we come! / Every beggar—every bum / From New York—and Jersey / Down to Purdue / By millions—we're coming / So that we can live on you."[48] Maybe all this fuss over a song simply attests to a long history of conflict about encouraging everyone—or anyone, for that matter—to enter the state's borders in search of a dream.

The Orange Curtain

Before postmillennial teen TV rechristened Orange County as "the O.C." and winnowed national impressions of the region to the McMansions of Newport Beach and the gated communities of Coto de Caza, other nicknames for Orange County circulated from the mid-1980s through the late 1990s. Like the nickname "the O.C.," these unofficial place-names for the county and its towns— "Anacrime," "Anaslime," and "Tragic Kingdom" for Anaheim, the home of Disney's "Magic Kingdom"; "Guadalahabra" for the city of La Habra; "Costa Mexico" for Costa Mesa—tell the story of the county's development, rise, decline, and assimilation into the global pop imaginary through a kind of toponymic shorthand.[49]

The title for this chapter—"Behind the Orange Curtain"—plays on just one of the colloquial place-names that adhered to the region in the mid-1980s at the height of the Reagan era. The appellation provides a sunbelt spin on the Cold War fantasies and nightmares that fueled Orange County's post-agricultural development as a military industrial power and as a suburban haven for displaced midwesterners seeking the good life in the mid-twentieth century.[50] At the same time, the mock-severity of the phrase draws attention to the region's obsession with public and private safety, and its attendant cultural and political conservatism, drawing a sharp contrast with its noirish, urban neighbor to the north, Los Angeles.[51] Many lexicons of slang and "fringe English" note this contrast with L.A. as a definitive feature of the "Orange Curtain." For example, one defines the phrase as "the characteristics, real or imagined, that differentiate Orange County from Los Angeles County and the rest of California."[52]

The first known published use of the phrase, like the opening of Studio K at Knott's Berry Farm, coincides with Reagan's reelection in 1984. It was not a regional newspaper or periodical that used the moniker, but rather the British *Financial Times* in a piece titled "Reagan Promises Peace from Behind California's Orange Curtain." As the article's coauthors, Reginald Dale and Paul Taylor, describe the region, "Roughly halfway between Los Angeles and San Diego, it is a place to which people tired of city life are reputed to retreat—to surround themselves with the locally renowned 'Orange Curtain,' as if with a security blanket."[53] And yet this blanket has often smothered those who disagree with the cultural values and development-driven capitalism practiced in the region. Orange County offers a grim (if scenic) backdrop for the immigrant communities and service laborers for whom the region's good life remains elusive.[54] Indeed, in Southern California's spatial imaginary, the Orange Curtain has replaced its Cold War counterpart—the Soviet Union's Iron Curtain—as a political and cultural entity to be reckoned with, particularly for working people, queers, and immigrants.[55] The immigration policies crafted from Cold War politics to contain the "red scare" and other threats to national security coincided with a "pink scare" provision in the 1952 Immigration and Nationality Act barring "homosexuals and other sex perverts" entry to the United States.[56] In the genealogy of a border concept like the Orange Curtain, then, the principles of quarantine apply to sexualized as well as racialized subjects, going so far as to insinuate a potential conflation between perverse sexualities and foreignness that would threaten to undo security in the region and the nation.[57]

As it has developed in the last twenty years or so, the Orange Curtain also aptly describes what Alexandra Moctezuma and Mike Davis have depicted as a "third border" that scars the region. It is a border both real and representational, a "crabgrass apartheid represented by blockaded streets and off-limits parks" policed by civic bureaucracies working, paradoxically, toward increased privatization.[58] Evan McKenzie dubbed this phenomenon, in which communities began to be legislated privately by home owners' associations, a "privatopia."[59] We can even see this rendered visually in the opening title sequence of *The O.C.*, when a guard at the gates of an exclusive enclave admits Sandy Cohen and Ryan Atwood into the fortressed world behind the Orange Curtain.[60]

More often than not, when the topic of borders in California arises, our attention turns first and foremost to the border shared with Mexico less than a hundred miles south of the southernmost reaches of Orange County's wealthiest areas.[61] But as Moctezuma and Davis's work reminds us, California is a land of many borders, both seen and unseen, public and privatized, officiated by "the law" yet also policed informally with Wild West zeal by some of its citizens. As a border concept, the Orange Curtain—playing as it does on specters of the Cold War and the suburban good life that accompanied the region's turn to aerospace, defense, and other security industries (even the Kwikset lock company was based in Anaheim)[62]—urges us to look in multiple directions: to the east as well as the west, or in this instance, the "Far East." From the mid-twentieth-century onward, Orange County also absorbed relocations of bodies, labor, and cultures from this sector of the Cold War world, especially Korea and Vietnam.[63] The storied political emergence of the Vietnamese community in Orange County, for example, is owed in part to the persistence of Cold War politics, particularly the vehemently anticommunist stance of the region's grassroots conservatives. As a recent *Los Angeles Times* article noted, "Vietnamese have historically voted largely Republican, identifying with the party's historic anti-Communist stance . . . though the number of Vietnamese Democrats and voters who decline to state parties has increased."[64]

In their bid to reconsider Orange County as a *post*-suburban region, Rob Kling, Spencer Olin, and Mark Poster point to a cultural shift in Orange County enabled in part by new waves of immigration after the Vietnam war, as well as by the global markets first opened by the booming defense industries at mid-century. Among the most notable of these shifts is an attitudinal and architectural reorientation from provincialism—think Knott and his berry farm—to an Asian-influenced cosmopolitanism: "In Westminster and Garden Grove, long boulevards post store signs almost exclusively in Korean and Vietnamese. The street signs in Garden Grove are bilingual, in English and Vietnamese."[65] In a broader sense, however, I imagine that the relocations etched ever so subtly in these migratory shifts, traced in toponyms like "the Orange Curtain," become part and parcel of a *regional* suburban imaginary—one that distinguishes Southern California as a gateway for Pacific Rim as well as Mexican and Central and Latin American immigration and migration from the mid-twentieth century to the present.

In the previous chapter, we saw how Lynne Chan's JJ Chinois projects grappled humorously with Ellis Island as a disorienting coordinate for her queer, West Coast immigrant imaginary. As Gustavo Arellano clarifies in his own memoir of his family's many migrations to and from Orange County and south of the border, "Orange County *is* the Ellis Island of the twenty-first century."[66] The statistical data on immigration to Southern California supports these popular observations. In the 1980s, the Asian population in Orange County increased 177 percent, while the Latino population increased by 97 percent.[67] A decade later, throughout Southern California "foreign-born Asians . . . led immigration to the region from 1990–1998" at 44 percent, followed by Latinos at 38 percent.[68] In short, the "borders" and migrations that compose this region spiral outward in a myriad of directions, from the south, east, and west, all the way across the Pacific. Buoyant with the winds of Manifest Destiny, the Tropic of Orange has moved so far west, we're touching east again.[69]

Park, Place

These myriad movements, these spiraling migrations to, from, and around, provide the signature gesture to the relocations traced to and through Orange County. Rather than assuming there is a linear development from provincialism to cosmopolitanism in the wake of new patterns of immigration (as is implicit in Kling, Olin, and Poster's argument about the emergence of a "postsuburbia"), we might reconsider the suburbs of Orange County as a site of oscillation, one that stages the back-and-forth between spatial and social concepts like provincialism and cosmopolitanism. We can experience this oscillation temporally: the suburbs are fueled by a nostalgia for a quaint, peaceful, and prosperous American past and yet function as modernity's test site by becoming an incubator for technological innovation, often in the name of convenience.[70] One of the more common criticisms of the suburbs, as well as of the sprawling, suburban character of

Orange County in particular, and southwestern "edge cities" in general, is their disorganized sense of history, their lack of cultural coherence, and their failure to adhere to temporal linearity, bringing mid-century modernism into close quarters with gaudy 1980s futurism and Spanish colonial revivalism.[71] Another way to reframe this lack of architectural, aesthetic, and cultural coherence is through the lens of Fernando Ortiz's "transculturation," a concept hatched at another Cold War coordinate, Cuba (albeit years before Cuba and the United States would officially tangle, and more than a decade before Fidel Castro assumed power).[72]

As a counterpoint to the anthropological term "acculturation," transculturation does not refer to the unidirectional movement of one dominant culture over the other (the conqueror over the conquered), but instead a *mutual* process of intercultural exchange despite "the unequal distribution of power characteristic of transcultural relations."[73] Among the many redactions of this term in postcolonial and Latin American studies, the one I find most relevant to Orange County is Felipe Hernández's use of transculturation to describe "the cultural economy between peripheries and centers" in architectural theory. Hernández writes, "The term transculturation places the theorisation of processes of cultural exchange between peripheries and centres on a more democratic basis ... [because it] creates a new form of cultural dynamics that understands cultural productivity not in binary terms, but as a fluid, complex operation among differing and contesting cultural sites."[74] In other words, transculturation as a concept does not take for granted any unidirectional forms of violence or submission based on where power is located spatially and architecturally. What Hernández describes as fluidity is, in my mind, akin to the oscillation between provincialism and cosmopolitanism, and the tangled movements to and from different sites of colonial conquest, from the Pacific Rim to Latin America, in the Southern California region. Likewise, it suggests that more traditional suburban models that play on an urban center/suburban periphery structure are frustrated by the "conurbated" geographies of Southern California.[75] Indeed, it is that flutter or buzz shared between elements in tension—and sometimes in surprising collusion—that helps situate a place like Orange County in a queer of color suburban imaginary.

As we draw back the Orange Curtain and navigate deeper into its contested terrain, we can begin piecing together a queer of color aesthetics amid the noise, pop, booms, and crashes that began to reshape the region from the 1980s through the present.[76] Indeed, the common denominator that binds the historical debris amassed thus far in this story of Orange County—its grassroots conservatism, televisual emergence, Cold War politics, local and global migrations, architectural schizophrenia, sexual subtexts, and suburban security—is the region's emblematic spatial form: the theme park. As Eric Smoodin explains, "Rather than signaling the end of history, the theme park exemplifies its collapse—all eras and figures exist simultaneously, reduced to funny anecdotes or sound bites about liberty."[77] Smoodin could very well be addressing Orange County itself, with its frontier ethos of freedom that helps propel a tourist economy founded on a winning, reassuring combination of safety, convenience, and amusement.[78] And yet what signals the end of history, I would argue, is not simply the theme park's architecture but also its soundscape. Much like how the sound track of *The O.C.* sonically reinforces borders both tangible and imagined in historical and popular discourse about the region, the soundscape of an amusement park combines with its meticulously planned, but historically incongruous, architecture to become another defining feature of an emergent queer of color suburban imaginary.

To take very literally Smoodin's use of the term "sound bite" in his description of Disneyland's architecture, we might think of amusement parks as participating in a project of regional and national mapping through snippets of popular music. Sound tracks not only accompany the theme park experience but also function as a crucial component of the park's architectural effect—one of coherence amid incoherence. For example, the Walt Disney Company's most recent venture, the California Adventure Park, which is located directly across the entrance plaza from Disneyland, besieges guests with California-themed popular music the moment they enter the "Sunshine Plaza."[79] Framed by a partial recreation of San Francisco's Golden Gate Bridge, California Adventure's entryway music predictably includes the Beach Boys' "California Girls" and Natalie Cole's rendition of "Route 66," while also featuring more offbeat choices, like the John Phillips–penned summer of love anthem, "San Francisco (Be Sure to Wear Flowers in Your Hair)."[80]

Though emblematic in our contemporary imaginings of the late-1960s counterculture with its signature lyric and subtitle—"If you're going to San Francisco / be sure to wear some flowers in your hair"—Phillips's "San Francisco" is actually known in rock lore as a glorified promo jingle for the 1967 Monterey International Pop Music Festival. Performed by Scott McKenzie, "San Francisco" lured those curious about the San Francisco sound and lifestyle to come to the festival—or in the more cynical words of the British rock critic Barney Hoskyns, to the "rock and roll trade show masquerading as a love in."[81] Although the effect of hearing a hippie anthem like "San Francisco" at a squeaky clean Disneyland theme park might initially seem jarring, the song's provenance as a promotional track makes sense in the larger scheme of a boosterist, Disney-imagineered California. At the concept *charrette* that Michael Eisner, CEO of Disney, convened in Aspen to design the new park, one of the themes that emerged focused on "the dreams, the myth, the iconography and the reality of the Golden State of California."[82] Meanwhile, the state of California's own dissonant "north and south" sociopolitical narrative, which pits the liberal San Francisco Bay Area against the conservative bedrock of Orange County, struggles to be resolved in the park's sonic gesture to "San Francisco" and the eclecticism of its overall soundscape (which also includes a lesser-known track, "Airplane" by the lesbian folk duo the Indigo Girls, in the aerospace-themed "Taste Pilots' Grill").

On a larger scale, the California Adventure Park's sound track works with its architecture to present a seamless story about California's abundant resources, including its history of immigrant labor and cultural diversity.[83] As the musicologist Mina Yang argues, cultural resolutions to classed, racialized, and political conflicts in California have been promoted by state boosters throughout the twentieth century: "Even as interracial conflicts have marred California's history and continue to threaten its present-day prosperity and delicate balance of power, discourses surrounding race have been subsumed by California boosters unequivocally delighting in the region's legacy of multiculturalism."[84] A mural painted above the park's replica of one of San Francisco's iconic structures, the neoclassical Palace of Fine Arts, originally built for the city's 1915 Panama-Pacific International Exposition—a structure that, appropriately, played a significant role in promoting public mural art—reinforces the California Adventure Park's melting-pot motif.[85] If we are to retrieve any message from the park's use of popular music as an accompaniment to recreations of the state's architectural and aesthetic landmarks, it is that the California dream offers a regional variation on a larger American dream that binds different people, places, and eras together within a common imaginary.

At the end of his remarks on the theme park's architectural absorption of all eras into one, Eric Smoodin refers to the sonic journey called "America Sings," first created at Disneyland and eventually exported to Disney World in Florida.[86] "America Sings" featured a rotating stage with animatronic creatures from different regions and moments in American history, who sing popular folk songs like "Yankee Doodle Dandy," "Polly Wolly Doodle," and "I've Been Working on the Railroad." Sam the Eagle, voiced by Burl Ives, serves as a narrator and sonic tour guide through the attraction. On its plasticine surface, the theme park and its attendant soundscapes would seem to fit squarely within the United States' homogenous national imaginary, one built in microcosm in Anaheim by Uncle Walt (Disney), after first being heard in the previous century by the nation's über-Walt (Whitman), who penned the poem "I Hear America Singing."[87] Describing the foundational, national mythos brought to life in Walt Whitman's dream of a United States united by music, Josh Kun writes: "'I Hear America Singing' didn't just create a trope that would come to dominate popular discourse about the national arts for the next century, it related a school of thought. To 'hear America sing' has come to imply a specific kind of listening, a listening that is nationalist and tuned into the frequencies of cultural consensus and univocality, keeping minoritized voices quiet, or audible only by proxy."[88] As Kun eloquently demonstrates throughout his own *Audiotopia*, however, Whitman's dream fails, though it also fails to die. Even Orange County's favorite president, Ronald Reagan, covered Whitman's song in his second inaugural address in 1985.[89] And yet there is something about this nationalist, imperialist fantasy always shadowed by its inevitable failure, by the awkward, if fleeting, dissonance produced through the pop music fantasy of counter-cultural expression—like the one employed in the California Adventure Park's use of "San Francisco (Be Sure to Wear Flowers in Your Hair)"—that makes it possible for us to reimagine how seemingly normative, mainstream recreational environments and soundscapes like theme parks might actually reveal other aesthetic and political narratives as well as possibilities. Doing so is not simply to succumb to the control of dominant forces in commerce, culture, and politics. After all, "San Francisco" transmits its own fraught story about the inevitable corporatization of rock and roll. Seeking what else might be possible in these fleeting moments of sonic awkwardness and incongruity is to locate in fissures, disappointments, and losses, as well as victories, the seeds of other ways of seeing and hearing what we are otherwise expected to ignore, or not invited to experience to begin with.

To harness a familiar Foucauldian framework via Freud, the very repression and oppressiveness of an overly controlled and controlling environment like a theme park (or a master-planned community, for that matter) has also led to some curious forms of aesthetic as well as sociocultural expression and innovation.[90] By revisiting the transcultural scripts and shifts through architectural and other cultural environments inspired by Orange County's storied theme parks, we cannot take for granted narratives in queer studies that pit "subcultural" against "mainstream" forces. Just maybe the convolutions and complications of Orange County can help us reframe some of the false dichotomies inherent in these terms, especially vis-à-vis the suburbs writ large. Consider, for example, the racialization of the term "subculture," with its white, punk genealogies that tend to obscure the centrality of the suburbs to its formation and occlude the brown bodies that began repopulating the suburbs in the United Kingdom as well as the United States—which, in turn, inspired certain racist forms of punk disaffection. In his critique of British cultural studies and its "suburban blinkers," Barry Langford explains that "a number of the subcultural practices contemporary cultural studies is concerned to explore, excavate, and, frequently enough, to validate— particularly youth subcultures such as punk and latterly dance culture . . . —are understood and valued precisely as negations of miseries portrayed as integrally suburban."[91] And yet a critical response to this cosmopolitan fetishization of subcultural objects and subjects cannot be limited to rehabilitating suburbia or celebrating the turnabout in which "cultural studies' dispossession of the suburbs has effectively reintroduced to suburbia the very critical marginality its denial disguises as absence."[92] Perhaps one of the critical gestures to be acquired from the suburbs and its theme parks is to work with and through gaudy juxtapositions of incongruous objects and subjects. The terms "mainstream" and "subcultural" are problematized and frustrated by their shared manifestation in such environments. Maybe these terms are ultimately meant to retain their descriptive quality and remind us that the traffic runs and cuts both ways: that subjects of color and the working classes sometimes identify—or, to use Jose Esteban Muñoz's term, "disidentify"—with problematic, incongruous, and improper objects and environments.[93] As John D'Emilio's work also clarified in the early 1980s, capitalism and gay identity are, for better or worse, inextricably linked constructions of modernity.[94] The two share a history of emergence, if ultimately one deeply fraught with mutual disavowals as well as pernicious collusion.

It bears notice that the literary progenitor of an America singing, Walt Whitman, is a gay cultural icon. Despite (or was it because of?) his venerable status in American letters, Whitman has emerged as a heroic figure for certain queer and working-class subcultures since the nineteenth century.[95] And yet Whitman remains a politically problematic figure, precisely for the ways in which his republican vision of a unified national voice played into the ethos of westward American expansionism in the nineteenth century.[96] Whitman's oblique relationship to the theme park's soundscape, then, also marks this moment of confusion, where gay isn't always good, queer isn't always subcultural, and the subcultural, in turn, isn't always politically radical. I say all of this not to discard "subculture" as a concept and to urge a return to normalcy or to working within the system. Nor is this a plea for us just to give up and have a good time at the expense of fighting for other ways of reorienting the world (as Disney seems to implore us to do at theme parks like California Adventure). What looking and listening behind the Orange Curtain may ultimately come to show us, to make us hear, is the mess and cacophony that reside in great American theme worlds created with "a rage for order."[97] Making up this mess are the tangled borders, asynchronous architectures, unlikely alliances, and affective communities found in such unlikely locations as Orange County.[98] It is not only the theme park that potentially functions as an architecture for a queer of color suburban imaginary, but also the soundscapes smuggled in, out, and through its short-lived nightclubs, like Studio K at Knott's Berry Farm. These structures and sounds, both "American" and "Other," both pop and underground, are where new affinities emerge. We are now poised to reinhabit these theme worlds not to romanticize subcultures that formed there, but rather to hear and see these moments as echoes of our many struggles with the popular, the politically problematic, the spatially bound and contingent.

Sweet Escape: Studio K

These leitmotifs of guilt, pleasure, and escape bring us back to one of the first voices that opened this chapter: that of the would-be diva Gwen Stefani and her expressed longing to make an album that would sound like Studio K at Knott's Berry Farm in the 1980s. Her smash solo debut, 2004's *Love. Angel. Music. Baby.*, provides some clues as to what she thought an amusement park club would sound like, especially in the album's four high-octane opening tracks, all of which achieved chart success: the synth-rock dance hit "What You Waiting For?," the *Fiddler on the Roof*–inspired "Rich Girl," the marching band and drumline–driven summer jam of 2005, "Hollaback Girl," and the mid-tempo post-breakup reconciliation song "Cool." Stefani's own popular persona and self-presentation mirrors the theme parks around which she was reared.[99] She collapses the aesthetics of many eras into one, toggling between old Hollywood glamour-puss, space-age Orientalist, spunky rude girl, slinky 1970s "coke whore" (à la Michelle Pfeiffer in *Scarface*), and mid-century mom.[100] Stefani also makes much of motherhood and fairy tales, extolling her marriage to Gavin Rossdale, front man of the British band Bush, as a hetero fantasy akin to Maria von Trapp's in *The Sound of Music*.[101] She experiments with the visual and sonic idioms of imperialism from different global contexts, taking her ska roots as license to name her first-born son Kingston, after the Jamaican capital. And she travels with a coterie of Japanese Harajuku girls, branding their style for her own clothing line of the same name.

Riffing on the name of the popular Japanese restaurant chain and suburban sit-down favorite, Benihana, the journalist MiHi Ahn christens the latter move "Gwenihana":

> Real harajuku girls are just the funky dressers who hang out in the Japanese shopping district of Harajuku.... Vintage couture can be mixed with traditional Japanese costumes, thrift-store classics, Lolita-esque flourishes and cyber-punk accessories. In a culture where the dreaded "salary man/woman" office worker is a fate to be avoided for this never-wanna-grow-up generation, harajuku style can look as radical as punk rockers first looked on London's King Road or how pale-faced Goths silently sweating in their widows weeds look in cheerful sunny suburbs.
>
> Stefani has taken the idea of Japanese street fashion and turned these women into modern-day geisha, contractually obligated to speak only Japanese in public, even though it's rumored they're just plain old Americans and their English is just fine.[102]

In other words, latter-day Gwen Stefani has morphed from No Doubt's queen of convenience, critiquing the suburban decay and corporate soullessness of the theme park town in which she was raised, into a queen of convergence, opportunistically pilfering global style cultures to reinforce her own brand—much as the theme park masters themselves simulated scintillating urban settings in "safe" suburban contexts.

Nearly all the tracks of *Love. Angel. Music. Baby.* refer to the Harajuku girls either directly or indirectly. The album track explicitly titled "Harajuku Girls" begins with the soft, solo refrains of a Japanese bamboo flute and morphs into a synthesized-string vamp cribbed from Madonna's 1986 hit "Papa Don't Preach." A coy voiceover courtesy of Stefani subsequently explains who and what the Harajuku girls are, as well as where they're from—the Harajuku district in Tokyo, or, in the words of the song, "The pedestrian paradise / where the catwalk got its claws."[103] As MiHi Ahn tells the story, Stefani has succumbed to outsourcing cool to Asian female laborers, abandoning her own historical narrative of suburban origins and replacing them with sartorial expressions of suburban ennui from other global destinations (like the Harajuku district, or King's Road in London).[104] And yet perhaps there is a way to "provincialize" Stefani through a crass, Gwenihana-esque remix of Dipesh Chakrabarty's efforts to "provincialize Europe." In his introduction to the project, Chakrabarty isolates "Europe" as a genealogical object that "is at once both indispensable and inadequate in helping us to think through the experiences of political modernity in non-Western nations."[105] We may think of Stefani, meanwhile, as a crucial sonic coordinate in a fantastic global mapping of Orange County—as a figure at once indispensable and yet also inadequate in helping us think about how the region's pop imperialism and relationship to the Pacific Rim (and, not forgetting her ska roots, to the Caribbean) might be read, heard, interpreted, and translated in imaginaries about provincialism and cosmopolitanism itself.[106]

At first glance and listen, Stefani's pop persona and sound converge to create a "contact zone" for what Henry Jenkins has described as "pop cosmopolitanism," or the "transcultural flows of popular culture inspir[ing] new forms of global consciousness and competency."[107] Stefani's song "Harajuku Girls" tells the tale of acquiring Japanese pop literacy alongside competency in global fashion brands through the adoring remarks of the lyrical voice: "I'm fascinated by the Japanese fashion scenes / Just an American girl in the Tokyo streets / My boyfriend bought me a Hysteric Glamour shirt / They're hard to find in the States, got me feeling couture (it's really cool)." The speaker scripts colonial consumption and fascination as pedagogical exchange—she *learns*, simply from watching the Harajuku girls, to expand her own fashion vocabulary, as when she sings, "Your underground culture, visual grammar / the language of your clothing is something to encounter . . . Did you see your inspiration in my latest collection?" "Harajuku Girls," and the entire *Love. Angel. Music. Baby.* album, models the wild oscillations experienced and performed by the pop cosmopolitan; at the same time, it reinforces the national exceptionalism of the narrating American girl, who, in a moment of Orientalist conflation, describes Harajuku style as a "ping-pong match between Eastern and Western." As Jenkins elaborates about pop cosmopolitanism, "The pop cosmopolitan walks a thin line between dilettantism and connoisseurship, between orientalistic fantasies and a desire to honestly connect and understand an alien culture, between assertion of mastery and surrender to cultural difference."[108]

Such intercultural encounters also manifest in the production values of the music itself: spoken Japanese is layered with the "ticktock" vocal round that opens "What You Waiting For?" The Harajuku girls are name-dropped again in the rap garnish, courtesy of the hip-hop artist Eve, in the chorus of "Rich Girl" (a song produced by West Coast rap legend Dr. Dre, combining the pop-ragga, or reggae-influenced "ragamuffin" beats, with the melody of "If I Were a Rich Man" from *Fiddler on the Roof*): "Come together all over the world / from the 'hood to Japan, Harajuku girls."[109] Musically, Stefani's *Love. Angel. Music. Baby.* has been both lauded and derided for its attentiveness to combining world music beats and other global dance styles with American popular music forms. For example, "Bubble Pop Electric" (an album track not released as a single) begins as an electro-homage to 1950s American rock but veers quickly into intricate, multipart vocals evocative of swing-era girl groups like the Andrews Sisters in a mashup at once nostalgic and futuristic: think the *American Bandstand* theme meets *Neue Deutsche Welle* (German New Wave). Meanwhile, the mass distribution of Stefani's album through the transnational corporate networks of the record industry (and global music video outlets, as well as online) might also be read in a media imperialist context. As Jenkins writes, "Within this formulation, Western economic dominance over global entertainment both expresses and extends America's status as a superpower nation; the flow of cultural goods shapes the beliefs and fantasies of worldwide consumers, reshaping local cultures in accordance with U.S. economic and political interests."[110] And yet, as Jenkins and many scholars of transnational feminism like Inderpal Grewal and Caren Kaplan have argued before him, to read such media flows unidirectionally, from the top down, may itself reinscribe the violences of colonial supremacy we hope to obliterate through this simple act of exposure.[111] Instead, we have to at least entertain the notion that a more elaborate system of translations and affective transferences may be at work, especially in relation to "provincial" or local cultures.

The pronounced hyperproduction of locality and difference is a practice I ascribed earlier to Lynne Chan's work and the "dykeasporic condition" of the queer of color subject. In the case of Stefani, however, the deliberate reproduction of localism seems lost in the spectacle of her international solo superstardom after the success of her band No Doubt. She, who was "just a girl" rebelling against the gender constraints of life in the "Tragic Kingdom," metamorphosed in her solo debut into the "rich girl" she dreamed of becoming while "scrubbing floors at a Dairy Queen" and "playing piccolo in the school marching band" at Loara High School in Anaheim.[112] And yet, I would argue that it is precisely these incidental elements of her pop mythology—her musical cultivation through the suburban public school system; her ska-fan older brother's request to have her sing lead in his band; her penchant for Broadway musicals; her storied collaboration with the lesbian icon and pop tunesmith Linda Perry; her visceral attachment to the sound track of Studio K at Knott's Berry Farm[113]—that resulted in the acute production of local difference in her sound, giving her a "competitive advantage in the global marketplace."[114] Even the song "Harajuku Girls" narrates her relative provincialism in the sphere of the global fashion marketplace: it is her "boyfriend" who bought her the Hysteric Glamour shirts, "hard to find" in the States, that she admires on Tokyo's fashion vixens with a schoolgirl's enthusiasm ("it's really cool"). In other words, it is the very provincialism of Stefani's first solo album, with its wide-eyed wonderment at all things Japanese and its homage to marching bands, high-school musicals, and Orange County's theme park nightclubs in the 1980s, that paved the way for her emergence as a pop cosmopolitan, and as Orange County's biggest global export since Disneyland.[115]

It may not immediately be legible to the naked ear, but Stefani's *Love. Angel. Music. Baby.* is an interpretive sonic archive not only of the Orange County suburbs broadly defined, but of a particular place, time, and people: of the youth who attended Studio K at Knott's Berry Farm in Buena Park, California, from 1984 to 1991. The synthetic grain of 1980s pop is unmistakable in Stefani's album, as Krissi Murison in the venerable British music magazine *NME* notices: "All the best bits of the decade of decadence are here—Salt-N-Pepa's cartoon rap ('Crash'), Madonna's breathless purr ('Cool') and camped-up Prince sexperimentalism ('Bubble Pop Electric'). . . . Like a more clued-in Material Girl, Gwen Stefani has looked to the youngsters and realised that if the Thatcher/Reagan years can work in rock clubs . . . they can certainly work on the charts."[116] What gets lost in an equation structured entirely around Stefani's mode of production in a global music marketplace, as Murison's review makes us acutely aware, are the local, suburban practices of *consumption* that are rendered historically in the final product.[117] Stefani herself characterized her album as evoking what it was like to dance at Studio K, a moment in time in which the weekly Top 40 ruled and "every song sound[ed] like a single."[118] But what did Studio K *actually* sound like? How do we get from the pop eclectic, mid-1980s teen sound of the amusement park clubs to the chart-friendly postmillennial pop baubles that made Stefani stand in for an Orange County sound in a pop global imaginary? What exactly was Studio K? And for whom did it truly resound?

Knott's Berry Farm itself has no official corporate archive of Studio K, despite the fact that the club remained open for six years, from 1984 to 1991, and redefined the institution for a brief moment in history by tapping into a new demographic of local teens, expanding on what was no longer, by itself, a lucrative market of families with young children.[119] Very few traces of Studio K remain in municipal archives as well. The Orange County Archives in Santa Ana, California, holds about a dozen photographs and photo proof sheets documenting the teen scene. Stefani's album is perhaps the definitive (if profoundly interpretive) sonic archive of that moment. Otherwise, most traces of Studio K reside in the memories of those who created it, those who DJed there, and those who attended the club during its heyday.[120] Finding what is left of Studio K requires following the ephemera and tracking the public intimacies of a suburban youth club culture through its "remote" reenactments online on blogs, web communities like OCThen.com, or on social networking sites like MySpace and Facebook.

As I mention in my introduction and throughout this book, the relocations I trace have transposed the concept of "remote intimacy" from Jennifer Terry's work about militarized gaming cultures. I believe that these networked forms of intimacy among strangers online, which Terry links specifically to a post-9/11 world of surveillance and militarization, can also be refigured to describe a form of engagement practiced by suburban subjects scattered across time and space. In a pre-digital age, remote intimacies were practiced through the shared consumption (or some would say overconsumption) of broadcast television and popular music, as well as by "hanging out" live, at differently situated chains or even at amusement venues like Knott's. Sometimes the resonance of these activities and of these shared popular objects is only discovered belatedly, thus recreating intimacies in the present based on the shared, remote gestures—some experienced in isolation—in the past. I would venture to describe such asynchronous echoes as remote intimacies across time.[121] Stefani's album could serve as an ideal example of this as well: the songs she listened to on the radio and at Studio K forged the sound for her first solo album, one that calls forth different temporal layers of local sonic archives for disparate audiences scattered across time and space. Our post-digital age not only enables these remote intimacies across time through various forms of conversation, networking, and convergence, but also, importantly, literalizes and reinforces the spatial "remoteness" structuring these intimacies.

Indeed, connections actually happen "remotely"—on message boards, social networking sites, even on virtual community sites. Some recollections of the theme park clubs on these sites are decidedly more innocuous and nostalgic, whereas others hint at the sexual scenes improvised in these family venues. A blogger incarcerated at the Salinas Valley State Penitentiary in Soledad, who goes by the moniker "Prisoner Dave," shares a tale of being transported from his cell to Orange County's theme park clubs through the echoes of the Cure's "Just Like Heaven" on a local college radio broadcast: "The song took me back to my adolescent days when I just got my license to drive. . . . Friday nights at Studio K in Knott's Berry Farm. Saturday in Videopolis in Disneyland. Paying off the wino old man, a fixture on the sidewalk in front of the liquor store to score us some beer. Strawberry Hill for the Ladies."[122] Another commentator, identified as "Gavin Elster," meanwhile, responded to a thread about Disneyland's Videopolis with a more explicit tale: "Videopolis! . . . I was one of those elements they tried to keep out. I remember being stopped and asked to leave twice. Once for dancing with another guy and another time for having spikes in my jacket. It was interesting to see aspects of club life seep into the park. It was a time when you could get a blowjob in the Fantasyland restroom. I guess I have Eisner to thank for that hummer."[123]

Locating materials about Studio K from beyond the recesses of my own youthful memory as an immigrant, Inland Empire kid dazzled by what might be found there, proved difficult and required following the threads of these remote intimacies through public and sometimes anonymous conversations conducted on community websites. Thwarted by official corporate and civic archives, I was ultimately able to track the proverbial bread crumbs scattered across Internet message boards to live encounters with the club's founders and DJs at resort venues like the Pirates Dinner Adventure in Buena Park, California—a spectacular theme dinner-theater nestled among the new Korean restaurants and old Denny's coffee shops in strip malls all along Beach Boulevard, just down the street from Knott's Berry Farm. It was at the Pirates Dinner Adventure that my research assistant, Alex Wescott, and I met Gary R. Salisbury, the Knott's entertainment executive who created Studio K. I tracked Mr. Salisbury down after daily visits to a thread titled "Cloud 9 and Studio K" created by a former avid club-goer, Stephen L. Becker, on OCThen.com (a site that focuses on "Memories of Orange County, California").[124] Becker plans to create a tribute site to the two clubs, which were open concurrently at Knott's. His reminiscence about Saturday nights at the park prompted numerous responses about "the K and 9."[125] Among the respondents to the thread about Studio K and Cloud 9 was Gary R. Salisbury, former director of entertainment at Knott's Berry Farm from 1985 to 1989. When he created Studio K in 1984, Salisbury was the entertainment manager at the park. On February 17, 2008, nearly a year after I began visiting the thread in search of further information, Mr. Salisbury offered this post:

I was the one who came up with the concept of Studio K.

This concept was proposed in a memo dated February 11, 1984. I still have this memo framed in my office.

We opened Studio K on Memorial Day Weekend 1984. The success was overwhelming. She was credited with bring in an additional $2.5 million per year.

I also ran Cloud 9, but Cloud 9 never did near the numbers that were attributed to Studio K.

The name Studio K came from a contest sponsored by Knotts [sic] prior to opening. The winner received a year pass to the park. I have the original plans in my office and they refer to this facility as: Teen Dance Area.

I am also the person who suggested that Studio K be torn down when we approached the 90's. I could see that her days were numbered. She was now bringing in the wrong type of crowd.

She had a good life. what a ride!!!

Gary R. Salisbury

I contacted Mr. Salisbury through his Blogger user name and, after verifying with the Knott's media relations office that he was, indeed, the founder of the club, I scheduled an interview right away. This information was not supplied through any corporate documentation; rather, someone at the Knott's office "asked someone else" and called me back to confirm. Mr. Salisbury is now the marketing and entertainment director at the Pirates Dinner Adventure on Beach Boulevard (a thoroughfare also known as California State Route 39, which originally connected Orange County to Los Angeles), a mere one block north of Knott's Berry Farm. On August 14, 2008, in the shadow of Knott's towering thrill rides, Mr. Salisbury not only shared his recollections about founding Studio K but also volunteered some of the paper and video documentation never archived by the Knott's corporation, such as the memo to executives pitching the idea for the club, along with his aforementioned paper plans for the "teen dance area."

As Salisbury comments on the OCThen.com website, Knott's Berry Farm already had an entertainment venue that featured dancing (initially meant for the ballroom variety) called Cloud 9, located in the northern portion of the park in the "Roaring 20s" theme area. I asked Salisbury why it was necessary to create a new club space for Studio K rather than simply converting Cloud 9 into the space he envisioned. As he explained, Cloud 9 was enclosed and located in a less immediately accessible area of the park. Because of its location, security and fire safety measures were always a concern.[126] Further, "Cloud 9 was just the name of a facility" (in Salisbury's words) that staged all the park's numerous other forms of entertainment regardless of genre, including such fare as hypnotists, magicians, "The Berry Sisters," a cappella groups, and other forms of "old-time" amusement featured at

MEMORANDUM

Date: February 11, 1984

To: Joe Meck

From: Gary R. Salisbury

Subject: Fiesta Village Teen Dance Area

The new dance area which would be located at the site
of the old Animal Farm is being proposed to take advantage of the current teen entertainment trends to increase
the Park attendance in this market.

The concept is to develop a dance area that simulates the
new Southern California teen dance clubs that are geared
toward the youth market. These clubs utilize recorded
music, which research shows is preferred over live bands
by todays teens. Soft drinks and snacks are served and
an area with tables and chairs is provided for those
wishing to view the dancing. Our dance area must include
all the elements found in these clubs plus, by utilizing
special effects such as fog, lazers, and video, we will
offer much more.

We will highlight a special area to feature one of the
fastest growing, crowd gathering, entertainment attractions
of the '80's - break dancing. Break dancing is a form of
street dancing which due to several major motion pictures,
is a style of dance that has been sweeping the nation. By
showcasing break dance teams, I feel that we can generate
a great amount of public awareness of the new area and
generate added attendance at the gate.

GRS:kc

Gary R. Salisbury memo to Joe Meck, "Fiesta Village Teen Dance Area," February 11, 1984.
Courtesy of Gary R. Salisbury.

seaside resorts of the 1920s.[127] Even in its guise as a popular evening dance venue
for teens, featuring alternative rock and New Wave music, "Cloud 9 never pulled
the numbers of Studio K," according to Salisbury, typically drawing an additional
250–500 guests to the park at its peak. Studio K, however, would be a new concept
altogether in Salisbury's eyes, a rebranding of the entire park by offering open-air
entertainment that could bring numbers directly to the entry gate in a very literal

way: Studio K would be located adjacent to the entrance at the site of what was formerly a petting zoo and animal farm (to add an Orwellian twist befitting its opening in 1984). To enter Studio K, patrons would have to be "teenagers, nineteen and under, with a Studio K club card that would allow them to enter both the park and the club after five or six p.m. for the price of only eight dollars."[128] Knowing Knott's could never compete with the affordable five-dollar cover charge for other underage clubs further afield in Hollywood, Salisbury lobbied for this alternate entrance fee to boost overall park attendance, making all the park's attractions more accessible to the 13–19 age demographic. By contrast, the price for an admission pass to Videopolis, Disneyland's competing teen club, which opened more than a year later, required a lump sum of forty dollars for a seasonal "Videopolis Pass."[129] Studio K was open seven days a week during the summer and on weekend nights year-round to cater exclusively to the youth and teen market. Salisbury was given the additional challenge of doubling Cloud 9's revenue numbers, which Studio K accomplished with ease in the club's heyday during the mid to late 1980s, pulling in more than a thousand teenage patrons on some summer evenings.[130]

What Salisbury refers to in his memo to Knott's executive Joe Meck as "the fastest growing, crowd gathering, entertainment attraction of the '80's—break dancing," actually served as the impetus for the architectural environment at Studio K, one that would be attractive to teens and their concerned parents alike. The club's elevated stage, multitiered dance floors, and mirrors, inspired by the forms of break dancing popularized in mainstream movies of the early 1980s, also functioned as a panoptical environment for Studio K's security and the DJs, whom Salisbury entrusted with "controlling the crowd" with their musical sets.[131] As Salisbury emphasized, his desire to capitalize on the break-dancing craze is what also precluded the use of Cloud 9 as the staging ground for the Studio K concept, because it featured "low dance floors" that rendered it impossible to create the multiplatform, double-mirrored environment conducive to both amusement *and* security.[132]

In addition to the financial rewards promised by a break-dancing-themed teen club, part of what drew Salisbury to the trend was its relatively innocuous, harmoniously multicultural, and even multigenerational popular reputation, due to films such as 1983's *Flashdance* (which famously featured a dance sequence with city kids and jaunty senior citizens enjoying a sidewalk performance by the Rock Steady Crew): "The gang problem was always our concern. I had researched it and at that time there was no gang activity associated with that [break dancing]. That's the reason why the main thing of the club was the break dancing."[133] Salisbury's informal market research is corroborated by some accounts from contemporary dance scholars, such as Halifu Osumare, who claims that "breakdancing originated as a creative dance alternative to actual gang violence."[134]

By the time of Studio K's opening on Memorial Day weekend in 1984, break dancing had become thoroughly domesticated: "You could buy several how-to-do-it books as well as even more numerous how-to-do it videotapes. All over the suburbs, middle-class housewives and professionals could take classes at their local Y's and dance centers."[135] And yet, as numerous scholars have rightly insisted, break dancing, even in its most popularized forms cannot be abstracted from the racialized conflicts over the privatization of public space as a consequence of Reagan's postindustrial economic policies.[136] Faith in the marketplace to provide quick solutions to resource impoverishment captivated many break-dancers themselves, who, "like practitioners of sports, graffiti, and rap music," as Robin D. G. Kelley reminds us, "were not only willing to work within the marketplace, but actively promoted the commodification of the form as an alternative to dead-end wage labor."[137] The break-dancing crews' willingness to harness the marketplace for financial mobility in a bleak, postindustrial landscape converged with the amusement park executives' efforts to profit from what began as a subcultural phenomenon. Yet break-dancing crews were never officially hired to perform at the club. As Salisbury remarks, "We relied on the spontaneous expression of break dancing in a space we created to be suitable for an activity that was all the rage both nationally and internationally. We didn't think we needed to hire any professionals to do it."[138] Salisbury's budget-savvy appeal to spontaneity may have ended up yielding more than he bargained for. What actually happened at Studio K—the provisional communities formed by its patrons, as well as by the DJs who were asked to double as entertainers and as security personnel in the club—frustrates any tidy narratives about the lamentable importation of what may have begun as subcultural forms into the controlled and controlling environment of the suburban amusement park. Indeed, a reading that would foreclose such reparative possibility would correspond quite well with the same corporate, development-driven interests that believed in effectively corralling "delinquency" within the cordon sanitaire of a supervised space.[139] In the end, Studio K far exceeded its mazelike rope lines, strict musical playlists, and even the boundaries of the park itself.

While his memo to Meck focuses on his desire to capitalize on the "break-dancing craze . . . sweeping the nation" as a justification for opening Studio K, in our conversation Salisbury offered a more personal reason for bringing a new "teen dance area" into Knott's Berry Farm. Like so many pleasure-seeking suburban youth who would commute to Los Angeles in search of fun, Salisbury's teenage daughter would regularly make the forty-five-minute drive from Orange County to dance at a club called the Odyssey on La Cienega Boulevard in Los Angeles: "My daughter was driving up to Hollywood to go dancing every night, and I knew the name of the club, so I went up there to check it out and as soon as I walked in, all these light bulbs went off in my head and I thought, 'Wow. Wouldn't this be a great thing to put into an amusement park?!?'"[140] Salisbury was stopped at the door and questioned by the bouncer about his interest in an underage club with only a five-dollar cover. He explained his curiosity about the Odyssey "as a dad whose daughter was driving to who knows where" and achieved admittance.[141] Captivated by the environment he discovered in the city through his daughter, Salisbury quickly hatched the concept of a club at Knott's Berry Farm to which the youth of Orange County would not be required to make an odyssey, so to speak: a venue with "security around, away from a busy boulevard, in an enclosed area with supervision, where there'd be other things to do like rides. Plus parents could drop the kids off and pick them up."[142] Even in Salisbury's rhetoric, we see how an Orange County ethos combining security with commerce, and mixing amusement with reassurance, influenced this entertainment executive's plan to reinvigorate the park's atmosphere. Salisbury hoped to allay parental concerns and avert any potential mishaps with meticulous organizational planning. In much the same way that amusement parks will recreate urban environments in a sanitized form (e.g., Disney's California Adventure Park's recreation of the streets of San Francisco), Salisbury envisioned a way of bringing urban excitement to the Farm without compromising its promise of family entertainment.

In his interview with me, Salisbury insisted that the executives' primary concern was not so much to curb any specific "gang activity" associated with certain styles of music or dancing in the venue, but rather to limit any dangers posed by unleashing "a huge teen population . . . from this area down here, which is kind of a mixed area," into the club.[143] He added that "musical format was tremendously important" to this principle of crowd control, especially when admitting throngs of libidinal teens, without commenting further on what he meant by the phrase "mixed area" or the specific concerns such an assessment of the local culture may have inspired in Knott's execs. Like much of the region, Buena Park, site of Knott's Berry Farm and the topographical center of Southern California—the city's official motto is "Center of the Southland"[144]—underwent dramatic demographic shifts in the 1980s. For example, a cumulative increase in the South Asian population in Buena Park gave rise to a shopping and restaurant district called "Indian Village" in the 1980s—a name shared with an attraction at Knott's Berry Farm's Ghost Town, although the latter refers to Native Americans and the Wild West.[145] From the 1980s onward, the "Center of the Southland" also experienced an upsurge in its Korean, Chinese, Filipino, and Vietnamese populations, keeping pace with northern Orange County's growing Latino population.[146]

While Salisbury himself tried to keep his comments about the racial demographics of the region and the club's attendees to a minimum during our conversation—he and the Knott's Berry Farm corporate organization did not collect any official demographic data (only sales revenue information)[147]—the pervasive anecdotal discourse about Studio K on blogs, in interviews with attendees, and even in books mentioning Disneyland's competing club, Videopolis, suggest that at the very least, *perceptions* about the racial dynamics of the club began to influence its regional reputation. In his OCThen.com post quoted at length earlier, Salisbury offers an aside about "the wrong type of crowd" eventually leading to the club's demise. A former club-goer to both Studio K and Videopolis (who prefers to remain anonymous) observed in an e-mail interview that "[Disneyland's] Videopolis was full of white kids in mostly 'New Ro' [New Romantic] or trendy fashions. K was full of Hispanic kids in red and blue bandanas and baggy jeans. I guess you could call it 'gangy' clothing . . . but we were too young to know the implications of all that."[148] Contrary to Salisbury's market research, then, which emphasized the universalized popularity of the break-dancing phenomenon, the gathering of racialized bodies at Studio K resulted in scopic reinterpretations of the venue and its patrons within sensationalized local imaginaries about "gangs."

Whether these gangs (or at least the patrons attired in "gangy" fashions) were exclusively "Hispanic" is also disputable. David Koenig's unofficial history of the Magic Kingdom, *Mouse Tales: A Behind-the-Ears Look at Disneyland*, alludes to several violent incidents at Knott's Studio K that gave the planners of Disney's own dance club pause: "When the Videopolis dance area opened in 1985, officials knew they would see more large groups of teenagers at the park, including more gangs. They had seen it happen at Knott's Berry Farm with its two similar dance clubs, Cloud 9 and Studio K. And just days before the unveiling of Videopolis, bloody clashes broke out between dozens of Hispanic and Samoan gang members at Knott's and then at Magic Mountain."[149] Within a year of its opening, Studio K acquired a far edgier reputation than its executives imagined, albeit one they always feared, in part because of the repopulation of Buena Park by communities of color, notably Asians and Pacific Islanders who didn't quite live up to the innocuous, nerdy image propagated in John Hughes films of the era. Whether Koenig's reporting of "violent clashes" at Studio K and Cloud 9 stems from fact or clever counter-marketing on Disney's behalf matters very little. Studio K's "street rep" had been established among the youth of the region, even if their parents remained oblivious for some time and continued to let their kids attend the club in droves into the late 1980s and early 1990s.

This sense of something "real" happening in a space that was manufactured for their innocent entertainment only added to the venue's appeal for some, especially in contrast to the more palpably restricted and automated Videopolis at Disneyland. Unlike Studio K, Videopolis (launched a year after Studio K, in 1985) rarely featured live DJs—only a predetermined playlist of recorded music, a

Videopolis press kit, front and back covers, 1985.

live cover band that played Top 40 hits for thirty minutes nightly, and an assemblage of futuristic video screens playing MTV hits the rest of the night.[150] It also employed its own theme song, "Videopolis (Going to the Top)," which featured such lyrical boasting as "Gonna use my very best moves / Show what I can do / Dance to the drum / 'Cause the music's so hot, hot, hot" to pump up its crowds.[151]

Marciano Angel Martinez, now an L.A.-based AIDS activist, artist, and queer-about-town, offers this succinct remark about what differentiated the crowds at Videopolis from those at Studio K: "The nerds went to Videopolis, and the cool kids were at K."[152] Stephen Becker, the former Knott's club-goer whose inquiries on OCThen.com ultimately led to the creation of a MySpace group devoted to Studio K and Cloud 9 called "KBF Locals," commented on the rivalry between Videopolis and Studio K, and the classed and racialized stereotypes that adhered to it, which pitted Disney's "sophistication" against Knott's lack thereof: "There was 'teenage tension' between the Knott's crowd and the Videopolis crowd. . . . From what I could tell, Studio K was the place for the non-yuppie crowd to spend weekends. Videopolis was more of the 'money' crowd."[153] Whereas regular patrons of Videopolis and Disney historians like Koenig read an underlying violence threatening to rupture the "diverse" image of Knott's Studio K, Becker and other devotees of the Knott's venues looked on this aspect of Studio K as an added incentive: "The Knott's crowd was far more diverse than the Disneyland crowd. . . . everyone was treated equally at Knott's clubs. There was a lot of subscene activity happening on the weekends, including Domination and Submissive [sic] behavior: [some] people were walked around the park or parts of it, with leashes on, etc."[154]

A former Studio K and Cloud 9 DJ from 1985 to 1991, DJ Craig Gregg (who transitioned from male to female in 2000, and now goes by the name of Bridgette "Mixtress B" Rouletgregg), also reminisced about the eclectic scenes that collectively ruled the platforms and dance floors at Studio K:

> It was the kids who had Mohawks, and the boys who wore more make-up than the girls, and dressed in black and danced really weird and did drugs, and dropped acid, and smoked pot, or brought razor blades, who came. And they came in part because the DJs were so bad-ass. We [as DJs] collaborated and actually helped to make the crowd diverse. We had all types of ethnic backgrounds . . . Latino, Black, Asian and white kids and all the little subcultures within those groups. We'd play all the different genres they followed and appreciated. Some would intermix, some would clash and throw down about dance styles. The experience at Studio K offered everything—class, stigma, style. And we [DJs] knew how to work all of it.[155]

Contrary to the historian Eric Avila's reading of suburban amusement parks—one that scripts the undoing of the vibrant classed, immigrant sexual cultures of the "urban industrial democracy" into a narrative about the theme park's structural suburbanization (including automobile-focused transportation and the "centerless development" pioneered by Disney and Knott)[156]—attractions like Studio K actually became expressive venues for emergent forms of classed, immigrant sexual cultures in the *sub*urban, postindustrial world of the Reagan-era 1980s.

Even a club as closely regulated as Disneyland's Videopolis had its share of controversy, not the least of which was an infamous lawsuit brought by three gay UCLA students who were prevented from couple dancing at the venue in 1988. The three young men, Christopher Drake, Eric Hubert, and Jeffrey Stabile Jr., were told by a Disney guard that "touch dancing is reserved for heterosexual couples only" at the club, and filed suit with a national gay rights legal fund lawyer, Leroy S. Walker.[157] Disney eventually settled the suit and lifted its ban on same-sex dancing, though Videopolis closed shortly thereafter, in 1990.[158]

If we are to believe narratives about the class divide between Studio K and Videopolis shared by Stephen Becker and the other club patrons whom I interviewed, the sheer fact that the gay "couple-dancing" controversy at Disneyland occupied newsprint and entangled legal resources only reinforces the perceived socioeconomic differences between the clubs' milieus.[159] Disneyland and the Walt Disney Company's complex relationship to its gay patrons and employees is well documented, in so far as organized, institutionalized forms of grievance and agitation (by its gay employee union, for example) is woven into local histories and even scholarly books and journals.[160] Documentation of the Knott's queer scene, meanwhile, is far more anecdotal and ephemeral, with nary a legal case to cite as official evidence of its existence. Instead, we only hear its patrons' inclinations in echoes and whispers through music across time and space. Playing on its Orange County setting, the nascent form of suburban expression practiced by queers and youth of color at Studio K transposed the very principles of security, spatial isolation, and a service-driven economy—as well as the weekly Top 40[161]—into their repertoires of rebellion.

Like Rouletgregg, Salisbury himself attributed the vibrant life and afterlife of Studio K to the club's DJs, albeit in Salisbury's comments their role as protectors of the club enterprise was tantamount. Asked to address Studio K's reputation as a hot spot for club kids of color (leading to its conflation in the regional imaginary with gang activity), Salisbury returned to the topic of musical formatting and his youthful DJs' street savvy as a firewall to any conflicts that would arise at the club: "Your DJ is so important because he can control that crowd. He's got to know there's a problem area. He's got to see 'there's something going down here' and change that music so that it mellows out."[162] Rouletgregg seconds Salisbury's statement with a cheeky programming example from back in the day: "Erasure breaks up gang fights pretty quick, you know? It just makes you wanna hug."[163] Her aside to Erasure and the impulse to "hug it out" in the afterglow of their infectious synth music and falsetto vocals also underscores what came across as the relatively unremarkable and peaceful coexistence of queer or questioning youth and youth of color with the much-ballyhooed "thug" element at Studio K. Indeed, the lines among these scenes often blurred, even in the decades before "homo thugs" came to consciousness as an object of interest in contemporary queer studies.[164]

Young queers of color found themselves poised within these multiple worlds that were sometimes apportioned according to musical taste cultures. Marciano Angel Martinez offers this rendering of the milieu at Knott's: "There was the Latino/Asian mini-truck crowd. Islanders (Samoan and other) were, at the time, interchangeable with the mini-truck crews. The KROQ [alternative radio station] crowd was all melded. The Blacks and Latinos were there . . . but tended to go to Cloud 9. Throughout the evening those of us who had 'crossover appeal' usually went between the two clubs a few times."[165] In multiple recollections (including Gwen Stefani's famous aside about the club), "the hits," and in particular "the kind you can dance to," ignited a special chemistry among the disparate scenes at Studio K. Rouletgregg in particular recalls mixing Soft Cell's 1981 hit "Tainted Love" with the theme from *Sesame Street*: "All the kids—all the little death rockers—would go arm in arm and bunny hop. . . . They were young enough to appreciate it, and old enough to have the freedom to be silly."[166] Couple dancing at Disneyland be damned: the kids at K wanted a chance to move together en masse.[167]

Despite the Knott's executives best efforts to produce a family-friendly environment by monitoring the DJs' playlists, going so far as to ban rap and hip-hop (further deracinating the break-dancing phenomenon by extracting it from some of its musical contexts), the club's teens and DJs, some of whom were older teens themselves, ultimately figured out a way to circumvent and thwart the Farm's security measures.[168] Rouletgregg, for example, contradicts Salisbury's account of the musical formats sanctioned and actually played at the teen club, and admits that "Studio K was a little more hip-hop, funk, soul, and rap-based. . . . Gary basically just opened the doors and said, 'Do with it what you want.'"[169] Nevertheless, in the remembrances offered by both Salisbury and Rouletgregg, there were certain limitations on *how* rap and hip-hop could be mixed into the DJs' sets. Rouletgregg, like many of the other DJs at the venue, improvised mixes to maneuver around the club's purported safety ban on rap by creating mash-ups that embedded samples and recognizable instrumental or vocal riffs from rap hits within more melodically driven Top 40 dance hits:

> We couldn't play any hardcore rap, and I remember being frustrated about not even being able to play radio hits like "Push It" by Salt-n-Pepa or "Wild Thing" by Tone Loc. It was 1987, '88. I was doing mash-ups live out of necessity. I wanted to play rap music. I wanted to play funky-ass shit. I wanted to throw down and groove because this what the kids wanted to hear—they wanted the freshest hits and they

Studio K dance floor, 1989. Courtesy of the Orange County Archives, Santa Ana, California.

wanted you to do it with style or else you'd have thirty-five hundred kids on the floor shaking their heads, sayin'"nah-uh." . . . One of my favorite mixes involved playing the 'You want it, you got it' vocal hook of Young MC's "Bust a Move" with Janet Jackson's "What Have You Done for Me Lately?" That would get the crowd going.[170]

The DJs musical improvisations at Studio K were in keeping with an ethos of "making do"—a special alchemy of making something out of nothing—enacted by the youth of the Southern California suburbs on a regular basis, be it through musical playlists or through retooling commercial and private spaces as their playgrounds. The stories Rouletgregg and others have shared about the forms of DJ culture at Knott's converge with some of the larger spatio-cultural narratives that also informed break dancing's emergence in postindustrial urban landscapes. Tricia Rose offers the definitive argument about the nascent hip-hop generation's reinvention of the streets, sidewalks, and evacuated buildings of the urban United States as social environments for youth of color in the wake of the nation's privatization.[171] The suburban equivalent of this spatial repurposing also transpired in regions like Southern California from the 1980s onward, albeit without a city-based public culture of streets and sidewalks as their canvas. Rouletgregg's stories bring to light some of the shadow economies and other forms of queer of color *sub*urban sociability that transpired in and around Buena Park and Knott's Berry Farm.

The DJs' unofficial resumes, itemizing their service-industry day jobs along-side their gigs at local clubs, provide a detailed socioeconomic mapping of Orange County's overlapping cultures of service and amusement. As an older teen, Rouletgregg worked full-time by day at Pacific Bell and began DJing at night, picking up various gigs in Orange County as well as in Los Angeles at a club called Dreams of L.A. in Silver Lake (which has since become the indie music venue Spaceland). Rouletgregg's entry into the Knott's DJ circuit was facilitated by her time at Cyprus College, where Craig Gregg met Dale Clark (a radio DJ at the college), who offered Rouletgregg regular work spinning at a club called Bentley's housed at the Holiday Inn in Buena Park.[172] As DJ Craig Gregg, Rouletgregg gained momentum working in the Orange County scene, especially at some of the area's signature clubs staged in unmistakably suburban venues like Holiday Inn ballrooms or in backyards at house parties put on by groups of local teens.

The backyard party scene in particular, with its queer variant known as "t-par-ties," took place throughout the Southern California region in Orange County, the Inland Empire, the San Gabriel Valley, and South and East L.A. Its more heteronormative histories have recently been commemorated in multimedia archival projects like the L.A. PBS station KCET's "Webstories."[173] Elaborating on why Southern California is amenable to this kind of DJ and party culture, one of the project's authors, Gerard Meraz, remarks, "The planning of our streets with its city grids and post-war middle class homes allow many residents to enjoy a backyard with an orange tree and enough space to throw a party."[174] Though not through corporate intention, Studio K at Knott's started to overlap significantly with the "greater Eastside"–driven backyard scene that was just achieving its apex in the early 1980s, as DJs combined suburban, radio-friendly Top 40 pop with other genres, like "Hi N-R-G, new wave, rock-a-billy, ska, reggae, funk, [and] freestyle."[175]

Another of Knott's legendary Studio K DJs, Tony Gonzalez, was also spin-ning at backyard parties and at the Bentley's club at the Holiday Inn with Craig Gregg. Gonzalez began working his way up the service ranks at the park, first as an usher at Knott's Good Time Theater, before he was tapped by Salisbury to open Studio K: "Tony was working for five dollars an hour as an usher and he was doing some of the music at Cloud 9, so I offered him ten dollars an hour to run Studio K and he couldn't believe it. I offered him that money because I really had to trust him to run that operation from the ground, which he did. He was amazing with the crowds."[176] Other favorites at Studio K and Cloud 9 include DJs Todd "Hot Toddy" Payson and Mike Martin, the latter of whom went on to become a radio DJ at KIIS-FM—a station that has boasted of being "Los Ange-les's No. 1 Hit Music Station" since the Rick Dees era in the 1980s.

As their circulation in different suburban work and play scenes might suggest, the DJs' role as entertainers and as security at Studio K was not limited to the parameters of the club. Rouletgregg in particular confesses to partying with some of the other DJs and their shared fans: "I did associate with the locals . . . a preppie group, a ska group, a surf group, a brainiac group. I had lots of different little cliques around me because I played such different kinds of music. I would also make them bring me music. That British EBM [electronic body music] band Nitzer Ebb was introduced to me by one of the regulars. I remember one girl brought me an import of Nina Hagen's 'New York, New York,' so I played it for her at the club."[177] The circuits of musical exchange and sociability Rouletgregg describes are at once utterly mundane and yet remarkable for the way they model the uses and limitations of suburban space, be it the unofficial listening parties thrown at the houses of kids whose parents were out of town for the weekend, or even the more organized repurposing of backyards and hotel meeting rooms in an effort to fashion alternate social environments for youthful experimentation.

In personal interviews with some of the club attendees who identified themselves as either "queer" or "questioning" during the Studio K era, the gender-bending pop landscape of the 1980s itself also helped give the amusement park clubs an aura of stylistic experimentation, despite the fact that much of the music was not of an "underground" origin.[178] Judith Ann Peraino's *Listening to the Sirens*, a remarkable and sweeping account of queer identity and music "from Homer to Hedwig," illuminates the context for some of the sentiments expressed by Studio K's queer and proto-queer club-goers: "The play with androgyny and irony in much of 1980s new-wave pop opened mainstream doors to queer identities, at least as a source of cutting-edge fashion and provocative sensibility."[179] Referring to his own queer awakenings at Studio K, Marciano Angel Martinez also cites New Wave and New Ro' as a catalyst: "Just the way that guys were allowed to wear makeup and dress in their New Romantic finery made you imagine. Even if that wasn't your scene. And you also had to know as a 'homo thug' that there had to be others at Studio K like you, whatever you were into. It set into motion the idea of that possibility."[180]

The capitalist-driven eclecticism of the Top 40 charts in the 1980s—which encouraged DJs to manufacture sonic proximities between British neo-bubble-gum like Wham!'s "Wake Me Up Before You Go-Go," industrial-lite exhortations about S and M (and the Hegelian dialectic) like Depeche Mode's "Master and Servant," and the *Hot, Cool, and Vicious* female rap of Salt-n-Pepa's "Push It"—materializes as another historical moment in which capitalism and gay identity are entwined around the dissolution of traditional family structures and environments, thus forging an alternate narrative about space and identity. To make this claim is not to celebrate capitalism as the agent of transformation and queer emergence, but rather to track the relations between queers, racialized subjects, and objects and spaces that may have been meant to shore up the family's defense against the kind of "social instability" (to use John D'Emilio's phrase) these milieus represented in Orange County, while actually enabling different configurations of sociability altogether.[181] As Marciano Angel Martinez reflects, "I heard songs like 'Tastes So Good' by File 13, 'Sex Dwarf' by Soft Cell, and Hillary's 'Drop Your Pants!' These were songs we only heard on KROQ alone late at night. To hear them manifest in some place outside of your head, where there were other people dancing to the same music which isolated you from others . . . well, it was liberating to know you were not the only freak."[182]

Ultimately, the latchkey quality of Studio K as a space of amusement in which parents could deposit their children "safely" in the care of broadcast media (like the weekly Top 40) and an amorphous community of other adult supervisors, actually made the suburban amusement park an amenable habitat for nascent efforts to fashion the "affectional communities" D'Emilio calls for in the conclusion of his essay on "Capitalism and Gay Identity."[183] Conceptualized between 1979 and 1980 and published in 1983 (a year before Studio K's opening), D'Emilio's essay speaks out against the ethos of privatized Reagan-era capitalism, urging us instead to work toward alternate forms of community building: "As we create structures beyond the nuclear family that provide a sense of belonging, the family will wane in significance. . . . The building of an 'affectional community' must be as much a part of our political movement as are campaigns for civil rights. In this way we may prefigure the shape of personal relationships in a society grounded in equality and justice rather than exploitation and oppression, a society where autonomy and security do not preclude each other but coexist."[184] Numerous critiques and friendly amendments to D'Emilio's thesis have multiplied in the decades since its emergence in the early 1980s, many of which challenge the essay's emphasis on the urbanity of queer developmental history. In the interest of focusing on the particular historical moment his essay shares with Studio K, however, it behooves us to dwell on how the key terms of his proposed solution to the political dilemmas faced by gay activists were imbricated with the provisional communities already being formed in the classed and racialized youth context of amusement park clubs. Indeed, the forms of sociability being enacted in Studio K anticipated, in many ways, the (in)formal strategies for undoing what we have come to think of as a set of primarily white, gay male priorities in building queer institutions.

Strikingly, "security" and "privacy" combined to become the touchstones of a gay political project, only the right to privacy D'Emilio alludes to has often been conflated with legal fights over the private sexual practices of gay men—most notably, in the battles over sodomy laws in state and federal courts throughout the 1970s and 1980s that culminated in *Bowers v. Hardwick* in 1986.[185] And yet couched in the conclusion to "Capitalism and Gay Identity" is an appeal to support "the rights of young people" as part of the project of "broaden[ing] the opportunities for living outside of traditional heterosexual units."[186] An intervention Studio K offers in the genealogy of queer battles over rights to privacy and security is that it challenges us to think beyond private sexual practices as our only retort to traditional configurations of the nuclear family, presenting instead collective, improvisational models of affection—through dance, musical exchange, or merely hanging out together in motley assemblages—that unravel "security" and its seemingly innocuous impetus toward amusement.[187] Historically, D'Emilio has mapped the opportunities to disrupt the nuclear family on to what he calls a "social terrain," mostly gay and lesbian bars and same-sex boarding houses like the YMCAs scattered throughout the United States but celebrated as "community building" in places like New York and San Francisco.[188] Contrasting the Videopolis archive with that of Studio K—the former documented in legal rights cases and sordid tales of Fantasyland blowjobs, the latter felt in the aftershocks of 1980s pop and scattered in threads on tribute websites—underscores the disparate archives that inform our competing prerogatives for a *contemporary* queer agenda. Caught in the push and pull between a right to privacy and the desperate quest to find something broader, potentially beyond "queer" itself, the suburban, racialized subjects of Studio K employed any means necessary to make something out of nothing. The question remains, then, whether a place like Studio K ultimately belongs to the genealogy of queer social terrain documented by D'Emilio and the many scholars who followed.

The "club" was not a bar (despite the creative smuggling of libations, or parking lot tailgating that may have lubricated social interactions there on occasion), but rather an entertainment venue in a family-themed amusement park. It was not exclusively a same-sex environment, despite the awkward, adolescent separation of spheres sometimes choreographed by group dance trends of the 1980s. Neither was the space grassroots or community generated, but rather manufactured for profit while keeping entertainment execs' amusement park safety records unblemished. Studio K, in other words, was a distinctly suburban space conceptualized around safety, convenience, and the automobile, a technology engineered for and inspired by the nuclear family's flight from the city. Its very lack of urbanity, its *sub*urbanness in nearly every aspect, would seem to preclude it from queer histories of emergence. And yet Studio K, I would argue, necessarily belongs to a political genealogy of queer sociability not despite what it lacks, but rather because of how it exceeds the boundaries of what we are willing to call "gay and lesbian history." What we find there is utterly ordinary, but not in the way our imaginaries have been trained to expect ordinariness to manifest in the suburbs, especially in Reagan's county during the 1980s.

Studio K press photo proof sheet, 1989. Courtesy of the Orange County Archives, Santa Ana, California.

In a suburban world that the Cold War built not simply through industry but through the flows of immigration wrought by its policies, Orange County's youth—queer and proto-queer, trendy and awkward, a couple of generations or fewer removed from the boat or the barrio—dismantled security simply by letting it amuse them. Orange County in general, and Studio K in particular, may ultimately end up meaning the same thing to and for queer and national imaginaries. It was and continues to be (to paraphrase its sonic archivist, Gwen Stefani) one of our guiltiest pleasures: a paradoxically well-ordered mess we want desperately to get rid of. It is proof of our embarrassingly provincial suburban origins, of our attachment to tacky objects like the weekly Top 40, as well as of the cultures of convenience that are the source of both our employment and entertainment. The suburban sociabilities found there threaten to rupture the veneer of queer cosmopolitanism while actively thwarting even the most mainstream of LGBT political agendas. But they also call out our questionable, queer collusions with the hetero nouveau riche fantasies that buttress such a world. From the Pacific Island gangsters who strutted tough, to the brown, bunny-hopping Goths with smeared makeup, to the suburban B-boys and -girls who longed to be discovered on its platforms, Studio K swelled with the ranks of those looking to claim their territory, any parcel of fantasy that could be made their own. Maybe they were just looking for a "sweet escape," a way of being in Orange County without feeling like they were. But on those endless summer nights, long before *The O.C.* was catch-phrased into being, the refrains of New Order would score a mess of bodies moving, wanting to be moved, as the cold world melted away.

4 Empire of My Familiar

In elementary school and junior high, I found that nearly everyone's parents
had immigrated here—from Louisiana and Oklahoma and Mississippi, from
Michoacán and Zacatecas and Guanajuato, from the Philippines and Germany
and Japan. I had friends whose fathers were military men and whose mothers were
immigrant brides from those countries. I had other friends whose fathers were
military men and who'd returned to the South and vowed never to live in poverty
and segregation again. All settled in Riverside, in San Bernardino, in Victorville—
wherever there were military bases. And their children grew up in the Inland
Empire—a new people.

> —Susan Straight, introduction to *Inlandia: A Literary
> Journey through California's Inland Empire*

Here is where the hot wind blows and the old ways do not seem relevant, where
the divorce rate is double the national average and where one person in every
thirty-eight lives in a trailer. Here is the last stop for all those who come from
somewhere else, for all those who drifted away from the cold and the past and the
old ways. Here is where they are trying to find a new life style, trying to find it in
the only places they know to look: the movies and the newspapers.

> —Joan Didion, "Some Dreamers of the Golden Dream"

Oranges Are Not the Only Fruit

Before the mid-1950s and the televisual emergence of Disneyland and Orange
County, there existed another Orange Empire crafted by gentleman farmers from
the East, and cultivated by immigrant laborers from Mexico and the Far East. It
all began in a place they once compared to the Garden of Eden: Riverside, California, approximately sixty miles east of Los Angeles, and (depending on how
you measure the distance) about thirty miles northeast of Orange County. In his
expansive chronicle of the Orange Empire, the historian Douglas Cazaux Sackman explains how the orange, which "most likely originated in the Malay-East
Indian Archipelago some twenty million years ago," passed through the hands of
indigenous peoples, colonial explorers, and missionaries until the 1820s, when "a
mutation in a grove in Sao Salvador de Bahia, Brazil, created a new and succulent variety of orange"—a seedless specimen fusing a smaller, embryonic orange

Deanna Erdmann, "Parent Navel Orange Tree," (2009). Courtesy of the artist. All rights reserved.

within the body of a larger one.[1] Eventually, an American woman named Mrs. Nellie Desmond from Syracuse, New York, brought several of these navels home as souvenirs after visiting her brother at a rubber camp along the Amazon.[2] Hearing of Mrs. Desmond's curious find, the U.S. commissioner of agriculture procured several of the seedless, tiny tree grafts for the Department of Agriculture in Washington DC in the 1870s, where a woman in search of better air and better health named Elizabeth Tibbets was on her way to Riverside to join her husband, Luther.[3]

Eliza Tibbets was given several grafted bud stocks before her westward relocation, and she and Luther subsequently cultivated them next to their new Riverside cabin. By 1878 these bud stocks blossomed into the "Parent Navel Orange Tree," a feat of agricultural ingenuity that in 1902 was transplanted from the Tibbets' yard to the corner of Arlington and Magnolia Avenues, where it remains standing today. Surrounded by wrought iron gates, the Parent Navel Orange Tree sits forlornly across the street from a strip mall anchored by a 7-Eleven and a nail salon.

The tree is almost indistinguishable from the other water-starved shrubs that share its side of the sidewalk flanking rows of low-rent apartments, some styled after Thomas Jefferson's Monticello residence, all aspiring to a more stately existence. Though you can still see some citrus ranches when you drive down Dufferin Avenue or Victoria Avenue, and while some of Riverside's residents still have orange trees in their yards, like the Tibbetses of yore, the title "Orange" belongs to others now.

The exact moment of the region's transition from an "Orange" to "Inland" empire has never been clarified, although curiously local historians have traced the moniker "Inland Empire" all the way back to citrus's heyday at the beginning of the twentieth century. Real estate developers and local business owners were the first to use the term to lure new residents to the region. According to the reporter turned local historian Robert Leicester Wagner, "Evidence of the term dates to April 1914 when the Riverside *Enterprise* published a 'Progress Edition' supplement on high-quality coated paper. The edition chronicled Riverside County's current issues and its past."[4] The boundaries of this new empire have been frequently redrawn since that first glossy insert announced a land of progress, eventually incorporating (depending on whom you ask) all of Riverside and San Bernardino Counties, certain outlying desert communities like Victorville and Barstow, and even the liberal arts college towns further west, like Claremont, Pomona, and La Verne (a few of which technically belong to Los Angeles County).

Though the empire's boundaries are nebulous, its sense of being inland—not just geographically, but pejoratively in the parlance of contemporary California real estate—was intensified with the mid-twentieth-century emergence of its

Deanna Erdmann, "Parent Navel Neighbor (Spa Detail)," 2009. Courtesy of the artist. All rights reserved.

Deanna Erdmann, "View from the Navel," 2009. Courtesy of the artist. All rights reserved.

coastal cousin to the west, Orange County. As I mentioned in the previous chapter, the televised debut of Disneyland, followed by the postmillennial rebirth of "The O.C." in the national imaginary, has left "the I.E." in search of its place in the universe, or at the very least in Southern California. The Inland Empire, left with little but show citrus, closed steel plants, and decommissioned defense factories, is further from Orange County than its contiguity on the map might suggest. And yet it is closer to worlds even further afield than its sturdy, implacable rows of 1960s tract homes belie. The sentiment expressed by Summer Roberts's disapproving "ew" on the teen soap *The O.C.* when the Inland Empire town of Chino is mentioned has been shared by many residents of Southern California since other towns blossomed and surpassed the aspiring empire from the 1950s onward. No one, it seemed, ever *wanted* to be in the I.E., and yet somehow everyone from everywhere relocated there. As Riverside's signature author Susan Straight recalls in the opening epigraph to this chapter, "nearly everyone's parents had immigrated here" from all corners of the globe in search of progress, redemption, or simply a base on which to settle once and for all.[5]

In light of all this, it seems fitting that a seedless, mutant navel incapable of reproducing on its own gave rise to Riverside, San Bernardino, and the other towns enveloped in the larger husk of the region known as the Inland Empire: a place cultivated by a dream of empire that withered on its diminishing vines throughout the twentieth century and on into this one. Once a land of plenty to which people like the Tibbetses and the author M. F. K. Fisher retreated for clean air, water, and health—Riverside was the richest town in the nation for a brief moment in the 1890s[6]—it has now become the repository for the region's toxins from the groundwater up, vestiges of a succession of imperial projects and failures. In 1956, right around the time its identity as an inland rather than orange empire became more actively promoted by real estate developers and local business owners, the Stringfellow Quarry Company opened and managed a state-approved hazardous waste disposal site within five miles of Riverside in Glen Avon. According to Daniel A. Vallero in *Paradigms Lost*: "The Stringfellow Quarry Company disposed of 120 million liters of industrial wastes into an unlined evaporation pond. The contaminants came from the production of metal finishing, electroplating, and formulation of the pesticide DDT."[7] The toxic run-off from the empire's industries—the metal for its guns, the plating for its planes and missiles, the pesticides turned weapons of war first concocted to grow the dream of plenty—began to turn on the inhabitants who came in droves, dreaming of Eden in their bedroom communities only to wake up in a blanket of smog. Another hue of orange. A world after the fall.[8]

Once adored by the nineteenth-century patrician travel writer Kate Sanborn as a place where "you'll see flowers enough to overwhelm a Broadway florist," the region is now, in the words of author and local resident Percival Everett, "known for meth labs and prisons and brutal summers and the occasional cougar wandering through town."[9] Once heralded as a haven of affordable housing for dreamers of the golden dream (to invoke Joan Didion's words), it is now ground zero for the nation's mortgage crisis, a "postcard from the recession." As Susan Straight explained in a 2009 *Los Angeles Times* feature: "Here in the Inland Empire, we joke that our people are canaries but we don't die. Our foreclosure rate was the highest in the country for many months; Riverside County's unemployment rate is 12.2%. But we do recession better than many places. We have experience."[10] The experience Straight speaks of is one that oscillates wildly from boom to bust. Booms wrought by the hands of men and women in the intrepid pursuit of prosperity, only to bust apart again in the constant grasp for more. More land. More convenience. More might. Another specimen of the classic, if hackneyed, narrative arc of empire in which every rise presages an inevitable decline.

Surveying its stubborn monuments today, like the Parent Navel Orange Tree on Magnolia Avenue, affirms that the Inland Empire was never just a homogeneous conglomeration of little boxes, but truly the crossroads of empire. From the Cold War and Reagan-era military bases and defense industries that once resided there, "making America strong,"[11] to the recreations of Spanish missionary culture in its old downtowns, to the genteel, citrus-era Victorianism still discernible in its oldest houses and civic landmarks—the latter affirming a strange, Brit stranglehold on culture and anarchy even now, long after the sun has set *beyond* the British Empire. Now the bases are museums, the factories and the old Kaiser Steel Plant in Fontana are empty, and houses old and new bear the stain of foreclosure. Many towns have proclaimed to be the "heartland of California," like they used to sing in a jingle familiar to most locals for the Stater Bros. grocery stores, now headquartered in San Bernardino on the former grounds of the decommissioned Norton Air Force Base.[12] While the question of who gets to have that honor or burden might never be resolved, one certainty is that this aspiring empire provides the baseline for all of Southern California. As Mike Davis explains:

> Base Line Street [in San Bernardino] is the Euclidean progenitor, the Ur-line, from which all the glamorous movieland boulevards and drives—Wilshire, Rodeo, Sunset, and so on—were originally derived. It was plotted in November 1852 by Col. Henry Washington, working under contract to Samuel King, the Surveyor General of California.... It was Southern California's turn to submit to the geometry of Manifest Destiny. The colonel and his party of a dozen men first established a cadastral Initial Point on the 10,000-foot-high Mt. San Bernardino, then laid down the Base and Principal Meridian lines. They are the absolute coordinates from which Southern California has been subsequently subdivided.[13]

Despite being the source, the "Ur-line" for the region's coordinates, the Inland Empire has perpetually been relegated to bit parts in movies, TV shows, and even books about Southern California, as the documentarian William E. Jones remarks in a voice-over to his documentary on Morrissey and the Smiths.[14] Perhaps it is because this empire, like the many that have come before and after, always seems to start something it can't finish—or will finish badly.

Even Luther Tibbets failed to profit from the agricultural feat he achieved with his wife. As the *New York Times* reported in 1902: "Luther C. Tibbets, who planted and grew the original tree, is a homeless, white-haired, tattered public charge in Riverside County. Every day he looks out from the county poorhouse across a broad valley on a vast expanse of green orange groves and superb homes and reflects that when he planted his first navel orange tree there not a tree grew in the valley."[15] Since then, the Inland Empire has inevitably receded into the background, a base—or like a bass, laying down the rhythm to an elaborate song, felt in time but barely heard. And yet, as this chapter will show, the Inland Empire's failures—failure to hold the line, failure to make profit, failure to take seed—have also been the source of its profoundest successes. Failure, in other words, is its contribution to a larger spatial imaginary about what Southern California might come to mean in this millennium, for what has truly failed in the Inland Empire is the destiny of empire itself.[16]

And so this chapter will peer into its chasms and dwell on its faults, much as the region itself sits precariously on the San Andreas awaiting its own annihilation. One never knows when it will turn to rubble, but we keep building, living, waiting, much like the Parent Navel Orange Tree with its misleadingly reproductive name continues to sit sterile after a lifetime of being cut and grafted for others to profit from its mutation. In 2009, *Time* magazine claimed that the region presaged the death of the American suburbs altogether: "Not every suburb will make it. The fringes of a suburb like Riverside in Southern California, where housing prices have fallen more than 20% since the bust began, could be too diffuse to thrive in a future where density is no longer taboo."[17] Because this place has (as Lee Edelman might say) "no future,"[18] dare we leap to the conclusion that there is something about the Inland Empire that is discursively, representationally, structurally, queer? Or is there some other way to read and inhabit what is queer in and about the Inland Empire?

On a larger scale, this chapter grapples with these questions not only by exploring how empire has come to be etched into suburban grids, but also by considering how empire and sexuality come to be entwined in the suburbs itself. Whereas the architectural soundscape of the amusement park emerged as a gathering place for queers and people of color in Orange County, this chapter relocates to the micro-spaces of commerce and immigrant entrepreneurship known as the strip mall: that parcel of convenience that once taunted the Parent Navel Orange Tree across the street as a glimpse at the future, but now shares its misery as a relic of an ill-conceived past. Scattered across Southern California as well as the globe, the strip mall is not native to the Inland Empire. As we have seen, the artist Lynne Chan already commemorated the strip mall and some of its resident chain stores within a queer of color "dykeasporic" imaginary through the tour dates on her original website for the celebrity persona JJ Chinois. In this chapter we will revisit the concept of the strip mall, both real and imagined, in the aftermath of big-box development and property expansion during the real estate booms of the last twenty years. The empire's repurposing of these commercial spaces for social, sonic, and sometimes even spiritual transactions provides the structure, in more ways than one, for the inland region's queer of color imaginaries.

Straddling the line between fiction and nonfiction, the literature of the Inland Empire traces its development and imperial aspirations while reporting some of its most storied scandals and scandalous failures. The 2006 anthology edited by Gayle Wattawa, *Inlandia: A Literary Journey through California's Inland Empire*, is among the very first to map this space through time and letters, calling on the prismatic perspectives of its many immigrants, migrants, visitors, and inhabitants. Its many voices make cameos throughout this chapter in epigraphs, footnotes, and asides, functioning not unlike a chorus, reflecting on a meta-level on the ways in which history has been refracted through the region. While the work in *Inlandia* informs the literary-historical character of this chapter, queer storytelling in the Inland Empire appears in less sustained formats and remains an emergent entity, with the exception of the 2007 novel *Still Water Saints* by Alex Espinoza, a queer Latino author educated at the University of California, Riverside.[19] The second half of this chapter focuses on *Still Water Saints* to consider the function of "the literary" as it maps queer contact in suburban empires. Given the paucity of visual representations of the Inland Empire in movies or on television—detours on *The O.C.* and David Lynch's abstract noir notwithstanding—this chapter implicitly argues that the Inland Empire, counter to its crass reputation, remains largely a land of letters: a place where poets, essayists, and fiction writers, queer and otherwise, still gather at literary salons and cafes hosted in homes and, yes, in mini-mall cafes. Espinoza reanimates the region's strip-mall culture in *Still Water Saints* with a fictitious botanica nestled in a town called Agua Mansa, a figment of memory drowned by Santa Ana floods and commerce. Espinoza situates his novel in this historical ghost town in an effort to capture the "'other' Southern California" that exists beyond the coastal fantasies otherwise perpetuated by the American popular imaginary:

> Agua Mansa . . . is not just one specific city, but one that embodies many elements
> of communities here in Southern California. . . . In the popular version, Southern
> California is oriented almost entirely toward the Pacific Ocean, anchored by
> Los Angeles (which often seems to be reduced to Hollywood), the beach cities
> of Orange County, and San Diego. It is the Southern California of surfing,
> skateboarding, punk rock, and movie stars. These things really do exist here, but
> my Southern California is different. It's oriented eastward, toward the desert, and
> it's changing as people move away from the coast in search of affordable housing.[20]

In *Still Water Saints*, the author spins what many reviewers have lauded as a "magical realist" tale, using a densely populated literary narrative to revisit the legacies of historical, imperial, and affective erasure in the region's dilapidated strip malls. But Espinoza insists on the realism and historicism of *Still Water Saints* and its approach to human density amid lands of sage and sprawl.

Like many parts of Southern California, the Inland Empire belongs to what the idiosyncratic Los Angeles historian Norman Klein calls a "history of forgetting," a history made of layers of settlement, occupation, and development bleeding into and out of one another until everything becomes nearly indiscernible.[21] These processes and forms of forgetting, so distinctly local in their unfolding, also resonate more broadly, I would add, with what Victor Bascara (among others) has described as the dialectical disappearance and reemergence of American imperialism—a project that has gone "by numerous and well-documented aliases and euphemisms."[22] The literary reading that forms the bulk of this chapter, then, will imagine Espinoza's novel in conversation with some of these other layers of imperial erasure and emergence in history, sound, and memory to be found in Southern California.

In the full interest of disclosure, it behooves me to admit that these stories, these grids, this place, are not just another archive on which to exercise my years of training in the dark scholarly arts of queer, literary, and cultural studies. Though all of the materials and regions in this book genuinely *mean* something to me, the Inland Empire is my cardinal coordinate, the Ur-line for this entire project. Like other dreamers of the golden dream who found themselves in the Inland Empire "a new people" (to mash up this chapter's opening refrains courtesy of Joan Didion and Susan Straight), my parents and I found ourselves in the empire after many migrations and relocations to and from other imperial landscapes and soundscapes. Some of our stories and sounds overlap intricately with the narrative through line of this chapter, less resembling a line than following the contours of the death-defying cloverleaf freeway interchanges etched into the region's concrete pathways—entry points on which traffic is not meant to stop, but rather to merge and weave in an elaborately timed choreography learned through experience. And yet I am also acutely aware that this story is not simply my own, and that my personal details for the most part should recede into the flow of anonymity among the many other road warriors making the mundane commute: the escape to nowhere that is our shared somewhere. So even though this chapter, more than any other, will occasionally break that scholarly "fourth wall," devolving (as some are sure to complain) into the sensationalism of the "return of the native," stay with me just long enough for a ride through the empire of my familiar.

Inland Emperors

This corridor along the 10 and 60 Freeways is the eastern edge of the Los Angeles metropolis: formerly irrigated agricultural land, then a center of heavy industry, now old and new suburbs. . . . There's a lot of pollution, terrible traffic, but real estate is more affordable the further east one travels. . . . Most of the population is Latino, and several cities have Asian majorities. The outlying area of the region is called the Inland Empire, but its boundaries are vague, and there is no emperor.
—William E. Jones, *Is It Really So Strange?*

In graduate school, I was trained as a Victorianist and learned about the elaborate cultural and political machinations of the British Empire. Schooled in the discourses and materialities of empire, I sought its traces in other environments and came to understand how it functioned correlatively in my other home context: the Philippines I left as a child, or a place, in the words of the author Jessica Hagedorn, that "spent 400 years in the convent and 50 years in Hollywood."[23] It took some time for me to realize, however, that in studiously seeking stories and evidence of empire elsewhere, I failed to noticed that I spent my entire adoles-

Avenue Brand citrus label, ca. 1930s. Courtesy of the Riverside Public
Library Local History Resource Center.

cence surrounded by its sounds and structures in the inland region of Southern California, a place I thought only played for profit with empire's name. The
Inland Empire amused itself with British imperial echoes, but it played for keeps
with the United States' commercial and military might. Or so I thought.

Riverside, the town that reared me, has a long history of collective fascination
with all things British, and its persevering attachment to Victoriana might explain
a few things about my own twisted career path from a venerable Victorianist to
whatever I am now. But that's another story. Even now, the town annually hosts
an elaborate "Dickens Festival" during the author's birthday weekend in February,
complete with a street fair, premiere performances, pub nights, scholarly presen-
tations, and youth and adult literacy programs.[24] Playing fast and loose with the
word "empire" since its halcyon days, Riverside's spirit of Victoriana actually coincides historically with what is understood locally as its "citrus heritage." The town
thoroughfare symbolizing this legacy is the lengthy, palm-lined Victoria Avenue,
which is listed on the National Register of Historic Places and designated a City
of Riverside Cultural Heritage.[25]

Victoria Avenue continues to be lovingly preserved by town boosters and
preservationists as a specimen of the "'Grand Highway' concept of . . . Victorian
landscape design," while serving as a combination "historical landmark, recre-

Victoria Brand citrus label, ca. 1930s. Courtesy of the Riverside Public Library Local History Resource Center.

ational park and linear botanical garden" for the Inland Empire's new people.[26] The Victoria Avenue Historic Restoration Project cites a 1995 botanical survey enumerating the parkway's continuing biodiversity, including "1302 Mexican Fan Palms, 388 Crepe Myrtle, 273 Eucalyptus, 191 Magnolia (2 species), 99 Redbud, 79 Chaste Trees, 64 Jacarandas, etc."[27] Large sections of the heart of Victoria Avenue are also still lined by citrus groves. Riverside's oldest high school, Polytechnic (or "Poly") High, holds a Victoria Avenue address, and the parkway ambles past the elite Victoria Club in Tequesquite Arroyo, a private country club founded in 1903 only a couple of years after its namesake, the empress of India, Queen Victoria of Great Britain and Ireland, passed into history.

After crossing the ornate Victoria Bridge straddling the parched Arroyo Seco River bed, Victoria Avenue narrows into a regular two-lane road without any botanical bisection, remaining oddly quaint in a Southern California infrastructure prone to stretching out into four- and eight-lane avenues to accommodate Hummers and SUVs—empire's latest vessels of war turned recreational status symbols. Scaled to more modest proportions over the Arroyo, Victoria winds through East Riverside, a neighborhood populated in the mid-twentieth century by middle-class African American families. The area has also become a housing destination for working-class Latino families. *Carnicerias* and a few neighborhood bodegas anchor some of the street corners en route to Victoria's endpoint on University Avenue at the Thunderbird Lodge, an "Indian-themed" motel that was a dilapidated specimen of mid-century roadside architecture until its more recent renovation in the corporate, Best Western idiom. Although Victoria Avenue at its narrow culmination offers a glimpse at many vestiges of the American empire, it also remains one of Riverside's roads that leads directly back to the British Empire.

In the 1880s and 1890s, an Irish jeweler raised in Canada by the name of Matthew Gage invested in agricultural land throughout Riverside and developed a canal that would eventually harness the waters of the Santa Ana River (which inspired the town's name) to enrich its arid lands for the cultivation of citrus orchards.[28] Victoria Avenue was Gage's notion, his vision of a "showcase parkway" to promote sales of the agricultural and residential land that would be irrigated by his canal.[29] To finance his ventures, including Victoria Avenue and the Victoria Bridge, Gage ultimately enlisted the assistance of a London financier named Wilson Crewdson, a British Oriental art enthusiast who honeymooned and convalesced from an "unidentified malady" during the winter of 1884–85 at Riverside's Glenwood Inn (a site that ultimately became the Mission Inn, Riverside's landmark hotel and resort).[30] Gage's most recent biographer, Joan H. Hall, explains how a British investment company called the Riverside Trust Company coalesced in London in 1889 nearly a decade after Eliza and Luther Tibbets' first navel oranges blossomed. The company eventually assisted Gage in developing and purchasing more large parcels of land in Riverside after he found himself heavily in debt from building his canal, all the while dreaming of his grand parkway, Victoria Avenue:

Deanna Erdmann, "Thunderbird," 2009. Courtesy of the artist. All rights reserved.

[Gage] had spent more than $200,000 building his canal, and his indebtedness was in excess of $800,000. . . . Matthew was desperate. He wrote a detailed letter to Wilson Crewdson, in London, recalling their encounter at the Glenwood Hotel during Crewdson's 1885 visit to Riverside. . . . Mr. Crewdson replied that he was fully invested in England, but thanked Mr. Gage for the correspondence and wished him well. . . . Matthew, disappointed and dejected with Mr. Crewdson's response, decided to personally present his proposal to the Englishman. With [his wife] Jane's encouragement, and a reasonable fare, he left Riverside in October 1889, crossing the Atlantic Ocean in six days on the steamer *Etrurita*. . . . After detailing his visionary plans, Mr. Crewdson introduced Matthew to his uncle, Theodore Waterhouse, senior partner of the international accounting firm of Price, Waterhouse Company. . . . In March 1890, Matthew returned to the London offices of Wilson Crewdson. There, he signed legal documents conveying his Arlington Heights property and his irrigation canal, including all water rights, to an English investment group incorporated as the Riverside Trust Company, Limited. The new company, headed by Crewdson and Waterhouse, was capitalized at $1,250,000 American dollars. The purchase agreement included the Gage Canal Water system, Matthew's 7171 acres of land known as the Victoria Tract, and 4790 acres known as Arlington Heights.[31]

And so we come to learn that there is something more behind the region's Victorianism than a fondness for Charles Dickens and period landscaping. English capital is what helped make Riverside the capital of the Orange Empire in Southern California at the end of the nineteenth century. To invoke the Riverside Trust Company's motto, the budding Orange Empire was fueled by "American Energy and English Capital."[32]

Though Riverside, like so much of Alta California, was first wrenched from indigenous peoples during the Spanish missionary era in the eighteenth century and converted into Mexican ranchos in the early to mid nineteenth century, it materialized at the fin de siècle as a western American outpost of a British Empire on the cusp of waning.[33] Residents of citrus-era Riverside fancied themselves part of their own "English colony" funded by what they described, without any hint of double-talk or criticism, as the "wealthy syndicate" of the British Riverside Trust Company.[34] The subjects of this imperial outpost celebrated Queen Victoria's birthday annually throughout her lifetime with picnics and fairs in Riverside, but on her Diamond Jubilee in 1897, the gentlemen orchardists and denizens of the "English colony" threw a much more elaborate celebration at the town's Loring Opera House, where "three becoming portraits of Her Majesty and Union Jack flags draped around each frame, stood on the stage covered in flowers." Alongside Victoria's likenesses were "several portraits of President William McKinley draped in American flags."[35]

Spectators of the jubilee in Riverside's opera house also bore witness that night to empires crossing over. In 1898, within a year of this Riverside fete for the British Queen, McKinley's modern American empire would begin to take shape in the Caribbean and the Pacific after the United States acquired partial control over Cuba, annexed Hawaii, and took ownership of Puerto Rico, Guam, and the Philippines.[36] Much as Spanish missionary culture was replaced by British capital in this parcel of Southern California, Spain was also dispossessed of the territories McKinley coveted in the Pacific and Caribbean for his own "civilizing" mission.

The confluence of imperial cultures in the region was not limited to this symbolic passing of the torch through portraiture at Victoria's jubilee celebrations in Riverside's Loring Opera House. Alongside architectural and social inflections of a British-inspired Victorianism as well as residual nods to the Spanish missionary era are historical and architectural flourishes of Orientalism. Some of these "Oriental" artifacts anticipated the United States' more vigorous involvement in and with Asia after McKinley's inroads to the Pacific, whereas newer, more whimsical relics captured a mid-twentieth-century fantasy of an Asia Pacific that the United States thought it had already conquered. At the lavish 1890 banquet honoring Matthew Gage's development of the region from an arid desert to prime citrus-growing lands, "brightly colored Chinese lanterns" festooned the lobby at the Glenwood Inn.[37] Less than a decade later, in 1906, as more Japanese laborers came to Riverside to work in the citrus orchards and packinghouses—the mayor at the time, Chauncey McFarland, greeted them as "workers . . . friends and neighbors"—another emperor's birthday was celebrated at the Loring Opera House: that of Emperor Mutsuhito of Japan.[38] According to newspaper reports, the local Japanese community mingled with subjects of the "English colony" at the Opera House and concluded the evening with the spirited cry, "Banzi—Banzi, long live the Emperor."[39]

Yet other historical traces of "the Orient" actually came with the people from China, Japan, Korea, and the Philippines who found themselves building the Orange Empire in the inland region starting in the late nineteenth century.[40] Even today a "Chinese Pavilion" stands across from the Mission Inn, directly in front of the city's main public library branch, a mid-century modern building with otherwise clean, bureaucratic lines.[41] Cofinanced in 1985 by the Republic of China (Taiwan), the City of Riverside, and a local nonprofit organization called the Chinese Pavilion Committee, the monument was built to commemorate the Chinese "pioneers" who, prior to and alongside figures like Matthew Gage, helped "settle" Riverside in the late nineteenth and early twentieth centuries by providing local services, building railroads, and harvesting agriculture.[42] The Inland Empire's shift from Occident to Orient, then, is not so much sequential, tracking its way to and through World War II, Korea, and Vietnam, as it is simultaneous with a British imperial imaginary. Indeed, these imperial imaginaries have always been entangled with one another among the citrus groves, on the railroads, and in the British and American articulations of Orientalism informing and actually funding the area's development from its incipience to the present. The filmmaker William E. Jones is right that "there is no emperor" in the Inland Empire. Instead, there have been all too many. Empire flourished here and the region's developers knew it, so they brandished the phrase "empire" even as the United States itself performed ambivalence, weighing the rewards and "burdens" of its nascent imperial projects at the beginning of the twentieth century that would create deeper entanglements with Japan, Korea, and the Philippines.[43] And yet a key element of this imperial imaginary is the nominal and spiritual shift from an Orange Empire to an Inland identity in the region.

As the country-and-western chanteuse Loretta Lynn once sang, "Success has made a failure of our home." Early successes at crafting a Victorian-inspired infrastructure sourced by his canal may have earned Matthew Gage the distinction and notoriety of being an "empire builder" who lured other far-flung imperial subjects like Chinese, Japanese, and Filipinos to the desert turned oasis.[44] But in the end, the Irishman could not escape his fate as but another subject or casualty of a British Empire that would also inevitably recede into memory and fantasy: "He has been praised as a great builder and benefactor of Riverside, and yet he lost the empire he had built and, in 1916, died not far above poverty."[45] In various accounts of Gage written by local journalists and historians, it seems he had a profound dream of developing land but failed to master the intricacies of his legal entanglement with the Riverside Trust Company and other investors: "In his deal with the English backers he seems to have had no legal advice. He expected to develop and sell land, but sales were slow. Instead, the company became primarily a citrus production organization. Gage's stock was composed of 'B' shares, which stood to profit heavily from land sales rather than citrus production."[46] And so the end of Gage's own story portends the moment of historical crisis that the Inland Empire, bereft of the title of "Orange," finds itself in now: in debt and foreclosure as the collateral damage of empire's grand ambitions. As the journalist and local historian Tom Patterson explains, "The longtime Gage home on a 10-acre lot on Fourteenth Street was lost to foreclosure."[47] This is a line that resounds today, echoed daily in newsprint, or glowing from computer screens as newspapers themselves cease to clutter doorways and driveways. Only the names and addresses have been changed.

I have lingered on Gage's story here not to resurrect him as a pioneering exemplar, a gesture to which many local historians are prone. Nor do I simply hope to make a convenient example of him as a cautionary tale about imperial ambitions and their brokered destinies. Gage and his collaborators, adversaries, and legions of unsung laborers literally crafted the tributaries of empire in the inland region, carving its architectures of commerce and technology—such as a canal and a grand parkway—into Riverside's desert landscape. And yet incidental histories of failure and foreclosure are what began to take seed, even during the region's first blush of imperial fantasy. Materially and metaphorically, the inland region began to realize how much of it comprised "'B' shares." In the end, the hazardous effects and unpredictable affects of empire cannot be reduced to measuring its parcels of land and enumerating the resources one pilfers or yields there. To invoke the methodology employed eloquently by Norman Klein, the routes of empire I have traced thus far in the inland region belong to "a history of forgetting" and accrue as layers of an erasure to which we have become attenuated in built environments, like the suburbs, that seem to rely on our blissful distraction.[48]

"All of this has happened before, and it will happen again," to echo the nihilism of the hit Syfy remake of *Battlestar Galactica*. The suburbs have always been about a here, now, and future, with a tenuous relationship to pasts that never were, or only as we might want them—quaint, sepia-toned narratives of success, development, and the triumph of successive generations. And yet the stubborn traces of empire call forth something else, maybe a curse more than a blessing, of what success actually brings and at what costs. It sometimes leads askew, as imperial narratives are prone, back to the space of distraction—to an otherwise and elsewhere that both unearths and recovers what any of it might ultimately mean. Klein writes that "forgetting is a twin; its tandem effect is best called '*simultaneous*' *distraction*, the instant when one memory defoliates another."[49] Now, after a haphazard genealogy of the emperors who passed through the region, loaned their names to its streets, or simply never were, we have arrived at another instance of memorial distraction in the wake of devastation. What memories would allow us to "defoliate" this one in order to get us to a queer here, now and then? Do we peel back the layers and gaze at that unremarkable, smaller part of the navel, encased by fleshier, more substantial fruit?

Echo of Another Subject: Accents in Theory and Time

> U.S. culture can be said to remain at least vestigially postcolonial so long as its citizens are impressed by the sound of an educated British accent.
>
> —Lawrence Buell, "Postcolonial Anxiety in Classic U.S. Literature"

> Music, then, primes; it sets off the autobiographical gesture. Which is to say, as well, the theoretical gesture.
>
> —Philippe Lacoue-Labarthe, "The Echo of the Subject"

In 1970, Tom Patterson concluded that as a developer and civic patron, Matthew Gage "gave the city new long-term prosperity and a new social accent."[50] While the journalist may have been referring to a commonwealth accent imported to the region through the circuits of British capital—through Ireland, Canada (Gage's childhood home), and England—it evolved into something else altogether by the time it mingled with the other imperial accents of the inland region from the past into the present. Is it really so strange that nearly a hundred years after Gage launched his efforts to build an empire that I heard that accent again, in 1983, when I landed in Riverside with my musician parents? A British accent whistling through Victoria Avenue's palms, down a vanished Chinatown's Wong Way, slicing diagonally past the graveyard and a sandwich shop called Butch's Grinders, sinking deep into my adolescent bones after being remixed and refracted through time on the radio and MTV: the slinky, synthy sounds of British pop, an imperial New Wave from the much-heralded second "British Invasion" sold to SoCal kids by a local DJ named Richard Blade. Formerly Richard Shepphard of Torquay, England, Richard changed his last name to "Blade" when he moved to Los Angeles in 1982 as an homage to that year's neo-noir hit film *Blade Runner*. On his local broadcast TV shows like *Video One* and *Video Beat* (on KHJ-TV and KTLA, respectively), and as the signature DJ on KROQ, the "Roq of the 80s," Blade curated the sound track for my reentry into the so-called first world from the Philippines.

Much as the club kids of Studio K—queer, proto-queer, or "just experimenting"—found a sound track for their fantasylands in the refrains of British New Ro, New Wave, and pop music, my extended radio and TV dates with bands like Scritti Politti, Spandau Ballet, Blancmange, ABC, Depeche Mode, and Duran Duran introduced me to a modern English (with Continental flourishes) that activated new forms of remote intimacy in the Inland Empire: a place that resembled everywhere and nothing to me. Of course, I wasn't the only one in the I.E.— or Southern California, for that matter—captivated by these British accents in pop. In a 2007 interview with the Inland Empire–based, African American, "homo hip-hop" artist Mélange LaVonne, the rapper confessed to me that her favorite band was the British duo Tears for Fears.[51] In a virtual intellectual forum on Chicana/o cultural studies hosted by Angie Chabram- Dernersesian, Michelle Habell-Pallan emphasizes the effect KROQ's dissemination of British New Wave and ska had on her own discovery of antiracist strains of popular music as a young woman of color in the working-class suburbs of Downey, California: "As a teenager in the 1980s, I listened to punk, alternative, and new wave on radio-station KROQ broadcast out of Pasadena. KROQ's playlist included a lot of new wave/ska music that was coming out of Britain on the Two-Tone label. ... That new wave/ska sound, to me, had a very Chicano feel to it—although at the time I doubt that I would, or could, have articulated it that way."[52]

As we will explore further in the next chapter, a band from Manchester, England, called the Smiths also proved to be a formative musical influence on

Latina/o youth throughout the region, inaugurating a phenomenon treated as a curiosity by documentarians today.[53] Despite some serious flaws, William E. Jones's documentary about Latina/o Smiths fans, *Is It Really So Strange?*, goes to some lengths to acknowledge that the heart of the Smiths' current fan base is in the brown, working-class suburbs of the Inland Empire: "When Morrissey asked the crowd at one of his shows at the Wiltern Theater, 'How are things in San Bernardino?,' he was doing more than making idle chatter. He was acknowledging the geography of his grassroots audience."

The music of the 1980s, ranging from pop, industrial, and alternative genres—essentially the repertoire of KROQ during that era—also functions as a leitmotif throughout *Still Water Saints*, Alex Espinoza's novel about the fictitious Inland Empire town of Agua Mansa. Espinoza's musical references are culled from a wider breadth of 1980s music from the United States and "the Continent," particularly Germany (KMFDM, Rammstein).[54] For Espinoza, the very act of writing was inaugurated by pop music from the United Kingdom and Europe filtered through the radio waves on KROQ and a high-wattage AM radio station called the Mighty 690, licensed in the Tijuana/Rosarito/Baja border region.[55] As Espinoza remarked in a personal interview with me:

> I loved a lot of the synthy pop like Depeche Mode, Echo and the Bunnymen, and Yaz. For me it was a culture and identity that was so different from anything that was around us. . . . It was a reverse exoticizing. Instead of England as a colonial power taking over countries, I guess we were sort of colonizing them. There was this fascination with the look, the music, and the identity. Everyone wanted to go to gloomy England and write really depressing stories after listening to the Smiths. You know, that was when I first really started writing. And it was all really bad stuff. But it seemed so romantic. I think we fantasized a kind of sophistication to it. It felt very different from the reality we knew in places like La Puente, California.[56]

Yet more incidental examples of these accented pop fantasies are culled from memory, from my own angsty teen encounters with others of my ilk in the Inland Empire. An African American girl I knew in high school spoke with a British accent our entire freshman year and tried to convince everyone she dated Nick Rhodes from Duran Duran over summer vacation.[57] Others dressed the part, like several sensitive Latino boys I shared bottles of Boone's Farm with who were ritually swaddled in Morrissey-inspired cardigans and immaculate white T-shirts. I mention these incidents not simply to dwell in memory as it makes itself heard or felt in certain geographies, but to beg the question of what we might make of these displaced gestures of belonging in the Southern California suburbs.

What is the analytic engendered by these sonic gestures to a place many of us never visited but only heard of—or heard—in the slightly accented inflections of a singer or DJ's voice? I imagine that we were, in our own way, practicing Jennifer

Terry's nascent conceptualization of "remote intimacy," a key phrase I have invoked throughout this book. Although Terry has used it to describe some of the circuits of affect generated by surveillance technologies, I have come to imagine remote intimacies describing the communities for whom intimacies cohere across virtual networks of desire through radio, music, and television, on the Internet, and now through online social networking sites. Remote intimacies account both technically and affectively for the symbiosis that can happen between disparate subjects—like the storied connection between Latinos and Morrissey, for example, or between suburban queer kids of color and Anglophilic ear candy in general.[58]

Like most adolescent girls of the early 1980s, I became smitten with the British band Duran Duran and created elaborate fantasies about Birmingham, England, their place of origin. Nothing seemed more exotic to me than a place-name with "ham" in it. So regal. So old-world. So Atlantic. In my own holding pattern of relocations around the Pacific Rim, my Le Bon–addled mind failed to process the fact that the locales in Duran Duran's music videos for the jet-setting 1982 *Rio* album had little to do with the Birmingham of my pubescent fantasies. Instead, their videos recaptured the colonial imaginaries of a bygone British Empire, restyled by Vivienne Westwood: "some New Romantic looking for the TV sound" on a redrawn "Planet Earth."[59] Much as Habell-Pallan confesses to being unable to draw some of these political and intellectual connections as a young teen—unable to "articulate it that way" back then—I, too, didn't quite grasp that Birmingham, in all its gritty, industrial glory, might have actually been closer to the Inland Empire than I dared imagine.

Orange County's beaches were only a forty-minute drive away, but my immigrant fancy preferred to wander worlds away to seaside destinations that I never visited yet which felt more familiar—places that once belonged to other empires, like Belize (where Wham!'s "Club Tropicana" video was shot), or Antigua, Duran Duran's alluring azure and white-sand backdrop for the "Rio" video and their dashing, colorful Antony Price suits. The Spanish broke the colonial seal in both Belize and Antigua, and the Brits followed up gamely, just like in the Inland Empire. And in the Inland Empire, as they did in the Philippines, the Americans came and asserted their own imperial aspirations onto the landscape, erecting military bases and laying the foundation for the industries of war craft to fuel their booms and busts after oranges weren't enough.[60] But the incidental British imperial history of Riverside and the Inland Empire, which compelled the intellectual labor in the earlier part of this chapter, first revealed itself to me—perhaps, could *only* be revealed to me—in the sonic residue of British pop as an "echo of another subject," to transpose Philippe Lacoue-Labarthe.

In "The Echo of the Subject," Lacoue-Labarthe theorizes how being haunted by a melody (as Freud's pupil Theodor Reik was) undergirds the narratival compulsion to confess.[61] The confession elicited by these echoes of and from elsewhere for me is one that admits a disturbing intimacy between queer provincial longings and the cosmopolitan spaces, objects, and temporalities that inform both queer spatial imaginaries and queer theoretical labor itself. One such confession, as I discussed in the introduction to this book, appears in Eve Kosofsky Sedgwick's 1992 preface to *Between Men*, where the author narrates her own belated, textual experience of remote intimacy through her "provincialism," which was oriented toward queer "metropolitan destinies." These destinies were awakened, in part, by British and Continental literary texts of male homosocial desire.[62] Whereas Sedgwick's enactment of a remote intimacy to times, places, and scenes beyond her "provincial" purview gets routed, in the case of *Between Men*, through the sign of "the literary," the remote correspondences I explore here and elsewhere in this book make themselves felt through broadcast networks across time. And yet structurally, remote intimacy in both of these provincial contexts makes it possible to describe how we experience our own spaces in correspondence with others. The spatial fantasies engendered by textual and audiovisual echoes that cleave a place like Birmingham to Riverside or San Bernardino would be something akin to, but not as diplomatically chic as, "sister cities" or "town twinning."[63] Unlike most urbanites who assume the suburban is always oriented toward its closest city, I like to think that these imaginary correspondences with a sister elsewhere sometimes have to happen across greater distances, both conceptually and topographically, with other ethnicities, accents, nations, and even other empires that seem more benevolent—though they surely are not—simply owing to the fact that they are not ours.

The sense of belatedness that intensifies these correspondences, meanwhile, brings both imperial and queer temporalities to a perilous crossing despite neatly apportioned suburban grids. The disidentification between brown subjects of the (inland) empire and imperial cultures that may or may not have been theirs, like Britain's instead of Spain's or the United States', might easily be scripted into the postcolonial problematic of displaced native mimicry and "white love."[64] But to do so, I would argue, is precisely to reenact the violences of colonial temporalities that assume the belated fascination of the response of the "native" to imperial cultures, the sense of wonderment that codifies the atavism of the "native," while reinforcing her susceptibility to the charms of empire's opportunities for advancement in linear narratives about nation and progress. As Homi K. Bhabha insists in *The Location of Culture*, the national and exilic postimperial inter-identifications produced by the "dissemination of texts and discourses across cultures" do not transpire on a "horizontal" temporal, spatial, or narratival grid.[65] Instead, they call forth a comparative apparatus for imagined communities both "migrant or metropolitan," a "metaphoricity" that "requires a kind of 'doubleness' in writing; a temporality of representation that moves between cultural formations and social processes without a centered causal logic."[66] The asymmetrical correspondences and strange affinities I ventured to describe above—that gravitational pull that draws queer of color subjects in Southern California toward audiovisual echoes of pop imperialism and cosmopolitanism—further brings postcolonial discourse into conversation with queer conceptualizations of time, particularly temporalities associated with provincial spaces beyond "the urban," an emblematic site of modernity and "advancement." Elizabeth Freeman has called this deeply gendered sense of belatedness in queer time "temporal drag."[67]

Temporal drag has been conceptualized by Freeman as an intervention into the politics of queer performativity. Freeman focuses on the threat yet also the potential that the "genuine *past*-ness of the past" brings to bear on radical postmodernity through form and politics in queer theory. As Freeman writes, "The political result of these formulations can be that whatever looks newer or more-radical-than-thou has more purchase over prior signs, and that whatever seems to generate continuity seems better left behind."[68] Judith Halberstam, in *In a Queer Time and Place*, offers a slightly different take on temporal drag by departing from the historiographic impulse of Freeman's model to explore the relationship to prior signs—or among "originals with no copy"—through the "anomalous" butch musician and songwriter Ferron: "She was neither the historical template that younger performers imitated or rejected nor the representative of an earlier era."[69] The anomalous break, or "vortex," Halberstam locates in this dyke genealogy of subcultural musical production becomes legible around Ferron's white, working-class butchness, and her identification with "female factory workers" (among whom Ferron worked and wrote music) rather than lesbians of the women's music scene or the dyke punks of more contemporary scenes. In Halberstam's reading, then, gender presentation and class posit the interruptions that preclude tidy narratives about the past, or a potentially harmonious queer future, instead creating "an interesting relay of sentiment and affect between [Ferron] and the young audience" during an instance of performance in an intergenerational setting."[70] This sense of "drag," manifesting in multiple iterations of gender and generation in Halberstam's invocation of Freeman's model, results at the end of her reading in a melancholic relationship to "success," a looking "out from behind the music onto the urban landscape of a queer time in which fame, fortune, and success will always be as fleeting as 'shadows on a dime.'"[71]

That an "urban landscape" serves as a backdrop for this movement toward success—or more accurately, as a backdrop for a turn to melancholy possible only when success becomes a lost object that inevitably gains purchase through its anomalous performance of radical, queer failure—reveals how freighted time tends to be absorbed by the accelerated timescapes of urbanity, regardless of what the artist's intentions might be. Halberstam's emphasis on the dialectic of success and failure in this instance gestures toward a radicality that she feels has yet to be acknowledged in urban queer contexts: that of the butch, working-class dyke so often relegated to the margins of gay male iterations of style, urbanity, and implicitly political relevance. This version of success is one in which Ferron-assign becomes scripted as a "shadow" or "failure."

And yet in order to dislodge one version of (in Freeman's words) a "more-radical-than-thou" ethos of urban, queer temporality obsessed with innovation, another appears to take its place, as if compelled by the very specter of "the urban landscape" from which a figure like Ferron would be excluded and queer theory itself would be arbitrated. Halberstam's efforts *In a Queer Time and Place* are calibrated to move beyond iterations of what she calls "metronormativity."[72] But the city continues to loom large, exerting its place as the natural habitat of queer subcultures. She writes, "*In a Queer Time and Place* both confirms that queer subcultures thrive in urban areas *and* contests the essential characterizations of queer life as urban."[73] Though Halberstam successfully dispels these essential characterizations of queer urban life in her readings of figures like Brandon Teena, the emphasis on subcultures and "radical styles" in the conclusion risks succumbing to the cosmopolitan insistence on invention as intervention, even as she makes crucial contributions to "scrambl[ing] our understandings of place, time, development, action, and transformation."[74]

What would happen, however, if "being radical" actually referred to little more than an empty catch-phrase, and a dated one at that? In other words, how does Freeman's formulation of temporal drag stubbornly insist on a problematic freightedness that cannot ever take flight as a radical style, even in shadow form, to haunt history? How is this "drag" inescapable, especially when anchored to habitats of belatedness like the country, the suburbs, or the "colonies"? Or to approach this problem from a slightly different angle, maybe such moments present us with an opportunity to explore how the imperial temporalities of "belatedness," which cohere around race and empire in particular, collide with the avant-politics of queer temporalities, including the seemingly *a*temporal opting out of the past, present, and future altogether.

Freeman's very notion of "temporal drag" confronts not only the weight of problematic pasts on queer subjects, but also the *attachments* to pasts and "anachronisms" that are in and of themselves problematic. As Freeman asks in her essay: "Might some bodies, in registering on their very surfaces the co-presence of several historically-specific events, movements, and collective pleasures, complicate or displace the centrality of *gender*-transitive drag to queer performativity? Might they articulate instead a kind of *temporal* transitivity that does

not leave feminism, femininity, or other 'anachronisms' behind?"[75] While Freeman focuses on feminist generations, I would add race, empire, and the suburbs
to her catalog of anachronisms "dragging" certain bodies away from avant-queer
politics and the implicit urbanity of that orientation. We can further track in
Freeman's definition the potential resonances such queer political arguments
may have with the (post)imperial queer of color practices of listening and
broadcast consumption I described above. After all, how better to characterize
suburban, brown affinities for British New Wave and New Romantic pop than
as stubborn attachments to objects already burdened by their own imperialist
baggage?

Yet in the context of an Inland Empire consistently reconfigured by intersecting imperial imaginaries, not only throughout its own histories of "settlement"
and development but also within the imperial matrices precipitating the many
phases of immigration and migration to the region, how do we sort "proper" or
"improper" objects of continuity or discontinuity? What happens, in other words,
when subjects of color, and queer subjects of color in particular, create a "break"
with one set of prior signs—from their so-called empires, regions, or nations of
origin, like Spain, Latin America, the Philippines, and even the United States—
by relocating their fantasies to mainstreams, empires, and elsewheres that were
never theirs? What happens if the choice to opt out temporally, spatially, feels
impossible for subjects trying to figure out their dissociations as well as complicities with multiple nations, nationalisms, and the desires they engender?[76] In other
words, what happens when subjects opt *in* to one problematic context even as
they try to opt out of another?

It would be easy to think of these attachments to improper objects and imperial pasts within a reactionary logic, something to be expected in an environment
like the Southern California suburbs, which incubated various forms of grassroots conservatism during its growth spurts in the twentieth century.[77] As a space
conceptually grounded in the tropes of mobility, aspiration, and reinvention, the
suburbs further mimic empire in these ways and more, especially when they exert
the pull of *someone else's* past on a present experienced by subjects of color, and
more specifically, queers of color. Maybe easy would be the better way to go with
this reading, an analytic befitting a culture of convenience like the suburbs. When
it all boils down to it, maybe we *were* just being "radical" in the shallow, 1980s,
half-shirt and bumper-sticker sense of the word, when we turned to British pop
and the appeal of its imperial New Wave. Immersing ourselves in 1980s UK pop
was not so much indicative of the drive to fit in as it truly was a reaction formation, an effort to be something other than the white, American rock–loving kids
who taunted us for being accented, brown, and fresh off the boat. Or in the case
of Alex Espinoza's formative imaginaries, British pop offered an opportunity for

exogamous intellectual fantasies in his primarily Latino, working-class context: "The music gave us an opportunity to change while we were growing up. To move beyond what we imagined were our limitations in a place like La Puente, where everyone was just like us. Fantasies of the 'homeland' were figments of our imagination anyway, so this was just another leap. Another stretch. What ways were there to experiment with becoming an 'intellectual'? British pop provided something different to grab on to."[78]

Despite being dispersed subjects (around the block, across the freeway, in another subdivision), this was our collective, contingent effort to become civilized persons of "culture"—because that's what British accents mean, right? When our own failed to qualify as civilization in others' eyes, we harnessed Britain's civilizing mission founded on culture itself to avert the shameful circumstances wrought by the empires of our familiar in these shadowless inland valleys. It was a form of class passing, but in a truly *academic* sense: not passing as rich, since most of us resided squarely within that lower-middle-income bracket, but passing as smart. Finding ourselves through British New Wave and New Romantic pop music of the 1980s was to become, in Oscar Wilde's words, "an echo of someone else's music," to be "actors of a part that has not been written for" us.[79] (One cannot help but add another layer of echo at this moment, courtesy of the Smiths' ebullient melodic gothica in the song "Cemetery Gates": "Keats and Yeats are on your side, but you lose / 'Cause weird lover Wilde is on mine.")[80] And yet this chamber of echoes may inevitably yield something more reparative than the compulsion to confess stubborn attachments to improper objects and archives, a "temporal drag" rescripted in the catchy idioms of empire. Heard all at once, these echoes whisper into practice an analytic we couldn't articulate then but might be able to now: an analytic of burden that we still desperately want to resist, and from which we queerly dream of taking flight. But it is precisely this tremendous sense of burden—not the "white man's burden," but the burden of the white man's empires carried by queer, racialized subjects through time—that an analytic of empire and sexuality in the suburbs seems to demand.[81] The attachment to these histories, these songs, these texts disseminated through boom boxes, big-box shops, and big-screen TVs also yearn toward a methodology—or rather, grasp at several methodologies, variations on which we have heard elsewhere in other times.

In its own way, this practice resembles what Chela Sandoval has called a "methodology of the oppressed," an undoing of the "apartheid of theoretical domains"—and I would add, cultural material objects—that allows one imperial accent to unleash the babble of so many other imperial legacies in spaces like the suburbs that would stucco-blast them into uniformity.[82] We may also think about this methodology in terms of the uneasy alliances across vertical structures of colonial power forming what Leela Gandhi has called "affective communities," those political bonds of friendship that sully the "hygiene of oppositionality."[83] And we hear them again in earlier echoes of queer of color scholarship, in the "disidentifications" carefully wrought by José Esteban Muñoz, bringing us back to where we started with the echo of the subject, the "autobiographical gesture" that, in Lacoue-Labarthe's words, is also "the theoretical gesture." As Muñoz writes: "To disidentify is to read oneself and one's own life narrative in a moment, object, or subject that is not culturally coded to 'connect' with the disidentifying subject. It is not to pick and choose what one takes out of an identification. It is not to willfully evacuate the politically dubious or shameful components within an identificatory locus. Rather, it is the reworking of those energies that do not elide the 'harmful' or contradictory components of any identity. It is an acceptance of the necessary interjection that has occurred in such situations."[84] Connecting with the rapier wit of "weird lover Wilde" through Morrissey's flaccidly accented intonations may have started as an attempt to come to terms with an imperial legacy that seemed more glamorous, if purely for its spectacular remoteness, than my own. But like the provincial girl who makes a cameo in Sedgwick's retrospective preface to *Between Men*, the incredulity stirred by those encounters creates an impetus to at the very least explore the incidentals: to ask why the British accent never dies in the Inland Empire, and to wonder how this might mean something queer. It also points not only to the interstices of empire, but literally to the margins of books and queer theoretical storytelling: to the anecdote Muñoz tells about his "suburban spectatorship" of the "swishy spectacle" that was Truman Capote on late-night TV, emotionally excavated years later by Marga Gomez's performance in the one-woman show *Pretty, Witty, and Gay*.[85] This incidental tale of shared broadcast consumption could very well seem disposable, another trinket of personal memory weighing us down as we flee toward something bigger, yearn for a more profound sense of story, time, and queer progress.

Like the tiny navel of the orange that bears its name, this excess flesh may seem like a useless side effect in service of a manufactured end: the promise of something bigger, more succulent, more convenient by virtue of its mutant seedlessness. But these mutations hint at other questions and ephemeral histories that demand other answers. The answers lie not only with me, and the circuitous paths I took through outposts of the British Empire as disparate as Duran Duran's Antigua or Thomas Carlyle's fictitious Weissnichtwo in an effort to figure it out.[86] It resides in anyone listening, in anyone who listened and could never let go of the provincial fantasy that there was not only something more out there, but everything right here.

Strip-Mall Stories: Alex Espinoza's *Still Water Saints*

> It's fortunate for the mini-mall that the sun never sets on its empire, because
> suddenly, it seems, the unthinkable is possible: Mini-malls in Southern California
> may be headed for obsolescence. . . . As the power centers continue their expan-
> sion, as they gobble up entire blocks with their own brand of dull uniformity, sud-
> denly the beleaguered mini-mall seems almost discrete, brought down to human
> scale. From this arises an unnerving possibility, a thought even more unbelievable
> than the mini-mall's demise: Might we someday feel nostalgic for it?
>
> —Mary Melton, "A Brief History of the Mini-Mall"

Strip malls, sometimes referred to as mini-malls, were originally designed so
that even on the go, you could find everything you needed in one place. They
are the distilled architectural essence of convenience. Like the suburban amusement parks of the previous chapter, strip malls were initially designed with the
automobile in mind rather than the pedestrian: "They had all the products you
wanted under one roof. . . . In separate concessions, but all in a single place. The
big deal was that you could get off the street and drive up to it, get your stuff and
go."[87] Intersections are crucial for strip-mall commerce, and contemporary suburban landscapes in Southern California owe their gaudy, Vegas-inspired signage
to a perspective scaled to passing automobiles: "Located along the broad avenues
criss-crossing the suburban areas, the strip malls set a row of shops back from
the street, leaving a broad expanse of asphalt between the buildings and street for
free parking. To attract the notice of cars passing by at 35 or 40 miles an hour, the
strip malls erected large signs in a visual cacophony of information. The architectural character of the buildings could hardly be seen—indeed, hardly mattered—
in this brave new world of automobile shopping."[88] Although the drive-in-market
form can be traced back to the 1920s, and again to the 1950s during the United
States' postwar suburban expansion, the modern strip malls that now dot the
Southern California landscape actually owe their proliferation to a moment of
crisis for denizens of the automobile: the OPEC embargoes of the early 1970s. As
other scholars and journalists have noted, the oil embargoes led to the closure of
gas stations with real estate typically situated at busy intersections and "already
zoned for commercial use."[89] Sensing an opportunity, developers swooped in, and
according to Los Angeles lore, a group of impossible dreamers from the La Man-
cha Development Company erected the "first-modern-day-mini-mall, on a corner
lot in Panorama City, in the San Fernando Valley," in 1973.[90] As Jade Chang, an
L.A.-based journalist who wrote a passionate defense of the mini-mall in 2003,
remarked, "Mini-malls, it turns out, were actually built on that urge to write over
an unsuccessful past."[91]

What has been written over and through the strip mall in Southern California is a palimpsestic narrative about the relocations of immigrant entrepreneurship in the United States from urban ethnic enclaves to suburban retail environments. In the wake of the OPEC crisis, the commercial real estate that once belonged to gas stations fueled other dreams and aspirations for immigrants seeking small-business opportunities in affordable spaces beyond cities transformed by gentrification. As downtowns and centralized business districts in "great American cities" (to use the parlance of Jane Jacobs) became the focus of rehabilitation and renovation efforts for middle-class professionals of privilege—whose families were likely to have initiated the first waves of "white flight" from urban cores to the suburbs in the mid-twentieth century—communities of color from the 1970s onward have moved further and further outward to suburbs and exurbs in search of alternative retail spaces and cheaper housing.[92] Meanwhile, the shifting patterns of immigration from Asia and Latin America—the transnational relocation of immigrants directly to the suburbs instead of urban centers—has also profoundly reconfigured the retail and service landscape in the sprawling southland and all throughout the American West.[93]

For chiefly economic reasons, the strip mall emerged as an entry-level entrepreneurial space for immigrants in the Southern California suburbs. The price per square foot of retail space in strip malls is on average about two-thirds less than in enclosed shopping centers.[94] But to understand why Southern California is an empire of strip malls requires reconsidering how the United States' imperial aspirations and follies continue to make themselves felt in these microcosms of the American dream, an aspiration achieved by commerce and measured by expansion. In her paean to the strip malls and mini-malls of the San Fernando Valley north of Los Angeles, Jade Chang refers to the plentitude and secret pedagogies embedded in these places of everyday exchange that were in their own small way a crossroads of the world:

> Just three blocks away from our Northridge tract home, this prototypical collection of Chinese restaurant, beauty salon, candy store, and dry cleaner was the first place I was allowed to go on my own. . . . My first job at 17 was next door to the candy store, personalizing bar/bat mitzvah favors and children's birthday presents with puffy paint . . . The center of things is where you find it. In the pre-Starbucks era, when coffee shops first began to appear, we spent our nights listening to bad poetry and decent guitar playing at Common Grounds. I learned about chakras at the Psychic Eye bookstore in the same mini-mall, which was New Age back when it was actually new. . . . I had sushi for the first time at Kabuki Sushi, a neighborhood mini-mall mainstay that my parents—and every raw-fish devotee in the surrounding area—walk to weekly. On television in 1992, in the wake of the Rodney King trial, I saw Korean small-

business owners on the roof of a mini-mall, armed with guns, ready to defend their shops and restaurants from looters. Historic Black-Korean tensions rose to near breaking point in the city, and I began to see how neighborhood borders can be drawn like battle lines.[95]

As Chang remarks, "the center of the world is where you find it," and the world wrought by American imperialism—by a United States expanding throughout the twentieth century into Asia and Latin America not only through force but also through trade; by the Cold Warriors cultivated in places of "intervention" like Vietnam and Korea; by a United States still struggling with its legacy of slavery, civil rights, and an African American community that fought its wars, only to be kept fighting for diminishing resources in its cities and suburbs—finds its lessons, and finds itself, in Southern California's strip malls. Instead of viewing strip malls suspiciously, then, as tawdry architectures of convenience paving over something "real" and "historical" with something shallow and transient, it behooves us to reconsider the strip mall's form and function in an emerging suburban aesthetics as well as politics. Strip malls are spaces that let us sketch new myths and realities, that offer alternate histories of relocation and immigrant exchange in the American West. As Alex Espinoza, the author of *Still Water Saints*, confides: "I named the strip mall in my novel the Prospect Shopping Center in honor of the immigrants who came to the West to seek their fortunes, like the prospectors coming out west to stake their claim, to find gold. It's my homage and critique of that myth of the West as a place where dreams are made, shattered, and remade."[96]

Still Water Saints is a novel narrated in many voices by people who have come to the Inland Empire from other colonial contexts. At various instances, the book alludes to the many who have left in times of hardship or simply because they have had enough: "There was Luz Peña and her blind mother, Carmen, who fell too many times, so that Luz finally had to put her in a home. There was Mr. Slusser, the war veteran who carried his medals around in his pocket, who retired to Washington to live with his son. There were the Perezes who moved to Las Vegas, and the Bustamantes who flew back to the Philippines."[97] For the most part, however, the book dwells on those who end up staying, or being pulled back for reasons at once obvious and inexplicable. At the center of the novel is a strip mall botanica where transient commerce and random social interactions hint at the archaeologies of empire one can find in Southern California's prefabricated retail environments. Set deep in the Inland Empire, the promise of "the West" confronts the harsh realities of a desert East. Though Espinoza's Prospect Shopping Center is fictitious, *Still Water Saints* reconstructs a powerful cartography of queer, immigrant affect and exchange in the region by employing the idea and architecture of the strip mall as a structuring element of the novel.

Propelling the narrative of *Still Water Saints* are the daily transactions that take place in a shop where people seek hope and healing for a reasonable price, a botanica called Oshún: "When doctors failed, when priests and praying were not enough, the people of Agua Mansa came to Botánica Oshún, to Perla. The shop sold amulets and stones, rosaries and candles. They bought charms to change their luck, teas to ease unsettled nerves, and estampas of saints, the worn plastic cards they carried in their purses or wallets for protection."[98] Botanicas can be found tucked away in strip malls and other tiny retail spaces all over Southern California and the Southwest, servicing the everyday spiritual needs not only of Catholic and Latino communities but also of believers of all persuasions.[99] Commerce leaves little room for orthodoxies, and nestled among the Catholic saints and pagan remedies in Espinoza's fictitious Botánica Oshún are varieties of incense and statues of the Hindu goddess Ganesh. In an incidental moment of exchange in the novel, Perla, the botanica's owner and the unofficial spiritual adviser of Agua Mansa, sells Ganesh to her loyal customers Lakshmi and Hasari Gupta, "who owned the Excelsior Liquor Store."[100] As Espinoza depicts in *Still Water Saints*, the proximities strip malls regularly stage between different ethnic and spiritual communities creates a suburban twist on the urban, immigrant enclave. Mexican restaurants are cheek-by-jowl with Thai massage parlors, Korean liquor stores, and Filipino *turo-turo* joints, bringing a range of businesses practices and social milieus into a concentrated contact zone otherwise thought impossible in suburban geographies of sprawl.[101] Elaborating on why he chose a strip mall as the setting for novel's botanica, Espinoza remarked: "It's so Inland Empire. I love the fact that you can have a donut shop run by a Cambodian family with a smoothie machine, and can wire money to Mexico next door. Strip malls are spaces of transition and transaction. A place of true exchange, not only of goods, but of ideas, religions, cultures, and actions."[102] While the strip mall may promise interethnic transactions and contact, it also serves as a monument to the legacies of exile and interethnic conflicts wrought by imperialism.

The botanica's namesake in *Still Water Saints*, the Afro-Caribbean spirit "Oshún—"spirit of sweet water, of lakes and ríos. Of love and beauty and fertility. . . . the one you see when you have money problems"[103]—alludes to a much broader history of imperial trade routes, forced displacements, colonial encounters, and spiritual exchange mapped across the Atlantic and into the Caribbean, across the American South and Southwest to its final destination in the deserted suburban strip malls of the Inland Empire. The original owner and proprietor of the botanica, a *curandero* (or folk healer) named Señor Darío, describes the transpositions of Oshún from a pagan goddess to Saint Cecilia as a legacy of the slave trade and Catholic missionaries: "In the Caribe, the monks tried to convert the slaves working in the sugarcanes to Christianity. When the slaves refused, they were beaten. They prayed in secret in the woods and worshipped their spirits by hiding them as santos so the monks would never know. They told themselves Oshún would be Nuestra Señora de la Caridad del Cobre."[104] Not everyone understands the botanica or approves of its ecumenical paganism in Agua Mansa, even in the contemporary moment during which the novel is set. Espinoza goes to great lengths to show that even communities that many readers would assume are predisposed to the botanica's supernatural allure are initially confounded by the relics first sold by Darío from a trailer festooned with images of Catholic saints, and then from a fixed spot at the Prospect Shopping Center: "Peacock feathers and amulets of animal bones and statues of a hooded skeleton wearing a red robe and wielding a scythe could be seen through the window. They said if you set foot in the shop you would be hexed. No one went in the first few weeks it was opened."[105] Old Mexican ladies who attend the Catholic Church whisper about Darío, wondering if he is a devil or just a con man.

Though many reviewers construe scenes like this, and figures like Darío in *Still Water Saints*, as supernatural or "magical" elements of Espinoza's novel, I would argue that doing so risks eliding the painstaking historicity of Espinoza's realism.[106] In fact, the author avowedly resists this critical formulation in which Chicano literature in particular, and "ethnic" literatures in general, are niched by the contemporary publishing economy into the "magical realist" genre because they offer representations of "atavistic" superstitions, beliefs, and fantasies.[107] In a brief interview with the *Austin Chronicle*, Espinoza confides, "My biggest challenge was that I was writing a book set in a botanica, but I didn't want it to be 'magical.'"[108] Instead, Espinoza insists on the pull and emotional power of the everyday as it transpires in particular spaces, hence the appeal of an architectural environment like the strip mall so endemic to the suburbs: "A strip mall is such a mundane and ordinary space, yet one that experiences an everyday transience of people pulling in, looking for what they need, and driving away."[109] The movement between tract home (or tract apartment) and strip mall regulates the flow of Espinoza's narrative, and captures how "need," as it is experienced in the suburbs, conflates the realms of commerce and domesticity. The central character of the novel, Perla, becomes a kind of touchstone or compass for the ways in which need, desire, and aspiration traffic between the home and the public sphere represented by the strip mall.

A housewife resigned to childlessness, Perla becomes Darío's apprentice because, in his words, she has "el don, the gift of healing."[110] This gesture of exchange, though seemingly endowed with its own sense of mysticism, actually brings to the fore Espinoza's approach to a realism that leavens the spiritual frameworks of the novel with the mundane aspects of suburban drama.[111] In many respects, Perla agrees to become Darío's apprentice just to get out of the house.

Though she initially resists her gifts—"'I want a family,' she said, starting to cry. 'Not power'"—Perla becomes overwhelmed by her feelings of failure as a nonreproductive subject in the suburban domestic setting and elects to enter the public sphere of commerce with the hope of finding something more. Although she first approaches Darío as part of her last-ditch effort to find an alternative cure for her reproductive failure, she finds another solution to (re)productivity altogether. Like so many novelistic heroines suffocated by the demands and failures of domesticity, Perla becomes a character who crystallizes the stakes of Espinoza's latter-day suburban discourse of separate spheres: "I want more. Something else to do besides sitting at home all day cooking and cleaning. If I can't have kids, I can have a job."[112] Her initial refusal of "power" on a more spiritual plane gives way to a desire for pragmatic forms of empowerment and involvement, first as a shopkeeper, and ultimately as the botanica's sole proprietor and Agua Mansa's resident healer.

Perla's stubbornness, thematized alongside the persistence of old superstitions that adhere to her trade, is replicated by the shop's stature in the community. The Botánica Oshún models a kind of structural resilience in an ever-changing suburban environment driven by the temporalities of development and expansion. The botanica becomes one of the final, stalwart tenants in the under-leased Prospect Shopping Center: "There were only three businesses in the strip mall—Best Donuts, Everything Ninety-Nine Cents, and the Botánica Oshún at the very end of the row."[113] Eventually, even the botanica's next-door neighbor, the Everything Ninety-Nine Cents store, is forced to relocate after competition from a Mexican big-box shop called Las Glorias makes it financially untenable for Alfonso, the second-generation owner, to remain in the Prospect Shopping Center: "My store's just not making it. . . . Las Glorias. All modern and high-tech. I can't compete with them. They've got everything cheaper. You can . . . refinance your house. Get cable television. They even got this shuttle that goes and picks people up who can't drive. I can't do that. I'm dying here."[114] Such proclamations, even by fictional characters, seem to affirm the inevitable obsolescence of the strip mall predicted by Mary Melton in her 1997 Los Angeles Times feature on the history of the mini-mall.[115]

Now among the last bastions of mom-and-pop businesses and immigrant entrepreneurship, strip malls throughout the Inland Empire have been underoccupied for decades as larger shopping centers and "power centers" anchored by major chains proliferate across the suburbs. Big-box shops like those Las Glorias is modeled after (the Asian-owned Ranch 99 Markets are one real-life correlative)[116] threaten to replace smaller niche shops like botanicas and discount stores by catering to immigrant consumers' nostalgia for the homeland: "Inside Las Glorias . . . murals covered the walls: Pancho Villa riding a horse; Vicente

Fernández singing to a woman in a red dress; Benito Juárez holding a scroll; an Aztec sun calendar; Indians in feathered headdresses climbing a pyramid; La Virgen de Guadalupe looking down onto the farmacia's counter."[117] (At one point in the novel, Perla considers lowering the retail price of her *veladoras*, or devotional candles, after noticing that Las Glorias sells them for only $1.25.)[118] And yet even in dire real estate environments like the Inland Empire, many shops continue to hang on while other tenants flee strip malls for greener pastures. Some of the Inland Empire's local residents actually credit the current recession for saving some of their favorite small businesses and social spaces in partially abandoned strip-mall environments. One of Riverside's local queer bars—a multipurpose sports bar, performance venue, dance club, and patio dining spot called VIP—remains in business today because the developers who planned to expand the Riverside Plaza, a large, outdoor "lifestyle center" across the street, ran out of money to redevelop the property, opting to renew VIP's lease instead.[119]

For Espinoza, these vanquished retail environments with faint glimmers of life became a source of fascination as he drove around the Inland Empire when he settled in the region in the early 1990s: "My mother and I would always go shopping at strip malls. I was always intrigued by the empty ones east of Riverside in Moreno Valley and wondered what happened to make them that way. There was something haunting and ghostly about those vacant spaces, something very lonely."[120] The sense of loneliness in these half-occupied strip malls reinforces what has become a common trope about the failure of suburban architectures to create community by isolating and scattering its subjects. Atomized suburbanites run errands between hubs, between the home and the shopping mall, seemingly bereft of opportunities for contact with others. And yet despite this isolation and the undercurrent of sterility throughout Espinoza's novel—from the "still water" of its title, to Perla, the anguished healer, who cannot have children—the author manages to craft alternative expressions of contact and intimacy amid loss, across distances, beyond families bound by blood. In fact, the eerie iterations of emptiness, ghostliness, and half-remembrance become rescripted in *Still Water Saints* as precisely the bonds that bring together disparate imperial subjects, as well as queer subjects. As Victor Bascara elegantly explains in *Model-Minority Imperialism*, part of what binds an identitarian community like "Asian Americans" together in the United States are the conditions of an empire that continually erases itself and hides in oblivion. And yet the very effort to come together relies on a shared sense of emergence that unearths these well-buried imperial histories lying "dormant, misunderstood, or forgotten until new constituencies formed to awaken, understand, and remember."[121] The constituencies that cohere in Espinoza's novel may not exclusively be understood through a racialized—indeed criticalized—category like Asian American, but they do cohere around a shared sense of imperial erasure articulated as the march of global commerce in the present yet also tied to the imperial trade routes and conquests of the past.

Espinoza stumbled on the town of Agua Mansa by accident when his partner, Kyle Behen, encouraged him to browse through maps as he struggled to find a setting for his novel that would incorporate several landmarks and boundaries of the inland region's landscape: "I knew I wanted the I-10. I knew I needed the Santa Ana River, and I knew I mentioned Rancho Boulevard in some of the earlier story drafts, so there were certain criteria that narrowed my search. We looked at the map and saw a huge empty spot where all the streets just sort of ended. And I thought, 'What is *that?!?*'"[122] This empty space on the map that fueled Espinoza's curiosity turned out to reveal not only a place that actually existed once upon a time in history, Agua Mansa, but also hinted by omission at the cartographies of erasure so endemic to Southern California. As I mentioned in the introduction to this chapter, Agua Mansa is actually classified by local archivists and county museums as a ghost town. Formerly the first nonnative settlement on the western banks of the upper Santa Ana River, the historical Agua Mansa is situated mostly within the contemporary geographical boundaries of Colton, between San Bernardino and Riverside Counties. At the crossroads for the Union Pacific and Burlington Northern Santa Fe Railroads, Colton is also where Espinoza settled with his mother in 1991.[123]

Agua Mansa began as a strategic site on the Santa Ana trade routes throughout the Southwest in the nineteenth century. As the San Bernardino County Museum literature explains, residents of Abiquiu, New Mexico, were offered free land to "settle the upper Santa Ana River and serve as a buffer against raiders and outlaws along the trading route from Santa Fe to Los Angeles."[124] Agua Mansa and its sister town on the east bank across the river, La Placita, flourished as agricultural communities for about thirty years until a devastating Santa Ana flood in 1862 consumed all of Agua Mansa, "leaving only the chapel, the cemetery, and Cornelius Jensen's adjoining store" standing in its wake.[125] Its remains after the flood—the sacred and profane trinity of religion, death, and retail—augured Agua Mansa's subsequent incarnation as a California state landmark cemetery and museum, and as the namesake for an expired "enterprise zone" offering business redevelopment tax credits.[126] Agua Mansa, in other words, became the very figure for both erasure and excavation, for the elemental and temporal annihilation of an imperial history, followed by its reanimation under the sign of "history" as an engine of commerce and redevelopment. Its historicity, in other words, offers something like a certificate of authenticity, or a patina of "pastness," that might bolster property values and pique visitor interest to a location reinvented as an enterprise zone. Like exploring half-empty strip malls, as Espinoza was prone to doing before he conjured the Prospect Shopping Center of *Still Water Saints*, one finds oneself drawn to the ghosts of these empty landmarks: to what may have been there and what might have happened. Yet in reaching toward the past, one cannot help but be seized by the future, by a foreboding sense of oblivion that feels inevitable in the commercial graveyards of imperial ambition.

Empire after the Flood

Espinoza alludes in *Still Water Saints* to the floods that destroyed the original Agua Mansa, in order to animate the suspense of its return throughout his book: "Rain unsettled Agua Mansa. It's only a matter of time, the ones who remembered would say. The Santa Ana is too unpredictable. It will spill over the banks and flood the streets. People will be ripped away by the currents. The whole city will be washed away all over again."[127] For Perla the healer, who is sitting in the botanica during a rainstorm that seems out of place in a drought-plagued region like the Inland Empire, these showers unleash a torrent of memories about Agua Mansa's original moment of destruction, memories her mother hoped to spare her by covering Perla's eyes while scenes of survival and struggle transpired during the flood. But Perla remembers, despite the historical inaccuracy such memories in the novel belie. The 1862 flood that historically consumed Agua Mansa is reconstituted in the novel as a more recent event of the twentieth century, one that shapes the collective consciousness of the town that no longer exists in "real time," but still hangs by a thread in the contemporary time frame of the novel. Floodwaters mingle with still waters and dictate the ebbs and flows of the central queer narrative in the novel. Eventually, the rain not only unearths Perla's memories at the botanica but also heralds the arrival of a stranger whose well-being will occupy Perla throughout the rest of the story, even though it challenges her own sense of self and her own knowledge of healing.

Rodrigo, a young man from Michoacán, washes in from the rain into the Botánica Oshún the afternoon of the storm asking, almost begging, Perla for English lessons. Perla refuses at first, retreating into the safety of her role as an isolated suburban subject, a guarded businesswoman who understands that, after all, her shop is ensconced in a world of commerce: "I'm not a teacher. I run my botánica. I'm a businesswoman. Take a night class. At the high school." Nevertheless, Rodrigo persists, ultimately appealing to her in the language of transaction she tacitly demands in her retail space, especially from strangers: "You help people all the time. All the time there's people in here. You are very smart and know things books have. I think this: She can talk in both Spanish and English. I can pay you for teaching me English."[128]

Makeshift English lessons ensue as Perla instructs Rodrigo to learn English vocabulary from whatever books she has available in the botanica, including palm-reading manuals and Rodrigo's own ratty copy of *1,001 Big Questions*, a book that could very well be found in the discount bins at Wal-Mart, written in the pop idioms of self-help as a stimulant for suburban game nights. Their sessions consist mostly of Rodrigo sleeping away his inexplicable exhaustion as Perla herself tackles the big questions in his book: "*What do you fear most?* She wrote: Being forgotten." As Perla grapples with her own fears of oblivion, triggered by memories of the flood and exacerbated by Rodrigo's strangely absent presence during their lessons, she begins to revisit her own biography: "I am ashamed that I only agreed to do this job because it would get me out of the house. . . . I am ashamed that I'm still angry at my husband for not being able to give me a baby and that I had once thought about leaving him because of this." She submits to this self-inquisition even as she spins dark assumptions about Rodrigo's potential transgressions in her head: "*Drugs? Gangs? Maybe he's an illegal. Maybe he's hiding out from La Migra.*"[129]

In the same way she initially creates a barrier to contact with Rodrigo by retreating into a language of business and transaction, Perla's private speculations about Rodrigo's criminal activities and (she also assumes) illegal status resonates with a stereotypically suburban paranoia about security, safety, and borders.[130] We have, then, at the formation of this focal relationship in *Still Water Saints*, a staged confrontation between a suburban, "model-minority" sensibility of individual uplift through entrepreneurship, and the call to community and responsibility imagined from the "homeland." Rodrigo's requests, his very presence in Perla's eyes, are bound up with the messier international demands of "community" that tether us to the foreign elsewheres that were once ours or our families'.[131]

Perla's first blush of ugly feelings about Rodrigo could be chalked up to a history of forgetting between and among immigrant generations, like the one so often centralized in the conflict between ethnic whites (who were among the first on either coast to make the suburbs their own) and the communities of color who followed them into master-planned territories of prosperity.[132] And yet Espinoza shows us how this generational and racialized conflict can happen not only among those assumed to be our "kindred"—between Rodrigo, a Mexican boy from Michoacán, and Perla, a Mexican American "born in Agua Mansa, California"—but also within ourselves.[133] Perla wrestles with her sordid conjectures about Rodrigo's character just as she turns to the topic of what she is most ashamed of in the book of *1,001 Big Questions*. Over the course of those afternoons spent shadow-dancing through English lessons in a strip-mall botanica, Perla manages to plumb something deep about her own sensitivity to race, and her own self-awareness from something as shallow as a big book of questions, the retail version of a catechism.

As we learn in the second half of *Still Water Saints*, Perla's darkest fears about Rodrigo's origins and how they might be linked to his present dangers fail to come close to the horrors of his actual situation. Rodrigo turns out to be another casualty of empire whose local migrations in Mexico ultimately lead to his illicit and illegal traffic across the border in Southern California's Inland Empire. Like so many other queer figures who relocate from provincial outposts to the city, Rodrigo's story begins with the same trajectory in Mexico, when he moves from his pueblo in San Miguel, Michoacán, to the border megalopolis of Tijuana— only his migration is not motivated by the desire to find an urban habitat for queer sexual expression.[134] Indeed, Rodrigo's sexual identity is implicitly contingent on the economic conditions that foreground his many relocations, both consensual and forced, throughout the novel. He goes to Tijuana with the intent of eventually crossing the border into California to find work, but also perhaps to find something *else*: "'I'm going to California,' he said. 'There's nothing here.' Things in San Miguel were hopeless."[135]

Another dreamer of the golden dream without an exact route mapped for its fulfillment, Rodrigo's extended family in Tijuana sends him to fend for himself and scavenge for shelter and sustenance in the dump: "People with soot-covered faces hauled piles of trash and combed through smoldering rubble. He thought of his mother and father back home, waiting for money. He knew coyotes were expensive; his brothers had written this in their letters. Sifting through all this, it would take years to raise so much."[136] The most lucrative discovery Rodrigo would come to salvage at the dump did not come from "anything shiny or made of glass, clothes and shoes" awaiting repurposing, but from a sexual encounter with a man named Félix, who mentored him in sifting for valuables through the soot: "He grabbed Rodrigo's hand and placed it between his legs. From his pocket, Félix pulled out a wad of crumpled bills. 'Andale,' he whispered. 'Just touch me. That's it.'...'I told you. I'll take care of you.'"[137] More than a scene of sexual manipulation—or in its most reparative sense, of sexual discovery—Rodrigo's encounter with Félix introduces him to the economy of sexual power, as well as to the gnarled economies conflating financial and sexual power. As it turns out, Félix is spiritually and financially bound to care for another: a pregnant girl to whom he is married. Even in the seemingly amorphous social world of the dump, a repository for the urban underclass, this reproductive heterosexual economy takes precedence over same-sex mentorship with benefits. Rodrigo is thus banished from the dump for "tempting" Félix in an expense of spirit and his meager income—an income better spent on cultivating whatever future might be salvaged among urban remains.[138]

Newly schooled in alternative economies of salvage, and perhaps even salvation through sexual favors, Rodrigo finds himself drawn into a "trade" as he becomes enlisted by another young street hustler into the border city's sexual service industry for men who are "powerful and rich" from "los Estados Unidos."[139] He moves from the improvisatory economy of the dump into the highly structured (but still shadow) economy of sex work at a nightclub called Estrellitas. For a stretch of time Rodrigo feels free, simply by rubbing shoulders (among other body parts) with men from the United States who have dollars to spend and benevolence to impart: "He was safe. He was free to come and go as he pleased, as long as he came back in time."[140] As he first set out to do when he left Michoacán to earn his passage to California, Rodrigo works for freedom, or at least the sensation of financial independence. And yet Espinoza carefully scripts Rodrigo's own reflections on liberation to emphasize how financial and sexual independence are often confused for one another, especially when both become mobilized in the form of queer labor.

Queer sexual acts literally set Rodrigo "free" to some extent by helping him earn his passage to the United States, but Espinoza ultimately urges us to recognize that any rhetoric of sexual freedom is irrevocably bound up with other political and imperial economies fueled by the term "freedom" itself. In other words, when we produce expectations around "queer" as a *liberatory* concept, we also unleash its American imperial dimensions. U.S. imperialism established itself by negating bureaucratic colonialism and adopting the more informal and affective structures of liberal burden.[141] As scholars like Amy Kaplan and Victor Bascara have observed, in its own eyes the United States does not colonize; it liberates, primarily through capital.[142] Eventually, Rodrigo is "liberated" from Tijuana not only by American capital, but specifically by a white American soldier named Dwight.

Not unlike the musical *Miss Saigon*, and the many other transpositions of *Madame Butterfly* that came before it, Rodrigo's relationship with Dwight begins as a love story before it devolves into a tragedy. In the sordid atmosphere of Estrellitas, the club in which Rodrigo tricks, Dwight bares his soul while baring his USMC tattoos to the young hustler: "The first night nothing happened. They just sat on the bed and talked. . . . The next time they sat on the bed and kissed. Dwight put his head on Rodrigo's chest and cried." Significantly, the intimacy between Rodrigo and Dwight does not begin with Rodrigo seeking his path to freedom across the border through Dwight, but the other way around. It is Dwight who begs to be set free, released from his All-American burdens as a husband, a marine, a man: "'This macho bullshit, it's all an act. I'm married. But she's not satisfying me anymore. My true feelings, I'm repressing them,' he said."[143]

Very quickly, however, Dwight redirects his own vulnerability, his own desire to be saved, into a desire to save—to be the hero who gets to claim the spoils of victory. He promises Rodrigo: "I'm taking you away. Keeping you for myself. Don't want none of these fuckers having their way with what's mine."[144] In making a vow to Rodrigo to take him away from poverty and oppression to the other side of the border, Dwight simultaneously stakes his imperial claim on Rodrigo through the language of queer "love," salvation, and freedom. Rodrigo, in other words, can only earn his freedom—or rather, must accept Dwight's benevolent *gift* of freedom (conflated with queer love)—by submitting to an American economy of ownership.

This is how Rodrigo comes to be spirited across the border to the United States, an outcome we are not even sure he still wants after he attains a sense of financial dignity working at Estrellitas. Dwight's imperialist assumption, his understanding as a good soldier, is that this is of course what Rodrigo would want—that the American dream, and specifically the California dream, is what anyone on the "other side" of the border yearns for: "Dwight was waiting for him on this side with a blanket and clothes. He took Rodrigo out for cheeseburgers and fries. They drove in the dark over long freeways, their numbers painted on blue and red crests—15, 215, 10. He saw the names of the cities—San Diego, Los Angeles, Las Vegas, Riverside, San Bernardino. . . . They came to the rows of houses, all of them small and pressed together with flat roofs." Rodrigo's first glimpse of the United States, of a life with a gentleman soldier in Southern California, seems almost romantic in its sheer banality of cheeseburgers, freeways, and tract homes. During one of the few opportunities Rodrigo has to be out and about in Agua Mansa, he rides along the riverside with Dwight and sees a giant mural of "La Virgen de Guadalupe painted on the side of a wall" (the outer wall of Botánica Oshún) while enjoying the aroma of "carne asada, pollo a la parilla, [and] carnitas" wafting from a nearby restaurant.[145] Mexico, or at least the idea and flavor of it, is not that far away, either literally or figuratively, from Agua Mansa. But the dystopia of suburban Americana soon sets in as Rodrigo is confronted by the sordid realism of an Inland Empire that is at once alien to him and strangely familiar. Whereas in Tijuana he finds something resembling a love nest with Félix in the dump, the duplex Dwight sets up as their love nest in Agua Mansa turns out to be a dump, with a ramshackle kitchen, sullied furniture, and cockroaches "roam[ing] freely around the place."[146] Rodrigo's liberation from a life of hustling promised by relocating to the United States is deferred, and he finds himself instead in another form of servitude to Dwight, in effect imprisoned by his "status" as an illegal immigrant: "Don't go out. You could get lost. And Migra's been known to do sweeps around here."[147] As the narrative subsequently reveals, Dwight sequesters Rodrigo in the apartment not only to protect him from immigration officers but also to protect himself from being outed as having gone over to the other side to bring back a gay lover: "'Temporary,' he said to Rodrigo. 'Until the divorce. Then it'll be just you and me. You understand, don't you?'"[148]

With this turn in the narrative, Espinoza explores the failures of the imperial imaginary to hold itself accountable to what happens *after*. What happens at home after you go abroad? What happens after you intervene? What happens after freedom? And on behalf of whose freedom are you intervening? In Dwight's case, we see how the American soldier displaces his own yearning for freedom—to be unburdened by the responsibilities that adhere to American masculinity—onto Rodrigo as an "Other" he presumes is seeking salvation. Abroad Dwight fancies himself the American marine whose aim is "to do good," whereas at home he is forced to confront his own desire for ownership, along with his own failure to achieve that category of success as a working-class figure in the American context. An agent of empire abroad, Dwight also becomes another of the Inland Empire's casualties at home. He is trapped in a marriage that seemingly cannot be undone, and thus lapses from sobriety back into his meth addiction: "'Fucking two years sober out the fucking window,' he said, sobbing. . . . Dwight took his shirt off and cried into the bulldog on his biceps."[149]

The love story Dwight thought he was weaving with Rodrigo unravels, devolving into violence. The colonial structures of domination that lie dormant, or at least concealed in the rhetoric of (queer) love and liberation, erupts in Dwight's vicious display of power: "He pulled Rodrigo by the hair down the hall into the bedroom. He ripped the boy's pants off and pushed him down onto the mattress. He bent him over, the boy's face pressed into the pillows. Rodrigo reached out, swatting the air with his left hand as Dwight raped him."[150] Dwight's reprehensible act of violence against Rodrigo can no longer be read within the framework of a "love story" gone bad. Nor is it sufficient to analyze Dwight's struggle within the framework of compulsory heterosexuality, as he acts out against his own queer sexual desires. Rather, Dwight's rape of Rodrigo underscores the disturbingly intimate intersections between American imperialism and forms of sexual domination, particularly those that employ queer sodometries while setting forth to annihilate the category of queer itself.

In *Terrorist Assemblages: Homonationalism in Queer Times*, Jasbir K. Puar constructs an extensive contemporary archive that shows how sodometries have been deployed in militarized contexts, most infamously and sensationally in the Abu Ghraib scandals, as an expression of colonial force through humiliation: "Humiliation becomes sanctioned because the military functions as a reserve for what is otherwise seen as socially unacceptable violence, sanitizing all aggression in its wake under the guise of national security." But as Puar further points out, the outrage American LGBTQ organizations have directed at these displays of domination often miss the point by relegating such acts to the scourge of homophobia alone: "To foreground homophobia over other vectors of shame—this foregrounding functioning as a key symptom of homonormativity—is to miss that these photos are not merely representative of the homophobia of the military: they are also racist, misogynist, and imperialist."[151] Dwight's violation of Rodrigo, in other words, cannot simply be read as an isolated act of violence against the threat of queerness, or as an outward manifestation of his personal struggle with "deviance" in so far as it is activated by the figure of an Other (Rodrigo). It also brings to the fore the racist imperialism of Dwight's project of "rescue" that previously functioned under the sign of love. By acting against the other, he acts out against his own failures as a liberal citizen-subject: his failure to fulfill his duty to liberate (himself and others). Further, Dwight's violent turn against Rodrigo makes us acutely aware of how significant the question of choice becomes in the novel's critique of American imperialism at home as well as abroad.

Choice is at the crux of how different categories of identity and power are managed in the novel—be it national or local identities, or gendered and sexualized identities. Perla takes up the rhetoric of choice when she finds herself caught between the failure of reproduction and the potential of productivity. Dwight conceals his choices as duty and desire, thus absolving himself of any accountability for his actions. Beyond his initial decision to leave Michoacán, we are never certain about Rodrigo's choices. During one particular scene between Rodrigo and Perla, when she offers him refuge in her home after he escapes from Dwight's duplex, Rodrigo seeks her advice about what to do next: "I don't know what to do, señora. . . . Do I go back there? To my parents? Or do I stay here? Look for my brothers?"[152] Rodrigo, as he is wont to do in the novel, relinquishes his own decision making to others. Indeed, he always appears to be acted *on* as both a beneficiary and victim of circumstances. But to say as much is not to designate Rodrigo a "bad character." In fact choosing an identity in the world of *Still Water Saints* is figured as at once a luxury and a burden. To be sure, it is a choice Dwight struggles against making, but we are reminded that it is also his privilege as a liberal citizen-subject to make such decisions, especially as one who so profoundly embodies his "Americanness" as a white soldier.

We are never told whether Rodrigo chooses or wants to be queer. Rather pointedly, Espinoza seems to suggest that the very question itself is burdened by an imperial predilection for narratives of liberation, the kind arbitrated by soldiers, saviors, and captors. Through these particular figures in the novel, then, queer sexuality (and the rhetoric of choice on which it trades) becomes implicated in what Puar would call homonationalism. As Puar explains, "The paradigm of gay liberation and emancipation has produced all sorts of troubling narratives: about the greater homophobia of immigrant communities and communities of color, about the stricter family values and mores in these communities, about a certain prerequisite migration from home, about coming-out teleologies."[153] This teleology of "coming out" is one that Espinoza refuses to narrate in *Still Water Saints*, not only through Rodrigo but also through the other queer characters who populate the novel, both white and Latino (including Lluvia Medina, the muralist whose La Virgen de Guadalupe adorns the outer wall of the Botánica Oshún and serves as a beacon to Rodrigo while he's on the run from Dwight).[154]

Whereas Puar focuses on the international horizons of homonationalism, I would like to consider conceptually its effects on a more "local" scale in the fictive desert suburb of Agua Mansa, an avatar for transnational suburbia in general, and the Inland Empire in particular. Some may misconstrue Espinoza's resistance to "outing" many of his queer characters as an expression of internalized and, indeed, suburbanized homophobia. After all, isn't this what a literature of the suburbs would demand? Isn't the very structure of the suburbs predicated on privacy, repression, and discretion?[155] And yet as Espinoza expressed to me in a recent interview, so much of what constitutes "queer" in the novel for him rests on the conditions of exchange and transaction anchored by the Botánica Oshún in the Prospect Shopping Center, as well as on the movements these suburban characters make through the Southern California landscape.[156] There is Azucar, the pre-op transsexual dancer who inhabits roles like Pat Benatar and Madonna while performing at an Agua Mansa club called La Chuparosa. Azucar hops on a bus heading west on the I-10 after she finds an abandoned baby, but in the end, we never learn what happens to her, or whether she will return.[157] There is Lluvia, the young, dyke muralist who paints her mother's face as the Virgen de Guadalupe's—the mural Perla commissions for the Botánica Oshún.[158] Lluvia takes her emotionally abandoned mother for a joyride on her motorcycle, careening west down the I-10 at speeds over a hundred miles per hour: "My mother shouts and squeezes my waist tight, and she doesn't let go until we're far enough away."[159] We never know the nature of her letting go—whether it is purely metaphorical or literally suicidal. The frustration produced by the absence of certain resolutions in the narrative, then, is meant to stimulate another practice of queer reading—of reading queerness into the suburbs in a manner that looks beyond the complications of "identity" as the cornerstone of queer experience.

As queer interlocutors of the novel, we do not receive verification or validation through Rodrigo's story, just one among many in the densely populated, multi-voiced narrative of Still Water Saints. Espinoza encourages us instead to wrangle more intimately with the economies and circumstances Rodrigo embodies and transports through various locations in the novel. In other words, we are urged to consider more closely the effects and affects of queer migration itself, especially the movements both consensual and coerced that happen to, from, and within these suburban crossroads of empire. In so far as the very question of queer choice portends the emergence of an enlightened liberal subject from out of the darkness, Espinoza elects to leave Rodrigo, Perla, and, by extension, the novel's readers in the dark. Instead of finding answers, we, like Perla, find more questions strewn across the abandoned battlefields of the everyday: "Perla focused the flashlight on the windowsill dotted with flies, their legs curled into tiny question marks."[160] Like Perla, we are left to sift through suburban architectures such as Dwight's decaying duplex at Galena Court—the place Rodrigo was held against his will—for traces of conquest, rebellion, despair, and maybe even glimmers of hope in the Inland Empire.

Perla loses Rodrigo after harboring him in the botanica and in her modest home for a brief period of time. Rodrigo runs away, afraid of two young, white men loitering in the Prospect Shopping Center parking lot who are waiting to enter the tattoo parlor that replaced the Everything Ninety-Nine Cents store next to the botanica.[161] Perla tries to find Rodrigo by retracing his steps, remembering his naïve cartography of the United States: he confuses a street named "Buffalo" with the city in New York that shares its name, all the while hoping to find one of his brothers (last known to be working in Buffalo) on this sprawling suburban street: "The blocks of houses and apartment buildings slowly gave way to tire repair shops, a taqueria, the Panaderia Flor de Jalisco, the Excelsior Liquor store as she walked up Buffalo."[162] But Perla never finds him. Throughout most of the novel, we see Perla excel at divining signs, confident and nonchalant in her rituals of diagnosis with other customers. But with Rodrigo she is confounded. Like the rest of us, she is left to read for clues, for anything these architectures might yield in a landscape she ceased noticing ages ago until Rodrigo washed in with the rains. The routine of her daily movements to and from home and the workplace are altered by her search, rerouted by the "contact" she fosters and seeks to continue with Rodrigo.[163]

Days after Perla roams down Buffalo Street in search of her lost customer, her lost pupil, her lost friend, an item appears in the local newspaper about a "badly burned body" that washed up along the banks of the Santa Ana River: "The unidentified body was that of a young male, slightly built, and approximately 5′4″ in height. Anyone with information as to the victim's identity is asked to call the San Bernardino County Sheriff's Department."[164] She never calls. She never gives up: "That wasn't him. He's fine. He's still alive. He found his brother."[165] Through him, she has come to see the world in Agua Mansa: in the Excelsior owned by the Guptas and watched over by Ganesh; in the bakery bringing Jalisco home to those who left it; in Buffalo as a state of mind through the glimmer of a lost soul's misrecognition. And we in turn see the world of Agua Mansa: a town of ghosts, some living and some dead; an imperial settlement swallowed by floods; a place prosperity forgot but faith never left. Alex Espinoza's Agua Mansa, avatar of the Inland Empire and keeper of its spirits, does not suffer the fate of its historical predecessor and namesake. The Santa Ana floods never return to reclaim it, even though "death was always stirring. It hid in the wind, on those palm trees, on the banks of the Santa Ana río."[166] What Perla is left with—what *we* are left with—is not the element of magic in *Still Water Saints*, but rather its stark realism. A realism born of the suburbs and mistaken as sterile by virtue of its prefabricated architectures, its strip-mall cloisters of convenience harboring the dreams of immigrants looking to stake their claim as subjects of the American empire.[167] And yet these little boxes, these micro-parcels of contact and commerce, teem with lives cosmopolites won't deign or dare to imagine: "If you stood there long enough, if you stood there and watched and listened, you could see what that river had once been, and you could see so much life in the still water that remained."[168] In Espinoza's *Still Water Saints*, we find an archive and pedagogy of reading, of reimagining empire, race, and sexuality amid the ruins of an Inland Empire seemingly impervious to success. And when empire fails, where empire fails, there is nothing left to do but to keep going, even as we stay put. We have no choice.

Epilogue: It's All Coming Back to Me Now

When my family arrived in the Inland Empire in 1983, I had no idea whether we would stay. My parents and I had been on the road for so long, going wherever there were gigs on an entertainment and leisure circuit that was itself a residual of the United States' imperial forays into Southeast Asia and the South Pacific.[169] One would think the Inland Empire and its sedate (if industrious) temporality would turn out to be a big bummer after a childhood spent traveling with musician parents, sipping Shirley Temples at hotel lounges, and learning metaphor through Cole Porter tunes. But for me this empire offered the sweet sound of settling, a room of my own where I could listen to the music *I* liked. A place where I could ride alongside the Santa Ana River bottom on a banana yellow ten-speed from Sears with my Walkman on, listening to the Psychedelic Furs' "The Ghost in You" over and over again. A place where I could play with other kids at school, on our block, or in the Dairy Queen parking lot around the corner. And even though those same kids surrounded me on our scraggly lawn when I first landed, enacting their own twisted inquisition— "Are you a Christian? Are there toilets in the Philippines?"—I felt glad to have arrived. To have stopped anywhere.

That new sensation of stability, that first taste of an American dream I would spend my entire academic life learning to understand, only to eschew, inevitably gave way to adolescent yearnings for something else, to elsewheres befitting the queer of color consciousness animated by all those evenings spent

Deanna Erdmann, "Night in the Empire: Fabulaus at the Menagerie," 2009. Courtesy of the artist.

Deanna Erdmann, "Night in the Empire: Remote Intimacy at the Menagerie," 2009. Courtesy of the artist.

Deanna Erdmann, "Night in the Empire: Movement at VIP," 2009. Courtesy of the artist.

Deanna Erdmann, "Billboards, 60 East: Casino," 2009. Courtesy of the artist.

alone in my room taping pop songs off the radio and watching sitcoms from the socially conscious Norman Lear oeuvre. Remote intimacies were in formation, mapping this young provincial's departure, hatching the various escape routes and enumerating the skills it would require for these dreams to come to fruition. So I read and I wrote. I learned by reading all the books they mentioned in those 1980s pop songs ("I got a reason girl, and it's Immanuel Kant's, and I like it").[170] I learned that reading and writing is what many people in circumstances far more dire and urgent than my own did to earn their freedom. And maybe this is why this chapter, despite my best intentions to cover everything I wanted to share about the Inland Empire—its music, its poetry, its teachers, its wageworkers, its queer nightlife, its military bases, its universities, libraries, and other public institutions, its people and a lifetime spent learning of, with, and through all of them—ended up being mostly about a novel that refuses to give answers.

As I learned only after I left it so many times over, the Inland Empire will keep bringing me back with a force at once mundane and powerful. Or as the

Deanna Erdmann, "Billboards, 60 East: Your Ad Here," 2009. Courtesy of the artist.

Deanna Erdmann, "K," 2009. Courtesy of the artist. All rights reserved.

scholar, Riverside native, and my childhood friend Jennifer Stoever-Ackerman once wrote in a poem, this place exerts a pull like a

> dirty
> *Press-Enterprise*
> rubberband
> yanking me
> hard . . .
>
> Forever grabbing,
> hurling me back—
> just as I start to run away.[171]

It pulls me back to Route 60 where billboards for Indian casinos, strip clubs, Farmer Boys burgers, and real estate agents (who speak *Español*) tell me I'm getting close to home.

It brings me back to the corner of Van Buren Boulevard and Arlington Avenue, where a Kmart stands as the gateway to West Riverside. It is the same Kmart where my mom worked her very first day job, transitioning from blue notes to blue-light specials because live music was not a service this imperial economy believed it could afford. It stands as a monument to an economy and taste culture too stubborn to hope. A relic of an empire that never was, and never will be.

5 The Light That Never Goes Out

Butchlalis de Panochtitlan Reclaim "Lesser Los Angeles"

Take me out tonight
Where there's music and there's people
And they're young and alive.

—The Smiths, "There Is a Light That Never Goes Out"

Prologue: Cloverleaves and Soundscapes

This musical citation from twenty-five years ago might feel like yet another spasm of memory born of the bustling nostalgia industry epitomized by the endless loop of commemorative programming on cable networks like VH1, MTV's more mature and sentimental sibling network. Thanks to these clever manufacturers of memory, everything that has made us feel good, guilty, tingly, or strange from the "Totally Awesome 80s" all the way up to just this past week (vis-à-vis the rapid-fire reflections on the now-defunct pop culture digest *Best Week Ever*) is available "on demand" in the flickering, ephemeral archives of our televisions sets, made smarter in the last decade by our TiVos, which let us hoard such moments until cluttered and bursting hard drives insist we make room for more. What, if anything, do such plebian electro-comforts have to do with reshaping our queer imaginaries? With dreaming other queer cartographies into fruition? Do I really mean to suggest—in an eerie evocation of the creepy cinematic crescendo in Wim Wenders's *Until the End of the World*, where the film's protagonists glare obsessively at their own dreams on mini-TV sets in playback mode—that the "light that never goes out" might have something to do with a television set? Is this another echo born of the navel, that seedless fruit grafted into what became the Orange Empire, then the Inland Empire, those empires of my familiar?

No, not entirely. And absolutely, yes.

This book's efforts to trace the contours of suburban modes of queer sociability, affinity, and intimacy has required taking multiple detours through the terrain of sometimes solitary and isolated practices of popular consumption and memory making: the remote intimacies that provide the form and content for what I have referred to throughout *Relocations* as "queer suburban imaginaries." Before we can launch the movement, however, before (in the spirit of the light that never goes out) we can even accept the car ride alongside another implicitly so significant that the thought of mutual annihilation en route to a vibrant destination is utterly divine—"And if a double-decker bus, crashes into us / To die by your side is such a heavenly way to die"[1]—we must revisit the desires that opened this book; the same compulsion toward elsewheres that moved Lynne Chan's avatar, JJ Chinois, and other queer suburban subjects to seek out that somewhere else "where there's music and there's people / And they're young and alive." The commute to find pleasure and affinity has dictated the flows of *Relocations* from California's suburbs to New York City, from Southern California's bedroom communities to its amusement park nightclubs, from a bedroom on the block to the strip mall around the corner. Whereas the commute to labor is the vehicular movement most often associated as the source of traffic (conceptual and actual) between suburbs and cities, the labor required in a commute to pleasure has lacked the same historical and cultural legibility.[2]

Like the epigraph with which I opened this chapter, and the sonic echoes that haunted the previous one, some of the most illustrative accounts of the commute to pleasure are colored by a British accent. British cultural studies scholars and popular music writers like Simon Frith and Jon Savage have theorized how formative a suburban ethos has been to the emergence of subcultural scenes like punk, New Wave, and mod in the United Kingdom.[3] I quote Frith at length:

> Geographically, suburbia is, in effect, an empty sign, a series of dots on the map from which people travel—to the office, to the fleshpots, to the city. Suburban living is characterized by what it lacks—culture, variety, surprise—not by what it offers—safety, privacy, convenience. . . . What I'm outlining here is a pop fancy, of course—suburban communities are no more classless, genderless, or cultureless than anywhere else in contemporary Britain—but the significance of suburbia in song is as an account of the situation of suburban youth. . . . It is not surprising, then, that rock and pop, as youth forms, should be obsessed with suburbia, nor that the suburban experience should be, in its mass mediated form, defined by teenage mores. . . . Boredom ostensibly refers to an absence of activity—nothing's happening; I've got nothing to do—but in suburbia it describes a more complex state: not only is nothing unexpected happening, but I sense uneasily that I don't really know what it means for something to "happen" anyway. . . . Home operates here as the implicit term of comparison with the electric space of most suburban rock: the metropolis, the metropolis as both real city—a place at the end of a tube or train or bus ride—and mythical backcloth, with its neon-lit streets and shadow alleys of adventure, exchange, and disaster. And for the suburban teenager too the distinction between public and private spaces is blurred: to grow up suburban is to use public spaces, to get out of the house and into the park, the railway station, and now, I guess, the multiplex and the mall; but such spaces are in effect occupied, marked out by a subcultural determination to draw boundaries against

"the public." It is this way of taking over territory that is reflected in the suburban teenage use of London itself, in the weekend gatherings in clubs and on dance floors that have marked musical movements from Mod onwards.[4]

Frith's depiction of suburbia as an operative sign in the formation of British popular music and musical subcultures is, of course, bound to the particular context from which he speaks: the United Kingdom and its systems of railways and subways that make certain weekend commutes to pleasure more materially accessible, if not always psychically so. And yet my attachment to Frith's theory of suburbia and its incarnations in British pop music cannot simply be pathologized as but another residual effect of my previous training in British literary and cultural studies, or my adolescent penchant for British pop. Rather, Frith's account of suburbia as a figure of "pop fancy" resonates with the U.S.- and Southern California–based pop fantasies I already discussed throughout this book not only for its speculative emphasis on the way "boredom" and spatial aspirations for metropolitan lifestyles function in discourses about suburban space and desire, but also for the sheer fact that the suburban-made music of which Frith writes—by Bowie, the Cure, Siouxsie and the Banshees, and the Smiths, among many others—continually resurfaces within the sonic archives of queer of color suburban imaginaries in Southern California, from Buena Park's Studio K, to Morrissey's devout Inland Empire fans. As I explained at length in "Behind the Orange Curtain" and "Empires of My Familiar," the mainstream popularity of British pop in the United States during the period I discuss (from the early 1980s to the present) forged a soundscape that underscored the imperial legacies—some obvious, others more remote, both historically and cartographically—embedded in the Southern California landscape. In other words, the intersection with British pop in this and other chapters is not simply theoretical, but deeply material.

Thus I imagine that the topographical and cultural particularities that preclude a seamless analogy between Frith's theorization of suburban sensibilities in British pop music and what follows as my own account of commutes for pleasure in a Southern California queer of color suburban imaginary—the freeways instead of railways, the distance of "London" as a concept, and the sprawl of Los Angeles as the space of metropolitan immediacy—enhance, rather than frustrate, our fantasmatic, conceptual merging. Frith's suburbia and my own do not become one in this chapter, but rather merge together before pulling apart toward different destinations in the familiar cloverleaf pattern that animates the theoretical gestures throughout *Relocations*. Put another way, Frith's exploration of suburban sensibilities in British pop reveals where certain musics and styles actually come from: the suburbs in Britain. Meanwhile, this chapter, with a glance toward the blind spot in which this history of suburban cultural production resides, drives alongside it before crossing over to take us somewhere else, to another suburban landscape where an FM radio station broadcast from Pasadena, California, KROQ 106.7, scored freeway excursions with British New Wave, New Ro', mod, ska, pop, and punk. It takes us even further to a queer of color performance archive that reanimates those sounds, sentiments, and movements through the Southern California landscape.[5] Los Angeles may present itself as the final destination of the queer suburban pleasure seekers I write about in this chapter, but it is a Los Angeles saturated with dreams of elsewheres. A sign of the possible rather than the actual.[6] A place we find "occupied" in multiple senses of the word.

Setting the Stage for the Butchlalis de Panochtitlan: "DRRRTY White Girls" and "Suedehead"

As we conclude this journey of *Relocations* through Southern California, it seems inevitable that the gravitational pull of a city without a center, Los Angeles, becomes the coordinate that consistently undermines the suburban commute to pleasure, while remaining its destination. Where does one go if "Hollywood" is just a sign, and downtown is always under construction? Where do dykes find "contact" if WeHo (West Hollywood) is, like most gay ghettos, a boys town?[7] And where do queers of color move freely in a city segregated between east and west? Confronted with these questions, I am inclined to a certain reticence. This reticence has itself been inspired by the cultural work that is the focus of this chapter, the archive of "lesser Los Angeles" created by the Butchlalis de Panochtitlan ("Butch Stars of Pussylandia," known in shorthand as BdP), a Southern California–based Latina dyke performance ensemble led by Raquel "Raquefella" Gutierrez and Claudia "C-Rod" Rodriguez. BdP has included up to four members in the past, including Mari "Big Papi" Garcia and Nadine "Nadino" Romero. In their work, as well as in their daily lives, the BdP have come to realize that when they do readily offer up information on where to go or where to locate something, they find themselves returning to a place they no longer recognize— to places "occupied" but not in the way they desire. So instead of answering these questions about Los Angeles with an annotated map, or a guided tour, or by reading the gay and lesbian literature and history that recuperates the city that doesn't look like a city,[8] this chapter explores and explodes these questions through the BdP's expansive performance oeuvre that depicts the friendships and transient intimacies transpiring amid the contested landscapes of "lesser Los Angeles" and its aggregate of scattered suburban municipalities, particularly in South, East, and Southeast L.A.

On their Butchlalis.com website since lost to "webtrification" (someone purchased their domain name from underneath them when the credit card the group used to pay for their URL expired), the BdP maps the thematic invest-

Hector Silva and Raquel Gutierrez, "Butchlalis de Panochtitlan," 2008. Courtesy of the artists.

ments of their work onto the specific neighborhoods, "second cities," and sub-urbs clustered around Los Angeles, or as Edward Soja describes the sprawling metropolis, the "conurbated city."[9] As I mentioned in my introduction, although Los Angeles was once regarded as an urban anomaly for its sprawling and some-times acquisitive relationship to neighboring municipalities, it has since become the paradigm for what Soja (among other critical geographers) has named the "postmetropolis."[10] L.A.'s built environments—horizontal rather than vertical in character, despite the recent changes to its skyline as a result of the latest incar-nation of the "downtown revival"—as well as its technology, leisure, and service-based economies, have come to inspire the designation "exurb" or "edge city" for many of the sprawling cities that structurally resemble Los Angeles through-out the West and Southwest.[11] Further, the intra-national migrations of post-agricultural, post-industrial workers from the East and Midwest to the West and Southwest, combined with the immigration of both "skilled" and "migrant" labor populations from the Pacific Rim, Mexico, and Central and South Amer-ica (among other socioeconomic factors), has led to a pronounced shift in the ethno-racial makeup of the suburban communities cleaved to greater Los Ange-les—the local zones the author and humorist Sandra Tsing-Loh has dubbed "lesser Los Angeles."[12]

The BdP offer their own thematic mapping of some of the locations absorbed under the sign and sprawl of "Los Angeles" and relegated to serving as the city's minor sites. Describing the impetus of their work, the group professes to "explore the liminal space of queer boi-dom and the identities and the neighborhoods we claim and are claimed by. Sketches include gestures toward Working Class Butch Latina/o Identities (City Terrace); Interracial Desire (Montebello): Family Guilt-Latino Queerness (East Los Angeles); Bar Culture/Softball Culture (El Sereno); Gentrification (Silver Lake); Class/Classism (all of LA Metro)."[13] The BdP stages a series of responses, some comedic, others decidedly dramatic, to relocations as a consequence of the bloated Southern California real estate market, and exacerbated by the gentrification of queer of color social spaces by creative classers.[14] The gentrification of social spaces and lived environments in Southern California has re-demographized not only the city but also its suburbs and exurbs near and far, from Bell Gardens to Riverside—two among the many place-names conjured in BdP's imaginative remapping of the region.[15] This chapter focuses on how the BdP's performances archive the social transitions and spatial erasures that happened when Southern California's real estate "bubble" was most distended at the turn of the twenty-first century, just prior to its spectacular burst in the last several years. Rather than scripting escape through moments of fantasy, the BdP harness fantasy in their minimal theatrical productions as a mode of critique and as an archival practice with the potential to kindle enduring systems of collective support and queer bonds.

BdP's projects run the gamut from evening-length sketch programs, to full-length plays, short films, workshops, and performance events in universities, local art spaces, and nightclubs. A chronicle of the ensemble and the contours of their past and continuing work are the primary focus of this chapter. Before this work of documentation begins, however, we must "set the stage"—or rather, reflect for a moment on how the BdP sets their stages—since "setting" in its multiple forms is what engenders the affect in and of the ensemble's performance oeuvre. The rich soundscapes and multimedia enhancements, slides, and both found and original film footage that accompanies BdP's sparsely adorned stage sets draw from an expansive repertoire of visual citations and popular music. At times their song selections are culturally embedded in what Juana María Rodríguez calls "queer latinidad."[16] At other moments their sound track is culled from sources seemingly incongruous or distinctly Anglo-American, but evocative of circuits of affect formed locally after a series of migrations not only between nations, but also between freeway exits in the expansive Southern California landscape.

One of their earliest sketch pieces from 2005, "drrrty White Girls," features (in BdP member Raquel Gutierrez's words), "Two East L.A. butches who happen to be aging KROQ flashback party jotas still bumpin' the Smiths, wearing mor-

BdP promotional image, "Driving in Your Car," 2006. Courtesy of the artists. All rights reserved.

rissey T-shirts."[17] The two butches featured in BdP's sketch, Lolo and Perla, are frustrated by a night out at Hollywood's Florentine Gardens, a landmark supper club that opened in 1938 and "enjoyed its heyday in the 1940s and '50s as an upscale place where celebrities could be seen quaffing and canoodling."[18] In 1979, Florentine Gardens was transformed into a dance club that began catering to an eighteen-and-over market, drawing "carloads of the eager 18-and-up set from such non-Hollywood hometowns as Pomona, La Puente, Montebello, and Whittier." The club ultimately evolved from the mid-1980s onward as a hot spot for young Latinos. In a 2004 *Los Angeles Times* piece about the potential razing of the Florentine Gardens to clear land for a new city fire station, Marina Grijalva, then a twenty-seven-year-old Mexican American tutor and Catholic school teacher, reminisced about her commutes to the club during her first few years at Pomona College in the early 1990s: "[Florentine Gardens] is where you go when you're underage and you want to go out somewhere. It was the whole experience. It seemed so big city."[19]

In "DRRRTY White Girls," Lolo and Perla have returned to Florentine Gardens as late-twentysomethings in the early 2000s, and they spend as much time reminiscing about past sexual liaisons with white, liberal-arts-educated "riot grrrls" from Pomona in the early 1990s, as they do cruising new flesh on the Hollywood dance floor. (Describing her past affair with one of the eponymous "dirty white girls," Lolo remarks, "She went to one of those fancy private colleges: Vicky Lawrence College or some other lady's name.") The memorialized encounter between East L.A. dykes and the white "riot grrrls" who held workshops in Pomona's industrial parks and garages concludes with an homage to Morrissey, the iconic former lead singer of the British band the Smiths. Just as Lolo and Perla resolve to leave the club after an unsuccessful night of cruising, Morrissey's "Suedehead" (from his 1988 solo album, *Viva Hate*) crescendos in the room as the two sway their way off the stage.

It remains unclear to the audience whether "Suedehead" has surfaced as part of a "KROQ flashback" set in the club itself, or whether its echoes are extradiegetic—a sonic device to usher the characters offstage and facilitate a technical transition, while accentuating the sketch's themes with its catchy refrain: "Why do you come here? / And why do you hang around? / I'm so sorry."[20] Is the unmistakable voice of "the Moz," accented and languid, asking Lolo and Perla why they come back and "hang around," only to dwell in the pastness of a place they no longer inhabit with ease as "aging jotas"? Once again we witness temporal drag exerting its force through lesbian bodies seemingly out of time with stylistic and sonic contemporariness, and "out of place" with their residual attachment to a British pop icon who, on the surface, has little to do with them.[21] Is this what makes the pair sorry, and the audience sorry for them? Or is Morrissey's jaunty inquisition directed at something else? At a loss impending rather than already experienced in a venue that seems perpetually under threat of erasure as a result of "eminent domain"?[22] Is this why we should all be sorry?

The answer is inevitably "both." The sonic styles and expired fashions that adhere to certain bodies cannot be extracted from the spatial negotiations that transpire simultaneously on a micro-scale—between patrons within a specific setting—and the macro-scales of development: from contemporary struggles over civic redevelopment, to historical, colonial conflicts and fantasies. Racialized bodies, accented idioms, and the ephemeral material of personal archives sometimes fail to ease seamlessly into what is in style, "modern," and of the moment. I am reminded yet again of the anecdote Martin Manalansan tells in *Global Divas: Filipino Gay Men in the Diaspora* about the "Third World"—the nickname given to a section of a Greenwich Village gay bar populated by Pinoy *baklas* in New York.[23] Bodies get "clocked" and become relocated and quarantined, even in public leisure spaces, because they are (sartorially, stylistically, physically) out of time, and hence out of place. Like Lolo and Perla at Florentine Gardens, the "Third World" described by Manalansan is not simply about a local negotiation on "the scene" among its various players, but also an encounter fraught with deeper histories of empire and the "improper" fantasies that may arise from these loaded moments of social segregation.

Meanwhile, the thematic ambiguities and the performative convergence of personal as well as collective memories of soundscapes, locations, histories, and popular artifacts summoned forth by the BdP's sound tracking of this early sketch

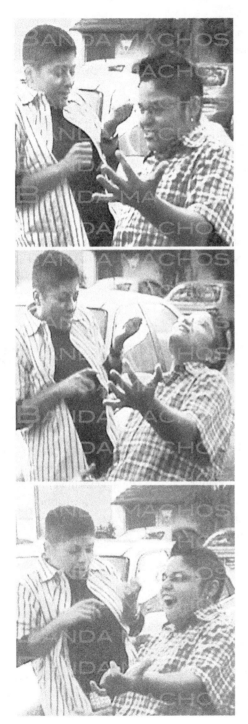

BdP interstitial slide,
"Banda Machos," 2006.
Courtesy of the artists.

sets the tone for the ephemeral, archival practices that have become a hallmark of the ensemble's work.[24] Much like the club-goers at Studio K or Lynne Chan's JJ Chinois, queer bodies intrude on sites not explicitly designated for queer pleasure and consumption in the BdP theatrical repertoire. This is partly out of a necessity born of peripheral spaces, yet it is also the ensemble's own stubborn demonstration that histories of queer sociability and intimacy sometimes happen in unexpected locations, and in correspondence with remote popular archives from the past—including those that are not their own. Further, like the figures featured in "Empire of My Familiar," racialized solidarity in the BdP's work draws its affective force from some unlikely sources, including potentially incongruous objects of desire like British pop and punk, and other ostensibly "white" subcultural and mainstream popular forms.

In "drrrty White Girls," Morrissey's "Suedehead" and Lola and Perla's Morrissey T-shirts posit a remote intimacy of interracial, interspatial, and intersubjective desire from the past on into the present. The subjects called out by the very name "suedehead" gestures to a British working-class subculture (an offshoot of the skinhead subculture) also enamored of musical styles and sensibilities from elsewhere—of reggae from the former "colonies," of black American soul, and of the hybrid form ska.[25] Relayed through Morrissey's song in the BdP's sketch, another set of interidentifications takes place between butch dykes of color in Southern California and British ruffians like "suedeheads," as well as more flaccid versions of British masculinity like Morrissey's (he has famously declared himself a vegan celibate, and his sexuality has always been a subject of subcultural debate). The convergence of these forms in a humorous, theatrical contemplation on the saliency of certain social spaces for communities of color brings to the fore the relays between remote histories of racialized conflict mobilized by the sign of "Morrissey," who emerged as a contentious figure in public debates about popular music and racism in the United Kingdom during the early 1990s while remaining a popular icon for Latino subcultures in Southern California and the Southwest from the 1980s on into the present.

In *Sounds English: Transnational Popular Music*, Nabeel Zuberi explains how Morrissey's controversial 1992 performance at the Madstock festival in North London—he draped himself in a Union Jack during the song "Glamorous Glue" while twirling before a "huge photographic backdrop of two 1970s skinhead girls"—ignited furious responses from a mixed audience of "skinhead fans of [ska supergroup] Madness" as well as "antiracist sections of the audience," because of the flag's (and the skinhead portrait's) nationalist and racist evocations. As Zuberi analyzes the aftermath:

> This musical moment spills over with national/transnational ironies: a pop star in London tells his audience that local language and culture are dead at the hands of American cultural imperialism while he spectacularly sells out a concert in

Los Angeles; a performer known for his androgyny and Oscar Wilde obsession is abused by the macho, determinedly hetero English skins he seems to celebrate, and the war in Northern Ireland looms large (if offstage) as an English singer of Irish-Catholic descent wraps himself in the Union Jack.[26]

The BdP's (unlicensed) use of "Suedehead" in their sketch not only underscores their own local, intersubjective entanglements with the "dirty white girls" who were part of a riot grrrl subculture at once enticing and profoundly alien to them as queers of color from Southern California's service underclass; it also affectively excavates how such attachments are routed through other interracial and transnational imaginaries that make Morrissey's music and iconography resound with their own desires in a strange version of fraternity.

As recurring characters in the BdP's oeuvre, Lolo and Perla offer a microsample of the BdP's performance methodology with their willingness to brandish clichés while brazenly using and misusing queer and popular icons like riot grrrls and Morrissey. Working reparatively, the BdP do not go in for the takedown; rather, they let these icons stand in order to show us how their mediated reactivation through other bodies and other imaginaries unleashes alternate histories of belonging through incommensurate forms of subjugation and fantasy.[27] These reparative mediations, which I have also described throughout Relocations as "remote intimacies," trigger pathways to other archives of "transnational ironies," like those within the British popular context described by Zuberi. The histories of transnational exchange and national tensions fueled by race and sexuality animated by Morrissey's song "Suedehead," then, serve as a foil for the disavowals of "consciousness" in the BdP's DRRRTY White Girls." The sonic architecture of their sketch both questions and confirms the characters' inappropriate desires for white subjects, if not for whiteness itself: it spotlights Lolo and Perla's predilection for well-educated, "dirty white girls," as well as their willingness to display on their own bodies (through their hairstyles and T-shirts) residual affections for a fey British white boy who began tailoring his music and his message for a Latino fan base (a following that kept his career alive long after it was supposed to be over).[28]

A plethora of writers and filmmakers have tried to explain why, or simply tried to document how, Morrissey and the Smiths remain such revered figures among some of Southern California's Latino communities.[29] The author, radio host, and longtime OC Weekly columnist Gustavo Arellano likens Morrissey's tremulous tenor and occasional falsetto to the voices heard in Mexican ranchera music, which critiques bourgeois culture from a populist perspective through lyrics soaked in metaphor and passionate imagery.[30] But this explanation—and explanations of this character—presupposes that the racialized youth are transformed into quivering masses upon first hearing the Smiths and Morrissey, because they already have ranchera running through their veins or deeply imprinted in their cultural memory.[31]

It presupposes a racially coherent, authentic, and self-aware subject that always has "home" or a diapsoric point of cultural origin as an affective coordinate, while presuming that one national context—Mexico—offers the foundation for a broader Latino/a intersubjective affinity with "Saint Morrissey" from Manchester, England. For BdP's Raquel Gutierrez (half-Salvadoran, half-Mexican, and self-identified as "matrilineally Salvi cultured, not Chicano/a"),[32] Morrissey functions as a reference point because he invokes with his own brooding suburban outsiderhood a version of Southern California spiritually significant to a spectrum of queer Latinas and Latinos—from "City Terrace to Whittier, Pico Rivera to Lynwood, Long Beach to Maywood and thru the 5/10/101/60 FWY interchanges."[33]

Indeed, as Gutierrez suggests on her blog, Morrissey's "spiritual significance" may have as much to do with the collision of imperial histories called forth by the soundscapes heard on the radio in automobiles crisscrossing freeway interchanges in the Southern California region as it does with any naturalized, "original" music from Mexico or Latin America coursing through anyone's veins. Arellano makes it a point to clarify that comparing Morrissey's music to "Mexican music is an interesting game, but it's beside the point."[34] Though he remains focused on Mexican American Morrissey fans rather than the star's broader reception within an international "latinidad," Arellano rightly explains that Southern California's soundscapes—replete with "1980s New Wave, oldies-but-goodies, and . . . rockabilly rhythms," as well as KROQ's "flashback lunches" (which kept British New Wave alive long after its heyday in the 1980s)—accommodated Morrissey rather than vice versa.[35]

Several articles and documentaries addressing the Morrissey/Smiths phenomenon depict the artists' Latino fans as "devout worshipers" while insinuating heretical and pathological dimensions to these affections. Chloe Veltman in *Believer Magazine* writes, "The aura surrounding Morrissey, vocalist and wordsmith of 1980s British pop group The Smiths, now turned solo artist, is of a wholly (holy) different order. . . . This aging and comparatively marginal British singer is blurring the lines between what it means to be a pop icon and religious icon."[36] Meanwhile, Chuck Klosterman, a journalist best known for his cheeky, masculine work on "low culture," is bemused by the incongruity between Morrissey and his "macho" Latino fans: "Perhaps you are wondering what a cut-like-marble Latino could possibly see in a quintessentially British, marvelously effeminate white guy best known for reading Oscar Wilde and wearing his espoused asexuality on his sweater sleeve. Frankly, there's no concrete answer to that question. But Cruz Rubio is definitely seeing *something*, because he is not the exception; within the walls of the sixth annual Smiths/Morrissey convention in Hollywood's palace theater, he is the rule."[37] Morrissey's Britishness (an identity that registers in a long cultural history as "effeminacy")[38] would seem to preclude sympathetic identifications across the boundaries of race and nationality, precisely because of (hyper)sexualized assumptions about what Latino masculinity purportedly signifies.[39] Rather than participate in these exclusionary discourses about gender, race, sexuality, and identification, the BdP follows in the footsteps of other Latino fans who transpose Morrissey into their own imaginaries, rather than conforming to the assumptions disseminated through his fan culture's critical reception in the mainstream media. In other words, the BdP are not the Moz's loyal subjects; instead, the BdP demonstrate through their performances that Morrissey potentially functions as an objective correlative for the sentiments of displacement and incongruity—both spatial and sexual—that might be shared by Latinos throughout Southern California's suburbs. When the BdP sing and move along to Morrissey in their performance work on the page and stage, they, among many other Latinos in Southern California, are singing a history of the suburbs as a place where empires collide, and where gender and sexuality is interpreted through the lens of these imperial desires. The queer compulsion to find something else and go someplace else may eventually lead to that something "Other" (be it racialized, gendered, or sexualized), sequestered remotely within ourselves as we move to, from, and between the spaces of familiarity that bore its traces all along.

As we continue the slow and congested commute toward some conclusion—toward a destination that might ultimately evade us when we reach the end—this chapter will provide an archive of the BdP's journey, first as individual commuters to a lesbian support group in Montebello, then, ultimately, to their collaboration as a performance ensemble documenting the search for queer of color pleasure and affinity in lesser Los Angeles. Spanning their early sketch work to their first full-length play, 2008's *The Barber of East L.A.*, this chapter's chronicle of BdP's aesthetic practices traces their efforts to forge an archive of queer of color suburban sentiments through performance. More than any of their pieces to date, *The Barber of East L.A.* overtly thematizes how to create queer, feminist histories of locations more often commemorated as masculinist, subcultural sites of intervention and innovation. Whereas the chapters leading up to this conclusion have focused on the outer reaches of Southern California's queer suburban imaginary (from Orange County to the Inland Empire), the BdP's work dwells on and within the inner suburbs cleaved to the city of Los Angeles, like Montebello and Bell Gardens. Further, this chapter explores how racialized neighborhoods in the city itself, like the predominantly Latino East L.A., are historically segregated from the city's discourse on "urbanity," and enfolded instead into what the scholar Raúl Homero Villa calls a "barrio logos."[40] After an extended reading of the ensemble's work, and *The Barber of East L.A.* in particular, I move to a coda that wraps up this chapter and this book.

In music, a coda is not only a concluding statement but also a superfluous gesture "extraneous to the form as usually defined."[41] I close with this musical structure in mind, because it offers the possibility of never being finished, of listening again to the motifs that animated earlier gestures, tones, and improvisations throughout the piece. In this spirit, the coda to *Relocations* will, at various instances, mouth along with Morrissey and the Smiths' "There Is a Light That Never Goes Out," as well as a few other pop songs, in a conceptual sound track for the relocations, displacements, and reclamations of space that foment intimacies among remote and sequestered queer of color subjects.[42] This critical experiment with a kind of critical karaoke, as it were, methodologically mimics and reproduces the trivial exchanges, the social fabrications, and the popular affinities that cohere in the spatially "disadvantaged" queer subject's profound encounters with media forms like music, radio, and television that we find throughout the BdP's oeuvre. These encounters are perhaps out of time as well as out of place, both vexed and resplendent.

If the queer suburban subject of color is presumed to be "out of touch, out of time" (to harness another lyrical echo from the mid-1980s, this time courtesy of the venerable "blue-eyed soul" duo Hall and Oates), we must nevertheless resist reading such spatially circumstantial anachronism as the pitiable consequence of not being *where* it's at. Neither can these anachronisms be easily assimilated into structures of postmodern irony or clever self-referentiality. Not every popular reverberation or citation is accompanied by a wink and a nudge. In some cases, the nod to the popular may be distinctly unpopular if it comes with tears of guiltless sincerity or a ticklish naïveté. As the BdP's work demonstrates, such moments of self- and mutual discovery—through a pop song, or through a figure or voice so seemingly remote, both spatially and temporally, from who "we" are—might make us so OK with going nowhere, so captivated by the company we've cobbled together in our suburban spaces, that we yearn for the "pleasure and privilege" of a "ten-ton truck" smashing into us to make it last forever.

Commutes and Collaborations: The Butchlalis Archive

The three individuals who coalesced into the Butchlalis de Panochtitlan in its most recent incarnation met in Montebello, California, a city eight miles east of downtown Los Angeles, distinguished for being at the crossroads of nearly every major freeway artery approaching L.A. In true lesbian fashion, the trio connected at a support group to which they all had to commute from "freeway-close" locations throughout Southern California, including Silver Lake (Gutierrez), Compton (Rodriguez), and Glassell Park (Garcia). In 1998, Claudia Rodriguez, Raquel Gutierrez, and Mari Garcia crossed paths at a Latina lesbian "rap session" sponsored by Bienestar, a grassroots Southern California nonprofit organization founded in 1989 and "dedicated to positively impacting the health and well-being of the Latino community and other underserved communities in Southern California."[43] In addition to servicing the health needs of Southern California's Latino communities, Bienestar's multiple sites in Los Angeles, San Bernardino, and San Diego Counties also function as gathering places for local queers of color in search of peer support and other social services.

In their time together and apart, members of BdP have lived in different parts of Los Angeles and have worked in various sectors of the "lesser Los Angeles" economy. The ensemble's thematic emphasis on negotiating Southern California's sprawling spaces for labor, community, and pleasure has been informed by their respective experiences commuting to socialize and aesthetically collaborate within what the performance studies scholar Meiling Cheng has called the "multicentric" spaces of Los Angeles.[44] The BdP's most current description of their collective project (culled from their MySpace page, which replaced the original Butchlalis. com site) shares in Cheng's rhetoric of *multi*centricity: "Butchlalis de Panochtitlan is an ensemble that has emerged from community-based activist spaces to create visibility around politicized identities and the limitations in identity politics within a Los Angeles–centric context. They work to produce multi-dimensional language as a way that activates a new way of seeing their multi-layered, contradictory, and celebratory selves in an often hostile world."[45] As Cheng clarifies about her own use of the word "multicentricity," the term resists conflation with the concept of "multi-culturalism," problematized in ethnic and American studies as well as postcolonial studies, for its erasures of disparate histories of racial conflict and coalition: "[Mul-ticentricity] does not purport to be an ethical or redressive measure as does 'mul-ticulturalism.' Multiculturalism, at least in its idealistic phase, aspires to institute fundamental changes in the directions and definitions of 'national cultures' through education, hiring principles, and media advocacy."[46]

BdP disabuses anyone who reads their website from any sense of idealism about what the prefix "multi" is meant to accomplish in their own rhetoric of multiplicity. For example, they undermine serious statements about their mis-sion by using the MySpace "Who I'd Like to Meet" window to solicit the atten-tion of "recovering identity politicians, the indigenous chic, stoic trolls and party starters," among others. Front and center, however, is their commitment to spa-tial circumstances in their work. The performance collective describe their earli-est endeavors as "sketch-based pieces focusing on recuperating queer narratives washed over by waves of gentrification, state and local terror and violence," while locating their own bodies in those histories of erasure in the Southern California landscape: "We explore identity and its consequence while mapping the city we live in on the brown female masculine bodies we walk in, as we perform our-selves, each other, imagined characters and caricatures."

From their nascent encounters as acquaintances through the Bienestar sup-port group, to their individual backgrounds as children of immigrants who settled throughout the region to perform domestic, industrial, and service labor, the BdP consistently map and remap competing "centers" of the centerless city of Los Angeles in their collaborative work. As Cheng has described the interpretive practice of multicentricity in relation to L.A.-based performance art: "Each Los Angeles has to deal with conflicts, differences, and incommensurabilities within itself. Likewise, it has to handle a complex ramification of relationships with other Los Angeleses, including opposition (antagonism among competing entities), coexistence (parallel subsistence among different entities), coalition (cooperation between different entities for mutual benefit), and hybridity (merging with other entities)."[47] The ensemble has not only had to negotiate topographical distances while rehearsing and performing with one another, but also the temporal disjunctions, breaks, and relocations determined by their disparate economic and living circumstances among extended family members, lovers, and other friendship circles.

Gutierrez hails from Bell Gardens and has lived at different instances in Huntington Park with her family and in other parts of L.A.'s "greater East Side" (which debatably includes Silver Lake, Historic Filipinotown, and Lincoln Heights).[48] Rodriguez grew up in Compton (where her family is based) and moved around various parts of South Central L.A. and the Westside (including the more affordable rental district of Palms) during her studies as an undergraduate at UCLA and her graduate work in creative writing at CalArts in Valencia. In 2006, Rodriguez moved back to Compton before settling in the West Adams district near the University of Southern California. Garcia grew up in Glendale, California—a suburb north of downtown Los Angeles that has since become an enclave for Filipino and Armenian communities[49]—before striking out on her own in nearby Glassell Park and Silver Lake. Garcia ultimately moved in the early 2000s to the San Fernando Valley in Winnetka, and commuted to work as a teacher at Lincoln High School in East L.A. As of this writing, Gutierrez and Rodriguez room together in Lincoln Heights, and Garcia has moved to Echo Park. From 2005 to 2007, the BdP included a fourth member, a photographer and video artist named Nadine Romero. Romero worked in the service sector at Starbucks in West Hollywood while living six miles east in Silver Lake.

The group's formations, dissolutions, and reunifications have coincided with their movements through, and negotiations between, the multiple "Los Angeleses" each has experienced. Those who have moved repeatedly, including Gutierrez and Rodriguez, have had to do so as a result of conflicts (some with lovers who have since become exes), and at other times because of broken coalitions with aesthetic collaborators who have competing visions for how queer of color and feminist politics is accomplished. Whether staying or going, each has based their decisions about relocation on the gentrification they experienced in their neighborhoods. Gentrification has made it financially untenable to relocate within hipster enclaves like Silver Lake and Echo Park—and during the most distended period of the rental bubble in Los Angeles, Glassell Park (which was rapidly being bought up by young families)—while also making it socially undesirable to remain in these areas because of the dramatic changes this process brought to some of their favorite locations. Garcia remained in Winnetka at a remote distance from the gentrified zones clustered around downtown Los Angeles, which were nearer to her workplace in East L.A., because it made more financial sense not to relinquish her place after a relationship ended with a longtime partner. Gutierrez and Rodriguez also preferred not to hunt for "shares" in certain neighborhoods after their respective breakups with longtime partners, not only for financial reasons but also because (in Gutierrez's words) "the douche quotient in these places reached an all-time high."[50] Negotiating the demands of her employment in the service sector, Romero preferred not to waste money on moving costs to get away from Silver Lake, and ultimately she left the ensemble in order to turn her attentions to supporting her family.[51]

The ensemble's formation also happened in aggregate, much like the multicentric and conurbated spaces that provide the local material for their work. The BdP first formed as a duo, with Rodriguez and Gutierrez initiating the collaboration. After repeated encounters with each other at Bienestar events and other queer women of color gatherings in East and Southeast Los Angeles, Rodriguez and Gutierrez undertook their first collaborations in the broader editorial milieu of *Tongues*, "a politically and socially conscious magazine and website 'zine for queer women of color, specifically Xicanas and Latinas," founded in 1999.[52] *Tongues* envisioned its mission as a creative correlative to social service organizations like Bienestar, at the same time that it hoped to offer alternative, aesthetic, and political interventions into more mainstream LGBTQ organizations less attentive to race, labor, and the consequences of globalization.[53] Rodriguez and Gutierrez ultimately chose to take their shared notions of creative intervention a step further by focusing on live performance in addition to writing for the publication and organizing community events with *Tongues*. As a duo, they first performed under the Butchlalis de Panochtitlan moniker in the program for "Lesbiradas," a *Tongues*-sponsored spoken word, performance, and multimedia benefit for the Lesbiradas de Guatemala (a queer women's organization based in Guatemala) at Highways Performance Space in Santa Monica, California, in September 2002.[54]

Despite the success of this first performance in the Lesbiradas group show, BdP's expansions and contractions as an ensemble (first as a duo, then as a quartet, then as a trio, and finally, at the time of the final edits to this book, back to a duo featuring Gutierrez and Rodriguez) would have to await the transformations occurring in its founders' lives, who were in their early-to-mid-twenties in 2002–2003. A month prior to their first performance as Butchlalis de Panochtitlan in September 2002, Rodriguez began working as a community organizer at Bienestar, where

we are a performance tropa
exploring los angeles...watch our
female-born bodies explode
with masculine chispa

BUTCHLALIS DE PANOCHTITLAN
TEENAGE PAPI: THE 2ND COMING OF ADOLESCENCE

BdP promotional image, "Teenage Papi: The Second Coming of Adolescence," 2005.
Courtesy of the artists. All rights reserved.

she remained in various posts until May 2006, when she subsequently transferred to APLA (Aids Project Los Angeles). Gutierrez, who studied in the late 1990s and early 2000s at Rio Hondo Community College (in Whittier) and California State University, Northridge, left Southern California in 2003 to pursue a graduate education in performance studies at New York University's Tisch School of the Arts. After completing her master's degree, Gutierrez reevaluated whether the academy was a suitable place for her aesthetic and activist efforts. She returned to Los Angeles in fall 2004, rekindling her friendship with Rodriguez in the process and expanding the BdP to include their former Bienestar buddies Mari Garcia and Nadine Romero.

Reconfigured as a quartet, and with each holding down full-time day jobs— Gutierrez landed an administrative post as the assistant director of the Center for Feminist Research at the University of Southern California, Rodriguez continued working in the nonprofit HIV/AIDS community sector, Garcia continued teaching high school, and Romero continued working at Starbucks—the ensemble wrote and assembled their first full-length show after working hours in the fall of 2004, while commuting between their respective apartments scattered across Southern California (Rodriguez lived in Compton, Gutierrez and Romero lived as neighbors in an apartment complex in Silver Lake near the I-5, and Garcia lived in the San Fernando Valley). The result was *Teenage Papi: The Second Coming of Adolescence*, an assemblage of sketches, short films, monologues, and multimedia slide shows that premiered at the Highways Performance Space in January 2005.[55]

Teenage Papi: The Second Coming of Adolescence opened to minimal fanfare but was well attended, especially considering that the ensemble had not previously performed as a quartet, and that Butchlalis de Panochtitlan had been placed on hold as Gutierrez pursued her graduate studies on the East Coast in 2003–2004. The group's access to Highways came as a result not only of Rodriguez and Gutierrez's first BdP duet for the Lesbiradas group show in 2002, but also because of Gutierrez's precocious involvement with various Southern California music and art scenes as a teenager and college student. In the years leading up to Gutierrez's departure from Southern California for graduate studies at NYU, she worked a series of jobs in the greater L.A. music and arts community, from her late teen years at the music venue Atomic Café (as a musician with the band Tummyache and as an independent promoter), to her early twenties working at the Album Network and AtomicPop.com (an online record label).[56] In the summer of 2002, Gutierrez acquired a Los Angeles County Arts internship at Highways (setting in motion her efforts to broker the *Tongues* event at the venue, and BdP performances in ensuing years), before continuing on as their house manager until graduate school called in 2003. Rodriguez's deepening involvement in community organizing and AIDS activism, meanwhile, began to inform her sense of some of the limitations of "outreach" available in such organizations bound to the bureaucracies and economies of the city and the state. Together with Garcia and Romero, Gutierrez and Rodriguez made the commitment after reuniting in 2004 to devote as much of their off-work hours building the Butchlalis repertoire and honing their artistic and political mission.

They viewed themselves and their performances as "works in progress," and thus turned their attention to retooling, revising, and expanding some of the sketches from *Teenage Papi* into a more ambitious full-length program, which would include new material written for *Rocking the Macho Cockless*, a 2005 group show and multimedia installation at Highways put together with other artists and performers (including Lynne "JJ Chinois" Chan, D'Lo, Ricky "Daddy Rick" Garcia, Vicky Babuts, Chris Diaz, Jessica Lawless, Felix Endara, Chris Vargas, Riku Matsuda, and Tre Vazquez). The result was truly the "second coming" of *Teenage Papi*. Aptly dubbed *Teenage Papi: The Remix* (performed January 26–29, 2006), the BdP's second full-length show at Highways included a new piece, "Cockfight," that explored the futility and underlying violence of competing butch masculinities, and signaled the ensemble's turn to a performance ethos devoted to butch intimacies. The forms of closeness, support, and care scripted between brown butch dykes in their "remix" of the *Teenage Papi* sketches explored not only the scampish fraternity between "bois" and their imagined communion with iconic figures ranging from Morrissey to Chavela Vargas to Fernando Valenzuela, but also the erotic possibilities of butch-on-butch desire in a piece co-assembled by Rodriguez and Romero, titled "BDSM." A more sustained reading of some of these sketches, including the BdP's "reboot" of the Lolo and Perla characters in the social milieu of a gentrified Silver Lake and Echo Park, is revisited in the coda to *Relocations*.

The ensemble's reputation grew not only as a result of their second full-length performance at Highways (and third BdP-helmed production in the space within the span of a year, including *Rocking the Macho Cockless*), but also because of a fairly vigorous touring schedule, despite their demanding work commitments. After *Teenage Papi: The Remix* at Highways Performance Space, BdP toured in various configurations, securing their first artists' residency in San Jose's MACLA (Movimiento de Arte y Cultura Latino Americana), April 3–9, 2006. Other high-profile shows quickly followed, including a featured performance at the QueLaCo (Queer Latina/o Arts Coalition) National Queer Arts Festival in San Francisco (June 16, 2006), and a stint at the storied biennial queer music, culture, activism, and arts festival Homo A Go Go (August 1–6, 2006) in Olympia, Washington, organized by the legendary transman impresario Ed Varga, and replete (in the BdP's words) with delicious "drrrty White Girls."[57] Not all four members of the BdP could travel to every out-of-town gig, since they were operating on the nonprofit-scaled funding and honoraria from these engagements while pooling their own resources as individuals. As a quartet, the BdP would sometimes tour in altered configurations—as a duo, trio, or in rare cases, as individuals—if certain members could not travel because of financial limitations or time commitments to their day jobs. The ensemble thus created a working format for their full-length productions that could easily be adjusted to available personnel on any given occasion.

Romero, whose preferred medium was photography and video, would appear in the group's slide shows and short films interspersed between live sketches. In the event she couldn't travel or perform because of her work commitments in the service sector, she could still be projected remotely into the performance through set video pieces. Garcia, the BdP member with the most experience and training in acting and singing for the stage, quickly acquired the role of "utility player" and chameleon, taking on parts ranging from an undocumented, male-to-female preoperative transsexual from El Salvador (in the Rodriguez-authored "Cosa Rara" from 2006, currently in redevelopment as a full-length play), to the middle-aged, potbellied, crooked Chicano cop Frank Martinez in *The Barber of East L.A.* (the BdP's first full-length play, authored by Gutierrez in 2007). Rodriguez and Gutierrez, meanwhile, perform the bulk of the writing duties and share the administrative operations for the group, updating the website, booking gigs, applying for grants, and responding to inquiries from arts organizations and academics. Such provisions were not simply an effect of a robust touring schedule booked by

fernando valenzuela's
number was #34,
the same number
as the channel
for spanish language
station, univision...
coincidence?
the BdP Unit
think not.

BdP interstitial slide: "34," 2005. Courtesy of the artists.

Gutierrez (who, as a result of her previous experience in the administrative and DIY aspects of the arts community, became the designated "hustler and flower" of the BdP), but also because of the local circumstances that shaped their collaboration in lesser Los Angeles.

Because each member of the ensemble is bound to different work schedules and situated in disparate locations, the group composes their performance pieces with an eye toward flexibility, functionality, and portability. The production value of their shows is scaled minimally with interchangeable props and set pieces, few costume and makeup changes (many of the costumes are culled from thrift stores or sewn by Gutierrez's mother, an expert seamstress), and portable "scenery" and "effects" in the form of PowerPoint slide projections and cue-ready mix CDs and MP3 playlists for sound tracking as well as scene transitions. Their first two *Teenage Papi* shows impart something of a "latchkey" aesthetic of found pop culture materials from the 1970s, 1980s, and 1990s, gathered from the Internet, captured from television and radio, or incorporated from their own personal accumulation of objects.

This assortment of popular materials easily accessible and "reheatable" through Photoshop and other computer programs befits not only the group's shoestring budget and limited schedule for making art—those with certain software and

BdP promotional image, "Choco-Taco, Represent!," 2004. Courtesy of the artists.
All rights reserved.

computer access at work could put together entire scenescapes during lunch
hours and other downtime—but also a queer suburban aesthetic of "making do"
with popular objects and materials acquired through hours of mass consumption.

As I have argued throughout this book, converting convenience and prefabricated, pret-a-manger materials into art and performance is a hallmark of queer
of color suburban aesthetic practice. The BdP's appearances at queer, or Latino,
or both queer and Latino performance festivals created a uniquely suburban disruption to the thematic programming of each of these events. The BdP, in other
words, not only fulfilled certain representative demands for "race" in a queer context, or "queer" in a Latino context, but made a concerted effort to frustrate desires
for tokenistic models of "good," unproblematic subjecthood by calling attention to what I referred to in my earlier chapter on "Relocating Queer Critique"
as a "dykeasporic," queer suburban sensibility of deeply shallow attachments to
popular objects and their racialized, sexualized potential. Allow me to offer this
illustration as an example, a T-shirt design created for the group by Gutierrez but
later converted into an interstitial slide for *Teenage Papi: The Remix*.

The image works on multiple levels, scrambling several signifying codes, popular styles, and subcultural references. Most immediately striking is the hand-
scrawled, Sharpie-shaped font, evocative of the angular letters found in graffiti
tags. The numbers scrolled together in the second line of text shouts-out the telephone area codes of Los Angeles and its surrounding areas as a play on hip-hop
culture's neighborhood boasting: from the original "213" area code that used to
encompass all of greater Los Angeles, to the 323 and 310 topographically separat-
ing the so-called Eastside ("323" includes gentrified areas like Echo Park, Silver
Lake, and Los Feliz), to the more upscale Westside ("310" incorporates Beverly
Hills, Brentwood, Bel Air, Santa Monica, and other notoriously moneyed neigh-

borhoods). But as Rodriguez clarifies, "What some westsiders don't realize is that 310 also covers South Central and my hometown, Compton."[58] The other area codes completing the "code call" reach farther and farther outward from Southeast L.A. all the way into Long Beach (562), into the suburban capital of porn, the San Fernando Valley (818), and even as far east as the Inland Empire (originally 909, before a 2004 zoning split created the new 951 area code for western Riverside County).

This encompassing display of regional, Southern California pride extends to the Spanish written around the image, from the ensemble's name gesturing to a utopian elsewhere at once a part of and beyond Aztlán, to the invocation of Los Angeles, remapped and reclaimed (in Gutierrez's words) through a "popular thug and Chicano movement place name" for California: "Califas."[59] In her lexicon of *Chicano Folklore*, Rafaela Castro explains that this term of endearment and "proprietariness" toward California can be traced back to the *"pachucos* (1940s youths) in the jargon they developed in the 1930s," which was influenced (according to Mary Ellen Garcia) by Caló, the "criminal argot associated with the gypsies in nineteenth-century Spain."[60] "Califas" is a designation that continues to adorn T-shirts, bumper stickers, and other ephemeral artifacts of "Chicano pride" throughout the Southern California region at swap meets, county fairs, and in neighborhood shops. Meanwhile, the Spanish phrase sandwiched between the roll call of area codes and the place-name, "Los Angeles, Califas," also invokes a twist on a familiar phrase found on signage and product packaging throughout Southern California: instead of "tortillas hechas a mano" (handmade tortillas), the BdP contorts the phrase into "Tortille*ras* Hechas a Mano"—translated roughly as "handmade tortilla-making women." "Tortillera" is Chicano slang for "lesbian." As Alicia Arrizón explains in *Queering Mestizaje: Transculturation and Performance*, "[*Tortillera*] alludes to women making love as analogous to the making of tortillas. The 'clapping' on the hands that traditionally occurs when cooking corn tortillas represents lesbian desire."[61] The BdP not only queers the phrase for fresh, handmade tortillas by inserting this slang variation, but, as Gutierrez explains, the group also gestures to how dykes might be "homegrown" or "homemade" in the Southern California region, from "Los Angeles, Califas," out to the other suburban area codes represented on the graphic. The metal tortilla press depicted visually between the layers of text adds an exclamation to this phrase, alluding at once to female labor, queer sex, and other perverse connotations of "the homegrown."[62]

As we look more closely at the interplay between images, slang, and the slippery registers of meaning in what appears at first to be a fairly simple promotional image, we begin to notice how the BdP confounds fundamental assumptions about their own practices of affiliation through cultural signifiers like "tortilleras," "tacos" (which carries its own slangy, anatomical associations), and even the "handmade." The phrase "hechas a mano" not only alludes to lesbian sex, or the (gendered) painstaking labor of making tortillas by hand—fetishized, perhaps, by creative-class consumers as "artisanal," while simply regarded as repetitive and exhausting by its practitioners—but also is a nod to the DIY ethos preached by punk and riot grrrl subcultures, which the ensemble depicts as both irritating and stimulating in pieces like "drrrty White Girls" and *The Barber of East L.A.* After all, the BdP are themselves participants in a DIY culture as self-producing performers who retain their day jobs while grappling with the nuts and bolts of staging shows—from writing sketches, to booking venues, to making slides, props, promotional images, and costumes. Indeed, in the case of Gutierrez, she acquired some of her skills as one of the BdP's resident impresarios by working in the predominantly white "indie" and punk music scenes during her teen years.

Meanwhile, the "tacos" visually flanking the tortilla press in the BdP's slide are not handmade in any sense of the word. These taco-shaped sugar cones locked in an embrace with vanilla ice cream and fudge are, in fact, the Good Humor ice cream favorite "Choco Tacos." A variation on the ice cream sandwich, Choco Tacos were first concocted in the 1980s by the Jack & Jill Ice Cream Company in Philadelphia in order to tap into the "rage for Tex-Mex fare," according to a *Time* magazine article.[63] For a period of time, Choco Tacos were even available at the fast-food chain Taco Bell.[64] Gutierrez remembers the Choco Taco fondly from her 1980s childhood in the suburbs of Bell Gardens. Dilapidated ice cream trucks sputtering "Dixie" out of tune, and helmed by either Latino or Asian immigrants, would cruise past suburban tract homes and tempt Gutierrez with "something that looked familiar, but oh so different, special and sweet."[65] With this promotional image, the BdP implies that to be a dyke "homegrown" in Southern California's suburbs is to be nurtured and shaped by the commercial simulacra of racial authenticity. In the same way that Lynne Chan as JJ Chinois resignified a Playboy bunny pendant as a "lucky" amulet of Chinese astrology, the BdP reclaim the commercial symbology of the Choco Taco as, at once, expressive of twisted forms of suburban racialization and also a viable means of *self*-expression and rediscovery through mediated suburban objects and landscapes.

The BdP's "Choco Taco, Represent!" image is but one micro-instance in the group's performance archive that transforms commercial objects of the everyday into powerful, ludic symbols for the transcultural lived experiences of queer of color suburban subjects. As the BdP built their repertoire in the years 2006–2008, the ensemble turned increasingly to other "found objects" from popular genres like movies, TV, and popular music as the foundation for their work. Their sketches and films, which began to develop in length and scope into feature-length projects, focused not only on the different meanings to be culled from popular objects but also on *how* these objects are transformed both in and through their consumption in specific settings, from the home, to the streets, to the disappeared social spaces of lesser Los Angeles.

"Fat Chocha Ghetto Gurl"

"Fat Chocha Ghetto Gurl," a "meta-piece" in BdP's third full-length Highways program, *BdP Get U.G.L.Y.* (February 23–24, 2007), reflects on the ensemble's collaborative process as individuals commuting to make art together in the Southern California landscape. As Rodriguez and Gutierrez explain, "Fat Chocha Ghetto Gurl" was inspired by the improvisational, inebriated scampishness of Cheech and Chong's cult films from the 1970s and 1980s, which played repeatedly on late-night TV when they were growing up.[66] The Cheech Marin and Tommy Chong oeuvre, as Rosalinda Fregoso explains, employs "improvisational parody" and "satirical portraits of various ethnic/racial groups and subcultures in California (surfers, dopers, hippies, mystics, nationalists, motorcycle club members, and so on)."[67] As the title suggests, "Fat Chocha Ghetto Gurl" plays on the same "self-derogatory ethnic humor" Cheech and Chong mobilized in their comedy while referencing different modes of consumption—from watching trash films, to drinking beer, to listening to one another "shoot the shit."[68]

"Fat Chocha Ghetto Gurl" is set in an apartment—exact coordinates unspecified—although Gutierrez's apartment in Historic Filipinotown (or "HiFi") at the time served as the actual location for the off-the-cuff shoot. The piece came about as the group tinkered with Rodriguez's new MacBook during one of their regularly scheduled writing meetings and rehearsals.[69] While sharing a few beers, they began to take pictures of themselves on the Apple Photo Booth application (which recreates the effect of photo booth–style filmstrips using successive snapshots taken with the computer's built-in camera). On the spot, the group came up with the idea to string together a narrative from these images and the anecdotes they told one another in the interstitial moments between "actual work." Thus their collectively indulgent, slacker break from labor became the material for the work itself.[70]

"Fat Chocha Ghetto Gurl" takes the form of what the BdP calls a DIY "fotonovela": an assemblage of low-resolution pictures snapped in the Photo Booth application, combined with a conversational track recorded in Apple's GarageBand audio program, and edited together in iMovie. Historically, the fotonovela emerged as a popular form throughout Latin America in the twentieth century and blossomed within the romance fiction market first directed at middle-class women, then ultimately broadened to a mass female readership.[71] As scholars of Latin American popular culture have noted, this mass, feminized iteration of the fotonovela in the Latin American market has, in recent years, begun to cater to an adolescent male market with the subgenre of the *fotonovela picaresca*, or "picaresque fotonovela," which is more bawdy and sexually explicit.[72] Meanwhile, in the United States, Chicano artists like Harry Gamboa Jr. have adopted the format with an eye toward politicizing the popular idiom by "blend[ing] identity, politics, relationships, and philosophy in a sort of photo-graphic poetry."[73] Throughout Southern California and beyond, the fotonovela form has also been incorporated into activist and community-based programs "as an organizational tool for outreach, education, and proselytizing."[74]

The BdP's "Fat Chocha Ghetto Gurl" could be said to fit thematically within the picaresque subgenre of the fotonovela, although the piece departs formally from both the traditional fotonovela as well as more contemporary, politicized Chicano/a approaches to the genre, by splicing the images together in a moving picture format (like a timed slide show), and by using recorded dialogue instead of conversation balloons or captions. Instead of conceptualizing their fotonovela as something more cutting-edge, however, the group imagines the project as a happy, lo-fi accident, an evocation accomplished through play and a certain level of cluelessness about how certain Mac applications work. The piece thus capitalizes on the herky-jerky "flipbook" aesthetic coincidentally mimicked by the slide transitions between photos in the Photo Booth application, even as it blends together certain incongruous elements of fotonovela subgenres, from its fleeting focus on female desire and romance, to its studious turns to space and community as well as lapses into ribald, teen-style sex banter.

The story of "Fat Chocha Ghetto Gurl" focuses on one of the BdP members (Rodriguez) arriving late for a meeting and interrupting a living room turned waiting room scene. The other members are reclining, and beer bottles and other leisurely accoutrements are scattered on the coffee-table. Rodriguez intrudes on this slacking with a typical Southern California excuse about traffic on the freeway. Soon enough the real reason for her tardiness is revealed: a sexual encounter. The character played by Rodriguez has just been fisted, and each of the other BdP "fellas" (Garcia, Romero, and Gutierrez) reacts to the tale with taunting and hazing. Some are "grossed out" and drop clever one-liners about their own stance on butch sexual practices and how much play one's own "chocha" (slang for the vagina) should receive. Others are inspired to share their own stories of "rough play." Intermittently, the background noises of consumption—clinking bottles, gurgling bong water, incidental music—score the conversation. Some speak in slightly slurred voices, while others assume a laid-back tone as the vicissitudes of brown butch desire are mulled over in the casual conversation. The piece captures an improvisational feel, but is it in fact constructed: the dialogue is scripted (Garcia's parts are obviously being read aloud at one moment, and the stiltedness of its delivery is assimilated into the humor and implied intoxication of the scene), and the photographic, "flipbook" slideshow is blocked and collated into sequential order.

"Fat Chocha Ghetto Gurl" dwells on buffoonery rather than innovation, which is underscored when the piece crescendos to its conclusion with a drunken sing-along. The song we hear is not a prerecorded or preexisting piece from the radio or an album, but begins like a schoolyard chant. After Rodriguez completes her sordid tale of sexual encounter, Gutierrez's character calls Rodriguez's character out for being the "Fat Chocha Ghetto Gurl" of the fotonovela's title. Gutierrez sings the line "fat chocha ghetto gurl" in a simple a cappella melody that tonally resembles a mash-up of the "na na na na na naaaa na" schoolyard taunt and the mid-1980s dance hit "Don Quichotte" by Magazine 60. The other voices in the background begin to join the chorus, including Rodriguez's, as a homemade GarageBand freestyle beat is layered into the group chanting of "fat chocha ghetto gurl, fat chocha ghetto gurl!" The chant accelerates and the fotonovela freezes on an image of the quartet making silly faces.

The BdP appropriates the "buffoonery" traditionally played by male comedians like Cheech Marin and Tommy Chong for a brown butch imaginary. As scholars of Chicano/Latino media and film like Christine List and Stephanie Greco Larson have noted, Cheech and Chong were at the forefront of subversively recuperating a stereotypical figure like the "Hispanic buffoon" (the object of derision in Hollywood cinema and television because "he speaks English so badly") by making him the star.[75] The BdP mimics this gesture by placing themselves (or a parodic version of themselves) at the center of "Fat Chocha Ghetto Gurl" as buffoonish stars. Any lesbian sense of "sisterhood" is turned on its ear in the fraternal razzing featured in "Fat Chocha Ghetto Gurl." And yet the fotonovela also offers its own version of a twisted sisterhood by focusing on how a butch dyke's embodied "femaleness"—specifically her "chocha"—functions in sexual negotiations and encounters beyond the intimate space of private parties that ensue in lieu of work. "Fat Chocha Ghetto Gurl" in form as well as content harnesses certain perversions that transpire in ostensibly private spaces like the "home" and the "suburbs," while also archiving the sedentariness and consumption that transpires in these private spaces (sitting around, doing nothing). As a meta-reflection on their own aesthetic practice, the failure to "go anywhere"— with their work at the meeting, or beyond the confines of the apartment—actually becomes the generative material for "something else," for another kind of labor and aesthetic practice not foreclosed but rather enabled by waiting and sitting in an apartment or in traffic, and amplified by derelict consumption.[76]

BdP Get U.G.L.Y., featuring "Fat Chocha Ghetto Gurl" among other pieces, proved to be one of the ensemble's most successful programs at Highways Performance Space (with two sold-out evenings), and one of their last full-length performances as a quartet before Romero's departure. As much as the BdP's earlier material concentrated on "adolescence," queer "boi-dom," and the pleasure and pain of arrested development, the ensemble took a thematic turn in *BdP Get U.G.L.Y.* toward intergenerational contact and the archives generated by these encounters. This change in their work also resulted in a formal adjustment, as the ensemble began to make a concerted effort to think through a full-length play. At the audience "talk-back" and Q&A session we conducted together onstage after their *BdP Get U.G.L.Y.* show at Highways (I was the moderator), Gutierrez was questioned about the ensemble's archival energies, and whether it heralded the group's "selling out" to more conventional formats and desires. She responded by asking audience members:

> What's to say being experimental and working in short form isn't also a privilege for many artists? It's a way of expressing an "edge" even if you have all the resources in the world. Like any form of artistic expression, short form can be used by poseurs looking to manufacture a subcultural attitude. Long form can seem like a bourgie aspiration, but honestly isn't the tension between subcultural lives and mainstream desires part of what makes our work troublesome as well as entertaining? Dykes of color—the characters in our shows—have fewer options about what they can and should do, how they can and should "represent" or be, in order to be properly political and righteous. But it's way more complicated than that. Sometimes we want and desire things that aren't going to mesh with what we're supposed to be happy and content with, or what's supposed to make us seem "cutting edge." . . .
> Working in long form is something we [the BdP] rarely have the luxury for. As much as we're totally proud of the work we've created after hours and on weekends, why shouldn't we crave a more sustained process where we can develop these characters, their back stories and the histories that made them as well as us?[277]

The contradictory elements that can be traced back to BdP's performance of "improper desires" in their "drrrty White Girls" sketch, or through their predilection for "inauthentic" treats like Choco Tacos, and soundscapes from elsewhere like those provided by Morrissey, resurfaces as a theme in Gutierrez's comments about the ensemble's transition into full-length pieces. As she implies, the ensemble resists liberal desires from both within and without their own constituencies that seek to locate righteous forms of suffering within queer brown bodies. In other words, the BdP refuse to "represent," or perform righteous suffering—that is, accepting less as a badge of honor, rather than exposing the systemic problems with valorizing the deprivation of resources within certain communities—even as they grapple in explicit ways with the problems of representing race, sexuality, and desire in their performances. Subsequently, their first full-length play, *The Barber of East L.A.* (first staged as a working production in April 2008), not only endeavored to archive certain lost histories but also reflected on how something like a "queer Latino/a" past proves more convoluted and contentious than certain liberal imaginaries might admit.

The Barber of East L.A.

During the *BdP Get U.G.L.Y.* program of 2007, the ensemble debuted a documentary interview with the Chicana butch legend Nancy Valverde—a community leader originally from East L.A. who was active in various scenes throughout the 1970s and 1980s. The ensemble first met Valverde at the same Bienestar lesbian support group in Montebello where they all connected as strangers. In the early 1980s, Valverde owned a barbershop in East L.A just down the street from the legendary community space Self-Help Graphics.[78] Her tales of being thrown into the "daddy tank" (a quarantine in L.A.'s local jails for butch women who were busted during police raids at local lesbian bars) influenced several of BdP's sketches—including the aptly titled "Daddy Tank," performed in both *BdP Get U.G.L.Y.* and the traveling program *Dickwhipped* (fall 2007). The personal history Valverde shared with the group about her experiences as a butch dyke struggling and sometimes even thriving in the sexist and heterosexist milieu of the Chicano movement in East. L.A. during the early 1980s inspired BdP's *The Barber of East L.A.* As Rodriguez and Gutierrez explained at the Q&A session for *BdP Get U.G.L.Y.*, their numerous interactions and collaborations with Valverde prompted them to think in more sustained ways about how their performances might function archivally. Rodriguez remarked that "in addition to documenting how butches laugh, love, and play, we also pay close attention to the everyday political movements and acts from the past that made it both possible and impossible to do what we do now."[79]

In the summer and fall of 2007, after winning a grant through the Visions and Voices Arts and Humanities Initiative at the University of Southern California (for which Gutierrez applied in her capacity as the assistant director of the Center for Feminist Research),[80] Gutierrez began to write *The Barber of East L.A.* Because the grant did not include substantial stipends, all the BdP members (reconstituted as a trio after Romero's departure) continued to work their day jobs while writing, rehearsing, and ultimately performing the production at USC. One of the primary features of the grant included the opportunity to solicit experienced collaborators, and the BdP selected two well-known Latino artists based in Southern California.

Their first collaborator was the visual artist Hector Silva, who lives and works in Pomona and commutes regularly to art venues all over greater Los Angeles for solo and group shows. Known internationally as an emblematic L.A. artist, Silva's work reinvents and queers what Richard T. Rodriguez describes as the "homeboy aesthetic."[81] Not only did Silva custom-create a set piece for *The Barber of East L.A.*, but he also premiered a retrospective of his own prolific body of work, including the historical ephemera surrounding it (i.e., a fan letter from

Lucille Ball, an invitation from Mayor Villaraigosa to design a piece for the city's arts calendar, and early photographs of his installations and decorative work in the city's gay discos frequented by such queer icons as Freddie Mercury, Diana Ross, and Grace Jones, among others). Silva and BdP initiated their collaboration during the *BdP Get U.G.L.Y.* era, when Silva asked to photograph and sketch the ensemble as part of his own efforts to expand his repertoire of sexy queer thugs to include queer female "homebois."[82]

The second collaborator of their choosing was the renowned Chicano playwright, dramaturge, and MacArthur Foundation fellow Luis Alfaro, who was, at the time, in residence at USC as a visiting lecturer in the School of Theater. Born and raised in the Pico-Union district of downtown Los Angeles (situated near the university), Alfaro is a prolific playwright and an acclaimed director and producer who acts in productions for film, television, and the stage. In 2002, he was awarded the Kennedy Center Fund for New American Plays twice, for *Electricidad* (a retelling of Sophocles's Electra set in contemporary East L.A.) and *Breakfast, Lunch, and Dinner*. Working with Alfaro had been a goal for the ensemble, who always admired his writing about local cultures, and his groundbreaking work building community resources in L.A.'s landmark venues, such as the Mark Taper Forum (where he cofounded the Latino Theater Initiative with Diane Rodriguez). The ensemble enlisted Alfaro to direct the play, workshop manuscript drafts, and provide formal movement training. Aside from Garcia, none of the other BdP members received acting training of any kind prior to their collaboration with Alfaro. Working with Alfaro presented the ensemble their first opportunity to be directed, trained, and mentored by a luminary in the dramatic arts, after spending their formative years handling all facets of production on their own.

Alfaro created a signature look for the production of *The Barber of East L.A.* by transposing the ensemble's lack of regular resources and frequent touring schedule into the stage design. Everything—like the ensemble's sketch-driven and self-produced work—was built to be portable, minimal, and easy-to-stage regardless of the space, from college lecture halls to fully equipped theaters. The focal set piece, upstage center, is a tall assemblage of tables with an assortment of wigs perched atop "unisex" foam heads. The wigs are not only props but also costumes donned by members of the ensemble at key moments to transition between the multiple parts (eleven total) split between the three of them. Each member is clad simply, in black pants and white T-shirts to start, before they cover their undershirts with white barber smocks for the duration of the play. As with their previous productions, projected slides and music alert the audience to the setting for each scene, although in the Alfaro-helmed premiere the slides were rescaled and reoriented in the shape and form of supertitles projected above the

Promotional flier (front) for *The Barber of East L.A.* and Hector Silva Retrospective for the University of Southern California Visions and Voices Series, 2008. Courtesy of the artists and the University of Southern California. All rights reserved.

Butchlalis de Panochtitlan

THE
Barber of
EAST L.A.

Directed by
Luis Alfaro

TWO NIGHTS ONLY!

Friday, April 11, 7 to 9 p.m. & Saturday, April 12, 6 to 8 p.m.
Ground Zero Performance Café, USC

The Saturday performance will be followed by the opening reception for the Hector Silva Retrospective. See below for details.

Admission is free. Reservations requested. RSVP at www.usc.edu/visionsandvoices.

Butchlalis de Panochtitlan (BdP) is a multimedia ensemble that explores stories of love, loss, work and play in the queer-of-color communities of Los Angeles and its sub-urban peripheries. In *The Barber of East L.A.*, their first full-length play, directed by MacArthur Fellow Luis Alfaro, the group calls Chicano history into question while tipping their hats to the Chicano punk scene and the rise of grassroots spaces. *The Barber of East L.A.* weaves outsider narratives into a striking tapestry and honors BdP's predecessors by sharing local histories as they collide with mainstream and underground records.

HECTOR SILVA RETROSPECTIVE

Saturday, April 12 through Tuesday, May 20
OPENING RECEPTION: **Saturday, April 12, 8:30 p.m.**
ONE National Gay and Lesbian Archives
909 West Adams Boulevard

Hector Silva's work is erotic, playful and politically charged. This retrospective will feature the entire range of Silva's work and the historical ephemera surrounding it, including his correspondence with Lucille Ball and early photographs of his decorative work in gay Los Angeles discos frequented by such icons as Freddie Mercury, Diana Ross and Grace Jones.

Presented as part of the series Records y *Recuerdos*: Music and Memory in Queer East L.A., organized by Karen Tongson (English) and Raquel Gutierrez (Center for Feminist Research). Co-sponsored by the ONE National Gay and Lesbian Archives, the LGBT Resource Center, the Popular Music Project at the USC Norman Lear Center and *Makeshift* Magazine.

For more information, please visit our website or contact us at visionsandvoices@usc.edu or (213) 740-6786.

VISIONS AND VOICES
The USC Arts & Humanities Initiative

USC UNIVERSITY OF
SOUTHERN CALIFORNIA

WWW.USC.EDU/VISIONSANDVOICES

Promotional flier (back), *The Barber of East L.A.* and Hector Silva Retrospective for the University of Southern California Visions and Voices Series, 2008. Courtesy of the artists and the University of Southern California. All rights reserved.

stage. A massive banner featuring a sketch of the ensemble by Hector Silva (in which each member brandishes tools of the barber trade) usually flanks the stage, depending on the setup of each venue. At the premiere of *The Barber of East L.A.*, the banner filled out the wall adjacent to stage right. The music for the show—itself another "character" as well as an element of setting—was curated by Gutierrez, who incorporated as-told-to histories of the Hollywood and East L.A. punk scene into the play's narrative about space, gender, sexuality, and longing.[83]

Staging their minimalist fare at USC, which is geographically closer to downtown, South Central, and parts of East Los Angeles than the Highways Performance Space, was envisioned by the ensemble as a unique opportunity to diminish the commute many of their audience members would take from the greater Eastside and the outer reaches of L.A.'s eastern suburbs to Santa Monica. Because of the subsidies the grant provided, *The Barber of East L.A.* ran for free admission, a situation not previously afforded by their self-produced shows at Highways. Even though the event was scheduled to be held at an institution—the university—rather than a community art space, the BdP hoped they could broaden their audiences while also making their show more geographically and financially accessible to their core audience of young queers of color. Additional draws of the Visions and Voices grant included supplementary public events like workshops and "listening parties" leading up to the play's premiere.[84] Further, the ensemble saw their partnership with USC's Visions and Voices program as an occasion to open up institutions like the private university by "infiltrating" its stellar lineup of established artists and speakers with local, independent, and queer of color community artists.

Recording Queer Movement(s)

Scripting a whole new cast of characters and combining them with others who debuted in previous sketches at Highways, including an older butch nicknamed "Chonch" and her group of friends, lovers, and adversaries, *The Barber of East L.A.* explores how queer of color histories intersect with both mainstream and underground events and movements in East L.A., while also begging the question of how records of the underground—both historical *and* musical—are made, in addition to how they might ultimately survive. Thematically, the play explores the "prehistory" of urban gentrification, and what Gutierrez calls the "disappearance" of queer Chicanos and Chicanas from the official records of East L.A.'s activist subcultures, including within the Chicano punk scene that gathered at grassroots, mixed-use spaces like the Vex and Self-Help Graphics.[85] Framed historically by the National Chicano Moratorium against the Vietnam War, the death of the Mexican American journalist Rubén Salazar at an anti-war protest in 1970, and the impending election of Ronald Reagan to the White House in 1980, *The Barber of East L.A.* dramatizes what Gutierrez describes as the "draconian gender policing" of queer communities of color by local law enforcement in the streets and social spaces of Los Angeles. Sometimes this policing and violence happened between and among Chicanos as well as at the hands of "outsiders" in East L.A.

Before the narrative of *The Barber of East L.A.* unfolds, the play opens with a prologue performed by the trio in the alternating unison of a Greek chorus:

ALL:	Every barrio has its drama!
ONE:	Cada Barrio tiene su fama!
TWO:	Every 'hood has a creation myth
THREE:	Every 'hood would plead the fifth
ONE:	Every neighborhood has its story
TWO:	Tales of defeat
THREE:	Tales of Glory
ONE:	The people gone and lost their shame
TWO & THREE:	When Brooklyn Avenue changed its name
TWO:	The people gone and lost their faith
ONE & THREE:	Just as all of Watts went up in flames
THREE:	The people scarred by an open wound
ONE & TWO:	Cut deep in the shallow waters of Sleepy Lagoon
ALL:	But there's one thing every barrio has
TWO:	And in every barrio she's been harassed
THREE:	You've seen her in your neighborhood
ONE:	Camina asi con actitud
ALL:	There's a butch in every barrio
	There's a butch in every 'hood
	Every barrio has its macha
	Not every barrio treats her good
TWO:	So the story you'll be seeing
THREE:	Is the condition of human being
ONE:	As queers come back into the fold
ALL:	When the big gay city just gets too cold
TWO:	San Francisco ain't for me
THREE:	New York City? Too gritty!
ONE:	West Hollywood? [Pause.]
ALL:	no!
ONE:	Make the home we can never return to
TWO:	Confront the whispers and the stares
THREE:	Ignore the gossip and tall tales

ALL:	Every 'hood has its name
	Every 'hood has its fame
ONE:	Now we proclaim
THREE:	What of East L.A. a butch became
TWO:	Cease the self-hate, no longer we wait!
ONE:	We shan't self-negate, it's time to create!
ALL:	A butch hero so great!

[FADE TO BLACK; MUSIC CUE: The Duprees'"Daddy's Home."][86]

The prologue establishes the tension between feeling "at home" within one's own ethnic enclave and being ostracized for brandishing one's butch, female body in the '"hood." Queer figures, and in this particular instance, the butch dyke, are excluded from other masculinist, cultural nationalist narratives of heroism scripted into the affective topography of the barrio or the neighborhood.[87] But leaving is not a viable option either. The prologue maps itself against queer topographical narratives locating "safety," acceptance, and freedom within emblematic queer cities, by establishing the brown butch's preference for *her* 'hood over the implicitly "cold" and indifferent "big gay city" (e.g., San Francisco and New York—or for that matter, the big gay neighborhood in L.A., West Hollywood).

The intergenerational protagonists at the center of the play, Chonch Fonseca (an older butch returning to the barrio after jail time and a stint at Moler Barber College) and Betty Basta (a bisexual high-school student and aspiring punk rock star), embody the competing queer trajectories of staying or leaving, of returning or fleeing. While the play features an expansive cast of characters played exclusively by the three members of the ensemble, the relationship between Chonch (Gutierrez) and Betty (Rodriguez) is pivotal to understanding *The Barber of East L.A.*'s commentary on space and sentiment. The encounters between Chonch and Betty are mediated through the ghostly presence of Isabel "Chiquis" Velasquez (Garcia), who appears primarily in flashback: Isabel is Chonch's dead lover, as well as Betty's "Aunt Izzy," the woman who raised Betty. Both Chonch and Betty have a chip on their shoulder about the barrio's failure to nurture their dreams and desires. And yet both, through Izzy/Chiquis, find their pathways by what the barrio makes possible through accidental forms of activism and everyday gestures of protest.

Chonch, like her historical precedent, Nancy Valverde, opens a barbershop in East L.A. on Brooklyn and Rowan as she resolves to take back her barrio:

I'm the barber! And I'm going back, yes sir, to the streets that put the yellow in me in the first place.... Back on Herbert Avenue, I'm going to see how I can [stage dir.: takes a hit off a joint] contribute to the informal economy.... Then I will claim a Winchell's for my morning *cafecito*, and the roach coach on Whittier and Soto for my afternoon torta, and nobody's gonna get me down about it. Do

193   The Light That Never Goes Out

what I do in my barrio—just like you do what you do in your barrio—without somebody saying something about it. . . . I am going back to all those streets to work the pain. The pain is never going to work me. *Ya versa.* . . . I am going to see a little piece of the world with my name on it. Rub me out all you want, but you're never going to run me out of here.[88]

Chonch's expulsion from the barrio as a young *jota* comes as a consequence of a crooked cop's wicked machinations. Officer Frank Martinez (Garcia) frames Chonch for a violent crime, but she is released from jail because the charges "didn't stick."[89] Returning, then, is not simply a matter of neighborhood pride. After all, the neighborhood in which she was busted repeatedly for "masquerading" in men's clothes, and harassed by family and friends, never actively sought to keep her. Returning becomes Chonch's gesture of defiance and reclamation. She comes back not only because she's "got nowhere else to go" (to paraphrase Richard Gere's infamous line in *An Officer and a Gentleman*), but also because she refuses to relinquish her own desire for, and claim to, the everydayness of a place and way of life scripted as both impossible and undesirable for queers: morning coffee at the Winchell's chain donut shop and a lunch-break sandwich from the neighborhood "roach coach." Chonch never wanted anything all that complicated, but the complications that ensue as a result of her "choice" to live openly as a "bulldagger" make the mundane all the more appealing, make the familiar all the more remarkable.

Further, Chonch's stubborn attachments to the everyday were formulated during her relationship with Izzy/Chiquis, when she cultivated her own American daydreams of a "good life" beyond the barrio after Chiquis received her beauty school certificate:

CHONCH:	You deserve the best *mariachis, Chiquis.* The best of everything. [Looks nervously over her shoulder.]
CHIQUIS:	No one is looking, baby.
CHONCH:	Yeah?
CHIQUIS:	Let them look.
CHONCH:	*Te quiero llevar bien lejos de aqui.*
CHIQUIS:	*Llevame, baby. No quiero regresar.*
CHONCH:	To the desert. The mountains.
CHIQUIS:	Riverside?
CHONCH:	Riverside.[90]

Chonch's lack of ease when she hits the town with Chiquis is scripted into the blocking of the scene, as she nervously looks over her shoulder. Meanwhile, the allusion to the Inland Empire town of Riverside as a final destination in the couple's pursuit of happiness is meant, at once, to be a joke and heartbreakingly sincere. Local, contemporary audiences would understand the reference to Riverside—hard-hit by the recent recession, home foreclosures, and unemployment—as truly the "road to nowhere," an ill-fated choice for these queer lovers canoodling in East L.A. in the 1970s. Yet within this flashback scene between Chonch and Chiquis, Riverside remains a sweet, untarnished dream—much as it was for many other Latinos during that era who were lured by lower property values and the promise of being left alone by the LAPD as they made their way deeper into the desert fringes beyond Los Angeles. Eventually, Chiquis does "leave" the barrio, but not in the way she dreamed she would with Chonch.

Chiquis dies from a drug overdose after a series of violent events compel her to find other means of distraction and departure. As Chonch explains to Betty in "Betty and the Barber" (scene 6):

CHONCH: You were a little girl when Chiquis graduated from beauty school—your family had a party for her. I wasn't invited on account of my . . . *condition*. So Chiquis and me had our own little celebration together down at *ese* little Redheadz bar on *la primera*.

It was supposed to be one drink. But Chiquis could sure put them away. We were feeling the tequila and decided we needed privacy. We walk out, three blocks, and we're followed by these *vatos*. I knew one of them so I thought we'd be okay. Chato. He was flying. He was my little brother's homeboy that got hooked in Viet Nam and stayed on the junk any way he could.

[. . .]

CHONCH: These *pendejos*. They didn't like the way me *y tu tía* looked together. Like she was too pretty . . .

BETTY: To be with a barber?

CHONCH: Precisely. Too pretty to be with a barber.

BETTY: Did they call you names? They call me names at school, ugh—

CHONCH: You can't leave it alone, can you, little girl? You're so grown now and you think that's all there is to it? To get called names? I wish it was just names, 'cuz some days I think that *jota maricona* must be my first and last name and it don't feel so bad. Beats a steel toe to the ribs. Throwing up blood just as those boys went straight for their fucking *pingas*, 'cuz they were killing us for kicks. I don't think you really want me to tell you what Chato did to poor Isabel while they made me watch. Do you, Betty?

[. . .]

BETTY: Now I know why I hate this place so much!

CHONCH: This place is all I know.[91]

Even as Chonch rails against the violence she both endures and enacts in order to protect herself and Chiquis from a homophobic crime (she cuts Chato "into hamburger . . . but he didn't die"),[92] she cannot completely condemn her neighborhood, which is all she knows. In a material and affective economy where a brother's friend—destroyed by fighting the Vietnam War—becomes your enemy in a vicious skirmish on the streets you share, the roles of "victim" and "oppressor" are not easily designated. Chonch does not justify violent retaliation, or excuse Chato for sexually assaulting Izzy/Chiquis because of the hardships he endured in and beyond the barrio as a Chicano male conscripted into the military. Rather, she gestures toward the shared structural violences enacted by the state that effectively quarantine and tenuously bind her and Chato together in the barrio, where they unleash competing versions of despair, desire, and aspiration on one another. As Raúl Homero Villa explains in *Barrio Logos: Space and Place in Urban Chicano Literature and Culture*, "The barrio was not then, nor is it now, a space of pure security and wholly positive cultural practices. Griswold de Castillo reminds us of this when he notes that even as the barrio represented 'a place of familial warmth and brotherhood, it was also a place of poverty, crime, illness, and despair.' . . . This qualification avoids shining a singularly idealizing light upon barrio culture that would render its manifestations as always necessarily positive or politically contestative."[93]

In this pivotal scene between Chonch and Betty in *The Barber of East L.A.*, each negotiates her complicated relationship to the barrio as a queer of color. But Chonch's exposition of the story behind Chiquis's decline—the mortal consequences of a drug addiction that mimicked that of her oppressor—also functions as a pedagogical intervention for Betty. Bereft after losing her Aunt Izzy (Chonch's Chiquis), Betty struggles without any answers, and founders without the queer family structure of Aunt Izzy and "her bulldagger," who nurtured her as a kid.[94] As she explains to her best fag friend, Julian, "Izzy was there when my mom left. She gave me all the Tang and raw weenies I wanted so I wouldn't feel bad."[95] Betty approaches Chonch at the barbershop looking for answers, seeking some resolution in the barrio after she plots her escape to Hollywood with Julian. Chonch intuits this and takes Betty to task: "Oh, I get it. You wanna leave this godforsaken barrio with a clear conscience."[96] But despite her own tendency to be reticent, Chonch reluctantly obliges Betty's search for the missing pieces of their shared histories that propel the play's competing queer trajectories of staying or leaving.

Asked by Betty why she disappeared from the barrio for such a long time only to return now, Chonch insists: "That's what happens with the past. Things, people, and places just stay put where they belong."[97] For a brief moment, Chonch, the butch bearer of history in *The Barber of East L.A.*, disentangles herself from the past. In this context, to "belong" is not to move on, and she exempts herself from that static economy of belonging when she explains why she left East L.A. during the time Izzy/Chiquis was wasting away with addiction. For a moment, she and Betty switch positionalities: Betty, whose foot is practically out the door toward a new life in Hollywood, remembers she is the one who "got left" by both Chonch and her departed Aunt Izzy. "Why did you leave?," she asks Chonch, as she grasps toward the past and a fragment of belonging—of belonging to Chonch and Chiquis as their "Betita" ("little Betty"). She is, after all, the little niece Chonch helped raise as Chiquis' butch "daddy."[98] Chonch, meanwhile, revisits her moment of departure, her moment of flight from a place that consumed Izzy/Chiquis. But their role switching, between being the one who leaves and the one who gets left behind, is short-lived, as they come to realize that both of them were in effect left by Izzy/Chiquis. As Chonch observes, "Hey, how about that? I always get left, too."[99] Neither has actually resolved to come or go, and that is what brings them together to put shattered fragments of memory together in Chonch's barbershop. Indeed, Izzy/Chiquis may have taken the only true way out of the queer conundrum between staying or leaving the barrio after all.

Their coincidental, familial bond, improvised in the past through Izzy's mediation—Chonch remembers that "Isabel . . . would have us all playing house"[100]—resurfaces in the scene at the barbershop through Chonch's retelling of the story leading up to Izzy/Chiquis's demise. The figure of Izzy/Chiquis manifests once again as a mediating force that brings Chonch and Betty together to reconsider what the barrio means to each of them. Betty learns something through her narrative exchange with Chonch, not only about her aunt but also about her own ambivalent relationship to the barrio. Betty Basta (her punk-inspired last name translates to "enough") thinks East L.A. is a place that refuses to let her creativity blossom: she's an aspiring poet who, with Julian (also played by Gutierrez), dreams of making it big in a punk rock band called the Toxic Crayons. For Betty, punk promises another kind of life in a mythologized "Hollywood" beyond an East L.A. she feels she knows all too well. She and Julian fantasize about tearing "Hollywood to shreds" and opening for local punk iconoclasts like the Germs and the Bags.[101] Even though the Vex, a storied East L.A., all-ages punk venue hosted by Self-Help Graphics, is right around the corner, Betty and Julian swear they'll never play there:

BETTY AND JULIAN:	We'll never play at the Vex.
BETTY:	Because you gotta have a gross dirty cock to get a gig at the Vex.
JULIAN:	And I love gross dirty cock! But *that* won't get us a gig.[102]

Of course, the ephemeral history of the Vex is far more complicated, and the venue actually served as a locus of queer, female experimentation (both aesthetic and otherwise). This queer, female history of East L.A. punk was recently documented in the expansive 2008 exhibit at the Claremont Museum of Art, *Vexing: Female Voices from East L.A. Punk*.[103] Curated by Pilar Tompkins and Colin Gunckel, *Vexing* offered "an historical investigation of the women who were at the forefront of this movement of experimentation in music, art, culture, and social politics, while exploring their lasting legacies and contemporary practices."[104] In fact, BdP's *The Barber of East L.A.* (within months of its premiere at USC) served as one of the feature performances in the *Vexing* program as an imaginary archive of queer participation in the scene. On a meta-level, Betty and Julian's disparaging remarks about the Vex call attention to the belatedness of histories that only recently began to recognize and prioritize the creative contributions of women like Diane Gamboa, Teresa Covarrubias, and Alice Bag (among many others) to the East L.A. art and punk scenes. Meanwhile, the play itself strives to perform this reparative work by conjuring a queer and feminist history of the scene through its story line about Betty and Julian. In the drama, the pair's disillusionment with the Vex stems from their libidinal restlessness and adolescent curiosity about elsewheres, which prompts them to reevaluate whether young queers like themselves will ever manage to leave a mark on a scene they envision is masculine and straight.

As a teen dreamer, Betty trades in an economy of words, music, and fantasy. When audiences are first introduced to her character in scene 5 of *The Barber of East L.A.*, "Los Punks," Betty is reading her own maudlin and pretentious poetry and song lyrics aloud to Julian. Not unlike some of the adolescent-minded characters we encountered in BdP's earlier sketches, Betty and Julian trade witty repartee, replete with references to pop products and icons from TV and movies as well as punk idols on the L.A. scene: they chug Lucky Lager together in the Alpha Beta grocery store parking lot in Bell Gardens, tell lurid asides about the 1980s screen hunk who eventually died of AIDS, Brad Davis, and lust after, respectively, Alice Bag (of the Bags), and Darby Crash (of the Germs)—their very own damaged, punk heartthrobs. Betty and Julian's distaste for their "unglamorous" life in the barrio also extends to a certain self-hating rhetoric about being Mexican. Betty calls Alice Bag "the only Mexican I have ever admired," while Julian rails against the "skinny and sad Mexican boys around here who won't let me love them."[105] In the very next breath, however, Julian pants over a neighborhood boy named Billie Rincon: "He is my *indio* punk rock Brad Davis! And he could stick his cactus *nopal* needles in me anytime."[106] Although Betty and Julian may seem to seek their sexual utopias elsewhere, their playful, self-referential, and racially (in)sensitive remarks indicate that they at least imagine some provisional, disidentificatory relationship to their neighborhood and their peers.[107] Their ambivalence toward the barrio, toward "Mexicans," and toward themselves, in other words, cannot simply be regarded as another instance in which queers search for "liberation" beyond the racialized enclave. Instead, *The Barber of East L.A.* stages the tension between refusing to stay and refusing to leave as a historical matter, one that remains perpetually in negotiation between and among intergenerational queers of color.

Betty's vision of the barrio is juvenile in spirit, if not necessarily naïve, and Chonch's matter-of-fact approach to her own history is meant to break Betty of her youthful narcissism and poetic self-indulgence. Betty's response to Chonch's story about the gruesome events on the night of Izzy's beauty school graduation—"Now I know why I hate this place so much!"—implies that she may not have had a grasp on why she hated it before. Sure, Betty is "called names" by kids at school, but Chonch's belated retelling of her and Chiquis's conflicts in the barrio becomes a dramatic foil for Betty's adolescent self-righteousness. When Chonch asks Betty if she "thinks that's all there is to it," she calls attention to Betty's pose of queer exceptionalism, an attitude formed as a reaction to her feelings of exclusion within the barrio and among her "own people." During their confrontation at Chonch's barbershop on Brooklyn Avenue, Chonch juxtaposes her own history of violence—"a steel toe to the ribs"—with Betty's wounds both psychic and emotional, wounds yet to be formed by stories yet to be told and histories yet to be recorded. At the same time, Chonch also seems to suggest that there is nothing particularly special or exceptional about either of their stories, or their shared experience of loss. Both have always, already been a part of the narrative fabric of East L.A., and the losses they share so intimately—losing Izzy/Chiquis, losing themselves—also belong to a collective experience of loss, to the barrio's history of forgetting.[108]

That a femme lesbian, Izzy/Chiquis, becomes the fulcrum of loss in the play underscores the fact that women (and queer women, in particular) are the figures "forgotten" or scripted out of patriarchal histories of the barrio. As Raúl Homero Villa points out, "Chicana feminist, gay, and lesbian scholars have consistently targeted this patriarchal, heterosexual familism as a central ideological nexus for the subordination of 'irrelevant' or 'divisive' differences within the Chicano community. Attention to these differences was considered at best superfluous, and at worst traitorous to the political cause."[109] But contemporary queer scholars like Richard T. Rodriguez have also pointed out how the tropes of "la familia" have themselves been reconstituted and reimagined by queer Chicana feminists like Cherríe Moraga, confounding, at once, the patriarchal force of Chicano nationalism as well as alternative models of gay and lesbian kinship that cannot account for the "sustained relevance of family and kinship" among queer communities of color.[110] *The Barber of East L.A.* also revisits the extended and consensual kinship models theorized by both Latino/a and queer scholars, but it contextualizes their intervention within the spatial discourses that adhere to queer of color bodies. Do we stay among our "kin" in the barrio, or do we seek out other models of consensual kinship in a perpetually whitewashed "queer world" somewhere out there?

The play's climax happens, appropriately enough, at the Vex on the infamous night in October 1980 that Black Flag, the legendary white punk band from Hermosa Beach, California played a "particularly destructive set" (to quote *Vexing* curator Colin Gunckel).[111] In *The Barber of East L.A.*, Betty and Julian anticipate a troubled evening with the arrival of Black Flag's fans, and vow to meet each other at the club after Betty pursues her emotional reckoning with Chonch. Betty arrives late:

JULIAN: Betty! Are you okay? I thought you got *chonched* into a million little pieces!

BETTY: I'm fine, Julian, I got so much to—Where did all these Nazi skinheads come from?

JULIAN: Don't ask me! None of them are particularly hot either! Get used to them, Betty. We're going to be seeing a lot of these creeps once we get to Hollyweird.[112]

While the Vex was, from its inception, a venue where bands, artists, and scenes from all over Los Angeles and Southern California would perform and mingle, this intrusion would prove to be traumatic. As Josh Kun explains:

The original incarnation of the Vex closed with a Black Flag show that ended in a riot of broken glass and vandalism. White Huntington Beach punks threw chairs out the windows and into the parking lot, broke copiers and art equipment, and destroyed paintings and sculptures. "It was like when Manson struck and broke the whole hippie feel," says Velo [cofounder of the legendary Chicano new wave band, Los Illegals]. . . . "That show just broke what the Vex was all about. It was like having your friends come to your house and tear up your parents' furniture. It broke our hearts."[113]

Before the riot scene even breaks out in *The Barber of East L.A.*, Betty already has second thoughts about leaving the barrio only to be surrounded by white, racist "creeps" (to invoke Julian's words). She tries to back out of her plan to move to Hollywood with Julian, anxiously suggesting, "Maybe we can leave next year?"[114] Amid that night of chaos in local lore, Betty stages her desire for deferral. She is tempted to wait and stay, to be dragged back to the place she thought she had already left in her heart. But in order for her to truly leave, she, like Chonch, has to reclaim the space and stake her intervention as a queer woman of color. Or rather, she must reclaim the Vex and East L.A. in the name of the queer women of color whose stories have disappeared into the structural chaos of forgetting enacted by men—by white men who violently stake their claim anywhere and everywhere, as well as by men of color who think girls like Isabel "Chiquis" Velasquez are too pretty to be with a barber.

During the play's climactic scenes at the Vex, Betty not only manages to take down Frank Martinez, the crooked cop who tormented Izzy/Chiquis in the past and continues to torment Chonch now (Betty and Julian enact a sting operation exposing him for selling drugs to club-goers), but also confronts the skinhead milieu. She bum-rushes the stage and seizes the mic:

BETTY: Fuck you, you fucking Nazi punks! I'm sick of this! I'm sick of you! I'm so sick of my scene, it makes me wanna scream!

Yeah, I'm in a band, but we've never played at the Vex, 'cause of stupid boys like you!

So, *basta*! *Basta*! My name is Betty Basta and I'm the lead singer for the Izzies and we're from fucking east l.a.!¹¹⁵

Betty lives up to her chosen name, "Basta," by calling for enough. Enough of the invasive racism that destroys her punk scene and her barrio; enough of the sexism in her own community and beyond that erases her, Izzy, Chonch, and other queer women of color from the barrio logos; enough of the queer exceptionalism that makes her eschew her *familia*, her barrio, and her brownness. She takes the stage not only in her own name but also in Izzy's—she and Julian drop Toxic Crayons as their band name and become the Izzies as a tribute to her aunt and the barber who couldn't bear losing her.

The Barber of East L.A. concludes with a scene titled "A New Scar." Betty revisits Chonch's barbershop one last time before she finally crosses the L.A. River to another life in Hollywood. She comes not only to bid farewell to Chonch but also to share her last inheritance from her aunt: "My dad threw everything of hers away. These were left under my bed in a box with some dusty *conjunto* records. It had BV written on them. You know, my initials. I know she meant for me to have them."¹¹⁶ Izzy leaves Betty records—the records she and Chonch made in an "old recording booth at the Woolworth on Whittier Boulevard."¹¹⁷ While the audience will never know whether Betty will make her own records with the Izzies, we do come to learn that Izzy herself literally kept records: chronicles of her everyday excursions with Chonch. As the current keeper of these records, Betty decides to leave them with Chonch in the barrio. Though Chonch has been the historical voice throughout most of the play, the only archivist of "what happened then" during the events leading up to Izzy/Chiquis's death, she now becomes the recipient of an archive—the bearer of a mark, a trace. The play closes with the grain of a voice, of Chiquis in a Woolworth booth offering one final revelation:

I can't believe I love a girl named Chonch. *Pero no se llama* Chonch. Her name . . .
her real name . . . is Perfidia, *como la canción.*

[Isabel hums a few bars. chonch stands in the middle of her barbershop,
laughing and listening. Trio Los Panchos' recording of the song "Perfidia" plays.
The slide "Fin" appears.][118]

Even in its last breath of love, in what is meant to be a confession spoken and
hummed from beyond the grave, *The Barber of East L.A.* evades the search for
truth, offering no explanation or exoneration. "Perfidia," Chonch's real name, is
Spanish for "treacherous" or "false." Beautifully and queerly, true love speaks its
name as a pretense and a lie.

Like so many of the BdP's sketches leading up to it, *The Barber of East L.A.*
shatters utopian ideals about "safe community spaces" for queers and people
of color by documenting the inevitable incursion of other bodies, desires, and
scenes into their social spaces. The infamous events in 1980, during which white
skinheads from Huntington Beach took over the Vex in East L.A., offers something of a prehistory for the hostile takeover of social spaces depicted in the
BdP's wider performance oeuvre. As one of their definitive works, *The Barber of
East L.A.* stages the ephemeral, archival labor behind all their previous performance pieces on queer of color life in "lesser Los Angeles." The labor of relocating accounts of queer L.A. from scenes like West Hollywood, or of reorienting
queer space more generally from the vertical cities mythologized as its centers,
is profoundly affective and undeniably messy. The ethical impulse to adhere the
labels "good" and "bad" to particular places, people, or objects of consumption is
ultimately frustrated by this ensemble's efforts to explore the queer conundrum
of staying or leaving, of standing still or moving. Indeed, in tracing the push and
pull of suburban spaces, the BdP seems to open more wounds than they try to
heal, dwelling as they do on the rifts within as well as between queer of color
communities: between "us" and "them," between elsewhere and here. Wounds so
deep rarely ever heal properly, but perhaps they are, in the end, in the service of
other mutations and beautiful pretenses. Perhaps all we can ever truly wish to
find is a new scar.

6   Coda: Love among the Ruins

Contact, Creativity, and Klub Fantasy

Driving in your car
Oh please don't drop me home
Because it's not my home
It's their home and I'm welcome no more.

      —The Smiths, "There Is a Light That Never Goes Out"

AS WE MERGE once again on the road to nowhere in particular, we find ourselves seeking contact through the definitive mode of transport in Southern California—our cars. These moving isolation chambers are what purportedly keep Southern Californians, and anyone else in the country bereft of public transportation, from truly experiencing "contact," the transient encounters with strangers that make urban life vibrant and queer cruising possible. Vibrant street life, incidental contact, and the expression of sexual liberty remain the cornerstones of the queer spatial imaginary, even as the corporate redevelopment of emblematic cities like New York threatens to eradicate and reformulate the city's sexual cultures. Samuel Delany's *Times Square Red, Times Square Blue*, for example, mourns the lost interclass and interracial contact that once thrived in Times Square's porn theaters and the city streets surrounding them.[1]

While the first section of Delany's book memorializes the porn theaters that facilitated transient intimacies, the second half offers an impassioned argument on behalf of revivifying urban contact, a concept he borrows from the urban historian Jane Jacobs's work in *The Death and Life of Great American Cities*.[2] Contact, for both Jacobs and Delany, produces an ethics of mutual regard, an incidental empathy, and "a web of social pleasantry" across race and class boundaries.[3] Contact is a mode of relating and interacting that functions best—for Jacobs and Delany, it transpires *exclusively*—amid the walking cultures, small-business sectors, and densely populated neighborhoods of "great American cities" like New York. What Delany doesn't quite register in his eloquent lament for an urban queer sexual subculture under erasure at the hands of bureaucratic and corporate interests is the extent to which his and others' *idealized* forms of urban sociability and mobility are complicit with homonormative and neoliberal discourses promoting urban gentrification.[4]

The sheer density of urban street life and "human capital" great cities have to offer—and here we can think of the incidental, creative exchanges represented as contact in Delany's and Jacobs's work—is precisely what public policy planners like Richard Florida have promoted as an urban "amenity" to the prosperous new "creative class" of highly educated "knowledge-industry" workers.[5] Chief among the creative class—or to use Florida's sci-fi phrasing, the "super-creative core"—are "scientists and engineers, university professors, poets and novelists, artists, entertainers, actors, designers and architects, as well as the thought leadership of modern society."[6] In many respects, the same improvisational modes of life, the same temporal and spatial innovations recorded and championed in historical accounts of gay urbanity, have been incorporated into new models of urban planning aimed to entice members of this creative class to revive presumably ailing neighborhoods (primarily working-class and racialized ones) in U.S. cities. It comes as no surprise that one of the telltale indices Florida and his team of researchers use to measure a city's desirability is something called the "Gay Index": "Gays, as we like to say, can be thought of as *canaries* of the creative economy, and serve as a strong signal of a diverse, progressive environment. Indeed, gays are frequently cited as harbingers of redevelopment and gentrification in distressed urban neighborhoods. The presence of gays in a metropolitan area also provides a barometer for a broad spectrum of amenities attractive to adults, especially those without children."[7] At once silly and ominous, Florida's intrepid gay canaries nevertheless speak volumes about how queer forms of inhabiting and transforming space function as "subcultural capital" in urban economies of spatial "rehabilitation."[8]

The urban queer temporalities I alluded to in the first part of this book—an anticipatory temporality that innovatively extracts itself from "normative" reproductive and labor logics—actually overlaps with what Florida and others have begun to articulate as an idiosyncratic but nevertheless newly normative temporality for a postindustrial economy.[9] The postindustrial creative laborer has, as Florida implies, much in common with pioneering gay urbanites in so far as the traditional family unit (parents with children) no longer structures her leisure time. Further, the creative laborer eschews the requisite spaces and built environments of "family life" and family entertainment (presumably the suburbs and the single-family home), seeking instead a range of built environments and stimulating activities during precious downtime, since the creative labor clock exceeds the industrial forty-hour workweek. After conducting focus groups comprising creative workers, Florida comes to the conclusion that the urban spaces desirable to workers on the creative clock offer easy access to amenities via foot traffic and public transportation: "Many of the young creative workers did not have cars and wanted to locate in regions where they did not need one. . . . Creative workers working long hours need to be able to access amenities almost instantly on demand."[10]

Contact with a "diverse" group of others (to use Florida's formulation) further enriches the lived environments for (presumably white) creative classers and encourages their occupation of spaces otherwise deemed unsafe or unevenly developed. Diversity itself—a diversity one encounters through walking culture—becomes an "urban amenity," a crucial component of what provides the grain for, and an experiential quality to, the creative-class urban lifestyle: "Focus group respondents noted the importance of diversity and the attractiveness of regions that reflect, and are supportive of, diversity."[11] The racialized and working-class communities inhabiting the "distressed neighborhoods" rehabilitated by upwardly mobile queers (Richard Florida's gay "canaries"), and the heterosexual creative classers hot on their heels, serve literally as local color, if they are not immediately displaced and relocated. Residential dwellings are not the only spaces susceptible to this ethos of renovation. Social gathering places like bars and clubs also become "flipped," to use the parlance of gentrification, in order to accommodate the economically advantaged communities who choose to reterritorialize "distressed" urban neighborhoods.

To read Richard Florida's depiction of diversity and "tolerance" as urban amenities—as expressions of an ethically enhanced taste—alongside Samuel Delany's and Jane Jacobs's models of contact is not to suggest that the latter are conscious collaborationists with urban gentrification. Rather, pursuing such connections underscores the intersections that make strange bedfellows of both neoliberal and progressive ideologies, as well as both normative and queer spatial formations.[12] In the spirit of inquiry Roderick Ferguson has elaborated on as "queer of color critique,"[13] this genealogy of the imbrications among queer and normative accounts of space and styles of living reveals how the sometimes-conflicting imperatives of race, class, gender, and sexuality frustrate the *lifestyle* imperatives produced by canonical accounts of queer urbanity and creativity. The cultural value assigned to urban modes of queer life—to its mobility, style, innovation, improvisation, liveliness, and "contact"—has appreciated urban property values while depreciating modes of racialized queer sociability that transpire in other spaces, and that rely on other affiliative practices for "contact."

In their earlier work, the Butchlalis de Panochtitlan respond very specifically to the "diversity fetishes" that inform the queer and creative-class gentrification of social spaces in Los Angeles, a city not considered prototypically "queer" because of its sprawling topography, purportedly absent "street life," and limited walking cultures. The BdP also commemorate the aftershocks of gentrification in the city's suburban peripheries both near and far. For example, the sketch "Softball Diamond Girl (*Me Haces Sentirrr* . . .)" is set in the predominantly Latino, work-

BdP interstitial slide, "Dodgers Pennant," 2006. Courtesy of the artists. All rights reserved.

ing-class suburb of El Sereno, a community overshadowed by the wealthier white suburb of South Pasadena in the storied controversy over the construction of the I-710 Long Beach Freeway in the 1990s.[14] Nevertheless, the BdP offers an optimistic vision of sociability, intimacy, and contact stubbornly immune to urbane gay social and spatial economies. The sketch is framed visually with a slide that invokes the infamous Chávez Ravine scandal: Thousands of Mexican Americans, many of whom inhabited the rural valley at the cusp of downtown Los Angeles for generations, were displaced in the late 1940s and early 1950s, ostensibly to provide space for public housing projects. When all was said and done, however, the site became L.A. Mayor Norris Poulson's costly welcome gift to the city's newest New York transplants, the Dodgers baseball organization.[15]

In addition to commemorating a community literally bulldozed to make way for what Richard Florida would call a "traditional" urban amenity—a sports stadium[16]—the BdP draws a profound historical correlation between the spatial and cultural violence of civic-sanctioned, large-scale relocation projects and the creative-class gentrification of leisure sites in communities of color. The textual aside that appears at the bottom of the slide—"and the Short Stop will always be a fucked up cop bar"—calls out one of Echo Park's trendiest bars, the Short Stop on Sunset Boulevard. Formerly an off-duty watering hole for the LAPD's notorious Rampart Division, the Short Stop has since been tastefully renovated with mid-century low-brow accoutrements for its clientele of scruffily stylized hipsters. As the slide implies, the creative-class clientele, who self-consciously chug Pabst Blue Ribbon pints for a buck on Dodgers game-nights with nary a thought about the communities they've priced out of Echo Park, are no better than the cops who abuse their state-sanctioned power to intimidate the neighborhood's inhabitants of color.

While these sordid and corrupt histories of urban antagonism provide a conceptual frame for the BdP's "Softball Diamond Girl," the sketch itself, set in the Latino working-class enclave of El Sereno, offers a vision of refuge in *suburban* venues of sociability. The sketch translates the Chávez Ravine slide's invocation of the fraternal and patrilineal tropes associated with baseball, "the national pastime," into a scene of intergenerational Latino/a butch intimacy that transpires through the venerable *lesbian* pastime of interleague softball. In the dialogue between Coach (Raquel Gutierrez), a stoic yet heart-scarred older butch, and Jessy (Claudia Rodriguez), a young, aspiring *papi* "player" who is also reeling from a recent heartbreak, the BdP reevaluate what "contact" might mean for sequestered and forgotten subjects, and for potentially immobile subjects (Coach has a "trick knee" and hobbles around, if rather pimp-tastically, with a cane):

JESSY: Damn Coach, I didn't know you played.

COACH: Been 10 years.

JESSY: So you think you'll ever get back in the game?

COACH: I got a trick knee, but I'm healed now. And you will too.[17]

Softball in this sketch—a signifier for working-class, old-school dyke recreations with a presumed lack of complexity and stylistic flourish in queer imaginaries—becomes a rich metaphor for love in its variegated forms, a love and regard that persists despite the encroachment of wholesale changes to the spatial and emotional landscape of El Sereno. It is literally about a love among "players," a different kind of affiliative intimacy among dykes who have a love for "the game" in all its connotations. The conversations that transpire in sports metaphors, and in both popular and cultural shorthand—Jessy, whom Coach calls "koo koo for cha cha puffs," only needs to invoke the "Los Bukis songs flooding my head" for Coach to understand that the young player's heart and mind is vulnerable to doing some "crazy *vato* shit"[18]—gestures to the multiple circuits of affect foreshadowed by the sketch's subtitle, "Me Haces Sentirrr . . ."

The line "me haces sentirrrr," which translates as "you make me feellll," is pulled from the Spanish-language disco break in the 1986 freestyle radio hit "Diamond Girl," performed by Nice & Wild. In the most definitive scholarly account of the freestyle genre to date, Alexandra Vazquez provides an affective cultural topography for this dance-pop form derided for its overproduction and its association with racialized working-class women and queers in "urban and suburban transnational hubs in the U.S."[19] Vazquez herself vividly locates freestyle's sonic power "in public spaces outside of the home: on the dance floors of middle schools, at the mall, in youth centers, in headphones, in their parents' cars probably hijacked for the evening."[20] The song "Diamond Girl," a freestyle megahit featuring male vocals, has now become something of a retro staple at Latin clubs and on Southern California radio,[21] and provides the sound track for the opening moments of the BdP's sketch. "Diamond Girl," with its tinny beat and synthetic, Casio-toned jams, sets the tone for *how* these butches make each other feel through their popular archives of desire, and through their shared regrets about "playing the field," despite landing the femmes of their dreams. The English lyric that transitions into the Spanish disco break frames the question of who actually makes "me" feel.[22]

A robust, male tenor with an urgent R and B vibrato sings, "I'll always be your diamond girl / You're my diamond girl." The grammatical ambiguity of "I'll always be your diamond girl," presumably lacking the comma (i.e., "I'll always be your diamond, girl") that would cast the male lover as the "diamond" and not the "diamond *girl*"—such grammatical subtlety is understandably elusive in dance hits—provides the opportunity to imagine a different set of "lovers" in this scene. There is a transitivity to who is whose "diamond girl" in the modulations of queer feeling rendered in the sketch. In some sense, Coach and Jessy *are* each others' "diamond girls," even as their bond is formed in part by a dialogue about the femmes who've broken their hearts, like "*la catorce* (#14) in all her chachalisciousness." Indeed, Jessy even asks Coach at the end of the sketch, "What are you, some kind of *mom* butch or something?," to which Coach cockily responds, "Nah kid. I'm all *puro papi!*," as she takes her baseball cap off and holds it over her heart.[23]

Through their conversation, soaked in sports metaphor and peppered with idiomatic improvisations on pop phrases in Spanish and English, this intergenerational pair of butches allow each other to feel, to express their sentiments in ways that might otherwise be subsumed in the macho game playing of butch/femme seduction. The BdP also seem to disavow any butch policing around the pronouns used to refer to these characters who are, after all, featured in a sketch titled "Softball Diamond *Girl*." It's as if the spatialized and racialized memory invoked by their citation of the freestyle song title becomes a more significant expression of the characters' butch bond than an orthodox articulation of female masculinity through the studious use of English pronouns.

Yet their nonchalance about masculine pronouns, paired with their unabashed attachment to the feminized, "disposable pop" genre of freestyle, also comes with their insistence on acknowledging the *racialized* masculinities—the machismo survival mechanisms—that inform such butch bonds. In their powerful piece "Cockfight," the BdP actually eschew the butch competitiveness of white masculinities and ask us instead to consider the machismo intimacies that create communities of support and foment different models of contact, be it through structures like "the gang" or the extended family: "*En Lak Ech Tu Eres Mi Otro . . .* Yo, Don't Laugh Fool. You Are My Other Me," insists the BdP's own "big *papi*," Mari Garcia.[24] Nadine "Nadino" Romero subsequently utters these lines as she

A PERFORMANCE

BANDA MACHOS

QUEER

NAHUATL

URBAN CODICES

::PUSSYLANDIA

IS LOS SCANDALOUS L.A.

DOWN OR FIERCE RADICAL MASCULINITIES?

butchlalis de panochtitlan
teenage papi the remix // january 26-29, 2006
Highways Performance Space @ 1651 18th street, santa monica 90404
Thurs.-Sat. @ 8:30pm; Sun. @ 2:30pm $15/$13 Call (310) 315-1459 for reservations
www.highwaysperformance.org & www.butchlalis.com

BdP promotional image, "Teenage Papi: The Remix," 2006. Courtesy of the artists.
All rights reserved.

gestures to her fellow Butchlalis, as well as to members of the crowd: "I look for myself in her and him. She is my father and so is he. He is my son and so is she. She is my brother and so is she."[25]

Indeed, the "you" who makes "me" feel in "Softball Diamond Girl" can be the other *macho/a*—whether father, brother, mother, even lover—who offers solace on the softball fields of El Sereno when no one else, when no place else, is there for you.[26]

Such moments of simple yet profound practices of suburban affiliation in BdP's performances—an affiliation that extends "the family" through ethno-racial paradigms and reframes "incidental contact" through such vehicles as incidental music, be it freestyle or the Moz—are nestled among humorously scathing critiques of the gentrification that has left Los Angeles's Eastside in "ruins" for queer of color subjects, even as the area's built environments have been renovated.[27] The intimacies mediated through "the popular" *and* "the cultural" remain the BdP's touchstones for navigating one's way through spaces once ignored or disregarded as "nowheres," and since transformed by creative classers into "somewheres."

The characters Lolo and Perla, the same East L.A. butches who found themselves surrounded by "dirty white girls" in the BdP's first full-length production,

Teenage Papi: The Second Coming of Adolescence, are our intrepid guides through this reconfigured landscape. As Perla laments in "drrrty White Girls, "This was *our* slum, our home . . . not that we had a choice."[28] Now that the pricey Eastside neighborhoods of Echo Park and Silver Lake are no longer their "slums," no longer contain their homes, Lolo and Perla (in *Teenage Papi: The Remix*) commute to their former bar and club haunts from an unspecified elsewhere. The sketch, "Lolo and Perla Return to Avenge Klub Fantasy," begins with an offstage voice-over invoking the "ruins" of a Latino/a club space, Nayarit Nite Club, in what has historically been the Latino and working-class neighborhood of Echo Park. The Nayarit has since been converted into a live music and dance venue frequented by hipsters and rechristened, with minimalist panache, as "The Echo":

ENTER WITH SONG: "La Chona" by Los Tucanes de Tijuana

(VOICE-OVER.)

Little do our patrons know that we stand on the ruins of a racialized queer space—Klub Fantasy at Nayarit—do you know it? Have you ever been? Were you there?[29]

As the lights come up, Lolo and Perla are dancing vigorously to the *banda* party anthem "La Chona." Clad in a fringe-tastic suede jacket, Perla (Rodriguez) ecstatically busts her *banda-quebradita* moves, and Lolo (Gutierrez) robustly works the *punta*, or what she calls "the bastard skanking version of the two."[30] Both are thrilled to be in what they presume is still a "lesbian Latina club . . . [or] a Latina lesbian club," until the retro-rock refrains of Black Sabbath's "Paranoid" interrupts their reverie:

LOLO: Uhh, Perla, you sure we're in the right place?

PERLA: (*Looks around, shocked*) Dude, oh my god, I didn't know it was all dirty punk chicks n' shit! Not again! This sucks!

LOLO: *You* think this sucks, I'm the one that looks like a fashion *pendejo* wearing my dad's *guayabera* at a goofy punk rock dyke club! Nobody better order a fuckin' margarita from me or I swear I'll wail on their asses. (Pauses, looks around) . . . But you know I love me some punk rock hynas with the titty tats! (Stoner laugh)

[. . .]

PERLA: The fuckin' lady standing outside selling weenies wrapped in bacon threw me off. I thought this was the right place. (Dramatic pause) I'm screwed, 'ey!?

LOLO: (Smart-alecky) This is the right place, dude. It's just the wrong crowd, or at least the *new* crowd. This isn't your *tias lesbianas veteranas* crowd, you know? We ain't gonna see your mom and my mom in their Sunday best here. We ain't even gonna see the Lucha Villa and Thalia impersonators either, man![31]

The BdP's "Lolo and Perla Return to Avenge Klub Fantasy" not only reenacts the compressed temporality of spatial turnovers—the bar scene changes as quickly as the bars of one song cover over another—but the sketch also invokes the cross-cultural encounters both fraught and titillating that make legible the classed and racialized politics of competing styles in queer social spaces. Lolo's quip about wearing a *guayabera* at a "punk rock dyke club" not only captures the sensation of being out of place in a shifting social economy, but also calls attention to the racial significations that are incorporated into the practices of nightlife service economies in Southern California.[32] When Lolo remarks, "Nobody better try to order a fuckin' margarita from me or I'll wail on their asses," she underscores the fact that Latino/a service workers are essentially asked to perform some version of racial "authenticity" as part of their service. For Gutierrez, the contested national origins of the *guayabera*—"Filipinos think they made it, Cubans think they originated it . . . don't know for sure, and Mexicans think they did too"[33]— enriches the problem of reading race and nationality through iterations of style as it functions in a "new crowd," in a new social and spatial economy.

Lolo may have chosen to wear a *guayabera* for a night on the town in what she thought would be a queer Latina space, but the shirt risks being read in the transformed spatial context of the *white* dyke club in Los Angeles as a "Mexican uniform"—as but another atmospheric amenity (like a good margarita) that conjures up the old flavors of a once-racialized space, while relegating race itself to the dustbin of history. Even though she's in the "right place" with the "wrong crowd," and caught in a bourgeois-bohemian milieu likely to mistake a Latina butch rockin' a *guayabera* as a Mexican waiter in his service uniform, Lolo eschews a rhetoric of racial victimization, and instead launches her own fantasy scenario about hooking up with an inappropriate object of desire, a white, "punk rock hyna" with slammin' "titty tats."[34]

Lolo's churlish response to the encounter marks her refusal to be the object of consumption for someone else's taste. Lolo instead asserts *her* agency as a subject of taste who in turn consumes the white queer subcultures that have invaded her queer of color venues. Or perhaps more fittingly, Lolo, with her "creepy *cabron* voice," raunchy jokes, and fraternal butch razzing of Perla ("Yeah dude, you and your feminist politics missed out, 'ey?!"),[35] produces herself as an agent of *tastelessness* who very literally "acts out" against the club's new social order informed by white liberal curiosity, and filtered through a studied indifference masquerading itself as subcultural cred. In "drrrty White Girls," it is Perla who plays the bad subject of taste, when she boasts about her rascally intervention in yet another gentrified Echo Park dive, Little Joy: "They still had that juke box, so me and my homegirl put in $5.00 worth of Vicente Fernandez . . . he's not Morrissey or nothing; but it was worth it cause it only took $2.50 to clear out the place."[36]

In both of BdP's Lolo and Perla sketches, the titular butch characters extract themselves from the gentrified space and time that, though seemingly predictable, still manages to catch them off guard ("Not again! This sucks!"). During their nights on the town, Lolo and Perla retrace the path of creative-class gentrification "all up and down Sunset," in bars "crowded with young white folks with bed-head hair and wrinkled clothes on purpose,"[37] both queer and straight. How they choose to extract themselves from the languid, if not explicitly hostile, takeover of their social spaces, however, does not necessarily take the form of movement, of leaving these places behind or relinquishing ownership of the social environment. Rather, Lolo and Perla transport themselves from the scenes of spatial conquest unfolding in the present tense by activating their own memories, their own retrospective fantasies about owning the scene back in the day, which in some instances may just have been yesterday, or the day before.

In other words, Lolo and Perla enact their own racialized "temporal drag" on these gentrified spaces, whether sartorially (the fringed suede jacket, the *guayabera*), musically (through Vicente Fernandez or Morrissey on the jukebox), kinetically (with their *banda-quebradita* and *punta* dance stylings), or sexually (with a cheeky, inter-racial butch chauvinism directed at the indifferent "dirty white girls," as well as with their lascivious reminiscences about the crushes they harbored for the tranny/*travesti* performers who ruled the stage at Klub Fantasy). The broader cultural history they conjure among the ruins of these queer racialized spaces is also a history of love, a history of their friendship as it has been archived in the contours of these spaces, and as it has been transacted through a shared popular and cultural memory that sustains them amid such alienating, topsy-turvy contexts. In lieu of the space that actually was Klub Fantasy, they create their own club through their own fantasies.

Ultimately, all Lolo and Perla can really do is to keep moving on without actually leaving anything behind. "Movement" for subjects like Lolo and Perla does not necessarily connote "choice," "freedom," or "mobility"—the hallmarks of democratic citizenship—as it so often does in queer urban rhetorics. In many instances, their movements are predicated on the force wrought by other people's choices, tastes, and desires. "Lolo and Perla Return to Avenge Klub Fantasy" ends with the friends hoping to outpace the movements of gentrification, preparing to take their car to another place with *their* music, and *their* people, who are young (or maybe not so much anymore) and alive (or at least surviving):

LOLO: We'll just grab the Ranchola and go to this other spot in Pico-Union. No freiges 'cause they only sell beer there, but the *travestis* are fuckin' fine!

PERLA: Where?

LOLO: (All suspicious) Well, I don't want to say the name out loud in here. 'Cuz you never know dude (Looking around) . . . we might be in this same, exact situation a year from now.[38]

Maybe the light that never goes out is about *never* getting there, never arriving at that *somewhere*. Just maybe it's about the journey itself; about the desire to be taken out, but never finding *it*; finding something else instead and gladly risking oblivion in the process. Maybe it's about studiously avoiding the encroachment of too many somewheres while protecting the nowheres you call your own.

When I first began to route the twists and turns of *Relocations*, I imagined I would tell all. Seduced by the fantasy of comprehensiveness, I thought this book would reveal the vibrant lives unseen, unheard, unread in the cul-de-sacs, backyards, garages, strip-mall bars, and other queer spaces both secret and commercial scattered throughout the Southern California landscape. As much as we have seen, heard, and read about some of these locales, I realized some part of me refused to reveal everything, lest I come to find, like Lolo and Perla, my precious nowheres occupied and taken over. But then again, no one, not even I, can ever really get *there*—wherever that may be. The thrill happens in the search. The companionship is found in the disappointment.

Reading space vis-à-vis queer studies now requires shifting our spatial fantasies about sexuality from one kind of street life to another: to the compensatory forms of motion and contact in spaces seemingly (if not actually) bereft of the urban luxury known as "walking culture." Driving in your car through lonely stretches of Southern California or elsewhere. Driving in your car with someone else, with significant others (not necessarily lovers—or are they?). Rollin' deep with your homies, sisters or bros, real or conjured, desperately seeking excitement elsewhere, *somewhere*, but realizing that it might just be all about the ride, the inevitably aimless transport of accidental reverie—and all about who you're riding with.

Notes

NOTES TO CHAPTER I

1. One designer on an August 2009 episode of the HGTV reality competition show *Design Star* referred to the architecture of mid-century suburban homes in Southern California as "atomic-type ranch house." For a beautiful expansion of atomic metaphor and materiality in letters, cinema, psychoanalysis, and Japanese representational history, see Akira Mizuta Lippit, *Atomic Light (Shadow Optics)* (Minneapolis: University of Minnesota Press, 2005). I mention Lippit's book here not only in an act of free association with his "speculative reading" of the atomic and the darkness cast by the bombings of Hiroshima and Nagasaki, but also because (as I explain later in this introduction) this project is haunted by the more violent legacies of Japanese American relocation during World War II.

2. Nearly every scholarly book on the suburbs, regardless of its disciplinary orientation, begins with this premise. Rather than reproduce a comprehensive bibliography in this single note, allow me to register the ones that have been most influential on my own approach to defining the suburbs (in alphabetical order): John Archer, *Architecture and Suburbia: From the English Villa to the American Dream House, 1690–2000* (Minneapolis: University of Minnesota Press, 2005); Eric Avila, *Popular Culture in the Age of White Flight: Fear and Fantasy in Suburban Los Angeles* (Berkeley: University of California Press, 2004); Robert A. Beauregard, *When America Became Suburban* (Minneapolis: University of Minnesota Press, 2006);

Andrew Blauvelt, ed., *Worlds Away: New Suburban Landscapes* (Minneapolis: Walker Art Center, 2008); Robert Fishman, *Bourgeois Utopias: The Rise and Fall of Suburbia* (New York: Basic Books, 1987); Dolores Hayden, *Building Suburbia: Green Fields and Urban Growth, 1820–2000* (New York: Vintage, 2004); Kenneth T. Jackson, *Crabgrass Frontier: The Suburbanization of the United States* (New York: Oxford University Press, 1985); Catherine Jurca, *White Diaspora: The Suburb and the Twentieth-Century American Novel* (Princeton: Princeton University Press, 2001); Rob Kling, Spencer Olin, and Mark Poster, eds., *Postsuburban California: The Transformation of Orange County since World War II* (Berkeley: University of California Press, 1991); Becky M. Nicolaides, *My Blue Heaven: Life and Politics in the Working-Class Suburbs of Los Angeles, 1920–1965* (Chicago: University of Chicago Press, 2002); Becky M. Nicolaides and Andrew Wiese, eds., *The Suburb Reader* (New York: Routledge, 2006); and Lynn Spigel, *Welcome to the Dream House: Popular Media and the Postwar Suburbs* (Durham: Duke University Press, 2001).

3. Spigel, *Welcome to the Dream House*, 33.

4. See Eve Kosofsky Sedgwick, "Paranoid Reading and Reparative Reading; or, You're So Paranoid, You Probably Think This Introduction is about You," in *Novel Gazing: Queer Readings in Fiction*, ed. Eve Kosofsky Sedgwick (Durham: Duke University Press, 1997), 1–40. Later in this introduction, I describe and animate my own sense of reparative reading from Sedgwick's concept of reparative "critical

practices"—which she denies are "theoretical methodologies (and certainly not as stable personality types of critic)," but goes on to describe "as changing and heterogeneous relational stances" (8).

5. Jane Jacobs, *The Death and Life of Great American Cities* (New York: Random House, 1961). A scholar who has been at the forefront of documenting and critiquing the policies and ideologies behind gentrification and urban renewal is the geographer Neil Smith. See *The New Urban Frontier: Gentrification and the Revanchist City* (New York: Routledge, 1996). In his introduction to the catalog for the exhibit *Worlds Away*, titled "Worlds Away and the World Next Door," Andrew Blauvelt refers to a "reverse suburban migration of empty nesters, who return to the city to enjoy the kind of life they lived before they had kids to raise" (11).

6. "7.3: Two Progressive Reformers Critique Working-Class Home Ownership, 1912," in Nicolaides and Wiese, *Suburb Reader*, 199; and "11.1: The Chicago Defender Celebrates the Supreme Court's Ruling on Restrictive Covenants, 1948," in Nicolaides and Wiese, *Suburb Reader*, 324. David Theo Goldberg and Richard Marciano (among other collaborators) have created a "digital archaeology of segregation in California cities" called T-RACES (Testbed for the Redlining Archives of California's Exclusionary Spaces). T-RACES combines digital mapping technologies with archival hypertexts of civic and real estate documents, bank memos, and other material traces of housing discrimination and segregationist policies in California. A demo is accessible at http://salt.diceresearch.org/T-RACES/demo, accessed May 29, 2009.

7. Nicolaides and Wiese excerpt full-length academic studies of these topics, including Timothy Fong, *The First Suburban Chinatown: The Remaking of Monterey Park, California* (Philadelphia: Temple University Press, 1994); Sarah J. Mahler, *American Dreaming: Immigrant Life on the Margins* (Princeton: Princeton University Press, 1995);

and Evan McKenzie, *Privatopia: Homeowner Associations and the Rise of Residential Private Government* (New Haven: Yale University Press, 1996).

8. "14–1: The *New York Times Magazine* Spotlights Black Suburbanization, 1992," in Nicolaides and Wiese, *Suburb Reader*, 412; and "14–3: A Reporter Documents Ethnic Diversity in Atlanta's Suburbs, 1999," in Nicolaides and Wiese, *Suburb Reader*, 415.

9. David Brooks is credited with coining the term "bourgeois bohemian," or "Bobo," although the term had been in circulation colloquially in France since the 1990s. See Brooks, *Bobos in Paradise: The New Upper Class and How They Got There* (New York: Simon and Schuster, 2000).

10. "The Art of Boredom" was captured in a collaborative photographic essay by Justine Kurland, Joshua Lutz, Taryn Simon, and Larry Sultan (76–80), while Richard Rayner contributed a piece on "The Swinger Next Door" (42–46).

11. Blauvelt, "City and Suburb," 1.

12. See George Chauncey, *Gay New York: Gender, Urban Culture, and the Making of the Gay Male World, 1890–1940* (New York: Basic Books, 1994); Diane Chisholm, *Queer Constellations: Subcultural Space in the Wake of the City* (Minneapolis: University of Minnesota Press, 2005); Julie Abraham, *Metropolitan Lovers: The Homosexuality of Cities* (Minneapolis: University of Minnesota Press, 2009).

13. Judith Halberstam, *In a Queer Time and Place: Transgender Bodies, Subcultural Lives* (New York: New York University Press, 2005), 36.

14. Ibid., 15; emphasis added to "confirms."

15. Ibid.

16. An inevitably incomplete catalog of some of these important, earlier contributions to discussions on nonmetropolitan queer space would include the following: Richard Phillips, Diane Watt, and David Shuttleton, eds., *De-centering Sexualities: Politics and Representations beyond the Metropolis* (London: Routledge, 2000); Karen Lee Osborne and William J. Spurlin, eds., *Reclaiming the Heart-*

land: *Lesbian and Gay Voices from the Midwest* (Minneapolis: University of Minnesota Press, 1996); Beth Bailey, *Sex in the Heartland* (Cambridge: Harvard University Press, 1999); John Howard, ed., *Carryin' On in the Lesbian and Gay South* (New York: New York University Press, 1997); John Howard, *Men Like That: A Southern Queer History* (Chicago: University of Chicago Press, 1999); Mary Pat Brady, *Extinct Lands, Temporal Geographies: Chicana Literature and the Urgency of Space* (Durham: Duke University Press, 2002), 90; Michael Moon, "Whose History? The Case of Oklahoma," in *A Queer World: The Center for Lesbian and Gay Studies Reader*, ed. Martin Duberman (New York: New York University Press, 1997), 24–34; and Sherrie A. Inness, "Lost in Space: Queer Geography and the Politics of Location," in *Queer Cultures*, ed. Deborah Carlin and Jennifer DiGrazia (Upper Saddle River, NJ: Pearson/Prentice Hall, 2004), 254–77. I offer my own, extended genealogy of queer urbanity and its regional interventions in my chapter on JJ Chinois.

17. See Lauren Berlant and Elizabeth Freeman, "Queer Nationality," in Lauren Berlant, *The Queen of America Goes to Washington City: Essays on Sex and Citizenship* (Durham: Duke University Press, 1997), 160–164.

18. Scott Herring, *Another Country: Queer Anti-Urbanism* (New York: New York University Press, 2010), 4.

19. Ibid., 25.

20. Ibid., 23.

21. The Sugarbaker to which I cheekily refer, of course, is Dixie Carter's character, Julia Sugarbaker, on the long-running sitcom set in Atlanta, *Designing Women* (1986–1993). While some may think Delta Burke's Suzanne Sugarbaker is the sassier of the two fictitious sisters, I always appreciated Dixie's strong, indignant rants. For a more scholarly approach to *Designing Women*, see Tara McPherson, "Steel Magnolias, Fatal Flowers, and Designing Women: On the Limits of a Politics of Femininity in the Sun Belt South," in *Recon-*

structing *Dixie: Race, Gender, and Nostalgia in the Imagined South* (Durham: Duke University Press, 2003), 149–204.

22. The interchanges' mimicry of an organic shape—the leaves of a clover—have been aesthetically repurposed by visual artists like Jessica Smith, who incorporates their pattern (only discernable from an aerial point of view) into prints obscuring their artifice. Smith's work appeared in *Worlds Away: New Suburban Landscapes* at the Walker Art Center and the Carnegie Museum of Art in 2008. See also the definition of "cloverleaf" in Rachel Hopper and Jayme Yen, "A Lexicon of Suburban Neologisms," in Blauvelt, *Worlds Away*, 274.

23. As I explain in my chapter on JJ Chinois, the "rural" and the "urban" offer the primary spatial templates for collecting U.S. census data. See the U.S. Bureau of the Census, "Census 2000 Urban and Rural Classification," last modified December 3, 2009, http://www.census.gov/geo/www/ua/ua_2k. html. Some international scholars have argued vigorously on behalf of including a "suburban" spatial category for the purposes of analyzing more specific data sets. See Zhou De-min, Xu Jian-chun, John Radke, and Mu Lan, "A Spatial Cluster Method Supported by GIS for Urban-Suburban-Rural Classification," *Chinese Geographical Science* 14 (December 2004): 337–342.

24. For more on the United States' transition into suburbanization as its industrial cities went into decline during the 1970s, see Beauregard, *When America Became Suburban*. See also Fishman, *Bourgeois Utopias*; Hayden, *Building Suburbia*; and Jackson, *Crabgrass Frontier*.

25. Blauvelt, "City and Suburb," 11.

26. Brooks, *Bobos in Paradise*, 11.

27. Berlant and Freeman, "Queer Nationality," 165.

28. Lisa Duggan, *The Twilight of Equality: Neoliberalism, Cultural Politics, and the Attack on Democracy* (Boston: Beacon Press, 2003), 50.

29. See Richard Florida's *The Rise of the Creative Class: And How It's Transforming Work, Leisure, Community, and Everyday Life* (New York: Perseus Books, 2002); and his sequel of sorts, *Cities and the Creative Class* (New York: Routledge, 2005).

30. Florida, *Cities and the Creative Class*, 86.

31. The phrase "lesser Los Angeles"—a play on the geographical designation "greater Los Angeles"—was coined by Sandra Tsing Loh, and it appears in the subtitle to her collection of satirical essays *Depth Takes a Holiday: Essays from Lesser Los Angeles* (New York: Riverhead Books, 1996).

32. Of course, there is a much longer history of queer entanglements with gentrification going back to the mid-twentieth century. See Christina Hanhardt's monograph in progress, "Safe Space: The Sexual and City Politics of Violence." Hanhardt considers the transmogrifications of LGBT politics and policies as they emerged concurrently with neoliberal urban policies from the mid-twentieth century to the present.

33. Robert Bruegmann, *Sprawl: A Compact History* (Chicago: University of Chicago Press, 2005), 23.

34. Ibid. For expansive cultural histories of the "American dream" and the pursuit of the "good life" through commodities in the suburbs, see Archer, *Architecture and Suburbia*, and Beauregard, *When America Became Suburban*.

35. Carey McWilliams traces the earliest real estate boom cycles in the history of Southern California's development in *Southern California: An Island on the Land* (1946; repr., Layton, UT: Gibbs Smith Publishing, 1973). An anthology offering multiple perspectives on Southern California's role in a globalized, development-oriented border economy is Michael Dear and Gustavo Leclerc, eds., *Postborder City: Cultural Spaces of Bajalta California* (New York: Routledge, 2003). See also Jennifer Wolch, Manuel Pastor Jr., and Peter Dreier, "Introduction: Making Southern California: Public Policy, Markets, and the Dynamics of Growth," in *Up against the Sprawl: Public Policy in the Making of Southern California*, ed. Jennifer Wolch, Manuel Pastor Jr., and Peter Dreier (Minneapolis: University of Minnesota Press, 2004), 1–44. At the heart of Wolch, Pastor, and Dreier's contribution to the discourse of sprawl in Southern California is their insistence that federal, state, and local factors contribute to a fragmented and "ungovernable" Southern California. For more on the impact of immigration on the region's growth, see Enrico A. Marcelli, "From the Barrio to the 'Burbs? Immigration and the Dynamics of Suburbanization," in Wolch, Pastor, and Dreier, *Up against the Sprawl*, 123–150.

36. The scholarly and popular essays, as well as the creative fiction and nonfiction, works about Southern California's racialized suburbs are too numerous to name. Among the most significant and recent book-length scholarly works on the topic are Avila, *Popular Culture in the Age of White Flight*, and Fong, *First Suburban Chinatown*. New work on the racialization of the Southern California suburbs is being written across a range of disciplines. See Wendy Cheng, "Episodes in the Life of a Place: Regional Racial Formation in Los Angeles's San Gabriel Valley" (PhD diss., University of Southern California, 2009).

37. See Edward Soja, *Postmetropolis: Critical Studies of Cities and Regions* (Oxford: Blackwell, 2000), as well as much of Mike Davis's oeuvre, particularly "Planet of the Slums," *New Left Review* 26 (March/April 2004): 5–34; and his piece coauthored with Alexandra Moctezuma, "Policing the Third Border," *Colorlines* 2, no. 3 (1999): http://www.colorlines.com/article.php?ID=331.

38. See Wolch, Pastor, and Dreier, *Up against the Sprawl*, and Bruegmann, *Sprawl*.

39. Beauregard, *When America Became Suburban*, 144.

40. As Michael Hardt and Antonio Negri have argued in *Empire* (Cambridge: Harvard University Press, 2000): "The United States does indeed occupy a privileged position

in Empire, but this privilege derives not from its similarities to these old European imperialist powers, but from its differences. These differences can be recognized most clearly by focusing on the properly imperial (not imperialist) foundations of the United States constitution" (xiv). Parrying with the semantics of "imperial" versus "imperialist," Hardt and Negri differentiate between newer technologies of globalized power and management (largely capitalist and American, though not exclusively so), and the bureaucratic regimes and methodologies of sovereign and nation-state-based empires radiating outward from Europe in the nineteenth century and earlier (xiii–xiv). See also Amy Kaplan, *The Anarchy of Empire in the Making of U.S. Imperial Culture* (Cambridge: Harvard University Press, 2002); Victor Bascara, *Model-Minority Imperialism* (Minneapolis: University of Minnesota Press, 2006); and Inderpal Grewal, *Transnational America: Feminisms, Diasporas, Neoliberalisms* (Durham: Duke University Press, 2005).

41. Bascara, *Model-Minority Imperialism*, xxxv.

42. Beauregard, *When America Became Suburban*, 6.

43. In the mid-1990s, the "Project on Disney"—including Jane Kuenz, Assistant Professor of English, University of Southern Maine; Karen Klugman, photographer and teacher at the Creative Arts Workshop, New Haven, Connecticut; Shelton Waldrep, Visiting Assistant Professor of English, University of Southern Maine; and Susan Willis, Associate Professor of English, Duke University—compiled a volume documenting the variegated experiences produced by the Disney amusement parks, while also contemplating the problematic political and imperialist legacies of Mickey and the Disney brand (including the use of some of the park's surveillance technologies in the first Gulf War). See Project on Disney, *Inside the Mouse: Work and Play at Disney World* (Durham: Duke University Press, 1995).

Mickey is not an object of focus in "Behind the Orange Curtain," but his legacy as an avatar of American cultural imperialism has been the topic of various cultural studies, including Mary Yoko Brannen, "'Bwana Mickey': Constructing Cultural Consumption at Tokyo Disneyland," in *Cultures of United States Imperialism*, ed. Amy Kaplan and Donald E. Pease (Durham: Duke University Press, 1993), 617–634; and more recently, in Ruud Janssens, *Of Mice and Men: American Imperialism and American Studies* (Amsterdam: Amsterdam University Press, 2004). Janssens offers a fascinating and brief cultural history of Mickey Mouse in the western European context before, during, and after World War II (14–15).

44. For a blow-by-blow account of the events that led up to, and transpired during, the Orange County bankruptcy, see Mark Baldassare, *When Government Fails: The Orange County Bankruptcy* (Berkeley: University of California Press, 1998).

45. Bryan Walsh, "Recycling the Suburbs," *Time*, March 12, 2009, http://www.time.com/time/specials/packages/article/0,28804,1884779_1884782_1884756,00.html.

46. See Saskia Sassen's "Immigration Policy in a Global Economy," *SAIS Review of International Affairs* 17 (Summer/Fall 1997): 1–19; and also her more recent essay on "Global Cities and Survival Circuits" in *American Studies: An Anthology*, ed. Janice A. Radway, Kevin K. Gaines, Barry Shank, and Penny Von Eschen (Oxford: Blackwell, 2009), 185–194.

47. Marcelo M. Suarez-Orozco, "Everything You Wanted to Know about Assimilation But Were Afraid to Ask," in *The New Immigration: An Interdisciplinary Reader*, ed. Marcelo M. Suárez-Orozco, Carola Suárez-Orozco, and Desirée Baolian Qin (New York: Routledge, 2005), 77.

48. Hardt and Negri, *Empire*, xiii–xiv; Grewal, *Transnational America*, 20–22.

49. Grewal, *Transnational America*, 21.

50. Hardt and Negri, *Empire*, xvi. See a more extended discussion of the transition from imperialist to imperial forms in "Part 3: Passages of Production," 219–325. Hardt and Negri offer their reparative solution by gesturing to the multitude in "Part 4: The Decline and Fall of Empire," before following up with their book-length sequel on *The Multitude* (New York: Penguin Books, 2004).

51. Sigmund Freud, *Jokes and Their Relation to the Unconscious*, trans. James Strachey (New York: Norton, 1960), 61–63, 191–205.

52. See Harry Feinberg, "Full Service Relocation: Introduction," *HRO Today*, May 2003, http://www.hrotoday.com/content/594/full-service-relocation-introduction.

53. Numerous sociologists, psychologists, medical researchers, and business scholars have written articles about the effects of corporate relocations while arguing for and against the practice. A small but diverse sample of such work includes the following: Steven R. Holloway and James O. Wheeler, "Corporate Headquarters Relocation and Changes in Metropolitan Corporate Dominance, 1980–1987," *Economic Geography* 67 (January 1991): 54–74; David Wood, Neal Halfon, Debra Scarlata, Paul Newacheck, and Sharon Nessim, "Impact of Family Relocation on Children's Growth, Development, School Function, and Behavior," *Journal of the American Medical Association* 270, no. 11 (1993): 1334–1338; and Daniel C. Feldman and Mark C. Bolino, "Moving on Out: When Are Employees Willing to Follow Their Organization during Corporate Relocation?," *Journal of Organizational Behavior* 19 (May 1998): 275–288. See also Beverly D. Roman and John Howells, *Insiders' Guide to Relocation* (Guilford, CT: Insiders' Guides, 2004).

54. Laura Sachiko Fugikawa, a PhD candidate in American Studies and Ethnicity at the University of Southern California, explores the intertwined histories of U.S. government–sponsored Native American and Japanese American relocations in her dissertation in progress, "Domestic Containment: Japanese Americans, Native Americans, and the Cultural Politics of Relocation." Numerous histories, memoirs, and scholarly accounts have been written about Japanese internment, including Roger Daniels, Sandra C. Taylor, and Harry H. L. Kitano's important anthology *Japanese Americans: From Relocation to Redress* (1986; repr., Seattle: University of Washington Press, 1991); and Angelo N. Ancheta's *Race, Rights, and the Asian American Experience* (New Brunswick: Rutgers University Press, 2006). My own intellectual work on the histories and tropes of "relocation" has been influenced by the scholarship of Kandice Chuh, Karen Shimakawa, and Marita Sturken on representations of—as well as the failure to represent—Japanese internment. See Chuh, "Nikkei Internment: Determined Identities/ Undecidable Meanings," in *Imagine Otherwise: On Asian Americanist Critique* (Durham: Duke University Press, 2003), 58–84; Shimakawa, "Welcome a Chinatowng, Folks! Resisting Abjection," in *National Abjection: The Asian American Body Onstage* (Durham: Duke University Press, 2002), 77–98; and Sturken, "Absent Images of Memory: Remembering and Reenacting the Japanese Internment," *Positions: East Asia Cultures Critique* 5 (Winter 1997): 687–707. Among the more recent scholarship on African American representational histories of violence and subjection that that have influenced my own work are the following: Saidiya Hartman, *Scenes of Subjection: Terror, Slavery, and Self-Making in Twentieth-Century America* (Oxford: Oxford University Press, 1997); Daphne A. Brooks, *Bodies in Dissent: Spectacular Performances of Race and Freedom, 1850–1910* (Durham: Duke University Press, 2006); and Tavia Nyong'o, *The Amalgamation Waltz: Race, Performance, and the Ruses of Memory* (Minneapolis: University of Minnesota Press, 2009). Jasbir K. Puar's work on terrorism and queer complicities with discourses of "rendition" has greatly influenced my own thinking about "relocation" as a contemporary imperialist

security measure. See *Terrorist Assemblages: Homonationalism in Queer Times* (Durham: Duke University Press, 2007).

55. I borrow the term "crabgrass apartheid" from Davis and Moctezuma, "Policing the Third Border."

56. Meiling Cheng, *In Other Los Angeleses: Multicentric Performance Art* (Berkeley: University of California Press, 2002), 10; emphasis added.

57. Puar's *Terrorist Assemblages*, Martin Manalansan's *Global Divas: Filipino Gay Men in the Diaspora* (Durham: Duke University Press, 2003), and Gayatri Gopinath's *Impossible Desires: Queer Diasporas and South Asian Public Cultures* (Durham: Duke University Press, 2005) are among the most recent and paradigm-shifting offerings to these areas of inquiry, and their approaches to empire, movement, and interracial and interethnic queer imperial encounters dramatically inform my own work on the emergence of queer of color worlds in unexpected spaces.

58. Gayatri Gopinath, "Queer Regions: Locating Lesbians in *Sancharram*," in *The Blackwell Companion to Lesbian, Gay, Bisexual, Transgender, and Queer Studies*, ed. George Haggerty and Molly McGarry (Oxford: Blackwell, 2007), 341–353.

59. Ibid., 344.

60. In this sense, *Relocations* imagines itself participating in the kind of remapping Gayatri Spivak conjures in *Other Asias* (Oxford: Blackwell, 2008): a theoretical labor engaged in "rearrang[ing] desires" and "reconstellat[ing]" imaginaries about regional cartographies (4, 226).

61. Jurca, *White Diaspora*, 3–5.

62. John Archer also tackles this central problem of suburban aesthetics (or a lack thereof) in his aptly titled "Suburban Aesthetics Is Not an Oxymoron," in Blauvelt, *Worlds Away*, 129–145.

63. Elizabeth Freeman, "Packing History, Count(er)ing Generations," *New Literary History* 31 (Autumn 2000): 727–744.

64. Ibid., 728.

65. Ibid., 729–30.

66. Jurca, *White Diaspora*, 4.

67. Ibid., 5.

68. Eve Kosofsky Sedgwick, preface to *Between Men: English Literature and Male Homosocial Desire* (New York: Columbia University Press, 1992), ix.

69. Sedgwick, "Paranoid Reading and Reparative Reading," 28, 35.

70. Ibid., 35.

71. Jennifer Doyle, "Preface: A Promiscuous Reader," in *Sex Objects: Art and the Dialectics of Desire* (Minneapolis: University of Minnesota Press, 2006), vi–xvi.

72. José Esteban Muñoz, *Disidentifications: Queers of Color and the Performance of Politics* (Minneapolis: University of Minnesota Press, 1999), 4.

73. Television's "heartland" values and its cultivation of certain whitewashed imaginaries about taste and space informs my approach to the medium and its role in shaping the suburbs throughout this book. See Victoria E. Johnson's remarkable book *Heartland TV: Prime Time Television and the Struggle for U.S. Identity* (New York: New York University Press, 2008).

74. Jennifer Terry, "Proposal: Remote Intimacy," an application for the University of California Humanities Research Institute working group seminar on "Queer Locations: Race, Space and Sexuality" (Winter/Spring 2004), 2; cited with the permission of the author.

75. Benedict Anderson famously isolates the "presentation of simultaneity" as a significant temporal discourse in the formation of imagined communities like "the nation" in *Imagined Communities: Reflections on the Origin and Spread of Nationalism* (London: Verso, 1983). See especially his discussion of Hegel's supposition that reading the daily newspapers has become a substitute for "morning prayers": "Each communicant is well aware that the ceremony he performs is being replicated simultaneously by thousands (or millions) of others of whose existence he is confident, yet of whose identity he has not he slightest notion" (35).

76. A work contextualizing the innovations and disruptions forged by VHS and earlier analog formats of recording and copying is Lucas Hilderbrand's *Inherent Vice: Bootleg Histories of Videotape and Copyright* (Durham: Duke University Press, 2009).

77. For an expansive account of the role repeat programming has played in shaping American popular history and memory, especially since its proliferation in the mid-1970s, see Derek Kompare, *Rerun Nation: How Repeats Invented American Television* (New York: Routledge, 2005).

78. The legendary music writers Jon Savage and Simon Frith have engaged in an intertextual conversation with each other about the prominent influence of suburban experience on British punk, new wave, mod, and pop music. See Frith's "The Suburban Sensibility in British Rock and Pop," in *Taking Popular Music Seriously": Selected Essays* (Aldershot: Ashgate Press, 2007), 137–148; and the updated and expanded edition of Savage's 1991 book *England's Dreaming: Anarchy, Sex Pistols, Punk Rock, and Beyond* (New York: St. Martin's Press, 2001).

79. For an eloquent take on the repurposing of not only suburban garages but also the tools and technologies found within them for musical innovation, see Christine Bacareza Balance, "Breaks, Cuts, and Scratches: Future Aesthetics in Filipino American Turntablist Culture," in her PhD dissertation, "Intimate Acts, Martial Cultures: Performance and Belonging in Filipino America" (New York University, 2007), 112–154.

80. The *Los Angeles Times'* lead popular music critic, Ann Powers, has written one of the most haunting pieces about the significance of the "deep catalogs" offered by chain stores like Tower Records. See "An Appreciation: 'Deep Catalog' Taught a Deep Love for Music," *Los Angeles Times*, October 11, 2006, http://articles.latimes.com/2006/oct/11/entertainment/et-reflection11.

81. I am always inspired, in theory and practice, by all the karaoke theorized and performed alongside Christine Bacareza Balance (or the other half of my as-yet unformed karaoke band, Wilson Philipina). See Balance's "Repeat Performance: Karaoke and Affect in Filipino America," a conference paper delivered at the American Studies Association Annual Convention in Philadelphia in October 2007; cited with the permission of the author.

82. Josh Kun, *Audiotopia: Music, Race, and America* (Berkeley: University of California Press, 2005), 3.

83. This reflection on Naugahyde's public discomforts is culled from Alexandra Vazquez, "Latin Freestyle: With Her Black Liquid Eyeliner in Her Hand," from her PhD dissertation, "Instrumental Migrations: The Transnational Movements of Cuban Music" (New York University, 2006), 188.

84. Vazquez invokes "transnational suburbia" in ibid. Mike Davis has also depicted the economic and cultural flows between peripheries in Mexico and Central America and the U.S. suburbs in "Transnational Suburbs," in *Magical Urbanism: Latinos Reinvent the U.S. City* (London: Verso, 2001), 93–108.

85. Balance, "Repeat Performance," 6.

NOTES TO CHAPTER 2

1. Eve Oishi is the first scholar to have published on Chan's JJ Chinois projects, in "Bad Asians, the Sequel: Continuing Trends in API Film and Video," in a special issue of *Millennium Film Journal* on "Gay and Lesbian Experimental Cinema," ed. Jim Hubbard, 39 (Fall 2003): 34–41. Oishi contextualizes Chan's work within the transformation of Asian American media arts as a result of web-based technologies and distribution. A subsequent version of my MLA conference paper on JJ Chinois was published in *Social Text* as "What's Queer About Queer Studies Now?," ed. David Eng, Jose Esteban Munoz, and Judith Halberstam, 84/85 (Fall/Winter 2005): 193–216. Mimi Thi Nguyen has also written about

Chan's experiments with fan culture through her JJ Chinois projects. Nguyen reads JJ through the lens of the kung fu legend, Bruce Lee's star text: a discourse saturated with racialized expectations about gender, sexuality, and mass appeal. See "Bruce Lee I Love You: Discourses of Race and Masculinity in the Queer Superstardom of JJ Chinois," in *Alien Encounters: Popular Culture in Asian America*, ed. Mimi Thi Nguyen and Thuy Linh Nguyen Tu (Durham: Duke University Press, 2007), 271–304.

2. See Sedgwick, "Paranoid Reading and Reparative Reading."

3. I also mean to conjure here a faint echo of the storied East Coast/West Coast rivalry in hip-hop, which also grappled with different visions of the good life. See Murray Forman, "'Represent': Race, Space, and Place in Rap Music," *Popular Music* 19, no. 1 (2000): 65–90. For a concise description of the rivalry, see Stephen Best and Douglas Kellner, "Rap, Black Rage, and Racial Difference," *Enculturation* 2 (Spring 1999): http://enculturation. gmu.edu/2_2/best-kellner.html.

4. For an expansive analysis of how the American dream cohered around the United States' increasing suburbanization after World War II, see Archer's "Nationalizing the Dream" and "Analyzing the Dream," in *Architecture and Suburbia*.

5. Nancy Foner, *From Ellis Island to JFK: New York's Two Great Waves of Immigration* (New Haven: Yale University Press, 2000). An essay that contextualizes and contrasts the experience of immigrants on Angel Island to the immigrants on Ellis Island is Roger Daniels's "No Lamps Were Lit for Them: Angel Island and the Historiography of Asian American Immigration," *Journal of American Ethnic History* 17 (Fall 1997): 3–18.

6. See chap. 1 for my introduction of Judith Halberstam's term "metronormativity," from *In a Queer Time and Place*. See also Herring, *Another Country*, for perhaps the most detailed genealogy of metronormativity to date.

7. For a concise account of the link between suburban growth and the automobile, see Blauvelt, "Worlds Away and the World Next Door," 16. Kathleen McHugh cleverly reconfigures feminist criticism and its conversations about the traffic in women in her piece "Women in Traffic: L.A. Autobiography," *South Atlantic Quarterly* 97 (Spring 1998): 391–412. A *New York Times* story on May 2, 1955, documented the day in a life of a suburban woman and her automobile (Merrill Folsom's "Suburbia on Wheels: Around the Clock with a Mother Serving in a Typical Westchester Car Pool"). The story has been reprinted as "A Day in the Life of a Suburban Carpool Mother" in Nicolaides and Wiese, *Suburb Reader*, 270–271.

8. Nguyen, "Bruce Lee I Love You," 275.

9. Lynne Chan, interview with the author via e-mail, May 2004.

10. Freeman, "Packing History, Count(er) ing Generations," 728.

11. It would be a formidable task to catalog all the movies in which "Don't Stop Believin'" plays a crucial role, either diegetically or extradiegetically. Two of the most striking recent examples can be heard and seen in 1998's *The Wedding Singer* (reorchestrated to cellos as a wedding march) and 2003's *Monster* (as the roller-rink sound track to Aileen Wuornos and Selby Wall's first lesbian kiss). For a discussion of the latter, see Karen Tongson, "Metronormativity and Gay Globalization," in *Quer durch die Geisteswissenschaften: Perspektiven der Queer Theory*, ed. Elahe Haschemi Yekani and Beatrice Micahelis (Berlin: Querverlag, 2005), 40–42. The Detroit Tigers baseball team has also used the song as a stadium theme—especially in broadcasts during their 2006 World Series campaign against the St. Louis Cardinals—because of the song's second verse, which alludes to a "city boy, born and raised in south Detroit," who also "took the midnight train goin' anywhere." Playing on perhaps the most famous use of the song in a TV show—*The Sopranos* series finale, 2007's "Made in America"—Hillary Clinton filmed

a campaign video in which she, like Tony Soprano, enters a diner as the suspense builds about which song she's selected as her official campaign theme for her 2008 presidential run. This video is still available at http://www.dailymotion.com/video/x2breg_hillary-clinton-reprend-les-soprano. A choral arrangement of the song is a pivotal plot point in the premiere of the hit network TV series *Glee* (2009), a comedy about nerdy and queer show-choir teens. In 2008, "Don't Stop Believin'" became the first catalog track to have sold over two million units in digital sales according to SoundScan. See http://www.hypebot.com/hypebot/2008/11/the-top-selling.html. For more on the song's reentry into the popular zeitgeist, see David Marchese, "Start Believin'," Salon.com, June 13, 2007, http://www.salon.com/ent/audiofile/2007/06/13/journey/.

12. "Don't Stop Believin'," composed by Jonathan Cain, Steve Perry, and Neal Schon, on Journey, *Escape*, Columbia Records, 1981.

13. See Archer's "Nationalizing the Dream" and "Analyzing the Dream." Robert A. Beauregard periodizes these developments within what he calls the "short American century" (the late 1940s through the mid-1970s), during which the suburban ethos of financial and spatial mobility arguably reached its apex. See *When America Became Suburban*.

14. Rob Latham links the automobile to bohemian expressions of wanderlust in the 1960s. He writes, "The automobile, as the incarnation of individual agency within this system, was constructed as both the safely domesticated possession of hard-working suburbanites and a vehicle for dangerous thrill seeking—not to mention for the keen, impulsive wanderlust that drove the Beat writers." See *Consuming Youth: Vampires, Cyborgs, and the Culture of Consumption* (Chicago: University of Chicago Press, 2002), 197.

15. Herring, *Another Country*, 25.

16. A watershed work that theorizes queer migrations to big cities is Kath Weston's "Get Thee to a Big City: Sexual Imaginary and the Great Gay Migration," in *Long Slow Burn: Sexuality and Social Science* (New York: Routledge, 1998), 29–56.

17. More recent studies have begun to relocate their accounts of Asian immigration to the suburbs. See Cindy I-Fen Cheng's remarkably comprehensive essay "Out of Chinatown and into the Suburbs: Chinese Americans and the Politics of Cultural Citizenship in Early Cold War America," *American Quarterly* 58 (December 2006): 1067–1090. See also William P. O'Hare, William H. Frey, and Dan Fost, "Asians in the Suburbs," *American Demographics* 16, no. 5 (1994): 32–38; and Fong, *First Suburban Chinatown*. For a study of the "ethnic enclave" as it shaped the transactions of urban Chinatowns, see Min Zhou, *Chinatown: The Socioeconomic Potential of an Urban Enclave* (Philadelphia: Temple University Press, 1992).

18. Among the more recent publications in queer studies to grapple with U.S imperialism are: Puar, *Terrorist Assemblages*; Gopinath, *Impossible Desires*; and two major anthologies, Arnaldo Cruz-Malave and Martin F. Manalansan IV, eds., *Queer Globalizations: Citizenship and the Afterlife of Colonialism* (New York: New York University Press, 2002); and Eithne Luibhéid and Lionel Cantú Jr., eds., *Queer Migrations: Sexuality, U.S. Citizenship, and Border Crossings* (Minneapolis: University of Minnesota Press, 2005). A recent work in suburban studies that focuses on the imperial dimensions of American suburban expansion is Beauregard's *When America Became Suburban*.

19. Chuh, *Imagine Otherwise*, 3.

20. For analyses of the rhetoric of "burden" as it functioned in the United States' imperial expansion at the turn of the twentieth century, see Kaplan, *Anarchy of Empire*, and Bascara, *Model-Minority Imperialism*. Bascara in particular works meticulously through how the rhetoric of burden functions to repress the American imperial project in the collective cultural consciousness.

21. U.S. Bureau of the Census, "Census 2000 Urban and Rural Classification." In

2004, geographers at the Geographical Information Science Center at the University of
California, Berkeley, partnered with scholars
at the Northeast Institute of Geography and
Agricultural Ecology in the Chinese Academy
of Sciences to conduct a "preliminary spatial
analysis method for building an urban-
suburban-rural category in the specific sample
area of central California." This group of
scholars concluded that they "perfected the
TIGERs [Topographically Integrated Geographic Encoding and Referencing system's]
urban-rural classification scheme by adding
suburban category [sic]." Zhou et al., "Spatial
Cluster Method Supported by GIS for
Urban-Suburban-Rural Classification" (337).
As I discussed in my introduction, definitions
of suburban space are constantly evolving in
multiple fields of cultural analysis. Debates
about what defines "the suburbs" continue to
take place in urban planning and suburban
studies, as well as in history and cultural
studies. Most accounts of what constitutes the
suburbs are historically and regionally specific,
whereas some have been absorbed into a larger
discourse about "sprawl."

22. By invoking these two conceptual and
spatial polarities, I am, of course, referring to
Raymond Williams's paradigmatic mapping
of English literature in *The Country and the
City* (Oxford: Oxford University Press, 1973).
What is striking about this watershed work
is how often Williams refers to the "suburban"
as a mediating concept that interrupts and
sometimes even undercuts the rural and urban
imaginaries with which a range of authors,
from Juvenal to Richard Jefferies, have strongly
identified. For example, Williams deflates a
certain mythos about Jefferies as a "lifelong
countryman [and] son of yeoman farmers."
"The reality," Williams writes, "is different and
more interesting. [He is a] suburban writer
and journalist, recreating the country of his
adolescence on the struggling smallholding"
(192–193). In his appendix to the book,
Williams also asserts that while the "suburban"
has had a "physical sense since the seventeenth

century," it acquired "a social sense from the
early nineteenth" (307).

23. Archer, *Architecture and Suburbia*, xix.

24. Barry Langford, "Margins of the City:
Towards a Dialectic of Suburban Desire," in
Phillips, Watt, and Shuttleton, *De-centering
Sexualities*, 69.

25. For a take on the new residential
vernaculars made possible by the customization of suburban homes by Latino communities in Los Angeles, see James Thomas Rojas,
NACLA Report on the Americas 28 (1995):
32–34.

26. Ibid. See also Rojas, "The Enacted
Environment of East Los Angles," *Places* 8
(Spring 1993): 42–53; and Archer, "Suburban
Aesthetics Is Not an Oxymoron."

27. My use of the term "re-Orient"
here is influenced by Gayatri Chakravorty
Spivak's discussion of efforts to expand critical
imaginaries about what regions and nations
constitute "Asia." See "Our Asias—2001:
How to Be a Continentalist," in *Other Asias*,
209–238.

28. Jurca, *White Diaspora*, 4.

29. There have been numerous scholarly
accounts of the demographic shifts pre-
cipitated by gentrification in urban centers,
pushing communities of color and the
working classes to suburban and exurban
locations with more affordable housing. See
Wolch, Pastor, and Drier, *Up against the
Sprawl*, especially the introduction coauthored
by the editors, as well as the essays by Laura
Pulido ("Environmental Racism and Urban
Development," 71–98) and Enrico A. Marcelli
("From the Barrio to the 'Burbs? Immigration and the Dynamics of Suburbanization,"
123–150). See also Lydia Mihelič Pulsipher
and Alex Pulsipher, *World Regional Geography:
Global Patterns, Local Lives*, 3rd ed. (New
York: Macmillan, 2006), 79. For the impact of
the development concept of "New Urbanism"
on these relocation patterns, see Emily Talen,
*New Urbanism and American Planning: The
Conflict of Cultures* (New York: Routledge,
2005); and Neil Smith, "New Globalism, New

Urbanism: Gentrification as Global Urban Strategy," *Antipode: A Radical Journal of Geography* 34 (July 2002): 427–450. Public policy and civic-funded gentrification have also led to the dispersal of communities of color from urban cores to suburbs throughout the United States. See Brett Williams, "There Goes the Neighborhood: Gentrification, Displacement, and Homelessness in Washington, D.C.," in *There's No Place Like Home: Anthropological Perspectives on Housing and Homelessness in the United States*, ed. Anna Lou Dehavenon (Westport, CT: Greenwood Press, 1999), 145–164. Recent social histories like Timothy Fong's *First Suburban Chinatown* and Wayne Brekhus's *Peacocks, Chameleons, Centaurs* have powerfully argued that late twentieth-century and postmillennial American suburbs are increasingly populated by "minority majorities" of queer and racialized subjects.

30. O'Hare, Frey, and Fost, "Asians in the Suburbs."

31. As I've argued elsewhere, middle-aged white men are not the only ones to wallow in the "abasement of advantage" the suburbs provide. Younger boys, particularly those who identify with the suburban subculture of "Emo" are also prone to self-pity amid prosperity. See Karen Tongson, "Tickle Me Emo: Lesbian Balladeering, Straight Boy Emo, and the Politics of Affect," in *Queering the Popular Pitch*, ed. Sheila Whiteley and Jennifer Rycenga (New York: Routledge, 2006), 55–66. See also Matt Greenwald, *Nothing Feels Good: Punk Rock, Teenagers, and Emo* (New York: St. Martin's Griffin, 2003).

32. For a cultural history of the symbiosis between broadcast media (particularly television) and the suburbs, see Spigel, *Welcome to the Dream House*. See also Vicky Johnson's account in *Heartland TV* of how the "heartland" mythos of the United States' Midwest is crucial in TV's evolution and self-fashioning.

33. Andrew Blauvelt at the Walker Art Center in Minneapolis and Tracy Meyers at the Heinz Architectural Center of the Carnegie Museum of Art in Pittsburgh co-

curated an expansive exhibit of suburban art and architecture in 2008 for their respective venues, titled *Worlds Away: New Suburban Landscapes*. The catalog is a tremendous resource for anyone interested in suburban aesthetics, theory, and architecture. See Blauvelt, *Worlds Away*.

34. "Master Plan" was exhibited to the public for the first time from June 4 to September 6, 2006, at the Orange County Museum of Art for a mini-retrospective of Opie's work, titled *In and Around Home*. Organized to celebrate the debut of Opie's two most recent series of work, "1999" (1999) and "In and Around Home" (2005), the exhibit sought to contextualize Opie's larger oeuvre within her Southern California environs. In addition to "Master Plan" and her most recent projects, Opie's "Freeways," "Houses," "Mini-Malls" and "Surfers" series were also on display as part of the exhibit. See the commemorative catalog, Catherine Opie, *In and Around Home* (Ridgefield, CT: Aldrich Contemporary Art Museum, 2006).

35. In 2008, the Guggenheim Museum in New York staged a major retrospective of her work, including many of these photographic series. Holand Cotter's review in the *New York Times* focuses on Opie's eclectic approach to chronicling queer subcultures and American landscapes: "She is an insider and an outsider: a documentarian and a provocateur; a classicist and a maverick; a trekker and a stay-at-home; a lesbian mother who resists the gay mainstream; an American—birthplace: Sandusky, Ohio—who has serious arguments with her country and culture." "A Retrospective of Many Artists, All of Them One Woman," *New York Times*, September 25, 2008, http://www.nytimes.com/2008/09/26/arts/design/26opie.html. See also Nico Israel, "Catherine Opie," *ArtForum*, Summer 2000, http://findarticles.com/p/articles/mi_m0268/is_10_38/ai_65071285/.

36. Grace Glueck, "Art in Review," *New York Times*, April 3, 1998, http://query.nytimes.com/gst/fullpage.html?res=9903EEDF153AF930A3 5757C0A96E958260&ref=catherine_opie.

37. Samuel Delany, *Times Square Red, Times Square Blue* (New York: New York University Press, 2001).

38. For more on the impact of Internet technologies on Asian American media arts, notably on Chan's JJ Chinois projects, see Oishi, "Bad Asians, the Sequel."

39. Now portions of Murray Hill have been transformed into Manhattan's very own Koreatown, most famously a strip of Thirty-Second Street between Fifth and Sixth Avenues, called "Korea Way." Manhattan's "K-Town" is primarily entertainment, service, and business oriented (with Korean restaurants, salons, and *noraebang*, or private karaoke rooms), and not a residential enclave for New York City's Korean communities, who tend to live in the outer boroughs.

40. Janelle Brown, "The Dazed and the Bored on the I-5," *New York Times*, November 15, 2002, http://www.nytimes.com/2002/11/15/travel/driving-the-dazed-and-the-bored-on-i-5.html.

41. What are termed "cities" in the central valleys of California (like Fresno and JJ's purported birthplace, Bakersfield) have recently been referred to as "edge cities" or hybrid suburban environments, characterized by large civic governments and growing residential populations. Architecturally, these "edge cities" or exurbs are more suburban in character than the classic, early twentieth-century American notion of the vertical metropolis. See Joel Garreau, *Edge City: Life on the New Frontier* (New York: Doubleday, 1991).

42. The first Steer 'n Stein Chan ever came across was located off the Van Buren Boulevard exit on Route 60 in Riverside, in a rural stretch of town called Pedley, where the residents still keep horses and ranches. Chan, interview with the author via e-mail, November 3, 2002. The Steer 'n Stein is a real Southern California chain—albeit a very small one—of affordable steakhouses. As of this writing there are locations in Victorville (northeast of Los Angeles in the desert, en route to Nevada), Palmdale (a desert turned oasis of affordable housing north

of Los Angeles in the Antelope Valley), Hemet (a mountain/lake town in the Inland Empire), and Rancho Cucamonga, a developing suburb in the Inland Empire (the location of the afore-mentioned Ice Cube film *Next Friday*). There is no Steer 'n Stein currently open in Coalinga.

43. Chan, interview with the author via e-mail, November 3, 2002.

44. See Fong, *First Suburban Chinatown*, 35–54.

45. Brekhus critiques these queer cosmopolitans in *Peacocks, Chameleons, Centaurs*, 5–7. See also Dereka Rushbrook, "Cities, Queer Space, and the Cosmopolitan Tourist," *GLQ* 8, nos. 1/2 (2006): 183–206.

46. For a detailed history of Silicon Valley's expansion as a result of its proximity to universities, military spending, venture capital, and immigration, see AnnaLee Saxenian, *Regional Advantage: Culture and Competition in Silicon Valley and Route 128* (Cambridge: Harvard University Press, 1994).

47. Chan, interview with the author via telephone, July 31, 2009. Chan's father came to the United States in 1970 on a "Third Preference" or professional visa. Her mother came on a tourist visa and promptly married Chan's father in order to be added to his application for a green card. According to Chan's mother (who communicated these details via e-mail, asking that her first name remain anonymous): "We waited a total of thirteen years before we got the green card and waited five years to qualify for citizenship. Because we came from Hong Kong, we had to compete with everyone else in the British Commonwealth for visas. Hong Kong, from what I remember, only got about 200 a year as part of the quota. It wasn't until the 80s when Margaret Thatcher was negotiating with the Chinese regarding the return of Hong Kong to China that some U.S. senators recommended to up the quota for Hong Kong. This is why it took so long."

48. "Because the 1965 legislation favored the later cohort of [professional- and managerial-class] migrants, the roughly

fivefold increase between 1970 and 1990 in the population of persons of Asian descent living in the United States has meant dramatic alterations to 'Asian America' along multiple identificatory axes, including nativity and citizenship." Chuh, *Imagine Otherwise*, 7. See also, of course, Lisa Lowe's watershed work *Immigrant Acts: On Asian American Cultural Politics* (Durham: Duke University Press, 1998). Glen M. Mimura further argues that if post-1965 immigration patterns indicate "an epoch of globalization in which the Euro-American nation-states no longer exercise absolute sovereignty and dominance," earlier histories of Asian immigrant and migrant labor from the nineteenth century until the 1965 act recontextualize the cheaper, exploitative forms of service labor most Asians performed, and continue to perform, in the United States. See Mimura, *The Ghostlife of Third Cinema: Asian American Film and Video* (Minneapolis: University of Minnesota Press, 2009), 23.

49. Chan, interview with the author via telephone, July 20, 2009.

50. O'Hare, Frey, and Fost, "Asians in the Suburbs," 32.

51. Chan, interview with the author via e-mail, November 3, 2002.

52. Ibid.

53. Ibid.

54. Ibid.

55. Inderpal Grewal describes how some immigrant subjects who (not unlike Chan's parents) were working in the technology industries of Silicon Valley clung to the concept of the "American dream" even after the "bubble" began to burst at the turn of the twenty-first century. See *Transnational America*, 4–14.

56. Lynne Chan, "Tour Dates," http://www.jjchinois.com/. Chan is not the first to find comfort in the chain store. Virginia Postrel offers a reparative reading of chains in her piece "In Praise of Chain Stores: They Aren't Destroying Local Flavor—They're Providing Variety and Comfort," originally

published in the *Atlantic Monthly* in 2006, but more recently anthologized in Blauvelt, *Worlds Away*, 70–72.

57. See Mike Davis, *City of Quartz: Excavating the Future in Los Angeles* (New York: Vintage, 1990), 84–88.

58. Margaret Salazar offers an extensive cultural history of "tiki" motifs in Southern California's tourist destinations, particularly those in San Diego. See Salazar's chapter, "Marine Lands: Tourism, Military, and Conquest across the Pacific," in "Representational Conquest: Tourism, Display, and Public Memory in 'America's Finest City'" (PhD diss., University of Southern California, 2010).

59. Chan attended UC Davis for her first two years and then transferred to UCLA for her undergraduate degree in fine arts.

60. In many respects these earlier photographs coincided with the styles explored by such L.A.-area artists as Hector Silva. For more on Silva's queering of Chicano masculinities, see Richard T. Rodriguez, "Queering the Homeboy Aesthetic," *Aztlan: A Journal of Chicano Studies* 31 (Fall 2006): 127–137.

61. Chan, interview with the author via e-mail, November 3, 2002.

62. Mimura, *Ghostlife of Third Cinema*, 3. In his discussion of the "Asian" as a mediating racialized and sexual term, Mimura also engages with Richard Fung's watershed essay "Looking for My Penis: The Eroticized Asian in Gay Video Porn," in *Q & A: Queer in Asian America*, ed. David L. Eng and Alice Y. Hom (Philadelphia: Temple University Press, 1998), 115–134.

63. Chan, interview with the author via e-mail, November 3, 2002.

64. Ibid.

65. Both Bascara and Chuh are engaging with and expanding Lisa Lowe's influential work on Asian American citizenship and culture in the wake of the transformations wrought by twentieth-century immigration legislation. See Bascara, *Model-Minority Imperialism*, and Chuh, *Imagine Otherwise*, as well as Lowe, *Immigrant Acts*.

66. Chuh, *Imagine Otherwise*, 12.

67. Beauregard, *When America Became Suburban*.

68. Chuh, *Imagine Otherwise*, 10.

69. Ibid., 10–11.

70. See Matt Cook's work on the sexual topographies of European sexology in his chapter on "The Inverted City" in *London and the Culture of Homosexuality, 1885–1914* (Cambridge: Cambridge University Press, 2003), 73–91.

71. Chauncey, *Gay New York*. See also Elizabeth Lapovsky Kennedy and Madeline D. Davis, *Boots of Leather, Slippers of Gold: The History of a Lesbian Community* (New York: Routledge, 1993); and Esther Newton, *Cherry Grove, Fire Island: Sixty Years in America's First Gay and Lesbian Town* (Boston: Beacon Press, 1993).

72. See Marc Stein, "Theoretical Politics, Local Communities: The Making of LGBT Historiography," *GLQ: A Journal of Lesbian and Gay Studies* 11, no. 4 (2005): 607.

73. Ibid.

74. John D'Emilio, *Sexual Politics, Sexual Communities: The Making of a Homosexual Minority in the United States, 1940–1970* (Chicago: University of Chicago Press, 1983), 167.

75. Stein, "Theoretical Politics, Locational Communities," 607.

76. Chauncey, *Gay New York*. Scott Herring also offers an extensive genealogy of metronormativity, from Chauncey and Kath Weston onward, in the introduction to *Another Country*.

77. Chauncey, *Gay New York*, 23.

78. Ibid.; emphasis added.

79. Ibid., 28.

80. Ibid.

81. Chauncey explains that "the differences between men's and women's power and the qualities ascribed to them in a male-dominated culture were so significant that the social and spatial organization of gay male and lesbian life inevitably took very different forms," hence his decision to limit his study

to the lives of gay men (*Gay New York*, 27). Kennedy and Davis affirm such differences with their attention to bar culture and leisure sports leagues, and the working-class modes of sociability that come to define lesbian cultures in places like Buffalo, which exist beyond metropolitan centers like New York City. See Kennedy and Davis, *Boots of Leather, Slippers of Gold*.

82. "Gay men developed a highly sophisticated system of subcultural codes—codes of dress, speech, and style—that enabled them to recognize one another on the streets, at work and at parties and bars, and to carry on intricate conversations whose coded meaning was unintelligible to potentially hostile people around them." Chauncey, *Gay New York*, 4.

83. Samuel Delany, *Times Square Red, Times Square Blue* (New York: New York University Press, 2001), xix.

84. Ibid.

85. Ibid., 123–125. Delany explores the mutually beneficial dimensions of "contact," or what may begin as incidental, social encounters among strangers in places like "the line at the grocery counter," when "a neighbor . . . has brought her chair out to take some air on the stoop," or during "the discussion that begins with the person next to you at a bar" (123). One "supermarket-line conversation" in particular hints at the possibility of such social transactions leading to material as well as intellectual connections: "Another supermarket-line conversation was with a young man who was an aspiring director, looking for some science fiction stories to turn into brief teleplays. I was able to jot down for him a quick bibliography of young SF writers and short stories that he might pursue. Whether or not it came to anything, I have no way of knowing. But it was easy and fun" (124). Delany concludes, "The more ordinary sorts of contact yield *their* payoff in moments of crisis" (125). While I am not taking issue with Delany's argument about contact's potential to transcend the social to become something more—in some instances,

even lifesaving—I do take issue with his wider emphasis on the special character of these encounters in dense, urban environments. Taken on its own, there is nothing in his description of how contact functions that would preclude such encounters from coming to full fruition in spatial environments beyond the urban.

86. Much of the demographic information on gay and lesbian populations in *The Gay and Lesbian Atlas* is culled from the 2000 U.S. census, which, for the first time, surveyed partnered, household-sharing gays and lesbians. Because the census collected data on gay and lesbians using only categories of normative social arrangements like couples and families, the *Gay and Lesbian Atlas* offers a very limited portrait of gay and lesbian communities throughout the United States, despite its admirable geographical coverage. See Gary J. Gates and Jason Ost, *The Gay and Lesbian Atlas* (Washington, DC: Urban Institute Press, 2004).

87. Ibid., 28.

88. Ibid.

89. Ibid.

90. Edward Said most famously commented on the "consolidated vision" of empire in the metropolis disseminated in nineteenth-century British novels—or, in his words, "the cultural artefacts [sic] of bourgeois society." Said named New York from 1940 to 1970 as a "para-formation" of the imperial metropolis of London. See *Culture and Imperialism* (New York: Vintage, 1994), 244. Historically, in the United States, New York has also been figured as an "imperial metropolis of the world." See David M. Scobey, "Imagining the Imperial Metropolis," in *Empire City: The Making and Meaning of New York City Landscape* (Philadelphia: Temple University Press, 2002), 158–187.

91. Manalansan, *Global Divas*, 65.

92. See Delany, *Times Square Red, Times Square Blue*, 111–144.

92. Manalansan, *Global Divas*, 83.

93. Ibid., 86.

94. See an early publication of Gopinath's, "Funny Boys and Girls: Notes on a South Asian Queer Planet," in *Asian American Sexualities: Dimensions of the Gay and Lesbian Experience*, ed. Russell Leong (New York: Routledge, 1996), 119–125. Gopinath's extensive body of work on "queer diaspora" has enriched this initially very narrow and normative concept of diaspora while alerting us to the underlying nationalist limitations of the term.

95. Gopinath, *Impossible Desires*, 20.

96. Ibid.

97. As Gopinath explains, diaspora "needs 'queerness' in order to rescue it from its genealogical implications," while "'queerness' also needs 'diaspora' in order to make it more supple in relation to questions of race, colonialism, migration, and globalization." *Impossible Desires*, 11. Mimura painstakingly traces diaspora's variations not only in Asian American studies, but also (in a related form) in black British cultural studies and postcolonial studies. See Mimura, "Diaspora, or Modernity's Other: Theorizing Asian American Identity and Representation," in *Ghostlife of Third Cinema*, 1–24. The citation in the main text is taken from page 14.

98. Halberstam, *In a Queer Time and Place*, 27.

99. See Ann Pellegrini, "Consuming Lifestyle: Commodity Capitalism and Transformations in Gay Identity," in Cruz-Malave and Manalansan, *Queer Globalizations*, 134–148. See also Lisa Duggan's work, which brilliantly traces how gay consumerism is imbricated with neoliberal political and cultural formations. *The Twilight of Equality: Neoliberalism, Cultural Politics, and the Attack on Democracy* (Boston: Beacon Press, 2003). For a concise take on how gay consumer culture has pervaded mainstream commerce, see Elizabeth Throop's entry on "Gay Consumerism" in *Material Culture in America: Understanding Everyday Life*, ed. Helen Sheumaker and Shirley Teresa Wajda (Santa Barbara, CA: ABC-CLIO, 2008), 208–210.

100. See Jasbir K. Puar's discussion of the "global ascendancy of whiteness" as it traffics in the form of American "homonationalism": an iteration of queer politics "that corresponds with the coming out of the exceptionalism of American empire." *Terrorist Assemblages*, 2–5. Arnaldo Cruz-Malave and Martin F. Manalansan IV address the "appropriation and deployment of queer subjectivities, cultures, and political agendas for the legitimation of hegemonic institutions presently in discursive crisis" in a globalized economy in their introduction to *Queer Globalizations*, 5.

101. Grewal, *Transnational America*, 5–8. See especially Grewal's discussion of the richly multifaceted, but also problematic, effects of "transnational connectivities." These are a set of "affiliative practices" routed through technology and other networks of consumption that enabled diasporic subjects "to become provisionally attached to new identities and nation-states" as they saw themselves becoming "American," often in suburban centers of technology like Silicon Valley, where Chan is from. As Grewal explains, "Becoming 'American' had both a hegemonic and a heterogeneous meaning articulated within and through forms of transnational consumption and struggles for rights" (8).

102. Chan's incidental references in our interviews to *The Joy Luck Club* (Amy Tan's best-selling 1989 novel turned box office smash after the 1993 film adaptation directed by Wayne Wang) were meant to be humorous, a kind of shorthand for certain sentimental renditions of mother-daughter bonds and intergenerational immigrant narratives. But as we turn to more intricate discussions about diaspora, it is important to register just how significant *The Joy Luck Club* has become in Asian American popular discourse. For a reparative approach to how *The Joy Luck Club* can be read beyond its own production of sentimentality, as "commenting on the national public's aestheticizing of mother-daughter relationships in its discourse about Asian Americans," see Lisa Lowe, "Heterogeneity, Hybridity, Multiplicity:

Marking Asian-American Differences," in *Theorizing Diaspora: A Reader*, ed. Jana Evans Braziel and Anita Mannur (Oxford: Blackwell Publishing, 2003), 148.

103. For more on the history of Thrifty, see John N. Campbell, "Thrifty Corporation," *Wall Street Transcript*, January 4, 1983, 68, 529. For historical commentary on their ice cream, see Mitchell Gordon, "Thrifty Drug Stores Head for Healthy Earnings Gain," *Barron's*, November 6, 1972, 31.

104. These lines about "shallowness" and "depth" are haunted by my previous life as a queer Victorian literature scholar. In earlier discussions of gay literature, particularly Oscar Wilde, the question of shallowness and depth was inextricably bound up with questions of style and the "artifice" of the homosexual. See Jonathan Dollimore's classic essay that reframed this debate after the emergence of gay studies in the 1980s, "Different Desires: Subjectivity and Transgression in Wilde and Gide," *Textual Practice* 1 (Spring 1987): 48–67. See also Oliver S. Buckton, "'Desire Without Limit': Dissident Confession in Oscar Wilde's *De Profundis*," in *Victorian Sexual Dissidence*, ed. Richard Dellamora (Chicago: University of Chicago Press, 1999), 171–190.

105. Chuh, *Imagine Otherwise*, 111, 10.

106. Ibid.

107. For more extended readings of Linmark's novel, see David Eng, "Out Here and Over There: Queerness and Diaspora in Asian American Studies," in *Racial Castration: Managing Masculinity in Asian America* (Durham: Duke University Press, 2001), 204–228; and Victor Bascara, "'Everybody Wants to Be Farrah': Absurd Histories and Historical Absurdities," in *Model-Minority Imperialism*, 113–134. Bascara not only traces the novel's reception in Asian American studies as well as queer studies, but also considers the work a precursor to queer of color critique "before such an idea was codified" (118). Eng focuses on the character of Orlando (who dresses as Farrah Fawcett), tracking through his narrative the disciplinary regimes and

apparatuses of gender as they are interwoven with citizenship and the state.

108. R. Zamora Linmark, *Rolling the R's* (New York: Kaya Press, 1997), 1.

109. For more on how shadowy queer figures, like rapacious lesbian inmates and proto-queer street hustlers and runaways, made their way onto 1970s television, see Elana Levine, "The Sex Threat: Regulating and Representing Sexually Endangered Youth," in *Wallowing in Sex: The New Sexual Culture of 1970s American Television* (Durham: Duke University Press, 2007), 76–122.

110. Manalansan, *Global Divas*, 46.

111. Ibid., 60. Manalansan beautifully describes swardspeak as a "vagabond tongue and an itinerant code [that] refuses any fixed space and contexts." But he ultimately focuses on a transient cosmopolitanism that swardspeak makes possible for Filipino gay men in the Philippines as well as the diaspora: "Switching and shuttling between languages, the swardspeaker acquires a cosmopolitanism that is sometimes denied him elsewhere because of his economic, racial, ethnic, and cultural hierarchies and exclusions. The kind of cosmopolitanism that is not always and already a privileged one but rather comes close to what Louisa Schein terms as 'oppositional cosmopolitanism' or non-elite 'worldly' negotiations with the 'nexus of privilege and constraint.' Therefore, Filipino gay swardspeakers in the Philippines and in the diaspora, despite being excluded from numerous arenas, are creating alternative worlds and localities by their rapid and creative rearticulation and appropriation of various images, meanings, and practices." While I fundamentally agree with Manalansan about swardspeak's effects, and its intervention in structures of style, power, and language, I prefer to focus instead on how other "vagabond tongues" might find salience through spatio-cultural models beyond cosmopolitanism.

112. Rachel Hooper and Jayme Yen, "A Lexicon of Suburban Neologisms," in Blauvelt, *Worlds Away*, 280, 277, 271, 277.

113. For a more extended discussion of the interracial signifiers of masculinity Chan employs in her short film on JJ Chinois, see Nguyen, "Bruce Lee I Love You."

114. Chan began incorporating "Chinois" into her daily vocabulary after a visit to Paris, and shortly thereafter she invented the character of "JJ Chinois." Chan, interview with the author via telephone, October 2001.

115. With the exception of San Francisco, California's major cities such as Los Angeles and San Diego are incorporated into suburban topographical imaginaries, as Edward Soja's work on the "postmetropolis" explains. See especially Soja's chapters "An Introduction to the Conurbation of Greater Los Angeles" and "Fractal City: Metropolarities and the Restructured Social Mosaic" in *Postmetropolis: Critical Studies of Cities and Regions* (Oxford: Blackwell Publishing, 2000). A helpful resource on the sprawling topography of gay and lesbian life in Los Angeles is Moira Rachel Kenney, *Mapping Gay L.A.: The Intersection of Place and Politics* (Philadelphia: Temple University Press, 2001).

116. See Judith Halberstam's discussion of rural risk in *In a Queer Time and Place*, 27.

117. For a local history of the Skowhegan State Fair, see http://www.skowheganstatefair.com/history.html, last accessed May, 18, 2009.

118. Chan, interview with the author via e-mail, October 15, 2004.

119. See http://www.skowheganstatefair.com/.

120. Chan, interview with the author via e-mail, October 15, 2004. JJ has nevertheless consistently cited his political preference as "Republican," both on his website and in the JJ Chinois film. For more remarks on JJ's Republicanism, see Oishi, "Bad Asians, the Sequel," 35.

121. The Skowhegan State Fair website offers links to local news articles about demolition derby participants raising money or offering tribute to American troops in Iraq. See http://www.skowheganstatefair.com/. This content last accessed May 18, 2009.

122. Chan, interview with the author via e-mail, October 15, 2004.

123. The journalist David Brooks is credited with popularizing the red state/ blue state paradigm in an article titled "One Nation, Slightly Divisible," published in the *Atlantic Monthly* in December 2001. A flurry of responses to Brooks's calculated oversimplification of the "new culture wars" were issued, among them a book-length study debunking the cultural component of the divide authored by the Stanford political scientist Morris P. Fiorina (with Samuel J. Abrams and Jeremy C. Pope), titled *Culture War? The Myth of a Polarized America* (New York: Pearson Longman, 2005). Nevertheless, the concept continues to get a considerable amount of play and has since been reconfigured as the "retro versus metro" paradigm in what amounts to a cultural template for electoral victory pitched to centrist Democrats. See John Sperling, *The Great Divide: Retro versus Metro America* (Sausalito, CA: PoliPoint Press, 2004). Portions of the book are also available for free online as a PDF download through a website run by PoliPoint Press. See http:// www.retrovsmetro.org/. The political scientist Kimberly Nalder of California State University, Sacramento, is currently conducting a critical study and survey of these paradigms, and I thank her for her input regarding these geopolitical models.

124. Sperling, *Great Divide*, online ed., http://www.retrovsmetro.org/.

125. Ibid.

126. Chan, interview with the author via e-mail, October 15, 2004.

127. Ibid.

128. Sperling, *Great Divide*.

129. Chan, interview with the author via e-mail, October 15, 2004.

130. Ibid.

131. Ibid.

132. Ibid.

133. Cited from the *Washington Post's* transcript of the 2004 Democratic National Convention keynote address by "Illinois Sen-ate Candidate Barack Obama," July 27, 2004, http://www.washingtonpost.com/wp-dyn/ articles/A19751-2004Jul27.html.

134. Tavia Nyong'o offers a compelling analysis of Obama as our "first post-*colonial* president." See "Barack Hussein Obama, or, The Name of the Father," *Rewriting Dispersal: Africana Gender Studies* 7 (Spring 2009): http://www.barnard.edu/sfonline/africana/ nyongo_01.htm.

135. One ad run by John McCain's campaign compared Obama to such tabloid mavens as Britney Spears and Paris Hilton. See Gil Kaufman, "John McCain Ad Compares Barack Obama to Britney Spears, Paris Hilton," MTV.com, July 30, 2008, http://www.mtv.com/news/ articles/1591820/20080730/story.jhtml. As of this writing, the ad, titled "Celeb," is still available on YouTube at http://www.youtube. com/watch?v=oHXYsw_ZDXg.

136. "Barack Hard Abs," TMZ.com, December 22, 2008, http://www.tmz. com/2008/12/22/barack-hard-abs/.

137. Nguyen, "Bruce Lee I Love You," 297.

138. Ibid., 293.

139. Chan created her LES FUN, or "Lesbian Fundamentalists," project as part of her Next Wave Festival residency in Australia in 2008. Combining the elements of live performance, installation, video, web, and television broadcasting, as well as music and "social intervention," LES FUN exposes the commercial marketing strategies that are operative not only in mainstream political campaigns but also in queer subcultures. For more on astroturfing, see Peter N. Howard, *New Media Campaigns and the Managed Citizen* (Cambridge: Cambridge University Press, 2006), 83–100. Chan's ongoing New Sound Karaoke collaboration with Bobby Abate also combines live performance, video, Internet broadcasting, and actual club nights in various karaoke venues throughout New York. New Sound Karaoke (the focus of one of my articles in progress) channels Chan's and Abate's earnest investment in karaoke as an

expressive social pastime into a performative exploration of race, sexuality, reproductivity, and the thin line between homonormativity and hipster heterosexuality. Chan and Abate have filmed multiple karaoke music videos in which they sing and perform as an "ex-gay" heterosexual couple, Black Waterfall and Bobby Service, narrating their origins and the dramatic happenings of their daily lives by rewriting lyrics to karaoke classics like Wilson Phillips' "Hold On" and Minnie Riperton's "Loving You." See http://newsoundkaraoke. com/.

140. See Ronald Brownstein and Richard Rainey, "GOP Plants Flag on New Voting Frontier," *Los Angeles Times*, November 22, 2004, reprinted as "George W. Bush Wins with Critical Support from Suburban Fringe, 2004," in Nicolaides and Wiese, *Suburb Reader*, 393–394. In the 2008 general election, polling results from the National Center for Suburban Studies at Hofstra University caused a stir when they showed Obama surging over John McCain in a poll of suburban voters, largely identified as "Independent" rather than party affiliated. See Jim Tankersley, "Obama: Rockin' the Suburbs," *The Swamp*, October 30, 2008, http://www.swamppolitics.com/news/ politics/blog/2008/10/barack_obama_ rockin_suburbs.html.

141. Not unlike JJ Chinois, who wins mainstream crowds over despite (or perhaps because) of his "outlandishness," Obama achieved victory irrespective of the "exotic" details of his life story (born beyond the U.S. mainland in Hawaii, Obama was raised there as well as in Indonesia). As Tavia Nyong'o remarks, "Only the best political image-making team money could buy could have convinced a critical percentage of the voting public to actively disattend—or remain sufficiently ignorant of—the postcoloniality of his blackness long enough to select him as their surrogate to redeem the national crimes of slavery, segregation, and anti-black racism." Nyong'o, "Barack Hussein Obama."

142. Citation from CNN.com's full transcript of "The Saddleback Presidential Candidates Forum," August 17, 2008, http://transcripts.cnn.com/TRANSCRIPTS/0808/17/ se.01.html. Video documentation of this exchange in which Obama names marriage as a "sacred union" is also captured in its entirety on YouTube at http://www.youtube.com/ watch?v=rJhQBZ1Laow.

143. Jason A. Bezis, "Obama's Historic Win in California," *The California Majority Report*, November 8, 2008, http://www.camajorityreport.com/index.php?module=articles&func= display&aid=3854&ptid=9&theme=print.

NOTES TO CHAPTER 3

1. Cheryl Katz and Mark Baldassare, "Using the 'L-Word' in Public: A Test of the Spiral of Silence in Conservative Orange County," *Public Opinion Quarterly* 56 (Summer 1992): 233.

2. From a memo titled "Fiesta Village Teen Dance Area" from Knott's entertainment executive Gary R. Salisbury to Vice President Joe Meck, dated February 11, 1984: "We will highlight a special area to feature one of the fastest growing, crowd gathering, entertainment attractions of the '80's—break dancing." Courtesy of the Gary R. Salisbury Collection (private).

3. See Gustavo Arellano's irreverent memoir and public history about migration, immigration, and all things Orange County, titled *Orange County: A Personal History* (New York: Simon and Schuster, 2008). For a queer, Filipino perspective on revisiting Orange County as a site for queer social justice, as well as queer and Asian American critical analysis, see Karin Aguilar-San Juan, "Going Home: Enacting Justice in Queer Asian America," in Eng and Hom, *Q & A*, 25–38. For an account of Asian American popular music in the region, see Deborah Wong, "Pham Duy at Home: Vietnamese American Technoculture in Orange County," in *Speak It Louder: Asian Americans Making Music* (New York:

Routledge, 2004), 89–113. All these materials will be discussed in greater depth throughout this chapter.

4. Lisa McGirr, *Suburban Warriors: The Origins of the New American Right* (Princeton: Princeton University Press, 2002), 136.

5. The program for "An Evening With Barry," held on May 30, 1964, is posted as a link in an interview with the Goldwaters lead singer, Ken Crook, at *CONELRAD*, a website devoted to Cold War culture. See http://www.conelrad.com/media/atomicmusic/sh_boom.php?platter=25b#ticket. See also McGirr, *Suburban Warriors*, 136.

6. For more on the sexual freedom these amusement parks afforded, see Kathy Peiss, *Cheap Amusements: Working Women and Leisure in Turn-of-the-Century New York* (Philadelphia: Temple University Press, 1986); and Chauncey, *Gay New York*. For Chauncey's account of gay contact in Coney Island's bathhouses see pp. 210–233. For more on Disney's aversion to Coney Island and other "urban" resorts of its ilk, see Avila, *Popular Culture in the Age of White Flight*, 107–110. For an account of migrant male sexual encounters at the Pike at Long Beach, see Nayan Shah, "Between 'Oriental Depravity' and 'Natural Degenerates': Spatial Borderlands and the Making of Ordinary Americans," *American Quarterly* 57 (September 2005): 703–725.

7. "Orange County Supervisor Suggests Name Change for Airport" *Airline Industry Information*, June 10, 2004, http://findarticles.com/p/articles/mi_m0CWU/is_2004_June_10/ai_n6062218. Gustavo Arellano offered an opinion piece on Orange County Supervisor Chris Norby's suggestion to capitalize on the success of the teen TV hit *The O.C.* by renaming the airport. See Arellano, "Will the O.C. Bump the Duke?," *Los Angeles Times*, March 5, 2008, http://articles.latimes.com/2008/mar/05/opinion/oe-arellano5. See also Arellano, *Orange County*, 212–213.

8. McGirr, *Suburban Warriors*, 98–100. See also Richard Francaviglia, "Walt Disney's Frontierland as an Allegorical Map of the

American West," *Western Historical Quarterly* 30 (Summer 1999): 155–182.

9. McGirr, *Suburban Warriors*, 99–100. Knott's Freedom Center was "home not only to the California Free Enterprise Association but also to two other nonprofit organizations: the Libres Foundation, whose goal was to place patriotic books in supermarkets and disseminate educational material, and the Americanism Educational League, 'Walter Knott Branch,' which offered speakers on problems related to the 'preservation of the Constitutional Republic and American Freedom'" (100). See also Walter Knott, "The Enterprises of Walter Knott," interview conducted by Donald J. Schippers, 1965, Oral History Program, University of California, Los Angeles.

10. Avila, "'A Rage for Order': Disneyland and the Suburban Ideal," in *Popular Culture in the Age of White Flight*, 106–144.

11. Ibid., 120–122.

12. Dianne Chisholm, "Introduction: Sodom and Gomorrah in the Era of Late Capitalism; or, A Return to Walter Benjamin," in *Queer Constellations: Subcultural Space in the Wake of the City* (Minneapolis: University of Minnesota Press, 2005), 1–61.

13. Ibid., 11.

14. Gustavo Arellano, "The 'Real' Real Orange County Reel, or: About Those Stupid Television Shows, Why Orange County is 'Hip,' and What's Really Real and What's Somewhat Real—for Real!," in *Orange County*, 211–228. *USA Today* dubbed Orange County "the capital of cool" in 2002.

15. Nestled near the Santa Ana Mountains of the Cleveland National Forest in southern Orange County, the unincorporated Coto de Caza is a master-planned community that has been expanding since the project began in 1968. Originally conceived as a hunting lodge, Coto (as its residents refer to it) has evolved into a luxurious gated community with multiple eighteen-hole golf courses and a Spa and Sports Club. Managed by Keystone Pacific Property, the exclusive

enclave sits on five thousand acres of land, which is "private" and "guard-gated" according to its website. See http://www.coto.com/, accessed September 27, 2008; and the Coto de Caza Golf and Racquet Club site, http://www.clubcorp.com/club/scripts/section/section.asp?NS=PCH&MFCODE=CCGRC, accessed October 1, 2008. See also Arellano, *Orange County*, 222–224.

16. Kimi Yoshino, "An Ordinary County Becomes Must-See O.C.," *Los Angeles Times*, May 9 2004, http://articles.latimes.com/2004/may/09/local/me-theoc9.

17. For more on Disneyland as a "living television set" (the park itself debuted on national television), see Avila, *Popular Culture in the Age of White Flight*, 126–131. Avila argues that Walt Disney seized on the power of television to debut the Disneyland vision—a white, heteronormative ideal inspired by midwestern, small-town "values"—as a tangible reality for the nation.

18. Gary R. Salisbury, Studio K creator, interview with the author, August 14, 2008, Buena Park, CA. The *California Breakdance Competition* television special, produced by Pat Boone (yes, *that* Pat Boone) and hosted by Byron Allen, aired on KHJ-TV (now KCAL-TV), an L.A.-area station, on April 19, 1984.

19. Arellano, *Orange County*, 215.

20. See Michael Rogin's definitive book on the mythos surrounding the fortieth president of the United States, *Ronald Reagan, the Movie, and Other Episodes in Demonology* (Berkeley: University of California Press, 1987).

21. Yoshino, "An Ordinary County Becomes Must-See O.C." See also Phil Gallo's review of *The O.C.* in *Daily Variety*, August 4, 2003, 4. Gallo emphasizes *The O.C.*'s role in producing a new fantasy of Southern California for "landlocked Midwesterners."

22. While working as a data-entry grunt on a project called the Getty Thesaurus of Geographic Names, I learned that toponymy is the study of geographic place-names and their origins. The word's first usage is dated to the late nineteenth century by the *Oxford English Dictionary*, defining it as "a place name; a name given to a person or thing marking its place of origin." See *Oxford English Dictionary*, 2nd ed.. A linguistic researcher and lecturer at the University of California, Santa Barbara, Bob Kennedy, has written about toponymy and the truncation of town nicknames (e.g., from Orange County to the O.C.) on his blog. See "Toponyms and Nicknames," *Piloklok*, April 29, 2005, http://biloklok.blogspot.com/2005/04/toponyms-and-nicknames.html.

23. See episode 13 of season 4, titled "The Case of the Franks," aired February 1, 2007. This flashback-driven episode concludes in the present day, with Kirsten giving Sandy an original "Mondale '84" campaign button as a Valentine's Day gift.

24. "Caleb Nichol [Kirsten's father and head of the Newport Group] invoked for many Irvine company head Don Bren, not in the plots or dirty details, but in his aura of power." Arellano, *Orange County*, 219.

25. According to the California Department of Corrections and Rehabilitation (CDCR), the California Institution for Men in Chino (simply nicknamed "Chino" throughout Southern California) was the "first major minimum security institution built and operated in the United States." See the CDCR website at http://www.cdcr.ca.gov/Facilities_Locator/CIM-Special_Notes.html, accessed October 1, 2010. The CIM was erected in 1941 but has gained notoriety in the last twenty-five years for its proliferating prison breaks and the corruption among some of its correctional officers. The *Inland Valley Daily Bulletin* reported in 2006 that nearly one-third of the state's prison escapes were from CIM. Mason Stockstill, "State's Prison Problem Ignored for Decades," *Inland Valley Bulletin*, July 23, 2006, http://www.dailybulletin.com/news/ci_4086356. Perhaps the most infamous escape from Chino occurred in 1983,

when an inmate jailed for burglary, Kevin Cooper, escaped through a "hole in the fence" and allegedly murdered four people in neighboring Chino Hills. Cooper was sentenced to death in 1985 but won a stay of execution on appeal in 2004. Some activists and anti–capital punishment advocates continue to dispute Cooper's guilt. For the official press release about Cooper's alleged crime and subsequent arrest, see the CDCR website at http://www.cdcr.ca.gov/News/2004_Press_Releases/Kevin_Cooper.html.

26. The O.C.'s snobby airhead with a heart of gold, Summer Roberts (played by Rachel Bilson), utters this memorable response in the pilot episode, "Premiere," which aired on August 5, 2003.

27. As Yoshino writes in "An Ordinary County Becomes Must-See O.C.," "There are virtually no minorities on the show. Inland cities are mentioned with only a sneer."

28. Structurally, the gated community has been examined as an architectural response to the "fear" engendered by the rapidly diversifying suburbs. See Setha M. Low, *Behind the Gates: Life, Security, and the Pursuit of Happiness in Fortress America* (New York: Routledge, 2003).

29. T-shirts with the catchphrase "Welcome to the O.C., bitch," are regularly sold in the area's souvenir shops, as well as online on such sites as CafePress.com. The line has also provided the title for numerous articles in the local press and even on blogs about the area's real estate development. See, for example, "Welcome to the OC, Bitch," *Curbed L.A.*, August 20, 2008, http://la.curbed.com/archives/2008/08/welcome_to_the_oc_bitch.php.

30. As Yoshino remarks in "An Ordinary County Becomes Must-See O.C.," "The show focuses on a selective slice of Orange County, chronicling the lives of affluent white residents along the coast, with little reference to its bland suburban tracts or diverse Latino and Vietnamese communities." See also Arellano's take on the lack of Latino characters on

The O.C.: "Latino roles were limited to hot gardeners, subservient maids, and a pregnant girlfriend." *Orange County*, 219.

31. Arellano, *Orange County*, 219.

32. Data sets are culled from the U.S. Bureau of the Census online at http://quickfacts.census.gov/qfd/states/06/0651182.html.

33. See Gallo's review of *The O.C.* in *Daily Variety*, 4; and Yoshino, "An Ordinary County Becomes Must-See O.C."

34. See the "The Strip," season 1, episode 26, aired April 28, 2004.

35. Susan Straight, "Dissed by 'The OC,'" Salon.com, June 7, 2004, http://dir.salon.com/mwt/feature/2003/09/09/oc/. Straight comments on the Riverside mayor pro tem's efforts at the time to "explore legal action" against the network and show's creators for "slandering our city."

36. Ahn offers a more comprehensive take on the relationships between race, music branding, and "quality programming" discourses surrounding *The O.C.* in her essay "Scoring Orange County: The Racialization of Space and Music in Prime-Time Television," a paper presented at a meeting of the Society for Cinema Studies, Philadelphia, March 2008, 3; cited with the permission of the author.

37. Arellano, *Orange County*, 219.

38. Ahn, "Scoring Orange County," 10. Ahn cites a *Los Angeles Times* review by Steve Hochman, who praises the show for "tap[ping] into the tastes of the show's creative team, and even cast members, to go off the beaten track and highlight relative unknowns such as Spoon, Belle & Sebastian and Alexi Murdoch." See Steve Hochman, "Subversive Sounds of 'The O.C.,'" *Los Angeles Times*, January 25, 2004, http://articles.latimes.com/2004/jan/25/entertainment/ca-popeye25.

39. Hochman, "Subversive Sounds of 'The O.C.'"

40. My extended reading of the link between *Monster*, suburban desire, and Journey's "Don't Stop Believin'" appears in a previously published essay, "Metronormativity and Gay Globalization." See also chap. 2.

41. For more on how *The O.C.* has transformed the indie rock economy of Southern California and beyond, see Susan Carpenter, "'O.C.' Sounds Them Out," *Los Angeles Times*, November 9, 2005, http://articles.latimes.com/2005/nov/09/entertainment/et-theoc9; and Ethan Smith, "Ticket Out of Obscurity: Featuring Underground Bands Confers Coolness on 'The O.C.' and Helps Propel Albums Sales," *Wall Street Journal*, August 2, 2004, B1.

42. Though the theme song functions extradiegetically here, I want to register the act of measuring drive time in Southern California to popular music as a crucial component of transit in the region. In her book for the 33 1/3 Continuum series on Jeff Buckley's 1994 album *Grace*, Daphne Brooks clocks her door-to-door commute from her apartment to the UCLA campus to the minutes of the album's opening tracks: "It takes exactly nineteen minutes and five seconds from 427 12 North Orange Grove Avenue in Los Angeles to the lot 3 parking structure on the north side of UCLA's campus." See *Grace* (New York: Continuum, 2005), 1. Popular music and automotive transit will emerge again as a significant motif in my subsequent chapters.

43. Several trade pieces focus exclusively on the musical programming of the show, which Ahn argues functions to position Schwartz as a small-screen auteur. "Scoring Orange County," 11. See also John Horn, "He's 'O.C.'s' Fresh Breeze," *Los Angeles Times*, March 21, 2004, http://articles.latimes.com/2004/mar/21/entertainment/ca-horn21.

44. See, for example, the "The Road Warrior," season 3, episode 16, aired March 9, 2006.

45. Jolson cowrote the song lyrics for "California, Here I Come" with Buddy DeSylva, and Joseph Meyer composed the music. For a brief account of Jolson's composition and popularization of the song, see George Lipsitz, "Music, Migration, and Myth," in *Reading California: Art, Image, and Identity, 1900–2000*, ed. Stephanie Barron, Sheri Bernstein, Ilene Susan Fort (Berkeley: University of California Press, 2000), 154:

"[Jolson's] 1924 and 1946 recordings of 'California, Here I Come' attained great popularity and played an important role in advertising the charms of the state to potential migrants. The song's lyrics contained biographical significance for Jolson as well: He first emerged as a star in show business during the 1906–7 theatrical season in San Francisco. . . . But like so many artists associated with California, Jolson was not a native of the state. He actually 'started' in Russia, where he was born in 1886." For a more expansive theoretical exploration of California, music, race, and politics, see Mina Yang's groundbreaking book *California Polyphony: Ethnic Voices, Musical Crossroads* (Berkeley: University of California Press, 2008).

46. Richard Reeves, *President Nixon: Alone in the Whitehouse* (New York: Simon and Schuster, 2001), 20: "Inside were Nixon's funeral plans. . . . There was a list of honorary pallbearers as well as a list of six musical selections from 'God Bless America' to 'California, Here I Come.' Next to the California song, the poor boy from Whittier who had become president had written, 'Played softly and slowly.'" For a description of the Reagans' return to California, see Lou Cannon, *President Reagan: The Role of a Lifetime* (New York: Simon and Schuster, 1991), 14.

47. William E. Studwell and Bruce R. Schueneman, *State Songs of the United States: An Annotated Anthology* (Binghamton, NY: Haworth Press, 1997), 25.

48. For more on the Upton Sinclair candidacy and the song parody of "California, Here We Come," see Mark Allan Jackson, *Prophet Singer: The Voice and Vision of Woody Guthrie* (Jackson: University Press of Mississippi, 2007), 86–89.

49. Arellano offers a handy insert of "Common Nicknames for Cities, Some Nice, Most Not," in *Orange County*, 255. No Doubt, Gwen Stefani's band, helped disseminate the phrase "Tragic Kingdom" with the success of their album of the same name in 1995.

Produced by the one-hit wonder Matthew Wilder (who sang the pop hit "Break My Stride," which peaked at number 5 on the Billboard Hot 100 in 1984), *Tragic Kingdom* proved to be No Doubt's breakout success, catapulting the band and Stefani to pop megastardom.

50. See McGirr, *Suburban Warriors*, 26: "In 1953, California topped New York as the leading state in net value of military prime contracts awarded. Throughout the next decade, awards to the Golden State amounted to twice as much as the annual amount any other state received." See also Ann R. Markusen, Peter Hall, Scott Campbell, and Sabina Deitrick, *The Rise of the Gunbelt: The Military Remapping of Industrial America* (Oxford: Oxford University Press, 1991), 104: "In the 1960s, Orange County developed through spin-offs and subcontracting into an industrial subcontracting of small firms, characterized by dependence on a common labor pool and infrastructural services."

51. See Mike Davis's *City of Quartz*, which famously offers a cultural history of L.A.'s emergence as a noir city.

52. See *The Double-Tongued Dictionary*, http://www.doubletongued.org/index.php/dictionary/orange_curtain/. The dictionary, which "records undocumented or under-documented words from the fringes of English, with a focus on slang, jargon, and new words," was created by the American lexicographer Grant Barrett and is administered by Barrett and a staff of "word hunters" (mostly graduate students and other academics). Barrett is also the editor of *The Official Dictionary of Unofficial English: A Crunk Omnibus for Thrillionaires and Bampots for the Ecozoic Age* (New York: McGraw-Hill, 2006).

53. Reginald Dale and Paul Taylor, "Reagan Promises Peace from Behind California's Orange Curtain," *Financial Times*, September 4, 1984. 4.

54. On the rise of housing prices in the region in the wake of the military industrial boom in the 1980s, see Markusen et al., *Rise*

of the Gunbelt, 105: "Ironically, Orange County has become the victim of its own success. In the 1980s boom, it was often hard for companies to get enough labor, and housing costs increased dramatically, as in Los Angeles."

55. For more on how the racialization of the suburbs factored into the United States' Cold War with the Soviet Union, see Cheng, "Out of Chinatown and into the Suburbs."

56. See Daniel C. Tsang's exhibition catalog *Immigrant Lives in the OC and Beyond* (Irvine: University of California, Irvine, 2008), 19. The exhibition was featured from November 2008 to April 2009 at the UC Irvine's Langson Library. Curated by Daniel C. Tsang, it featured a section on gender that explored aspects of queer migration to the region while offering homage to Lionel Cantú's pioneering work on the topic.

57. See Robert Beauregard, "America's Global Project," in *When America Became Suburban*, 144–171. As Beauregard has argued, the homosexual peril during the Cold War was also conflated with a rising sense of promiscuity by heterosexuals, thus threatening to undo "peace and security" as well as the family: "At a time of national insecurity, sexual freedom was unacceptable" (159).

58. Davis and Moctezuma, "Policing the Third Border." The suburbs have been literally scarred, since their inception, by segregation through the redlining practices of the federal Home Owners' Loan Corporation, which denied loans to minority residents. A remarkable new database—or "digital archaeology of segregation in California cities"—has been created by David Theo Goldberg and Richard Marciano, among other collaborators, called T-RACES. A demo is accessible at http://salt.diceresearch.org/T-RACES/demo, accessed May 29, 2009.

59. McKenzie, *Privatopia*.

60. For more on the segregation and "fortressing" of the United States through gated communities, see Edward J. Blakely and Mary Gail Snyder, *Fortress America: Gated Communities in the United States*

(Washington, DC: Brookings Institution Press, 1999).

61. There is a major rift between southern and northern Orange County that has been brewing since the early 1980s, with the former distinguishing itself as a newer, tonier region than the increasingly ethnicized "north county" referred to by the aforementioned, "not so nice" nicknames above. The *Los Angeles Times* has posted extensive coverage of this skirmish in its op-ed pieces and its local coverage of the fight over the former El Toro military base's development. See also Arellano's brief account of the rise of gated communities in southern Orange County in his memoir *Orange County*, 55.

62. McGirr, *Suburban Warriors*, 99. See also Rob Kling, Spencer Olin, and Mark Poster's discussion of the region's development through defense in "The Emergence of Postsuburbia," in Kling, Olin, and Poster, *Postsuburban California*, 20–22.

63. See Cheng, "Out of Chinatown and into the Suburbs." Data from the 2000 U.S. census determined that a staggering 20 percent of the total Vietnamese population in the United States resides in the Orange–Los Angeles-Riverside County region. See Mark E. Pfeiffer, "U.S. Census 2000: An Overview of National and Regional Trends in Vietnamese Residential Distribution," *Review of Vietnamese Studies* 1, no. 1 (2001): 2. For a comparison of Vietnamese "refuge politics" with the Cuban American experience, see Minh Zhou and Carl L. Bankston II, *Growing Up American: How Vietnamese Children Adapt to Life in the United States* (New York: Sage Press, 1998), 64: "As have Cuban Americans, the Vietnamese frequently issued calls for armed struggle to overthrow the Communist government of Vietnam." See also Marcelli, "From the Barrio to the 'Burbs?"; and Mark Baldassare, *California in the New Millennium* (Berkeley: University of California Press, 2000), 144–146. For a popular account of these relocations, see Arellano, *Orange County*, 18: "The Vietnam

War brought hundreds of thousands of refugees to El Toro and Camp Pendleton [military bases]. Despite efforts by the government to disperse the Vietnamese, many of them settled in central Orange County and re-created Indochina as best they could, much to the chagrin of the other residents. But it wasn't just Vietnamese who were overrunning OC: Muslims, Koreans, Chinese, and refugees from the Soviet bloc also swooped in."

64. My-Thuan Tran, "From Refugees to Political Players," *Los Angeles Times*, December 7, 2008, http://www.latimes.com/news/local/la-me-vietnamese7-2008dec07,0,400174.story. For a sociological account of the different cultures of protest in which Vietnamese communities in Orange County participated after 1975, see Nhu-Ngoc T. Ong and David S. Meyer, "Protest and Political Incorporation: Vietnamese American Protests in Orange County, California, 1975–2001," *Journal of Vietnamese Studies* 3, no. 1 (2008): 78–107. For a broader political history of Asians in American politics, see the anthology edited by Don T. Nakanishi and James S. Lai, *Asian American Politics: Law, Participation, and Policy* (Lanham, MD: Rowman and Littlefield, 2003). One is left to wonder whether Lynne Chan took such political developments in Southern California into account when she chose to name JJ Chinois's political affiliation as "Republican." See chap. 2.

65. Kling, Olin, and Poster, "Emergence of Postsuburbia," 22.

66. Arellano, *Orange County*, 13; emphasis added.

67. Baldassare, *When Government Fails*, 37.

68. Marcelli, "From the Barrio to the 'Burbs?," 134.

69. I borrow the phrase "Tropic of Orange" from the novel of the same name, written by Karen Tei Yamashita. The novel is situated in Los Angeles and Mexico, not in Orange County, although its sense of shifting space in Southern California has informed my conceptualization of this entire project.

Yamashita, *Tropic of Orange* (Minneapolis: Coffee House Press, 1997).

70. An expansive account of how television was among the defining technologies of the suburbs—as well as its vehicle for marketing other conveniences for the suburban home—is Lynn Spiegel's *Welcome to the Dream House*.

71. See Archer, "Suburban Aesthetics Is Not an Oxymoron." See also Langford, "Margins of the City." For more on the role "edge cities" have played in American spatial paradigms and imaginaries, see Garreau, *Edge Cities*. Kling, Olin, and Poster rightly amend Garreau's take on edge cities by citing his "failure to examine some of the new ethnic communities, such as those composed of Vietnamese, Laotians, and Cambodians in Garden Grove and Westminster," who "tend to live outside of Garreau's edge cities." See "Beyond the Edge: The Dynamism of Postsuburban Regions," in Kling, Olin, and Poster, *Postsuburban California*, xv.

72. Fernando Ortiz, *Cuban Counterpoint: Tobacco and Sugar*, trans. Harriet de Onis (1947; repr., Durham: Duke University Press, 1995). The Cold War fantasies that infuse my account of the Orange Curtain and its relationship to transculturation are inspired, obliquely, by conversations with Alexandra Vazquez, Christine Bacareza Balance, and Patty Ahn about being "Cold War babies." The Cold War axis we've discussed collectively and with other scholars focuses on Latin America and Asia rather than its more Occidental coordinates. For a sense of what we're talking about, listen to the Orange County band Cold War Kids.

73. Felipe Hernández, "Introduction: Transcultural Architectures in Latin America," in *Transculturation: Cities, Spaces, and Architectures in Latin America*, ed. Felipe Hernández, Mark Millington, and Iain Borden (Amsterdam: Rodopi, 2005), xi.

74. Ibid.

75. For an extensive account of the term "conurbation" in relation to Los Angeles, see Soja, *Postmetropolis*.

76. Baldassare, *When Government Fails*. See also Kling, Olin, and Poster's discussion of the county bankruptcy debacle of 1994 in "Beyond the Edge," xvi–xviii.

77. Smoodin, "Introduction: How to Read Walt Disney," in *Disney Discourse: Producing the Magic Kingdom*, ed. Eric Smoodin (New York: Routledge, 1994), 9.

78. See also Avila, *Popular Culture in the Age of White Flight*, 116–124.

79. California Adventure Park opened as part of the revamped Disneyland resort in Anaheim in 2001. The park itself cost an estimated $1.4 billion, not including the $1 billion dollar investment from the State of California itself to "widen and reconfigure Interstate 5 (Santa Ana Freeway) and other freeways in the area near Walt Disney Company properties, to add a new interchange to funnel guests directly into Disney's parking structure, to plant 15,000 trees and shrubs, to expand the convention center and make many other improvements" during its three-year construction. The state's revenue for their $1 billion investment purportedly came "mostly from hotel room taxes" and was "supposed to bring 8000 new jobs to the area" while generating "$6 million in annual revenue to the State." Miodrag Mitrašinović, *Total Landscape, Theme Parks, Public Space* (Aldershot, UK: Ashgate Press, 2006), 64.

80. For more on the crafting of California's sonic presence in the national imaginary, see Yang, "Introduction," in *California Polyphony*, 1–10.

81. Barney Hoskyns, *Hotel California: The True-Life Adventures of Crosby, Stills, Nash, Young, Mitchell, Taylor Brown, Ronstadt, Geffen, the Eagles, and Their Many Friends* (Hoboken: Wiley, 2007), 18. For more on John Phillips's role in the Monterey Pop Festival and the sixties counter-culture, see Paul Friendlander and Peter Miller, *Rock and Roll: A Social History* (New York: Basic Books, 2006), 195–198; and Edward P. Morgan, *The Sixties Experience: Hard Lessons about Modern America* (Philadelphia: Temple University Press, 1991), 178–193.

82. Marty Sklar, the Walt Disney Company's international ambassador for imagineering (formerly vice president of concepts and planning), quoted in Mitrašinović, *Total Landscape, Theme Parks, Public Space*, 60.

83. Disney's California Adventure Park pays dutiful homage to the state's industries, including the Hollywood film industry, agriculture, aerospace, and defense in the "Condor Flats" portion of the park, which features the "Soarin' over California" simulated flight experience over state landmarks. In addition to flying over California's majestic mountains and rugged coastline, the ride also features two close encounters with California's military might: aircraft carriers poised off the coast of San Diego, and fighter plans scrambling in what appears to be the Mojave Desert.

84. Yang, *California Polyphony*, 3.

85. For a history of the Palace of Fine Arts' role in the emergence of San Francisco's municipal art programs, see Anthony W. Lee, *Painting on the Left: Diego Rivera, Radical Politics, and San Francisco's Public Mural Art* (Berkeley: University of California Press, 1999), 30–42.

86. Smoodin, "Introduction," 9–10. The attraction was open from 1974 (in time for the U.S. bicentennial) to 1988 (the end of Reagan's two terms as president) and occupied the rotating theater that previously housed the "Carousel of Progress" in the Disneyland park Tomorrowland. See Dave Smith and Debbie Johnson, *Disney A to Z: The Official Encyclopedia* (New York: Hyperion Books, 1996).

87. For more on Disney's obsession with recreating the "real" small-town United States, see Avila, *Popular Culture in the Age of White Flight*, 117-122.

88. Kun, *Audiotopia*, 30–31.

89. Ibid., 40–41.

90. Many artists and cultural bystanders have already explored the crucial links between Orange County and the literature and art produced behind the Orange Curtain's sister spatial concept, the Iron Curtain. The artist Peter Sis, for example, very recently created a multi-genre memoir combining

photography, drawings, journal entries, and fantasy that explores such themes. See *The Wall: Growing Up behind the Iron Curtain* (Vancouver: Douglas and McIntyre, 2007).

91. Langford, "Margins of the City," 65.

92. Ibid., 66.

93. Muñoz, *Disidentifications*.

94. John D'Emilio, "Capitalism and Gay Identity," in *Powers of Desire: The Politics of Sexuality*, ed. Ann Snitow, Christine Stansell, and Sharon Thompson (New York: Monthly Review Press, 1983), 100–113.

95. For a genealogy of Whitman's role as a "queer ancestor" and pivotal figure in queer disciplinary debates, as well as American national conversations about secularism and spiritualism, see Molly McGarry, "Secular Spirits: A Queer Genealogy of Untimely Sexualities," in *Ghosts of Futures Past: Spiritualism and the Cultural Politics of Nineteenth-Century America* (Berkeley: University of California Press, 2008), 167–176. See also Michael Robertson, "Worshipping Walt: Lancashire's Whitman Disciples," *History Today* 54 (April 2004): 46–53. Robertson discusses how Whitman's work inspired a homosocial group of spiritual socialists in late Victorian England. See also Diane Chisholm's work situating Whitman's role in an emerging queer discourse about "the city" as a site of freedom and invention for the "gay gaze" in *Queer Constellations*, 21–23.

96. Kun, *Audiotopia*, 33.

97. Avila, *Popular Culture in the Age of White Flight*, 106–144.

98. See Leela Gandhi's work on dissident, cross-cultural collaborations between unlikely allies in *Affective Communities: Anticolonial Thought, Fin-de-Siècle Radicalism, and the Politics of Friendship* (Durham: Duke University Press, 2006).

99. Stefani was born in Fullerton, California, and went to high school in Anaheim, home of Disneyland. See Katherine Krohn, *Gwen Stefani* (Minneapolis: Twenty-First Century Books, 2008). See also Amy H. Blankenstein, *The Story of Gwen Stefani* (London:

Omnibus Press, 2005), 11: "Gwendolyn Renee Stefani was born on October 3, 1969, just fourteen years after Walt Disney opened the Disneyland theme park in her hometown of Anaheim, California. Walt, whose company still sells the fantasy of family-oriented entertainment, would likely have approved of her upbringing in which her parents emphasized the conservative family values of their Catholic faith. Her parents were so protective, as Gwen would later confess in a 1997 interview with David Keeps of *Details* magazine, that for high-school graduation, instead of attending the typical hotel parties, she had to celebrate at Disneyland and had a midnight curfew." Stefani's recollection of what is called "Grad Night" at Disneyland is not unusual for youth of the Southern California region, protective Catholic parents or no. Many of the area's high schools, extending into the Inland Empire, had an officially established party at Disneyland that required riding directly to the park in a school bus with classmates and teacher chaperones, and staying at the park until it closed. I attended one of these Disneyland Grad Nights myself in 1991.

100. In a 2006 cover story for *Entertainment Weekly*, Stefani named Michelle Pfeiffer's "drug-addled bombshell from *Scarface*" as a stylistic muse. Clark Collis, "Holla Back," *Entertainment Weekly*, December 1, 2006, http://www.ew.com/ew/article/0,,1562569,00.html.

101. Ibid.: "Indeed, their plots are similar: Naive and chatty but well-meaning young Catholic girl—who makes her own clothes!—goes out into the big wide world, where she survives assorted adventures and meets the man of her dreams. Of course, in Stefani's case, the 'assorted adventures' didn't involve escaping from Nazis but selling 26 million albums worldwide with a globe-trotting ska-pop band, then 7 million more with her 2004 solo debut, *Love.Angel.Music.Baby*. And the 'man of her dreams' is a British rocker (Bush frontman Gavin Rossdale, 39, whom Stefani married in September 2002), not an Austrian

naval captain. But both stories do have a happy ending, as is evidenced in Stefani's case by the 6-month-old bundle of joy named Kingston James McGregor Rossdale, right now nestled in a Bugaboo across the room from his mommy."

102. MiHi Ahn, "Gwenihana," Salon.com, April 9, 2005, http://dir.salon.com/story/ent/feature/2005/04/09/geisha/.

103. "Harajuku Girls," composed by Bobby Ross Avila, Issiah J. Avila, J. Harris III, Terry Lewis, Gwen Stefani, and James Quenton Wright, on Gwen Stefani, *Love. Angel. Music. Baby.*, Interscope, 2004.

104. We might also imagine Stefani's metaphorical outsourcing of cool in relation to the specter of sweatshop labor performed by Asian women globally, including Asian female immigrants to the United States (although Stefani's own clothing line, L.A.M.B—which takes its initials from the title of her debut solo album—has not explicitly been implicated in any of these practices). See Yen Le Espiritu, "Gender and Labor in Asian Immigrant Families," in *Gender and U.S. Immigration: Contemporary Trends*, ed. Pierrette Hondagneu-Sotelo (Berkeley: University of California Press, 2003), 81–100. See also Edna Bonacich, "Asians in the Los Angeles Garment Industry," in *The New Asian Immigration in Los Angeles and Global Restructuring*, ed. Paul M. Ong, Edna Bonacich, and Lucie Cheng (Philadelphia: Temple University Press, 1994), 137–163.

105. Dipesh Chakrabarty, *Provincializing Europe: Postcolonial Thought and Historical Difference* (Princeton: Princeton University Press, 2000), 16.

106. To be sure, there are many other storied musical acts to have originated in Orange County. The politically conscious rap-metal band Rage Against the Machine, fronted by Zack de la Rocha (a former UC Irvine student) is but one example. Nevertheless, Rage Against the Machine is more often associated with Los Angeles, especially given their role

as sonic agitators for political configurations beyond the two-party system during the 2000 Democratic National Convention. This protest concert in L.A. serendipitously followed the release of their 1999 album *The Battle of Los Angeles*. For more on Rage Against the Machine's Orange County roots, see Arellano, *Orange County*, 217.

107. Henry Jenkins, *Fans, Bloggers, and Gamers: Exploring Participatory Culture* (New York: New York University Press, 2006), 156.

108. Ibid., 164.

109. "Rich Girl," composed by Mark Batson, Jerry Bock, Kara DioGuardi, Mike Elizondo, Eve, Sheldon Harnick, Chantal Kreviazuk, Gwen Stefani, and Andre Young, on Gwen Stefani, *Love. Angel. Music. Baby.*, Interscope, 2004. Stefani's version of "Rich Girl" not only cites *Fiddler on the Roof*'s "If I Were a Rich Man," but also a dancehall cover of the song released in 1993 by the London-based, female reggae-pop duo Louchie Lou and Michie One. According to her Laguna Beach–based management company, Rebel Waltz: "Based on a dancehall cover of 'If I Were a Rich Man,' 'Rich Girl' allowed Gwen to really test herself by writing, not from a personal experience but taking on a role. 'Dre was really pushing me to write in a new way and I'm not going to question him' [says Stefani]." See http://www.rebelwaltz.com/gwen_stefani.html.

110. Jenkins, *Fans, Bloggers, and Gamers*, 156.

111. Ibid., 158. See also Inderpal Grewal's account of divergent local and institutional strands of resistance to multinational corporations and their products, "Traveling Barbie: Indian Transnationality and New Consumer Subjects," in *Popular Culture: A Reader*, ed. Raiford Guins and Omayra Zaragoza Cruz (London: Sage, 2005), 168–183. See also Grewal's pioneering work on the subject with Caren Kaplan in *Scattered Hegemonies: Postmodernity and Transnational Feminist Practices* (Minneapolis: University of Minnesota Press, 1994).

112. Krohn, *Gwen Stefani*, 14, 16.

113. Ibid., 7–23.

114. Jenkins, *Fans, Bloggers, and Gamers*, 156. As he writes, "The result is not so much a global culture that eradicates local differences but rather a culture that *continually produces local differences* in order to gain a competitive advantage within the global marketplace" (158; emphasis added).

115. As the music journalist Jody Rosen rightly notes, Stefani's ascendancy as a global diva came not by accident, but rather as a concerted "rebranding" effort as the popularity of her band No Doubt began to wane: "There's a new competitor in the global pop diva stakes. This is a somewhat unlikely turn of events. When we first met Stefani in the mid-'90s, she was a punk chick in a belly shirt fronting an undeniably pop-savvy but frankly annoying band. She seemed destined to go down in history as a period curio—the beneficiary of the grunge-weary public's fleeting fancy for ska. . . . But then Stefani launched her rebranding campaign, an effort undertaken with such gangling good cheer—and, apparently, without the usual battery of professional stylists and other hired help—that it endeared her to the editors of *Jane* magazine and other tastemakers who normally cast a jaundiced eye on the careerist machinations of pop divas." "Gwen Stefani," *Slate*, December 14, 2004, http://www.slate.com/id/2111008/.

116. Krissi Murison, review of *Love. Angel. Music. Baby.* by Gwen Stefani, *NME*, December 10, 2004, http://www.nme.com/reviews/gwen-stefani/7561.

117. We might also track Stefani's Japanophilia to an early object of trendy consumption during her suburban childhood, Hello Kitty: "Gwen was also interested in Japanese trends. Her father often traveled to Japan on business for his job with Yamaha Motorcycles. He would bring back souvenirs for Gwen. 'I loved Hello Kitty and all these different Japanese things,' Gwen remembered." Krohn, *Gwen Stefani*, 15.

118. Ben Wener, "Gwen Stefani Puts Out Her Own Album but Says No Doubt Will Go On," *Orange County Register*, November 24, 2004, http://www.nxdscrapbook.com/article/orange-county-register-2.

119. Gary R. Salisbury, Studio K creator, interview with the author, August 14, 2008, Buena Park, CA. Salisbury notes that the club was credited with bringing in an extra $2.5 million in revenue a year throughout the mid to late 1980s.

120. When I asked Gary Salisbury if they statistically tracked or performed any market research to appeal to some of the specific patrons that attended Studio K, Salisbury simply replied, "We knew the Goth and New Wave kids were coming because the DJs knew it. They knew it, and they would tell me. That's about as formal as we got." Ibid.

121. Alexandra Vazquez heightened my sense of these reverberations created by popular objects across time and space in her paper for the American Studies Association Annual Convention in 2008, which discussed the intergenerational resonance of a Ted Nugent song shared by an older Cuban woman and a younger Cuban American woman from Dade County, Florida. See "What I Brought Back Here," a paper presented at the American Studies Annual Convention, Albuquerque, NM, October 2008; cited with the permission of the author.

122. PrisonerDavid.com is a popular website administered by "a California inmate currently serving 25 years to life." As his bio explains, "When Prisoner David is not in the law library seeking ways to prove his innocence, he writes about prison life and can be heard on the Adam Carolla radio program." The post about Studio K appears in an entry titled "Sleepless in Soledad," n.d., http://www.prisonerdavid.com/index.php/Sleepless_in_Soledad.

123. This commentary appeared in response to a blog post on May 21, 2008, featuring photos of Disney's Tomorrowland circa 1986

(around the time Videopolis was situated near that area of the park), on a popular Disney-themed blog featuring "Vintage and Current Disneyland Photos" called *Daveland*. See http://davelandblog.blogspot.com/2008/05/disneyland-august-1986-tomorrowland-pt.html (last accessed January 26, 2009).

124. See "Cloud 9 and Studio K," OCThen.com, October 26, 2007, http://www.octhen.com/2007/10/cloud-9-and-studio-k.htm.

125. Ibid., "Ruben Sanchez," comment on August 17, 2008.

126. Salisbury, interview with the author, August 14, 2008, Buena Park, CA.

127. See David Nasaw's classic account of the seaside resorts opened up to the masses thanks to a masterful synergy with public transportation systems (such as ferries, buses, trolley cars, etc.) in *Going Out: The Rise and Fall of Public Amusements* (New York: Basic Books, 1993): "Because the nation's waterways had served as its main transportation networks until the triumph of the railroad in the mid-nineteenth century, almost every major and mid-size American city was located on or near a waterfront that could, with minor adjustments, be converted into a playland for excursionists.... In the late 1880s, the resort areas at the outskirts of the city, once the province of the wealthy, privileged, or politically connected, were opened up to the city's working people as ferry boats, steamers, and streetcar lines linked them to the central city" (80).

128. Salisbury, interview with the author, August 14, 2008, Buena Park, CA.

129. Needless to say, not all the youth of the region had forty dollars to pay up front for a seasonal pass, despite the fact that its holders were entitled to regular admission to the park after 5 p.m. throughout the summer. Casual patrons were thus discouraged. Also, if you wanted to enter the park *before* 5 p.m., you would still have to pay the regular price for admission to Disneyland. The parks' competing admission prices are mentioned in a July 5, 1985, article by Randy Lewis in the *Los Angeles Times*, "Videoland in the Magic Kingdom,"

http://articles.latimes.com/1985-07-05/
entertainment/ca-9235_1.

130. Salisbury, interview with the author,
August 14, 2008, Buena Park, CA. See also a
brief mention of Knott's attendance records in
a *Los Angeles Times* article about Disneyland's
efforts to match its competitors' success nearly
a year later: "Disney was beaten to the punch
last year when nearby Knott's Berry Farm
embraced the teen market by building Studio
K, which packs in 2,000 or more patrons on
Friday and Saturday nights during the busy
summer season." Bruce Horovitz, "Seeking
to Attract Affluent Adolescents Disneyland
Will Open Teen Nightclub," *Los Angeles
Times*, April 23, 1985, http://articles.latimes.
com/1985-04-23/business/fi-11598_1.

131. Though the consensus about the
history of breaking is that it originated in
the streets of New York (many disagree
about precisely where), its dissemination
in popular culture, particularly through
dance-themed films of the early 1980s, and its
own economy of "professionalization" through
dance competitions on the club circuit,
provided Salisbury with his inspiration for the
architecture of Studio K. For a brief history
of break dancing's popularization, see Sally
Banes, "Breakdancing: A Reporter's Story,"
in *Writing Dancing in the Age of Postmodern-
ism* (Hanover: Wesleyan University Press),
126–132. See also what many consider to be
the definitive popular account of the hip-hop
generation, Jeff Chang, *Can't Stop, Won't Stop:
A History of the Hip-Hop Generation* (New
York: St. Martin's Press, 2005).

132. Salisbury, interview with the author,
August 14, 2008, Buena Park, CA.

133. Ibid. For more on the racialization of
break dancing and its multicultural depic-
tion in films of the early 1980s, see Banes,
"Breakdancing"; and Robin D. G. Kelley,
"Looking to Get Paid: How Some Black
Youth Put Culture to Work," in *Yo' Mama's
DisFUNKtional! Fighting the Culture Wars in
Urban America* (Boston: Beacon Press, 1997),
43–78.

134. Halifu Osumare, "Global Breakdancing
and the Intercultural Body," *Dance Research
Journal* 34 (Winter 2002): 33.

135. Banes, "Breakdancing," 131.

136. See Tricia Rose, "A Style Nobody Can
Deal With: Politics, Style, and the Postindustrial City in Hip Hop," in Guins and Cruz,
Popular Culture, 401–416. Rose elaborates
on how "hip hop culture emerged as a source
of alternative identity formation and social
status for youth in a community whose older
local support institutions had been all but
demolished along with large sectors of its built
environment.... The postindustrial city, which
provided the context for creative development
among hip hop's earliest innovators, shaped
their cultural terrain, access to space, materials
and education" (407–8).

137. Kelley, "Looking to Get Paid," 68.

138. Salisbury, interview with the author,
August 14, 2008, Buena Park, CA.

139. My Foucauldian-inspired formulation about the cordon sanitaire—literally a
"quarantine line"—is owed to D. A. Miller's
classic account of Dickensian delinquency in
The Novel and the Police (Berkeley: University
of California Press, 1988), 5: "The closed-
circuit character of delinquency is, of course,
a sign of Dickens's progressive attitude, his
willingness to see coercive system where it
was traditional only to see bad morals. Yet
one should recognize how closing the circuit
results in an 'outside' as well as an 'inside,' an
'outside' precisely determined as *outside the
circuit*. At the same time as the novel exposes
the network that ties together the workhouse.
Fagin's gang, and the police *within* the world
of delinquency, it also draws a circle around
it, and in that gesture hold the line of a *cordon
sanitaire*."

140. Salisbury, interview with the author,
August 14, 2008, Buena Park, CA.

141. Ibid.

142. Ibid.

143. Ibid.

144. See Buena Park's official website,
http://www.buenapark.com/.

145. For more on the growth of the South Asian population in Southern California, with specific reference to the Indo-Pak Bridal Expos held in the region starting in 1989, see Karen B. Leonard and Chandra S. Tibrewal, "Asian Indians in Southern California: Occupation and Ethnicity," in *Immigration and Entrepreneurship: Culture, Capital, and Ethnic Networks*, ed. Ivan Light and Parminder Bhachu (New Brunswick, NJ: Transaction Publishers, 1993,), 141–163.

146. The most recent census data for the city of Buena Park, taken in 2000, measured the city's Asian and Pacific Islander population at 21.6 percent (nearly twice the average for California cities) and the Latino population at 33.5 percent. See the U.S Bureau of the Census's state and county online database, http://quickfacts.census.gov/qfd/states/06/0608786.html

147. "We just knew the trends and demographic because my DJs knew it, felt the crowd, and could tell me." Salisbury, interview with the author, August 14, 2008, Buena Park, CA.

148. "M," interview with the author via e-mail, August 27, 2008. The anonymous "M" is a thirty-six-year-old Caucasian female who resided in Anaheim and regularly attended both Videopolis and Studio K from 1988 to 1991. She currently resides in the Inland Empire.

149. David Koenig, *Mouse Tales: A Behind-the-Ears Look at Disneyland* (Irvine, CA: Bonaventure Press, 2006), 158.

150. Lewis, "Videoland in the Magic Kingdom."

151. Studio K also featured live entertainment, often teen-friendly pop acts of the 1980s, including stars such as Tiffany, Debbie Gibson, and the Jets. The Disney publicity department's press pack for Videopolis in 1985 focuses on the venue's "high-tech" appeal, especially its "90 television monitors . . . arranged in a video 'wallpaper' effect around the dance floor." See "Videopolis: The Newest, Flashiest, Most Sophisticated Electronic Dancespot under the Stars at Disneyland,"

Fall 1985, 5 pp. plus front and back covers. To listen to the "Videopolis" theme song, visit the following link on a Disney enthusiasts' blog, http://www.disneyfrontier.com/wp-content/uploads/2006/08/disneyland-videopolis_song.mp3.

152. Marciano Angel Martinez, interview with the author via e-mail, December 17, 2008.

153. Stephen L. Becker, interview with the author via e-mail, May 4, 2008. Becker's online group for former regulars at Studio K and Cloud 9, "KBF [Knott's Berry Farm] Locals," can be found at http://groups.myspace.com/kbflocals. Group membership and a MySpace account are required to access the page.

154. Becker, interview with the author via e-mail, May 4, 2008.

155. Bridgette "Mixtress B" Rouletgregg, interview with the author, August 18, 2008, Los Angeles.

156. Avila, *Popular Culture in the Age of White Flight*, 110.

157. John Spano, "Dancing Gays Sue Disneyland anew in Suit Similar to One the Park Lost," *Los Angeles Times*, February 26, 1988, http://articles.latimes.com/1988-02-26/local/me-30259_1_dance-floor.

158. "It was the scene of controversy last September when gay men sued the park over the right to dance with one another there. Disney has settled the suit and lifted its ban on same-sex dancing." Mary Ann Galante, "For Teen-Agers, Closed Videopolis Limits Boogie Options," *Los Angeles Times*, November 4, 1989, http://articles.latimes.com/1989-11-04/business/fi-398_1.

159. The Walt Disney Company, unlike the more casual operation that seemed to be at work at Knott's Berry Farm, explicitly voiced its desire to lure "affluent teens" to Videopolis. Bob McTyre, the manager of marketing and entertainment at Disneyland leading up to Videopolis' debut, remarked in a *Los Angeles Times* interview that "our first concern is to keep Disney a family place, but there are a lot of good kids in Orange County who want a

place to go." Quoted in Horovitz, "Seeking to Attract Affluent Adolescents Disneyland Will Open Teen Nightclub."

160. See Sean Griffin, *Tinker Belles and Evil Queens: The Walt Disney Company from the Inside Out* (New York: New York University Press, 2000), for a more expansive take on the Disney Company's relationship to gay and lesbian employees and cultural movements. For a more theoretical approach to these entanglements, see Arthur Asa Berger, "Of Mice and Men: An Introduction to Mouseology Or, Anal Eroticism and Disney," in *Gay People, Sex, and the Media*, ed. Michelle A. Wolf and Alfred P. Kielwasser (New York: Harrington Park Press, 1991), 155–165.

161. Top 40 formatting has gone through numerous conceptual transformations in the rock era, and it has arguably been a significant format for the regionalized United States, if not the suburbs' definitive radio format—a distinction, some scholars argue, that belongs to its offshoot, "MOR" (or "middle of the road")/adult contemporary. See Eric Weisbard's dissertation, "Top 40 Democracy: Pop Music Formats in the Rock Era" (University of California, Berkeley, 2008). As Weisbard argues, "Top 40 persisted as a format long after the rock cohort had condemned it as 'square' and moved on to the burgeoning FM album rock format. It needs to be understood as a format of outsiders opting into the mainstream, far from the rock narrative's prizing of subculturalists opting out" (19).

162. Salisbury, interview with the author, August 14, 2008, Buena Park, CA.

163. Rouletgregg, interview with the author, August 18, 2008, Los Angeles. Erasure is an iconic gay band and still regularly makes appearances at pride festivals throughout the world alongside some of the artists they inspired, and who came of age during the Studio K era at Knott's, like the queer female hip-hop artist Mélange LaVonne, who is based in the Inland Empire. For a list of LaVonne's musical influences, see http://www.myspace.

com/melangelavonne. I also conducted an interview with her for my blog about the Inland Empire, where she named another 80s British pop band, Tears for Fears, as her favorite rock group. See Karen Tongson, "Tours of Duty (Free) + an Interview with Mélange LaVonne," *Inland Emperor*, February 19, 2007, http://theinlandemperor.blogspot.com/2007/02/tours-of-duty-free-interview-with.html.

164. A groundbreaking essay on the aesthetic and social fantasies that combine queer eroticism with the "homeboy" aesthetic in the Inland Empire/Los Angeles artist Hector Silva's work is Richard T. Rodriguez's "Queering the Homeboy Aesthetic." For more on "homo hip hop" and its recent commercialization and spectacularization in the popular media, see Robin R. Means Coleman and Jasmine Cobb, "No Way of Seeing: Mainstreaming and Selling the Gaze of Homo-Thug Hip-Hop," *Popular Communication: The International Journal of Media and Culture* 5 (May 2007): 89–108.

165. Martinez, interview with the author via e-mail, December 17, 2008.

166. Rouletgregg, interview with the author, August 18, 2008, Los Angeles.

167. A *Los Angeles Times* article published near the end of the runs of both Videopolis and Studio K focused on how teen dancing in the 1980s—particularly in the teen clubs of Orange County—abandoned the couple form. See Dana Parsons, "Footloose and Partner Free: When It Comes to Dancing, Today's Teens Are Single-Minded in Their Devotion," *Los Angeles Times*, August 19, 1989, http://articles.latimes.com/1989-08-19/news/li-671_1_dance-music.

168. Describing how he monitored Studio K's set lists, Salisbury declared, "We *didn't* have any rap in there or hip-hop ... but then you get the songs that are partial rap and partial singing and we'd all have to make another determination." Salisbury, interview with the author, August 14, 2008, Buena Park, CA.

169. Rouletgregg, interview with the author, August 18, 2008, Los Angeles.

170. Ibid.

171. "While graffiti writers' work was significantly aided by advances in spray-paint technology, they used the urban transit system as their canvas. Rappers and DJs disseminated their work by copying it on tape-dubbing equipment and playing it on powerful, portable 'ghetto blasters.' At a time when budget cuts in school music programs drastically reduced access to traditional forms of instrumentation and composition, inner-city youth increasingly relied on recorded sound." "A Style Nobody Can Deal With," 408.

172. Rouletgregg, interview with the author, August 18, 2008, Los Angeles. The stories Rouletgregg and other Knott's DJs have shared about their networks, the institutions they attended, and the venues in which they both worked and played bear some resemblance to Jeff Chang's account of the role that black suburbia played in hip-hop culture of the late 1980s on the East Coast. See in particular his tracking of DJ networks through local community and vocational colleges in "What We Got to Say: Black Suburbia, Segregation, and Utopia in the Late 1980s," in *Can't Stop, Won't Stop*, 215–231.

173. Titled "Backyard Parties: A Brief History of DJ Culture in Southern California," the project contains materials with commentary from the personal collection of an early backyard party scenester, DJ, and local scholar Gerard Meraz, among contributions from others who participated primarily in the scene's East L.A. and South L.A. incarnations. The interactive project also includes archival video footage and MP3 "mixtapes." See http://www.kcet.org/socal/departures/youthvoices/backyard-parties.html.

174. Ibid., start page.

175. Ibid., 1980s page.

176. Salisbury, interview with the author, August 14, 2008, Buena Park, CA.

177. Rouletgregg, interview with the author, August 18, 2008, Los Angeles.

178. The popular music critic and historian Eric Weisbard also draws several crucial connections between the evolution of Top 40, capitalism, gay identity, and multiple modalities of imperialism vis-à-vis Elton John's emergence as a bankable transatlantic (and ultimately global) pop star in the 1970s. See Weisbard's "Madman Across the Water: Elton John and the American Top 40," in his dissertation, "Top 40 Democracy," 252–326.

179. Judith A. Peraino, *Listening to the Sirens: Musical Technologies of Queer Identity from Homer to Hedwig* (Berkeley: University of California Press, 2006), 136.

180. Martinez, interview with the author via e-mail, December 17, 2008.

181. D'Emilio, "Capitalism and Gay Identity," 109.

182. Martinez, interview with the author via e-mail, December 17, 2008.

183. Particularly striking in light of Studio K's function as a safe holding place for youth in the evenings is D'Emilio's call for "community- or worker-controlled daycare" and "housing where privacy and community coexist." "Capitalism and Gay Identity," 111.

184. Ibid.

185. For a reading that situates the sodomy laws and the obfuscation of racialization within a longer history of queer liberalism, see David L. Eng's "Freedom and the Racialization of Intimacy: *Lawrence v. Texas* and the Emergence of Queer Liberalism," in Haggerty and McGarry, *Blackwell Companion to Lesbian, Gay, Bisexual, Transgender and Queer Studies*, 38–59. See also Jasbir K. Puar's discussion of the "right to privacy" discourse and the occlusion of racialized bodies from the project of homonationalism in "Intimate Control, Infinite Detention: Rereading the *Lawrence* Case," in *Terrorist Assemblages*.

186. D'Emilio, "Capitalism and Gay Identity," 110.

187. My evocation of "assemblages" here is indebted to the theoretical complexity Jasbir K. Puar has devoted to the concept in *Terrorist Assemblages*.

188. D'Emilio, "Capitalism and Gay Identity," 106–109.

1. Douglas Cazaux Sackman, *Orange Empire: California and the Fruits of Eden* (Berkeley: University of California Press, 2005), 17–19.

2. "The First Seedless Oranges," *New York Times*, April 20, 1902, http://query. nytimes.com/mem/archive-free/pdf?res=F50 712F63B591B728DDDA90A94DC405B828C F1D3.

3. Sackman, *Orange Empire*, 18–19. Tibbets acquired the seedlings from William Saunders at the U.S. Department of Agriculture, her next-door neighbor in Washington DC.

4. Robert Leicester Wagner, *Sleeping Giant: An Illustrated History of Southern California's Inland Empire* (Las Vegas: Stephens Press, 2004), 17.

5. Susan Straight, "Introduction," in *Inlandia: A Literary Journey through California's Inland Empire*, ed., Gayle Wattawa (Berkeley: Heyday Books, 2006), xvi.

6. The fact that Riverside had the highest per capita income in the nation for a period in the 1890s is famously touted in all the local literature in the Riverside Public Library's heritage collection. It was also recently trotted out by the Berkeley group Strategic Economics in their report "Older Suburbs in the Los Angeles Metropolitan Area: Decline, Revitalization, and Lessons for Other Communities," prepared for the Local Government Commission Congress for the New Urbanism, July 2002, http://www.lgc.org/freepub/docs/ community_design/reports/older_sub-urbs_in_LA.pdf: "By the mid-1890s Riverside had one of the highest per-capita incomes in the United States. Investors built the first golf course and polo field in Southern California, and the spectacular Mission Inn was built in 1902" (33).

7. Daniel A. Vallero, *Paradigms Lost: Learning from Environmental Mistakes, Mishaps, and Misdeeds* (Boston: Butterworth-Heinemann, 2006), 216–217.

8. In 2009, Riverside was reported to have the highest ozone average in the state: "Riverside has the highest ozone average (104ppb), and the risk of dying from respiratory causes was 50% greater than it would've been if there were no ozone." Thomas H. Maugh II, "Low-Level Ozone Exposure Found to Be Lethal over Time," *Los Angeles Times*, March 12, 2009, http://articles.latimes. com/2009/mar/12/science/sci-ozone12.

9. Kate Sanborn, *A Truthful Woman in Southern California*, and Percival Everett, "909," both excerpted in Wattawa, *Inlandia*, 55–56, 392.

10. Susan Straight, "California's Inland Empire," *Los Angeles Times*, March 8, 2009, http://articles.latimes.com/2009/mar/08/ opinion/oe-straight8. See also Lawrence Downes's op-ed piece about how Latino families were taken advantage of in the Perris region of the Inland Empire, "A Sinking Feeling in the Inland Empire," *New York Times*, February 19, 2009, http://www.nytimes. com/2009/02/20/opinion/20fri4.html.

11. Citrus is what eased the industrial transition from agricultural machines to tools of war craft in the region: "[March Air Force Base] grew in importance in the 1920s and the years leading up to World War II, bringing a great many military and civilian workers to the area. Some of the city's capacity for building citrus machinery was even applied to the manufacture of military hardware, namely the Water Buffalo amphibious tanks used during World War II. At the height of its activity, the base supported 85,000 troops and was a major fixture in the region's economy until its realignment in 1996." Strategic Economics, "Older Suburbs in the Los Angeles Metropolitan Area," 33.

12. Josh Brown, "Stater Bros. Celebrates Grand Opening of New Headquarters," *Riverside Press-Enterprise*, October 25, 2007, http://www.pe.com/localnews/sanber-nardinoarea/business/stories/PE_Biz_D_ stater25.3ae299d.html.

13. Mike Davis, "The Inland Empire," in Wattawa, *Inlandia*, 421.

14. "Unlike the Westside or the Hollywood Hills, this region is rarely chosen to represent Southern California in movies and television programs—perhaps because it offers a better sense of what it is actually like to live in the region." *Is It Really So Strange?*, directed by William E. Jones, 2004.

15. "First Seedless Oranges."

16. Victor Bascara puts it most succinctly in his own explanation of the dialectic of American empire: "The dialectic of the project of empire and the problems it purports to solve have made empire building an ambivalent enterprise, undertaken repeatedly despite a long history of glories that have consistently ended in failure." *Model-Minority Imperialism*, xviii.

17. Walsh, "Recycling the Suburbs."

18. Lee Edelman, *No Future: Queer Theory and the Death Drive* (Durham: Duke University Press, 2004).

19. Espinoza studied creative writing at the University of California, Riverside (UCR), with Susan Straight, the region's most distinguished novelist. I offer this bit of authorial biography not simply to situate Espinoza's work institutionally, but also because the institution itself is a coordinate for the queer imaginaries and sociabilities crafted in the region. Like the town that surrounds it, UC Riverside also owes its expansion, indeed its very existence, to citrus. In 1907, the Riverside Citrus Experiment Station opened as the precursor of the university that would grow in increments in years to follow. Within a hundred years of its first experimental forays into citrus and agriculture, Riverside became the first campus in the University of California system to fight for an LGBTQ studies minor, igniting a regional controversy that would spread nationally and galvanize the disparate queer communities that live and work in the shadows of the empire. See Felix Sanchez, "UCR Educators Seek Gay Studies Program," *Riverside Press-Enterprise*, May 13, 1996, A-1, A-16. The university's LGBT Resource Center opened in 1993, several years prior to the

establishment of a minor in 1996, becoming the first "professionally staffed campus office of LGBT resources in the state of California." Nancy Jean Tubbs, director of UCR's Lesbian Gay, Bisexual, Transgender Resource Center, interview with the author, April 9, 2009, Riverside, CA. See also the UCR LGBTRC website for a detailed history of its administrative operations, http://out.ucr.edu/center/history.htm. Now the resource center houses one of the more active queer of color–driven youth organizations in the region, Queer People of Color, which partners with the university's other student affairs programs as well as community venues to provide services and programming for the Inland Empire's LGBTQ residents. For an extended history of the Citrus Experiment Station and the University of California's growth in the early twentieth century, see Jana Shaker, "The Founding and the First One Hundred Years of the Citrus Experiment Station," *Chronicle of the University of California* 8 (Fall 2006): 3–31. For more on the Citrus Experiment Station's current function at UC Riverside and its surrounding community today, see Sara Lin, "Even at a Ripe Old Age, Citrus Center Breeds Designer Fruit," *Los Angeles Times*, February 15, 2007, http://articles.latimes.com/2007/feb/15/local/me-citrus15.

20. Alex Espinoza, *Still Water Saints* (New York: Random House, 2007), 250.

21. Norman Klein, *The History of Forgetting: Los Angeles and the Erasure of Memory* (New York: Verso, 1997).

22. Bascara, *Model-Minority Imperialism*, ix.

23. Jessica Hagedorn, "Dia Conference Presentation," in *Critical Fictions: The Politics of Imaginative Writing*, ed. Philomena Mariani (Seattle: Bay Press, 1991), 147.

24. See the festival website, http://www.dickensfest.com/. Though the site itself offers little to expand on the festival's history, I was able to conduct interviews with the festival's founder, Carolyn Grant, and (as of this writing) the teacher/actor and community arts

advocate who has played the role of Charles Dickens in the festival for the past five years, Paul Jacques. Grant and Joan Patton, both members of the "Friends of the Riverside Library," launched the first Dickens festival in 1993, using the municipal auditorium for adapted performances of *Oliver Twist* and *Great Expectations*. As Grant explains about the financing of the festival, it began with seed money from the Friends of the Riverside Library, but organizers of the festival were urged to establish their own nonprofit to continue staging the event. Carolyn Grant, e-mail interview with the author, April 7, 2009; and Paul Jacques, phone interview with the author, April 3, 2009.

25. Information about Victoria Avenue can be found through "Victoria Avenue Forever," a citizen-run nonprofit organization "dedicated toward preservation maintenance, [and] educational efforts related to Victoria Avenue." The organization is primarily volunteer-driven and has focused on beautification projects like the planting of "over 600 trees [and] the creation and maintenance of two special gardens." See http://www.victoriaavenue.org/.

26. See the Victoria Avenue Historic Restoration Project's website, http://www.vahrp.com/.

27. Ibid.

28. One of his first parcels of land, called "Section 30," eventually became the first Citrus Experiment Station and helped spur the University of California, Riverside's expansion. See Gordon Wilson, "Irish Determination Helped When Matthew Gage Built His Canal," *Riverside Press Enterprise*, June 14, 1949, 1. See also the more recent and comprehensive biography of Matthew Gage by Riverside local and historian Joan H. Hall, *Pursuing Eden: Matthew Gage: His Challenges, Conquests, and Calamities* (Riverside, CA: Highgrove Press, 2008).

29. Gage and his brother-in-law, business partner, and chief engineer of the Victoria projects, Matthew Irving, even wrote a letter to the Queen respectfully requesting her permission to name their avenue after her. Victoria's private secretary responded, granting the Queen's permission to build in her name. See Hall, *Pursuing Eden*, 70–71. For more on Gage and Irving's treasured correspondence with Victoria, see also *Press and Horticulturist*, January 9, 1886.

30. Hall, *Pursuing Eden*, 79–89. Gage initially refused Crewdson's offer to invest in his projects until the large scale of his ambitious plans, as well as several lawsuits to reclaim his agricultural investments in the area from other claimants, financially necessitated additional investors (discussed below). See also Tom Patterson, "Early Leading Riverside Figure Had an Unfortunate Side, Too," *Riverside Press-Enterprise*, April 24, 1994. See also Victoria Avenue Historic Restoration Project's website, http://www.vahrp.com/, although the authors of the site's history page offer a more sanguine tale of collaboration between Gage, Crewdson, and the Riverside Trust Company.

31. Hall, *Pursuing Eden*, 79–81.

32. Ibid., 84. The motto was printed on a banner at a "Testimonial Banquet" celebrating Gage's accomplishments on June 25, 1890. As Hall writes, "Draped beneath the sign were crossed Union Jack and American flags."

33. Spanish missions were never officially established in Riverside, although the nearby San Gabriel Mission claimed lands in what is now modern-day Riverside, as well as other parts of the extended Inland Empire like Temecula, Lake Elsinore, and Murrieta. See Tom Patterson, *A Colony for California: Riverside's First Hundred Years* (Riverside, CA: Press-Enterprise Co., 1971).

34. Ibid. See also Elmer Homes, *Riverside Daily Press*, April 6, 1890.

35. Hall, *Pursuing Eden*, 120. See also Elmer Wallace Holmes, *The History of Riverside County, California, with Biographical Sketches of the County Who Have Been Identified with Its Growth and Development from the Early Days to the Present* (Los Angeles: Historic Record Company, 1912). The Loring

Opera House in Riverside, true to the region's Victorianism, opened in January 1890 with a production of Gilbert and Sullivan's *Iolanthe*. Theatrical productions ran at the Loring until the 1920s, when it was converted into a movie house. See Tom Patterson, "Loring Opera House's Distinguished History," *Riverside Press-Enterprise*, October 23, 1966.

36. Bascara, *Model-Minority Imperialism*, xx. Bascara reframes 1898 as a moment during which the United States "unburdened" itself from the ideologies of European colonialism by creating "informal" structures and rhetorics of "liberation" in relation to its new territories: "Indeed, the displacement of European colonial control sets the stage for the legitimacy of effective neocolonial relations under nominal postcolonialism. At the turn of the century, the putative liberations of the Kingdom of Hawaii and Spanish holdings in the Caribbean and the Pacific were therefore a precedent for an empire on the rise." See also Kaplan, *Anarchy of Empire*.

37. Hall, *Pursuing Eden*, 84.

38. Ibid., 161.

39. *Riverside Enterprise*, November 3, 1906. For a colorful rendering of the event, see Hall, *Pursuing Eden*, 161.

40. For a personal account of what life was like for Asian American pioneers in Riverside, see Mary Paik Lee, *Quiet Odyssey: A Pioneer Korean Woman in America*, ed. Sucheng Chan (Seattle: University of Washington Press, 1990). The University of California, Riverside, also has an extensive archive, some of which is available online, on the history of Asian Americans in the Inland Empire starting in the 1880s. See http://aar.ucr.edu/.

41. The main public library in downtown Riverside is, as of this writing, a focal point of a local debate about the value of mid-century modern architecture in the area. City leaders would like to expand the building, concealing many of its extant architectural features in favor of a newer design. Local activists and mid-century architectural enthusiasts like Sonya Sorrell and Steve Lech, president of the

Riverside Historical Society, are encouraging preservation. See Doug Haberman, "Giving Historic Value to Riverside's Midcentury Architecture Is Inland Woman's Goal," *Riverside Press-Enterprise*, August 13, 2008, http://www.pe.com/reports/riverside/stories/PE_News_Local_W_wmodern13.10b6435.html.

42. See the University of California, Riverside's Asian American Resources page on the Chinese Pavilion, http://aar.ucr.edu/sites/ChinesePavillion/. For a history and archive of Riverside's historical Chinatowns, see the two-volume, cooperatively authored *Wong Ho Leun: An American Chinatown* (San Diego: Great Basin Foundation, 1987), which contains historical photographs, maps, architectural renderings, demographics, and "firsthand accounts of Chinese laborers in early 20th century Riverside." See http://aar.ucr.edu/sites/RiversidesChinatown/.

43. Bascara, *Model-Minority Imperialism*, xx. See also Allan Punzalan Isaac, *American Tropics: Articulating Filipino America* (Minneapolis: University of Minnesota Press, 2006). Isaac explores how fantasy shapes the U.S. imperial imaginary about the Philippines and its other territories at the turn of the twentieth century, particularly in literature and popular culture. For more on the United States' nascent struggles with a desire for both likeness and difference from the rest of the world as it launched its ideology of Manifest Destiny, see Kaplan, *Anarchy of Empire*.

44. Hall, *Pursuing Eden*, ix. See also Patterson, "Early Leading Riverside Figure Had an Unfortunate Side, Too." Since 1999, Christian Arquillo Trajano, a former graduate student in public history at the University of California, Riverside, has been at the forefront of collating archival resources about the arrival of Filipinos/Filipinas in Riverside at the turn of the twentieth century, first as exchange students to area high schools, and then as agricultural laborers. Some of Trajano's work is available on UC Riverside's "Asian American Riverside" website at http://aar.ucr.edu/NotableAsianAmericans/Filipinos/. Trajano's

work led to the establishment of the Filipino Heritage Fund, which supports research on Filipino Americans in the Inland Empire.

45. Tom Patterson, "Mr. Gage's Canal—It Succeeded; He Didn't," *Riverside Press-Enterprise*, January 11, 1970, B3.

46. Patterson, "Early Leading Riverside Figure Had an Unfortunate Side, Too," B3.

47. Ibid., B7.

48. Klein, *History of Forgetting*, 1–23.

49. Ibid., 13.

50. Patterson, "Mr. Gage's Canal."

51. Tongson, "Tours of Duty (Free) + an Interview with Mélange LaVonne."

52. See "Staking the Claim: Introducing Applied Chicana/o Cultural Studies," in *The Chicana/o Cultural Studies Forum*, ed. Angie Chabram-Dernersesian (New York: New York University Press, 2007), 54–55.

53. William E. Jones's 2004 documentary *Is It Really So Strange?* is the best-known, although more recently, in 2008, Kerri Koch released a similarly themed documentary, titled *Passions Just Like Mine: Morrissey and Fan Culture*. Koch's documentary has come to supersede Jones's as a more definitive chronicle of the singer's Latino fan base, in part because it incorporates more music as well as more footage of Smiths cover bands in the Los Angeles area, such as the Sweet and Tender Hooligans and These Handsome Devils. Journalists and novelists have also been drawn the topic of Morrissey and the Smiths' Latino fan base in Southern California and the Southwest. The journalist Chuck Klosterman wrote a piece on Smiths/Morrissey fan conventions in Southern California, titled "Viva Morrissey!," featured in the annual Da Capo anthology of *Best Music Writing*, ed. Matt Groening and Paul Bresnick (Cambridge, MA: Da Capo Press, 2003), 66–73. One of the earliest essays written on Latino Morrissey fans (and still considered to be one of the definitive sources on the topic) is Gustavo Arellano, "Their Charming Man," *OC Weekly*, September 12, 2002, http://

www.ocweekly.com/2002-09-19/features/their-charming-man/.

54. Espinoza, *Still Water Saints*, 222.

55. Alex Espinoza, interview with the author, May 1, 2009, Los Angeles. During the 1980s, the Mighty 690's format transitioned briefly from the easy listening or "beautiful music" format to Top 40. The station (at the time, its call letters were XETRA-AM) functioned as a "border-blaster" station heard all across Southern California even though its broadcast base was in Mexico. See Gene Fowler and Bill Crawford, *Border Radio: Quacks, Yodelers, Pitchmen, Psychics, and Other Amazing Broadcasts* (Austin: University of Texas Press, 2002), which characterizes XETRA as "the last of the AM border blasters" (273). Its transition from a music format to twenty-four-hour news format, as well as its promotional efforts to use only X-TRA as its call letters (dropping the Mexican government–mandated "XE" in national AM radio stations), is documented by Fowler and Crawford on pp. 291–293.

56. Espinoza, interview with the author, May 1, 2009, Los Angeles.

57. For a sonic illustration of this phenomenon, listen to the Moldy Peaches' short, 2001 meditation in the song "D.2. Boyfriend" (from their self-titled album, composition credits unlisted, Sanctuary Records). As the lyrics explain, "When I was in middle school, I had a group of friends / We wore jean jackets and sunglasses and we listened to Duran Duran / There were six of us so when we played it didn't add up you see / Everybody had a Duran Duran boyfriend but me."

58. The music journalist Chloe Veltman draws explicit connections between the Smiths' and Morrissey's working-class critique of suburbia's seedy underbelly, and the connections it forges with American suburbanites of color, in "The Passion of the Morrissey," *Believer Magazine*, August 2004, http://www.believermag.com/exclusives/?read=article_veltman. Chuck Klosterman comments explicitly on Morrissey's sexuality as it overlaps with

stereotypical notions of Latino masculinity: "Though it's understandable how a culture that invented the term *machismo* might be uncomfortable lionizing a gay icon, it's ironic that Morrissey has now been adopted by two diametrically opposed subcultures. Fifteen years ago, closeted gay teens loved Morrissey because they thought he shared their secret; today, future marines try to ignore the fact that their hero might find them foxy." "Viva Morrissey!," 71. I address the lack of subtlety with which Klosterman views these ethnic and sexual divides—after all, these same closeted teens sometimes grow up to be macho soldiers—in my concluding chapter on the Butchlalis de Panochtitlan.

59. I allude here of course to Duran Duran's 1981 single "Planet Earth," composed by Simon LeBon, Nick Rhodes, John Taylor, Roger Taylor, and Andy Taylor, on Duran Duran, *Duran Duran*, EMI/Capitol, 1981.

60. For an account of the different labor practices that intersect with the military industrial complex, and its residual effects in the Inland Empire, see Thomas Ehrlich Reifer, "Labor, Race, and Empire: Transport Workers and Transnational Empires of Trade, Production, and Finance," in *Labor versus Empire: Race, Gender, and Migrations*, ed. Gilbert G. Gonzalez, Raul A. Fernandez, Vivian Price, David Smith, and Linda Trinh Võ (New York: Routledge, 2004), 17–36.

61. Philippe Lacoue-Labarthe, "The Echo of the Subject," in *Typography: Mimesis, Philosophy, Politics*, ed. Christopher Fynsk (1989; repr., Stanford: Stanford University Press, 1998), 139–207.

62. Sedgwick, preface to *Between Men*, ix.

63. See Wilbur Zelinsky, "The Twinning of the World: Sister Cities in Geographic and Historical Perspective," *Annals of the Association of American Geographers* 81 (March 1991): 1–31. See also the official "Sister Cities International" website for a list of current collaborations: http://www.sister-cities.org/. Extensive information about "town twinning," specifically Germany's involvement in the concept, can be

found in Martina Weyreter, "Germany and the Town Twinning Movement," *Contemporary Review*, January 2003, http://findarticles. com/p/articles/mi_m2242/is_1644_282/ ai_97228022/.

64. I borrow this phrase from the title of Vicente L. Rafael's watershed book *White Love and Other Events in Filipino History* (Durham: Duke University Press, 2000). As Rafael argues, the rhetoric of "benevolent assimilation" taken up by the United States during its "intervention" in the Philippines presumes a reciprocal affection from its subjects: "The allegory of benevolent assimilation effaces the violence of conquest by construing colonial rule as the most precious gift that 'the most civilized people' can render to those still caught in a state of barbarous disorder" (21). If we read the suburban, postcolonial affiliations among incongruent subjects (e.g., the Latino and Pinoy Anglophilia discussed in this chapter) through the rhetoric of American imperialism's "white love," we see how anyone straying from the presumed loyalty or monogamous attachment to a *single* "civilizing force" could be construed as "barbarous."

65. Homi K. Bhabha, *The Location of Culture* (1994; repr., New York: Routledge, 2005), 202–203.

66. Ibid., 202.

67. Freeman, "Packing History, Count(er) ing Generations."

68. Ibid., 728.

69. Halberstam, *In a Queer Time and Place*, 183.

70. Ibid.

71. Ibid., 186.

72. Ibid., 12.

73. Ibid., 15.

74. Ibid., 187.

75. Freeman, "Packing History, Count(er) ing Generations," 729.

76. What I allude to here are the intricate confusions and relationships to nostalgia and memory explored by Gayatri Gopinath in *Impossible Desires*, 4: "Rather than evoking an imaginary homeland frozen in an idyllic

moment outside history, what is remembered through queer diasporic desire and the queer diasporic body is a past time and place riven with contradictions and the violences of multiple uprootings, displacements, and exiles. . . . Queer diasporic cultural forms and practices point to submerged histories of racist and colonialist violence that continue to resonate in the present and make themselves felt through bodily desire."

77. See McGirr, *Suburban Warriors*. For an optimistic take on the possible emergent forms of civic engagement that may be recrafted in the suburbs, see J. Eric Oliver, *Democracy in Suburbia* (Princeton: Princeton University Press, 2001).

78. Espinoza, interview with the author, May 1, 2009, Los Angeles.

79. Oscar Wilde, *The Picture of Dorian Gray*, ed. Peter Ackroyd (London: Penguin Books, 1985), 23.

80. "Cemetery Gates," composed by Johnny Marr and Morrissey, on the Smiths, *The Queen Is Dead*, Rough Trade, 1986.

81. See Victor Bascara's elegant theorization of how empire becomes "unburdened," specifically by Asian American subjects in the United States, in "Unburdening Empire: The Cultural Politics of Asian American Difference," from *Model-Minority Imperialism*, 1–25. The "burdens" I am gesturing to here aim to broaden Bascara's claims to address interethnic vestiges of American empire as they manifest in the suburbs—a space that is configured as "aspirational" in the American imaginary, and thus as an emblematic habitat for multiple "model minorities."

82. Chela Sandoval, "On Cultural Studies: An Apartheid of Theoretical Domains," in *Methodology of the Oppressed* (Minneapolis: University of Minnesota Press, 2000), 67–80.

83. Gandhi, *Affective Communities*, 4.

84. Muñoz, *Disidentifications*, 12.

85. Ibid., 4.

86. See my unpublished dissertation, "Ethical Excess: Stylizing Difference in Victorian Prose from Carlyle to Wilde" (University of California, Berkeley, 2003).

87. Richard Longstreth quoted in Mary Melton, "A Brief History of the Mini-Mall," *Los Angeles Times*, November 16, 1997, http://articles.latimes.com/1997/nov/16/magazine/tm-54209. See also Longstreth's books *City Center to Regional Mall: Architecture, the Automobile, and Retailing in Los Angeles, 1920–1950* (Cambridge: MIT Press, 1997); and *The Drive-In, the Supermarket, and the Transformation of Commercial Space in Los Angeles, 1914–1941* (Cambridge: MIT Press, 1999).

88. Mark Gelernter, *A History of American Architecture* (Hanover: University Press of New England, 1999), 272. See also Alan Hess, "Styling the Strip: Car and Roadside Design in the 1950s," in *The Car and the City: The Automobile, the Built Environment, and Daily Urban Life*, ed. Martin Wachs and Margaret Crawford (Ann Arbor: University of Michigan Press, 1992), 167–179.

89. Melton, "Brief History of the Mini-Mall."

90. Ibid.

91. Jade Chang, "In Defense of Mini-Malls," *Metropolis Magazine*, April 1, 2003, http://www.metropolismag.com/story/20030401/in-defense-of-mini-malls.

92. "Gentrification of old urban residential districts is increasingly common as primarily well-educated people invest substantial sums of money in renovating old houses and apartments, often displacing poor residents in the process." Pulsipher and Pulsipher, *World Regional Geography*, 79. See also various accounts of how the New Urbanism (or the renovation and repopulation of American urban cores) continues to affect the relocation patters of immigrants into suburban and exurban spaces, especially Talen, *New Urbanism and American Planning*, and Smith, "New Globalism, New Urbanism." These new flows are part of a longer story in critical geography tracing the patterns of (in Laura Pulido's words) "environmental racism," or the principles of industrial quarantine that led to the evacuation of urban industrial environments by the white middle classes, as well as

the increasing suburbanization throughout Southern California. See Pulido, "Rethinking Environmental Racism: White Privilege and Urban Development in Southern California," *Annals of the Association of American Geographers* 90, no. 1 (2000): 12–40.

93. O'Hare, Frey, and Fost, "Asians in the Suburbs." As I mentioned in the introduction to this book, U.S. census data has documented these pronounced shifts in migratory patterns, which have become the fodder for speculation among demographers, critical geographers, and mainstream journalists. See Sam Roberts, "In Shift, 40% of Immigrants Move Directly to the Suburbs," *New York Times*, October 17, 2007, http://www.nytimes.com/2007/10/17/us/17census.html.

94. Melton, "Brief History of the Mini-Mall."

95. Chang, "In Defense of Mini-Malls."

96. Espinoza, interview with the author, May 1, 2009, Los Angeles.

97. Espinoza, *Still Water Saints*, 179.

98. Ibid., 3.

99. For two different accounts of how the Southern California suburban retail and residential landscape has been transformed by Latino communities living among other communities of color, see Mary Helen Ponce, *Hoyt Street: An Autobiography* (Albuquerque: University of New Mexico Press, 1993). See also Davis, *Magical Urbanism: Latinos Reinvent the U.S. City*. The subtitle of Davis's book is somewhat misleading, in so far as it focuses on "the city," since the middle third of the book looks primarily at what he calls the "transnational suburbs" (of the San Gabriel Valley, the Inland Empire, and Orange County) and their enduring economic, social, and cultural ties to towns of origin in Mexico.

100. Espinoza, *Still Water Saints*, 68.

101. As I mention in the introduction to this book, suburban studies has already for the most part debunked prevailing popular, national imaginaries about the racial and classed homogeneity of suburban space. See especially Nicolaides and Wiese, *Suburb*

Reader. Nicolaides and Wiese have culled a deep, interdisciplinary archive to address such topics as racial and ethnic diversity in early suburbia (chap. 7), "The Postwar Suburbs and the Construction of Race" (chap. 11), and recent transformations to the suburban landscape (chap. 14).

102. Espinoza, interview with the author, May 1, 2009, Los Angeles.

103. Espinoza, *Still Water Saints*, 76.

104. Ibid.

105. Ibid., 72.

106. Though the novel's reception is still very much in formation, the brief reviews that do exist online, in newspapers, and even pull-quoted in the paperback edition of the novel allude to "magic" and "miracles," notably the remarks cited from *Booklist* and the *San Francisco Chronicle*. A student review from Espinoza's graduate school alma mater, the University of California, Irvine, is titled "A Memoir of Magic and Mysticism" (by Ginny Wang, in *New University*, March 12, 2007, http://www.newuniversity.org/2007/03/features/a_memoir_of_magic29/).

107. I am not taking issue here with the entire genre of "magical realism" as it has been traced historically through several contexts, from the visual art of the Weimar Republic in the 1920s, to the emergence of *realismo mágico* in 1950s Latin American literature. Rather, what both Espinoza and I are addressing is the tendency noted by scholars of magical realism to "refer to all narrative fiction that includes magical happenings in a realist matter-of-fact narrative"—especially those authored by Latinos or Latin Americans—within that rubric. In fact, nothing "magical" really happens in *Still Water Saints*. Cures are not enumerated, no one transports themselves in mystical ways (true to suburban form, most everyone drives to and from the strip mall or walks through town), and miracles don't save anyone. See Maggie Bowers, *Magic(al) Realism* (New York: Routledge, 2004), 2. See also Wendy B. Faris and Lois Parkinson Zamora's edited volume *Magical Realism: Theory, History*

Community (Durham: Duke University Press, 1995). Amaryll Chanady's essay in that volume offers a partial genealogy of how early critical approaches to "magical realism" promoted the term in an attempt to dignify the literary value of work being produced in Latin America in the mid-twentieth century. See Chanady, "The Territorialization of the Imaginary in Latin America: Self-Affirmation and Resistance to Metropolitan Paradigms," 125–144.

108. Belinda Acosta, "Skewed Expectations: Alex Espinoza on Still Water Saints," *Austin Chronicle*, March 2, 2007, http://www.austinchronicle.com/gyrobase/Issue/story?oid=oid%3A451538.

109. Espinoza, interview with the author, May 1, 2009, Los Angeles.

110. Espinoza, *Still Water Saints*, 79.

111. For more on the quotidian as the source of drama in the suburban novel, see Jurca, *White Diaspora*.

112. Espinoza, *Still Water Saints*, 81. It is worth noting that the sentiment of Perla's remarks echo a line in the song "Suburbia" by the Pet Shop Boys: "I only wanted something else to do but hang around."

113. Espinoza, *Still Water Saints*, 37.

114. Ibid., 109.

115. Melton, "Brief History of the Mini-Mall."

116. In Asian American suburban communities, the grocery chain Ranch 99 has famously become a gathering place for multiple generations of Asian immigrants throughout California. See Shengling Chang, "Ranch 99: A Virtual Chinatown," in *The Global Silicon Valley Home: Lives and Landscapes within Taiwanese American Trans-Pacific Culture* (Stanford: Stanford University Press, 2006), 103–122.

117. Espinoza, *Still Water Saints*, 111. For more on ethnic businesses and economies of nostalgia, specifically in Latino communities, see Alex Oberle, "Latino Business Landscapes and the Hispanic Ethnic Economy," in *Landscapes of the Ethnic Economy*, ed. David H. Kaplan and Wei Li (Lanham, MD: Rowman and Littlefield, 2006), 149–164.

118. Espinoza, *Still Water Saints*, 111.

119. In Mike Atienza's October 2009 conversation with Shawn Schulenberg, a longtime bartender at VIP, he revealed that the VIP was on the verge of being displaced to a new site and was also being required to increase the age of entry from eighteen to twenty-one. Atienza and Schulenberg, e-mail interview with the author, October 11, 2009.

120. Espinoza, interview with the author, May 1, 2009, Los Angeles.

121. Bascara, *Model-Minority Imperialism*, xxiii.

122. Espinoza, interview with the author, May 1, 2009, Los Angeles.

123. Ibid. For more on Colton as an important railroad crossing, see Keith L. Bryant, *History of the Atkinson, Topeka, and Santa Fe Railway* (New York: Macmillan, 1974), 98.

124. The San Bernardino County Museum publishes a quarterly series on special topics about the region's historical sites. Several volumes focus on Agua Mansa and are all authored by a local historian, R. Bruce Harley: *From New Mexico to California: San Bernardino Valley's First Settlers at Agua Mansa* 47, nos. 3/4 (2000); *The Agua Mansa Story* 39, no. 1 (1991); and *The Agua Mansa History Trail: Featuring an Historical Tour of Agua Mansa, La Placita, and San Salvador Pioneer Sites, 1842–1893* 43, no. 3 (1996). A redaction of some of Agua Mansa's historical information can also be found on the San Bernardino County Museum website (from which this citation has been culled), http://www.sbcounty.gov/museum/branches/agua.htm.

125. See the San Bernardino County Museum's website, http://www.sbcounty.gov/museum/branches/agua.htm.

126. The Agua Mansa enterprise zone is, according to the City of Rialto Redevelopment Agency, "a multi-jurisdictional State Enterprise Zone that included portions of the Cities of Colton, Rialto, Riverside, the County of Riverside, and the County of San Bernardino." The zone expired in October 14, 2006, but as of this writing, "hiring tax credits and sales

and use tax credits" are still available for any equipment or employees employed prior to the expiration date. See the City of Rialto Redevelopment Agency website, http://www.ci.rialto.ca.us/redevelopment_764.php.

127. Espinoza, *Still Water Saints*, 60.

128. Ibid., 63.

129. Ibid., 67.

130. There is an expansive body of work on the suburban "fortress" mentality, especially as it informs the building and governance of gated communities. See Low, *Behind the Gates*, and Blakely and Snyder, *Fortress America*. For a critique of this securitization of suburban space through the lens of U.S. border ideologies, see Davis and Moctezuma, "Policing the Third Border." Davis's solo musings on the subject are excerpted in "The Third Border" in *Magical Urbanism*, 69–76.

131. Davis, "Transnational Suburbs," in *Magical Urbanism*, 93–107. Davis explains how certain pueblos in Mexico, as well as other localities in parts of Central America, have created economic and civic forms of transnational exchange with expatriates working in suburbs and cities in the United States.

132. As Nicolaides and Wiese explain in the introduction to the "Postwar Suburbs and the Construction of Race" section of the *Suburb Reader*: "Federal programs made it possible for millions of European Americans to attain symbols of middle-class status such as college educations, small businesses, and homes of their own. At the same time, mass suburbia tied these benefits together in a coherent spatial package. . . . Yet the making of whiteness in postwar America also reflected darker, more fearful currents. . . . The quality and value of one's home reflected on the status of the family itself. A further presumption—encouraged by public policy and years of promotion by the real estate industry—was that racial mixing lowered property values" (321). Following their editorial statements, Nicolaides and Wiese offer an impressive selection of readings on constructions of race and racialized conflict in the post–World War II suburbs, including

legal documents, newspaper accounts of racial exclusion, and a seminal essay by George Lipsitz on whiteness and the suburbs. See chap. 11, 323–348.

133. Espinoza, *Still Water Saints*, 66.

134. As I mentioned in the introductory chapter of this book, as well as in my chapter on JJ Chinois, this "metronormative" trajectory has been thematized in numerous gay and lesbian cultural histories and academic works about queer space, most notably in Chauncey, *Gay New York*; and most recently in Abraham, *Metropolitan Lovers*, and Herring, *Another Country*.

135. Espinoza, *Still Water Saints*, 161.

136. Ibid., 163.

137. Ibid., 162–163.

138. Ibid., 163.

139. Ibid., 165.

140. Ibid., 166.

141. For an account of how the United States negates its own imperial practices through a language (and economic practice) of liberalism, see Bascara, *Model-Minority Imperialism*, 10–18

142. Ibid., xxxii–xxxvi. See also Kaplan, *Anarchy of Empire*.

143. Espinoza, *Still Water Saints*, 166.

144. Ibid.

145. Ibid., 169.

146. Ibid., 167.

147. Ibid., 168.

148. Ibid., 167.

149. Ibid., 169.

150. Ibid., 169–170.

151. Puar, *Terrorist Assemblages*, 95.

152. Espinoza, *Still Water Saints*, 175.

153. Puar, *Terrorist Assemblages*, 22.

154. Espinoza, *Still Water Saints*, 213–230.

155. Jurca, introduction to *White Diaspora*, 3–19.

156. While addressing the character of Rodrigo in our interview, Espinoza remarked: "Exchange comes into play in Rodrigo's sexuality. Part of what determines his sexual path (if we can call it that) in the novel is his desire to leave Mexico. There is no way to

separate his movements and the social and cultural reasons he has to move from his sexuality." Espinoza, interview with the author, May 1, 2009, Los Angeles.

157. Espinoza, *Still Water Saints*, 87–102.

158. Ibid., 222.

159. Ibid., 230.

160. Ibid., 186.

161. Ibid., 176. Because of his association of tattoos with Dwight, Rodrigo worries the two men are somehow his captor's agents, looking to bring him back to Galena Court. As it turns out, one of the characters loitering in the parking lot is Shawn, another of the novel's queer characters, a working-class white boy struggling with methamphetamine addiction. As we discussed Shawn during our interview, Espinoza commented that he "is an interesting character because I didn't even know he was gay, but as I was writing him it dawned upon me that he was in love with his friend Beady. I decided not to reveal this information in the novel and let the character simply reveal himself through actions and thoughts. Shawn was a happy accident in that sense." Espinoza, interview with the author, May 1, 2009, Los Angeles.

162. Espinoza, *Still Water Saints*, 180.

163. As I mentioned in previous chapters, and will address at length in the concluding chapter of this book, Samuel Delany's version of "contact" (borrowed from Jane Jacobs) implicitly precludes the possibility of meaningful encounters in sprawling suburban spaces. What *Still Water Saints* offers is an alternative model of contact that not only happens in suburban retail contexts, but which also encourages us to read anew what these spaces signify, and how they might function. See Delany, *Times Square Red, Times Square Blue*, and Jacobs, *Death and Life of Great American Cities*. For more on the evolving architecture of the suburbs, see John Archer's expansive study *Architecture and Suburbia*.

164. Espinoza, *Still Water Saints*, 208.

165. Ibid., 211.

166. Ibid., 240.

167. Geographers and other scholars of suburban studies have offered many iterations on how suburban landscapes have been transformed as "ethnoburb" entrepreneurial zones throughout the United States. See Wei Li, "Anatomy of a New Ethnic Settlement: The Chinese Ethnoburb in Los Angeles," *Urban Studies* 35 (March 1998): 479–501. See also S. W. Hardwick and James E. Meacham, "Heterolocalism, Networks of Ethnicity, and Refugee Communities in the Pacific Northwest: The Portland Story," *Professional Geographer* 57 (October 2005): 539–557. There have been many accounts of these recent relocations among Latino immigrant populations in particular, notably Thomas Macias, *Mestizo in America: Generations of Mexican Ethnicity in the Suburban Southwest* (Tucson: University of Arizona Press, 2006); and the full-length study of the influx of Latino labor to the "new South," Karen D. Johnson-Webb, *Recruiting Hispanic Labor: Immigrants in Nontraditional Areas* (El Paso, TX: LFB Scholarly Publishing, 2003). In a review of the catalog for a 2006 exhibit at the San Jose Museum of Art on *Suburban Escape: The Art of California Sprawl*, Jeannene M. Przybylski focuses on one particular image by Camilo Jose Vergara—a photograph of "an African American couple setting off to church from their neatly painted single-story stucco home"—as a "poignant reminder that suburbs have represented the American dream not only for a largely white middle class, but also for countless generations of racial and ethnic minorities, newcomers, and immigrants who are transforming many American suburbs into ethnocultural villages." See Przybylski's review of *Suburban Escape: The Art of California Sprawl*, in *Pacific Historical Review* 77 (November 2008): 687. See also John Archer's expansive scholarly account of how the suburban dream becomes "nationalized" in American architecture and disseminated through different popular modes in "Analyzing the Dream," from *Architecture and Suburbia*, 291–330. I imagine *Still Water Saints* changing the stakes of this conversation

about "American dreams" with its exploration of empire and sexuality in the suburbs.

168. Espinoza, *Still Water Saints*, 240.

169. See Stephanie Ng, "Performing the 'Filipino' at the Crossroads: Filipino Bands in Five-Star Hotels throughout Asia," *Modern Drama* 8 (Summer 2005): 272–296. See also Adria L. Imada's work on entertainment cultures in Hawaii—particularly hula performers—and their role in transforming the territory from a "minor tropical colony to an American tourist and military stronghold." "Hawaiians on Tour: Hula Circuits through the American Empire," *American Quarterly* 56 (March 2004): 111. For a more expansive account of the varieties of Filipino labor currently circulating in Southeast Asia, including domestic work and entertainment, see the anthology edited by Rebecca Elmhirst and Ratna Saptari, *Labour in Southeast Asia: Local Processes in a Globalised World* (New York: Routledge, 2004).

170. "Boom! There She Was," composed by David Gamson and Green Gartside, on Scritti Politti, *Provision*, Virgin, 1988.

171. Jennifer Stoever, "Riverside," in *Budget Press International*, ed. Johnnie B. Baker, 1, no. 1 (1998): n.p. The *Press-Enterprise* is Riverside's local newspaper.

NOTES TO CHAPTER 5

1. "There Is a Light That Never Goes Out," composed by Johnny Marr and Morrissey, on the Smiths, *The Queen Is Dead*, Rough Trade, 1986.

2. Kathleen McHugh has troubled the gendered association between commutes, mobility, and traffic (in multiple senses of the term) in her piece "Women in Traffic." See also Jeremy Packer's cultural history of driving and the scripted roles of specific driving figures in the American citizenry (from women, to people of color, to men in search of the open road) in his monograph *Mobility without Mayhem: Safety, Cars, and Citizenship* (Durham: Duke University Press, 2008). Packer shows

how the privileges of "automobility" adheres only to certain bodies deemed "secure" and thus worthy of citizenship.

3. Frith, "Suburban Sensibility in British Rock and Pop," and Savage, *England's Dreaming*. See also the volume of essays edited by Roger Silverstone, *Visions of Suburbia* (London: Routledge, 1997). In his preface to the volume, which features essays from a range of U.S. and UK scholars, Silverstone refers to *Visions of Suburbia* as a "Sussex book," in reference to its interdisciplinary take on suburbia (ix–x).

4. Frith, "Suburban Sensibility in British Rock and Pop," 144–146.

5. KROQ has been heralded by some as "the most powerful rock station in the world" and for a period of time ruled as "the number-one-rated radio station in Los Angeles." As I mentioned in my previous chapter on the Inland Empire, KROQ looms large not only in a broader Southern California imaginary from the early 1980s onward, but also among very particular queer and racialized communities in the suburban extremities reached by the upstart station's signal. See Kate Sullivan, "KROQ: An Oral History," *Los Angeles Magazine*, November 2001, 90. Sullivan traces the history of the renegade station that used to broadcast from a hotel ballroom in Pasadena. Originally founded in 1972 by a club promoter and band manager, Gary Bookasta, KROQ grew into a regional and national phenomenon in the 1980s. As Sullivan explains, "Much of the station's mystique—and listener loyalty—dates from its early-'80s adolescence as an independently operated renegade station with no real owner. In the absence of the usual controls, KROQ's DJs and programmers played what they liked. In the process they ignited a musical, cultural, and eventually commercial explosion. Mixing rockabilly with reggae, early electronica with punk rock, ska, new wave, and every mutation thereof, KROQ championed unknown baby bands including the Clash, U2, REM, the Specials, Billy Idol, Adam Ant, the B-52s, Oingo Boingo, Eurythmics, Tears

for Fears, Soft Cell, Spandau Ballet, Simple Minds, the Human League, ABC, Split Enz, the Cult, Midnight Oil, Yaz, Berlin, Frankie Goes to Hollywood, Madness, X, the Bangles, Thomas Dolby, Missing Persons, the Stray Cats, UB40, Men at Work, and the English Beat."

6. As Meiling Cheng explains in her introduction to *Other Los Angeleses*, 10: "As a city of information—which is often nonhierarchical, even unverifiable—the *being* of Los Angeles is largely constructed upon the interpreters' own ideological investments. It *becomes* what the interpreter wants it to *be*."

7. For a historical mapping of queer space in Los Angeles that verifies the gendered divides between lesbian and gay male space, especially in West Hollywood, see Kenney, *Mapping Gay L.A.*

8. The most recent and expansive history of queer life in Los Angeles is Lillian Faderman and Stuart Timmons, *Gay L.A.: A History of Sexual Outlaws, Power Politics, and Lipstick Lesbians* (Berkeley: University of California Press, 2006). A collection of contemporary writing from a range of queer subjects, both famous and obscure, who live and love in Los Angeles, has been coedited by Christopher Freeman and James Berg, *Love, West Hollywood: Reflections of Los Angeles* (New York: Alyson Books, 2008). Despite the slipperiness of where queer L.A. resides in Freeman and Berg's book (as noted in the title, which at once locates "West Hollywood" before expanding its framework to all of Los Angeles), the editors do take care to specify in their introduction that West Hollywood is not necessarily the queer epicenter of L.A.

9. See Soja, *Postmetropolis*. Soja opens his "Introduction to Greater Los Angeles" with a provocative reading of the "occupied territory" that composes Southern California: "Nearly 15 million people come together here in five counties: Los Angeles, Orange, San Bernardino, Riverside, Ventura. And embedded in it all is a galaxy of more than 170 municipalities, and agglomeration of agglomerations,

each one with its own geohistory, its own special specificity of urbanism" (121).

10. Ibid., 125.

11. Garreau, *Edge City*.

12. Tsing-Loh, *Depth Takes a Holiday*.

13. Butchlalis de Panochtitlan website, "About Us," http://www.butchlalis.com/indexbdp.html, accessed January 2007. The BdP now use MySpace to host their information, although this particular description is not available on the current site, which has revolving content. See http://www.myspace.com/butchlalis.

14. Florida, *Rise of the Creative Class*. See also Florida, *Cities and the Creative Class*.

15. Raquel Gutierrez, Claudia Rodriguez, and Mari Garcia, *The Barber of East L.A.*, unpublished play, 2008, directed by Luis Alfaro. Riverside is mentioned as a potential destination for the play's central butch/femme love pair, whereas Bell Gardens is where the lead character, an older butch named Perfidia "Chonch" Fonseca, first witnessed a same-sex kiss, which ignited her queer desires. For an account of how the white, working-class suburbs of Southern California (like Bell Gardens) were transformed by the relocations of communities of color in the city of Los Angeles, see Nicolaides, *My Blue Heaven*. See also Raúl Homero Villa's compelling cultural history of Chicano/a communities and their migrations throughout and beyond the city of Los Angeles in *Barrio Logos: Space and Place in Urban Chicano Literature and Culture* (Austin: University of Texas Press, 2000).

16. Juana María Rodríguez, *Queer Latinidad: Identity Practices, Discursive Spaces* (New York: New York University Press, 2003).

17. See Raquel Gutierrez's blog from November 3, 2005, "Why Do Our Asses Like Morrissey?," http://raquefella.blogspot.com/2005_11_01_raquefella_archive.html. Gutierrez's blog, titled *Thuggery and Skullduggery*, occasionally features pre- and post-performance reflections, as well as extended meditations on the themes explored in the Butchlalis de Panochtitlan's work.

18. Steve Hymon, "Property Owner Ready for Fire Fight," *Los Angeles Times*, October 11, 2005, http://articles.latimes.com/2005/oct/11/local/me-florentine11. For more on the golden age glamour of the Florentine Gardens in Hollywood, see Jim Heimann, "Those Hollywood Nights," *Los Angeles Times*, May 21, 2006, http://articles.latimes.com/2006/may/21/entertainment/ca-125nightlife21.

19. Daniel Hernandez, "Club Fans Fight Proposed Takeover," *Los Angeles Times*, December 28, 2004, http://articles.latimes.com/2004/dec/28/local/me-gardens28.

20. "Suedehead," composed by Steven Morrissey and Stephen Street, on Morrissey, *Viva Hate*, HMV, 1988.

21. As I discussed in my Inland Empire chapter, Morrissey has a storied Latino following that has morphed and grown since he originally performed with the Smiths in the 1980s. For more on the interworkings of temporal drag, see Freeman's "Packing History, Count(er)ing Generations," and "Time Binds, or, Erotohistoriography," *Social Text* 23 (Winter 2005): 57–63. As I have already mentioned throughout this book, Freeman's work prompts us to consider the failed correspondence between now and then and here and elsewhere through lesbian bodies and feminist theories. If such gendered, queer historiographies fail to achieve an aesthetic symmetry and a historical coherence linked to the progress of time and its subtexts of modernity and progressiveness, the pleasure we derive from elsewhere and from "other times" can fail to signify as enlightened, effective, and radically queer.

22. For a concise account of the eminent domain battle over Florentine Gardens, see Christine Pelisek, "The Siren's Song: A Hollywood Landmark Comes under Fire," *L.A. Weekly*, August 26, 2004, http://www.laweekly.com/2004-08-26/news/the-siren-s-song. More extensive, scholarly accounts of the legal and philosophical ramifications of eminent domain in the United States include Ellen Frankel Paul, *Property Rights and Eminent Domain* (1987; repr., New Brunswick, NJ: Transaction Publishers, 1987); and Richard A. Epstein, *Takings: Private Property and the Power of Eminent Domain* (Cambridge: Harvard University Press, 1985).

23. Manalansan, *Global Divas*, 89.

24. For more on ephemeral archives in queer public and counter-public cultures, see Ann Cvetkovich, *Archive of Feeling: Trauma, Sexuality, and Lesbian Public Cultures* (Durham: Duke University Press, 2003); Muñoz, *Disidentifications*; and Lauren Berlant and Michael Warner, "Sex in Public," in *Intimacy*, ed. Lauren Berlant (Chicago: University of Chicago Press, 2000), 311–330.

25. For a more in-depth reading of suedeheads and Morrissey's sonic ambivalence toward working-class and racialized masculinities in the British context, see Nabeel Zuberi, "The Last Truly British People You Will Ever Know: The Smiths, Morrissey, and Britpop," in *Sounds English: Transnational Popular Music* (Urbana: University of Illinois Press, 2001), 17–73.

26. Ibid., 17–18.

27. For more on fantasy as it intersects with queer Latino imaginaries of subjugation and intimacy, see Richard T. Rodriguez's groundbreaking essay "Queering the Homeboy Aesthetic."

28. Citing Colin Snowsell, Gustavo Arellano in "Their Charming Man" explains how the music press harbors some resentment toward Morrissey's popularity as a result of his Latino fans' loyalty: "It's hard to tell if the [press is] more upset with Morrissey for not knowing when he was finished . . . or with the audience for not respecting—or being unfashionably oblivious to—the tacit understanding that Morrissey was taboo."

29. See Veltman, "The Passion of the Morrissey," and Klosterman, "Viva Morrissey!" See also the film documentaries *Is It Really So Strange?* and *Passions Just Like Mine: Morrissey and Fan Culture*.

30. Arellano, "Their Charming Man."

31. The BdP actually uses some *ranchera* music for the sound tracking of their live

theatrical shows. Rather than rely on a once-removed evocation of *ranchera* sentiments through Morrissey, however, they focus on an iconically queer and Latino/a repertoire offered by the legendary Chavela Vargas. For a Chicana lesbian reading of Vargas's music, see Yvonne Yarbro-Bejarano, "Crossing the Border with Chabela Vargas: A Chicana Femme's Tribute," in *Sex and Sexuality in Latin America*, ed. Daniel Balderston and Donna J. Guy (New York: New York University Press, 1997), 33–43. Yarbro-Bejarano intentionally substitutes the *v* with a *b* in Vargas's first name to emphasize not only the name's proper pronunciation but also Vargas's butchness.

32. Raquel Gutierrez, interview with the author via instant messaging, March 5, 2006.

33. Gutierrez, "Why Do Our Asses Like Morrissey?"

34. Arellano, "Their Charming Man."

35. Ibid.

36. Veltman, "The Passion of the Morrissey."

37. Klosterman, "Viva Morrissey!," 66.

38. See Joseph Britsow's important work tracing the genealogy of "effeminacy" in cultural imaginaries of and about Britain in *Effeminate England: Homoerotic Writing after 1885* (London: Taylor and Francis, 1995).

39. Richard T. Rodriguez problematizes the tropes of machismo even in some of its reparative revisions by queer artists and performers (including the Butchlalis de Panochtitlan) in *Next of Kin: The Family in Chicano/a Cultural Politics* (Durham: Duke University Press, 2009), 50–54. We might also read Klosterman's implicitly racialized/sexualized taxonomy of Latino bodies through the refracted lens of Richard Fung's critique of sexual continuums produced by anthropologists and sociologists, which bases its spectrum of normative sexuality on the standard of whiteness (with "brown" and "black" bodies pushing toward hypersexuality and hyper-masculinity, while "yellow" or Asian bodies are effeminized and rendered sexually passive).

See Fung, "Looking for My Penis." For more on how gender and femininity function in these racialized continuums, see also Celine Parrenas Shimizu, *The Hypersexuality of Race: Performing Asian/American Women on Screen and Scene* (Durham: Duke University Press, 2007).

40. Villa, *Barrio Logos*.

41. See Don Michael Randel, ed., *The New Harvard Dictionary of Music* (Cambridge: Harvard University Press, 1986), s.v. "coda."

42. The "remote intimacies" I've invoked here is a lush concept inspired by Jennifer Terry's work in progress on information transit, the Internet, and surveillance cultures. See chap. 1.

43. See Bienestar's "History" on their official website, http://www.bienestar.org/eng/page/31/About-Us.html.

44. Cheng, preface to *In Other Los Angeleses*, xv–xxx.

45. Butchlalis de Panochtitlan home page, http://www.myspace.com/butchlalis.

46. Cheng, *In Other Los Angeleses*, 13.

47. Ibid., 14.

48. Which neighborhoods and towns constitute L.A.'s Eastside has been a source of ongoing conflict, political discussion, and aesthetic debate for decades. The most recent flare-up over the "Eastside" designation occurred in 2009, after the *Los Angeles Times* debuted a new "Mapping L.A." project. In her response to this project, and the real estate market–driven designations, renamings, and imaginary incorporations occurring both formally and informally in the region, Patt Morrison remarked: "What lights my fuse is the attempted rebranding of Silver Lake as the 'Eastside,' mostly, I think, by people who stand to make a buck by appropriating the name of one part of L.A. and slapping it on another. As one who lives on the real Eastside, I protest this baldfaced defiance of history, logic. and geography." "In L.A., East Is East," *Los Angeles Times*, February 19, 2009, http://articles.latimes.com/2009/feb/19/opinion/oe-morrison19.

49. For more on Glendale's transformations as an "ethnic enclave," see John R. Logan, Wenquan Zhang, and Richard D. Alba, "Immigrant Enclaves and Ethnic Communities in New York and Los Angeles," *American Sociological Review* 67 (April 2002): 299–322. In the mid-twentieth century, Glendale was primarily a white suburb, and became increasingly Latino, Asian, and Armenian after the 1965 immigration reforms. For more on Glendale's status as a community with an aging white population being replaced by an increasingly younger "nonwhite" population, see William A. V. Clark, *The California Cauldron: Immigration and the Fortunes of Local Communities* (New York: Guilford Press, 1998), 53–57.

50. Gutierrez, interview with the author, October 1, 2009, Los Angeles.

51. During the time of her departure from the group in early 2007, Romero's partner had an unplanned pregnancy, and Romero elected to focus on wage-earning labor in order to help support and raise the child. Romero explicitly thematized this moment of her life in a short film titled "Beautiful Torture" for the show *BdP Get U.G.L.Y.*, shown at the Highways Performance Space in 2007.

52. See *Tongues'* official statement about its founding, "The Story," at http://www.tonguesmagazine.org/.

53. Ibid. As the *Tongues* website explains, "Realizing that many of the Los Angeles–area agencies dealing with Lesbian, Gay, Bisexual, and Transgender issues lacked in providing a creative and political arena for the development of Queer Latina expression, leadership, and community, *Tongues* has evolved into serving as a medium for creating said platform to dialogue and take proactive measures on a variety of issues that usually are not considered 'relevant' to Queer Latinas (i.e., globalization, worker's rights, and educational justice)."

54. Ibid. The original advertisement for the Lesbiradas event at Highways is still featured on the *Tongues* website. For more

on the history, formation, and conflicts within Lesbiradas de Guatemala ("Liberated Lesbians Collective of Guatemala"), see Susan A. Berger, *Guatemaltecas: The Women's Movement, 1986–2003* (Austin: University of Austin Press, 2006), 68–76.

55. Highways Performance Space has, over the course of more than two decades, established itself as an emblematic, historically and politically significant Los Angeles venue for experimental and community-based nonprofit performance. For more on Highways' role in L.A.'s broader spatial imaginaries, see Meiling Cheng's reading of the space as a "heterolocus" in *In Other Los Angeleses*, 184–187. See also David Román's conversation about Highways with Chat Yew in "Los Angeles Intersections: Chat Yew," anthologized in *The Color of Theater: Race, Culture, and Contemporary Performance*, ed. Roberta Uno with Lucy Mae San Pablo Burns (New York: Continuum, 2002), 239–245.

56. Gutierrez, e-mail interview with the author, May 23, 2008.

57. For more on the lesbian punk rock subcultures that rocked Homo A Go Go, among other music festivals, see Angela Wilson, "'The Galaxy Is Gay': Examining the Networks of Lesbian Punk Rock Subculture," in *Queer Youth Cultures*, ed. Susan Driver (Albany: SUNY Press, 2008), 51–68.

58. Claudia Rodriguez, interview with the author via e-mail, May 16, 2007.

59. Gutierrez, interview with the author via e-mail, August 1, 2009.

60. See Rafaela Castro's explanation of the origins of "Califas" in *Chicano Folklore: A Guide to the Folktales, Traditions, Rituals, and Religious Practices of Mexican Americans* (Oxford: Oxford University Press, 2000), 31; and Mary Ellen Garcia, "Influences of Gypsy Caló on Contemporary Spanish Slang," *Hispania* 88, no. 4 (2005): 800.

61. Alicia Arrizón, *Queering Mestizaje: Transculturation and Performance* (Ann Arbor: University of Michigan Press, 2006), 164. Arrizón develops her reading

of "tortilleras" around Alicia Gaspar de Alba's well-known poem "Making Tortillas." See also Lourdes Torres and Immaculada Petrusa's anthology *Tortilleras: Hispanic and U.S. Latina Lesbian Expression* (Philadelphia: Temple University Press, 2003); and the self-described "Xicana Indígena lesbian multidisciplinary artist" and writer Adelina Anthony's solo performance piece *Mastering Sex and Tortillas!*, initially developed in dialogue with Gaspar de Alba at UCLA in 2001, and revived as a full-length piece featuring "part stand-up, part performance art, part teatro" in its current touring incarnation. See http://www.adelinaanthony.com/soloshows/masteringsexandtortillas/masteringsexandtortillas.htm.

62. Gutierrez, interview with the author via e-mail, August 1, 2009.

63. "Tidbits," *Time*, April 12, 2005, http://www.time.com/time/magazine/article/0,9171,1048344,00.html.

64. Gail Doeff, "Changing Channels; As Freezer Cases Fill, Frozen Dessert Makers Seek New Growth Avenues," *Dairy Foods*, March 1996, http://findarticles.com/p/articles/mi_m3301/is_n3_v97/ai_18305040/.

65. Gutierrez, interview with the author via e-mail, August 1, 2009.

66. Mari Garcia, Raquel Gutierrez, and Claudia Rodriguez, interview with the author via e-mail, October 3, 2009.

67. Rosa Linda Fregoso, *The Bronze Screen: Chicana and Chicano Film Culture* (Minneapolis: University of Minnesota Press, 1993), 49.

68. Christine List, quoted in ibid., 51.

69. When I asked Gutierrez what she might make of the fact that the BdP employed one of the signature toys of the creative class—the Apple MacBook—in their work, she retorted that "the MacBook in our hands is totally something different. You know, 'the master's tools.' Plus, we had only had one new computer with all of these new creative apps to share between all four of us at the time. My own Mac that I bought for grad school was so

old, it didn't even have a wireless receiver for the Internet." Gutierrez, interview with the author, October 1, 2009, Los Angeles.

70. Alex Wescott, a PhD candidate in the Department of English at the University of Southern California, is writing a dissertation on the cultural history of the slacker within late-capitalist shifts in labor politics.

71. Cornelia Butler Flora, "The Political Economy of *Fotonovela* Production in Latin America," *Studies in Latin American Popular Culture* 8 (1989): 215–230.

72. Clare Taylor's entry on the fotonovela in Lisa Shaw and Stephanie Dennison, *Pop Culture Latin America! Media, Arts, and Lifestyle* (Santa Barbara, CA: ABC-CLIO, 2005), 174.

73. Michael Emme, Anna Kirova, and Carolina Cambre, "Fotonovela and Collaborative Storytelling: Researching the Spaces between Image, Text, and Body," *Exposure: The Journal of the Society for Photographic Education* 39, no. 2 (2006): 45–50.

74. See the "Independent Lens" interview with Carlos Avila, the filmmaker of the television series *Foto-novelas*, featured on the Public Broadcasting System in 1997 (http://www.pbs.org/independentlens/fotonovelas2/index.html). See also "What Is a Foto-novela?," an accompanying, unattributed essay to the web documentation of the series, http://www.pbs.org/independentlens/fotonovelas2/what.html. Avila also has an important piece on the genre, "On Fotonovelas: *Distant Water* and *In the Mirror*," in *Urban Latino Cultures: La Vida Latina en L.A.*, ed. Michael J. Dear, Gustavo Leclerc, and Raul Villa (London: Sage, 1999), 63–69.

75. Stephanie Greco Larson, *Media and Minorities: The Politics of Race in News and Entertainment* (Lanham, MD: Rowman and Littlefield, 2006), 60. See also Christine List, "Self-Directed Stereotyping in the Films of Cheech Marin," in *Chicanos and Film: Essays on Chicano Representation and Resistance*, ed. Chon A. Noriega (Minneapolis: University of Minnesota Press, 1992), 183–194.

76. For more on the creativity and theoretical contemplation inspired by traffic, particularly by women stuck in traffic in Southern California, see McHugh, "Women in Traffic."

77. Live Q&A session after *BdP Get U.G.L.Y.*, moderated by the author at Highways Performance Space, February 24, 2007.

78. Self-Help Graphics is a storied arts community center, first formed in an East LA. garage by a Franciscan nun and printmaker, Karen Boccalero (among other Chicano artists), during the Chicano movement in the 1970s. For more on the history of Self-Help Graphics, see Kristen Guzman, *Self-Help Graphics and Art: Art in the Heart of East Los Angeles*, ed. Colin Gunckel (Los Angeles: UCLA Chicano Studies Center Press, 2005).

79. Live Q&A session after *BdP Get U.G.L.Y.*, moderated by the author at Highways Performance Space, February 24, 2007.

80. In the interest of full disclosure, I applied for the grant with Gutierrez as a faculty cosponsor at the University of Southern California. I began to write about the BdP's work soon after their debut in 2005 and have had the unique opportunity to have access to their archive ever since. As the co-applicant for the Visions and Voices grant with Gutierrez during the spring semester of 2007, I helped put together the curricular programming that would coincide with the production of *The Barber of East L.A.* as well as the Hector Silva Retrospective at ONE National Gay and Lesbian Archives, which is partnered with USC. My official capacity (and billing) for these events was as a "producer," and I fulfilled that function in the traditional sense as a point person who collated grant resources, hired external staff, booked certain facilities, and helped frame and promote the series of academic and public events linked to the play's debut as a "working production" in April 2008.

81. Rodriguez, "Queering the Homeboy Aesthetic."

82. Silva's first sketch of the BdP appeared at one of his solo shows running concurrently in the Highways Performance Space galleries with a series of performances by the acclaimed performance artist Guillermo Gómez-Peña in August 2006.

83. Gutierrez collaborated in part with the photographer Diane Gamboa, who was not only an integral participant of the East L.A. punk scene but also its most thorough visual documenter. Gamboa's work, and a fraction of her archives, were featured in the renowned KCET "Webstories" series for a 2005 program titled "Rites of Passage: Unpopular Culture," http://www.kcet.org/socal/departures/production-notes/unpopular-culture.html. See Gamboa's introductory essay for the online exhibit at http://www.kcet.org/socal/departures/production-notes/diane-gamboa.html. Through her conversations with Gamboa and her own fandom of music from the era, Gutierrez was also able to interview and collaborate with some of the female luminaries of the L.A. and East L.A. punk scene during the early 1980s, including Teresa Covarrubias, the lead singer of the Brat, and the legendary Alice Bag of the Bags (and later the Alice Bag Band).

84. *The Barber of East L.A.* and all events leading up to it were part of a series Gutierrez and I assembled for USC's Visions and Voices, titled "Records y *Recuerdos*: Music and Memory in Queer East L.A." The free public events (some with a curricular component) included the listening party "*Revoluciones* per Minute" (in collaboration with the Norman Lear Center's Popular Music Project, directed by Josh Kun) and a conversational forum with the BdP, Alfaro, Hector Silva, and the performance studies scholar David Román, titled "Eastside Stories: Queer Latina/o Art and Activism in East L.A." The listening party explored the local soundscapes of East L.A. in the early 1980s, the tones and textures of which provided a conceptual sound track for *The Barber of East L.A.*

85. For more on the Vex, a legendary punk venue hosted by Self-Help Graphics for a period of six months in 1980, see Josh Kun, "Vex Populi," *Los Angeles Magazine*, March 2003, http://www.elaguide.org/Peoples/joshkun.htm. See also the catalog for the Claremont Museum of Art's *Vexing: Female Voices from East L.A. Punk*, ed. Pilar Tomkins and Colin Gunckel (Claremont, CA: Claremont Museum of Art, 2008). As Chon A. Noriega explains in his introductory note to "Self-Help Graphics: Tomás Benitez Talks to Harry Gamboa Jr.," in *The Sons and Daughters of Los: Culture and Community in L.A.*, ed. David James (Philadelphia: Temple University Press, 2003), 196: "Chicano art historians regularly distinguish between the politics-driven activities of the other Chicano art centers and Self-Help Graphic's emphasis on access to fine art by and for the community. The distinction is accurate, but it is also somewhat misleading, since Self-Help Graphics upheld the same movement-era tenets about the necessity of art to community building. Rather than subordinate art to politics, or form to content, Sister Karen understood art itself as a social practice that could build and sustain community—through the active making, buying, and experiencing of art within the community. Located in East Los Angeles, Self-Help Graphics operated at a geographic and radical distance from the art world nestled in the culture industry on the west side. But it has also served as a platform from which Chicano artists could either return to the community or toward the commercial art world."

86. Gutierrez, *The Barber of East L.A.*, 2–4.

87. For more on the contradictory affects of belonging and exclusion within the logic of the barrio, see Villa, *Barrio Logos*, 5: "Social commentators have long noted the importance of the barrio's internal 'geographical identity.' This identity, manifest in the unique conjunctural forms of its residents' cultural practices

and consciousness, has been a vital mode of urban Chicano community survival against the pressures of a dominant social formation. . . . And yet the barrio was not then, nor is it now, a space of pure security and wholly positive cultural practices."

88. Gutierrez, *The Barber of East L.A.*, 23.

89. Ibid., 26.

90. Ibid., 13.

91. Ibid., 50–52; deleted dialogue indicated by [. . .].

92. Ibid., 51.

93. Villa, *Barrio Logos*, 5.

94. Gutierrez, *The Barber of East L.A.*, 36. As Betty explains to Julian after coming across an ad for Chonch's barbershop, "[Chonch] was Aunt Izzy's bulldagger."

95. Ibid.

96. Ibid., 49.

97. Ibid., 47.

98. Ibid., 49. As Chonch and Betty reminisce, "chonch: You were the baby and I, of course . . . / [Betty interrupts] / betty: Had to be the daddy."

99. Ibid., 48.

100. Ibid., 49.

101. Ibid., 32.

102. Ibid.

103. The exhibit catalog for *Vexing* is itself an important archive of essays, photographs, fliers, and reminiscences about the gender and sexuality politics of the East L.A. punk scene. See Tompkins and Gunckel, *Vexing*.

104. Pilar Tompkins, "Ways of Living and Models of Action," in Tompkins and Gunckel, *Vexing*, 7.

105. Ibid., 33, 35.

106. Ibid., 34.

107. See José Esteban Muñoz's body of work tracking the disidentificatory impulses that propel utopian longings in queer time and space in both *Disidentifications* and *Cruising Utopia: The Then and There of Queer Futurity* (New York: New York University Press, 2009).

108. Klein, History of Forgetting.

109. Villa, Barrio Logos, 226.

110. Rodriguez, "Making Queer Familia," in *Next of Kin*, 171.

111. Colin Gunckel, "Vex Marks the Spot: The Intersection of Art and Punk in East Los Angeles," in Tompkins and Gunckel, *Vexing*, 15.

112. Gutierrez, *The Barber of East L.A.*, 55.

113. Kun, "Vex Populi."

114. Gutierrez, *The Barber of East L.A.*, 56.

115. Ibid., 62.

116. Ibid., 48.

117. Ibid.

118. Ibid., 69.

NOTES TO CHAPTER 6

1. See Delany's *Times Square Red, Times Square Blue*, a haunting account of Times Square's corporate redevelopment in the interest of promoting tourism and public "safety." Judith Halberstam provides a useful reading of Delany's program for revivifying urban life, and eschewing heteronormative rhetorics of "safety," in her chapter on "Queer Temporality and Postmodern Geographies" in *In a Queer Time and Place*, 1–21. Elsewhere, I have addressed how Delany's own rhetoric about "safety" and "risk," combined with his nostalgic reflections about queer "mobility," perpetuates a hostility toward subjects who inhabit rural and suburban spaces, while exposing a fundamentally bourgeois, racialized, and gendered imaginary at the heart of both queer and normative ideologies about space. See Tongson, "Metronormativity and Gay Globalization."

2. Jacobs, *Death and Life of Great American Cities.*

3. Delany, *Times Square Red, Times Square Blue*, 178.

4. For an extended account of the intersection between homonormative and neoliberal discourses of gentrification, see Martin F. Manalansan IV, "Race, Violence, and Neoliberal Spatial Politics in the Global City," *Social Text* 23 (Fall/Winter 2005): 141–155.

5. Florida, *Cities and the Creative Class*, 99.

6. Ibid., 34.

7. Ibid., 131.

8. Ibid., 115.

9. See Halberstam's discussion of the subjects who "will and do opt to live outside of reproductive and familial time as well as on the edges of logics of labor and production." *In a Queer Time and Place*, 10. Like Delany, Halberstam focuses on a language of "risk" that defines queer time and space. But I am somewhat more skeptical about how stable the category of "normative time"—or in Halberstam's words, "the organizations of time and space that have been established for the purposes of protecting the rich from everyone else" (10)—remains, given the complex disavowals of wealth and the co-opting of sub-cultural ethics in such neoliberal paradigms as the "creative class." A language of "risk" also figures prominently in Florida's rhetoric.

10. Florida, *Cities and the Creative Class*, 85.

11. Ibid., 86. Florida devotes an entire chapter to "Technology and Tolerance." See also his introductory chapter, which explains in dramatically understated language why the "Gay Index" measures the final frontier for "tolerance" in the United States: "Several reasons exist why the Gay Index is a good measure for diversity. As a group, gays have been subject to a particularly high level of discrimination. Attempts by gays to integrate into the mainstream of society have met substantial opposition. To some extent, homosexuality represents the last frontier of diversity in our society, and thus a place that welcomes the gay community welcomes all kinds of people" (41).

12. Martin Manalansan IV's work in particular has traced the "racial violence" that comes with homonormative capitalist impulses that fail to "delineate or complicate intragroup differences" in accounts of queer space and queer identity. See "Race, Violence, and Neoliberal Spatial Politics in the Global City," 143.

13. See Roderick Ferguson's watershed book *Aberrations in Black: Toward a Queer*

of *Color Critique* (Minneapolis: University of Minnesota Press, 2004).

14. Raúl Homero Villa's chapter "'Phantoms in Urban Exile': Critical Soundings from Los Angeles' Expressway Generation," in *Barrio Logos*, 111–155, explores the extent to which dislocations of Latino/a communities throughout Southern California coincide with transportation development projects in the region. See also Klein, *History of Forgetting*, 62–63. Klein's "Epilog: Building the White Whale," offers a brief, if compelling, narrative of the thirty-year conflict over the path of the I-710 that saw white Republicans agitate against development in the interest of historical preservation: "The litigious Republican town of South Pasadena, still smarting from the builders of the Arroyo Seco Freeway (1940) not fulfilling their promise to protect the old arroyo, simply refused to knuckle under; and forced the California Transit Authority to undergo at twenty new plans, and at least seven environmental reports, some taking as long as six years apiece. The 710, if built, would also destroy hundreds of historically significant houses, and endanger at least five historic districts; it would also have a profound impact on the largely Hispanic town of El Sereno" (62).

15. Klein, *History of Forgetting*, 133–134. See also Eric Avilla, "Suburbanizing the City Center: The Dodgers Move West," in *Popular Culture in the Age of White Flight: Fear and Fantasy in Suburban Los Angeles*, 145–184.

16. Florida, *Cities and the Creative Class*, 35.

17. Claudia Rodriguez and Raquel Gutierrez, "Softball Diamond Girl (*Me Haces Sentirrr . . .*)," unpublished script, 2005, 2.

18. Ibid.

19. Vazquez, "Instrumental Migrations," 188. This portion of Vazquez's dissertation has since been revised and redacted into article form as "Can You Feel the Beat? Freestyle's Systems of Living, Loving, and Recording," *Social Text* 28 (Spring 2010): 107–124.

20. Vazquez, "Instrumental Migrations," 186.

21. See JK Havell's comment on http://www.discomusic.com/records-more/634_0_2_0_C/.

22. Vazquez, "Instrumental Migrations," 185. Vazquez offers a richer account of the ambivalent racializing function Spanish serves in the freestyle genre: "Spanish-spoken testimonials or short smuggled in phrases (often dirtier or more heartfelt than English allows) make their way into DJ sets on local radio stations and mix tape compilations. There is a kind of musical bilingualism felt through its sound, but . . . I belong to the school that is not quite ready to be held accountable in terms of its formal musical structures."

23. Rodriguez and Gutierrez, "Softball Diamond Girl," 2.

24. Mari Garcia, Raquel Gutierrez, Claudia Rodríguez, and Nadine Romero, "Cockfight," unpublished script, 2005, 2.

25. Ibid., 3.

26. Unfortunately, I lack the space here to elaborate on how the BdP explore a range of "butch-on-butch" intimacies and test the limits of their queer audience's sexual/gender politics with the piece "BDSM." "BDSM" depicts a butch-on-butch sexual encounter live on stage, while a video in the background unveils butch breasts, unbound, as a voiceover addresses a love poem to "my butch scholar."

27. For more on reconfiguring the extended family, or "la familia," in queer Chicano/a contexts, see Rodriguez, *Next of Kin*.

28. Claudia Rodriguez and Raquel Gutierrez, "drrrty White Girls," unpublished script, 2005, 1.

29. Claudia Rodriguez and Raquel Gutierrez, "Lolo and Perla Return to Avenge Klub Fantasy," in *Teenage Papi: The Remix*, unpublished script, 2005, 1.

30. Gutierrez, interview with the author via instant messaging, March 5, 2006.

31. Rodriguez and Gutierrez, "Lolo and Perla Return to Avenge Klub Fantasy," 1.

32. In "Papi Chula! The Guayabera and Latina Butch Style Politics" (a paper delivered as part of the "Migrating Epistemologies Workshop Series" at the Center for the Study of Women, UCLA, June 2, 2006), Deborah R. Vargas elaborates on the contested origins of the *guayabera* vis-à-vis the stylistic economy of racialized queer subjects and a politics of butch presentation/representation.

33. Gutierrez, interview with the author via instant messaging, March 5, 2006.

34. Rodriguez and Gutierrez, "Lolo and Perla Return to Avenge Klub Fantasy," 1.

35. Ibid., 2.

36. Rodriguez and Gutierrez, "drrrty White Girls," 2.

37. Ibid., 3.

38. Ibid., 4.

Index

ABC, 128

Abiquiu, NM, 144

Accent, theory of: British, 127–129, 136; Caló, 181; Cebuano, 60; Chicano slang, 181–182; imperial, 128; improvisational dialect, 60–61, pidgin, 58–59; Pinoy patois, 58–59; swardspeak, 60, 232n11

Aesthetics: 1980s futurism, 84; dykeaspora and, 47; excess and ambiguity, 34; "homeboy aesthetic," 187; Gwen Stefani, 89; "latchkey aesthetic," 179, 182; mid-century design, 44; mid-century modernism, 84; Spanish colonial revivalism, 84; suburban, 33, 36, 182. *See also* Architecture; Butchlalis de Panochtitlan; Chan, Lynne; Orientalism

Afterschool Special, 59

Agua Mansa, CA (historical), 144–145

Ahn, MiHi: "Gwenihana," 89–90

Ahn, Patty, 78–79, 237n36, 237n38, 241n72

Alfaro, Luis, 188

Amusement cultures, 13, 74, 245n127. *See also* Disney; Knott's Berry Farm; Theme park

Anaheim, CA, 72, 74

Anderson, Benedict, 23, 221n75

Archer, John, 34

Architecture: 1980s futurism, 84; atomic-type ranch house, 251n11; Best Western idiom, 123; break-dancing and, 97; of convenience, 139 (*see also* Strip malls); English and Mediterranean country villas, 34; mid-century modernism, 84; mock-Tudor, 34; Monticello, 113; Orientalism, 125; promotion of individualization, 34; ranch house, 34; Spanish missionary, 125; Spanish colonial revivalism, 84; Spanish-style stucco, 35; Victorian, 116, 125. *See also* Aesthetics; Archer, John; Opie, Catherine; Soundscape; Transculturation

Arellano, Gustavo, 71, 74–75, 77–78, 83, 169–170

Arrizón, Alicia, 181

Asian Americans/Asian Pacific Islanders, 46–47, 143: Chinese, 42–43, 58; citation of popular culture, 59; Filipino, 53–54, 58–60, 166; Japanese, 16, 125; middle-class domesticity and, 43; post-identity, 47; Samoan gangs, 100; Vietnamese, 82, 240n63. *See also* Chan, Lynne; Immigrants/Immigration, 1965 Immigration and Nationality Act

"Asians in the Suburbs" (O'Hare, Frey, and Fost), 36

Assimilation, 46

Avila, Eric, 102–103

Baez, Joan, 24

Bag, Alice, 198

Balance, Christine Bacareza, 26, 222n79, 222n81, 241n72

Barrio, 196, 200, 268n87. *See also* Villa, Raúl Homero

Bascara, Victor, 12, 46, 119, 143, 148, 251n16, 253n36, 256n81

Base Line Street (San Bernardino, CA), 117

Battlestar Galactica, 127

Beach Boys: "California Girls," 85

Beauregard, Robert A., 12, 224n13

Becker, Stephen L. 94, 102. *See also* Clubs/bars, Studio K

Bell Gardens, CA, 171, 174

Benjamin, Walter, 73

Berlant, Lauren, 6

Bhabha, Homi K., 131–132

Bienestar lesbian support group, 172–173, 175, 187

Birmingham, England, 130

Black Flag. *See* Vex

About the Author

KAREN TONGSON is Associate Professor of English and Gender Studies at University of Southern California. She is co-series editor for NYU Press's Postmillennial Pop series and co-editor-in-chief of *The Journal of Popular Music Studies*.

CPSIA information can be obtained
at www.ICGtesting.com
Printed in the USA
JSHW021042140822
29288JS00002B/107

9 780814 783108